Paul

May the grace of the Lord Jesus Christ, and the love of God, and the *koinōnia* of the Holy Spirit be with you all.

2 Corinthians 13:14

1 John

We proclaim to you what we have seen and heard, so that you also may have *koinōnian* with us. And our *koinōnia* is with the Father and with his Son, Jesus Christ.

1 John 1:3

Irenaeus

And to as many as continue in their love towards God, does He grant communion [*koinōnian*] with Him. But communion [*koinōnia*] with God is life and light, and the enjoyment of all the benefits which He has in store.

Adversus haereses V.27.2

Calvin

For although the faithful come into this Communion [*koinōnia*] on the very first day of their calling; nevertheless, inasmuch as the life of Christ increases in them, He daily offers Himself to be enjoyed by them. This is the Communion [*koinōnia*] which they receive in the Sacred Supper.

Letter to Peter Martyr, 8 August 1555

Calvin's Ladder

A Spiritual Theology
of Ascent and Ascension

Julie Canlis

WILLIAM B. EERDMANS PUBLISHING COMPANY
GRAND RAPIDS, MICHIGAN / CAMBRIDGE, U.K.

Published 2010 by
Wm. B. Eerdmans Publishing Co.
2140 Oak Industrial Drive N.E., Grand Rapids, Michigan 49505 /
P.O. Box 163, Cambridge CB3 9PU U.K.

Library of Congress Cataloging-in-Publication Data

Canlis, Julie, 1973-
Calvin's ladder: a spiritual theology of ascent and ascension / Julie Canlis.
p.   cm.
Based on the author's thesis (doctoral) — University of St. Andrews, Scotland, 2005.
Includes bibliographical references (p.   ).
ISBN 978-0-8028-6449-9 (pbk.: alk. paper)
1. Calvin, Jean, 1509-1564. 2. Ascension of the soul. 3. Spirituality —
Reformed Church. 4. Reformed Church — Doctrines.   I. Title.

BX9418.C387   2010

230′.42 — dc22

2009042573

www.eerdmans.com

To my dearest Matt

Time, then, is told by love's losses, and by the coming of love, and by love continuing in gratitude for what is lost. It is folded and enfolded and unfolded forever and ever, the love by which the dead are alive and the unborn welcomed into the womb. . . . No one who has gratitude is the onliest one.

WENDELL BERRY

Contents

CONTENTS

Acknowledgments

This book, perhaps more than most, was a family affair. I attribute my sanity to the children — Chapman, Madeleine, Iona, and Caitlin — who kept on arriving throughout the writing of this work, wonderfully changing my notions of efficiency and academic seriousness. All of my brothers and sisters contributed from across the pond: Amie for emotional support and delight; Stevie for his theological friendship; Joe for loving our children; Tom for enduring my computer questions; and Melissa for giving three months of her life and love to our children (and my bibliography!). Both sets of parents flew over multiple times to inject love, prayer, and study getaways into our often hectic life. Mom and Dad, Chris and Alice, we cherish every memory with you and recognize that your relief over the completion of this book will perhaps be greater than our own. But above all . . . Matt. You who stayed home with our children and grew your vocation "within" while I was working without. Thank you.

Much of the material contained in this book grew out of my doctoral thesis, which I wrote at the University of St Andrews, Scotland, from 2000 to 2005. Were it not for James Houston, I would not have turned my eyes to St Andrews, nor have had the disposition ready to receive a thesis such as this one. Alan Torrance was a constant encourager and has had a profound influence on both Matt and me by inviting us into the *koinōnia* of his faith and family. Philip Butin, Douglas Farrow, David Scott, and Stuart Hall offered invaluable insight as they graciously read over numerous drafts. I also recognize that without the ORS Research Grant (University of St Andrews), the Meeter Center's Summer Scholar program (Calvin College), the Institut d'histoire de la Reformation (Université de

KNOWLEDGMENTS

Genève), and the sanctuary of St. Deiniol's Library (Wales), much of this book could not have been written. I am further grateful for the doors that were opened by the Templeton Foundation's Award for Theological Promise, toward the continuation and dissemination of my research.

That "communion of saints" who encouraged, questioned, and prayed for me are many: Steven Prokopchuk, Poul Guttesen, Ivan Khovacs, Gisela Kreglinger, Kristen Deede Johnson, Tee Gatewood, Matt Jenson, Sharon Jebb Smith, Stephanie Smith, Allen Sundsmo, Jodi Hailey, and the congregations of St. Leonard's, Cameron, Pitlochry, and Methlick. And I will always be knit together with those women who prayed with me during those cherished mornings over coffee in the Stearns's basement: Chelle Stearns, Julie Khovacs, Kathryn Gatewood, Gina Prokopchuk, and Kirstin Johnson.

x

Abbreviations

AH	*Adversus haereses,* Irenaeus
ANF	*Ante-Nicene Fathers,* A. Roberts, ed. (10 vols.)
CO	*Calvini Opera (Ioannis Calvini opera quae supersunt omnia),* in *Corpus Reformatorum* [*CO* 1-59 = *CR* 29-87], Baum, Cunitz, Ruess, eds.
LCL	*Loeb Classical Library*
SC	*Sources chrétiennes*
ST	*Summa Theologiæ,* Thomas Aquinas
T&T	*Tracts & Treatises in Defense of the Reformed Faith,* H. Beveridge, ed. (3 vols.)
TDNT	*Theological Dictionary of the New Testament,* G. Kittel, ed. (10 vols.)

Calvin

Institutio 1559: To minimize the number of notes, I will cite passages from the McNeill-Battles (1960) edition in the body of the text itself, simply following the quotation with standard citation format (III.2.5 = book 3, section 2, subsection 5).

Commentaries and Sermons: References from the commentaries (Calvin Translation Society, 1843-55) and sermons (Leroy Nixon, *The Deity of Christ and Other Sermons,* 1997) will be acknowledged in the footnotes in conventional format: (*Comm. Gen.* 1:2).

Calvini Opera: If I have quoted directly from the original, I will include the volume and page number from *Ioannis Calvini opera quae supersunt omnia* (*CO* 42.157 = *Calvini Opera,* volume 42, column 157).

Irenaeus

Adversus haereses: Again, to minimize footnotes, I will cite passages from the *Ante-Nicene Fathers* (1885) edition directly in the text, although they will always be preceded by *AH* to differentiate them from the *Institutio* (*AH* V.8.2 = *Adversus haereses*, book 5, section 8, subsection 2).

Epideixis: References from John Behr's translation of what is often translated as *Demonstration* or *Proof of the Apostolic Preaching* will be directly inserted into the text.

Sources chrétiennes (*SC*): Quotations from the original are taken from this critical edition, which includes the Latin text, Greek fragments, Syriac and Armenian variants, and French translation: (*SC* 100:147 = vol. 100, p. 147).

Introduction

Calvin is a cataract, a primeval forest, a demonic power, something directly down from the Himalaya, absolutely Chinese, strange, mythological; I lack completely the means, the suction cups, even to assimilate this phenomenon, not to speak of presenting it adequately. What I receive is only a thin little stream and what I can then give out again is only a yet thinner extract of this little stream. I could gladly and profitably set myself down and spend all the rest of my life just with Calvin.[1]

Irenaeus may be described as the first great theologian of the Early Church; indeed, he has a greater right than any other to the title of the founder of the theology of the Church. All the others build on the foundation which he has laid.[2]

This book is concerned with a story line that has always been at the heart of Christian mystical theology and spiritual praxis: the "ascent of the soul." It is about how, perhaps surprisingly, Calvin reworks it into the

---

1. Karl Barth, in a letter to Thurneysen, dated 8 June 1922 (*Revolutionary Theology in the Making: The Barth-Thurneysen Correspondence, 1914-1925* [London: Epworth, 1964], p. 101).

2. Emil Brunner, *The Mediator* (Philadelphia: Westminster, 1947), p. 249.

heart of his Protestant manifesto on theology and piety. What is even more interesting is the *way* he does so: through the concept of Trinitarian *koinōnia*. The Greek word *koinōnia* (used by St Paul to mean human participation in God's life) suggests an entirely distinctive way of conceiving of the relationship between God and humanity. The purpose of this book is to consider what *koinōnia* might mean for us in a century fractured by individualism, reductionism, and fundamentalism, and to consider what it might signify for a comprehensive, embodied, repersonalizing *Christian* spirituality.

The "ascent of the soul" has had a colorful and venerable history in the Christian tradition, reaching back as far as the apostle Paul, who was "caught up to the third heaven." Although the terminology can be traced as far back as Pythagoras (sixth century BCE) and then Plato (fourth century BCE), it was thoroughly appropriated by Jewish apocalypticism around the time of Christ, having been wedded to the traditional "ascended" figures of Enoch and Daniel. Over the centuries, remarkably few Christian theologians or mystics have turned from that imagery; instead, they have baptized it and incorporated it into their own reflections on and experiences of Jesus Christ. Not least of these was John Calvin. His liturgical imagery *(sursum corda),*[3] explication of the Lord's Supper, and radical rendition of the ascension of Christ are all examples of the unique way he appropriated this metaphor for his own theological purposes.

So why has this language remained little accounted for in Calvin scholarship? A taxonomy of "ascent" is important but is not necessarily the whole task. Of this, von Balthasar wisely says, "It is in no sense enough merely to gather together those passages (often paltry or conventional or dependent on alien philosophies) where the subject . . . is expressly considered. Rather, what is decisive . . . occurs most centrally in the heart, in the original vision."[4] For Calvin, ascent was more than a metaphor: it was the decisive and final action of Jesus Christ into which we are included and, as such, is the foundation of his doctrine of participation. Ascent not only represents the moment when the *human* Jesus was taken up to his Father but also when all of humanity is opened to this relationship as well.

Calvin's emphasis on the ascent of humanity is precisely this vocation of union and communion with the triune God. In this, he is not much dif-

3. Lift up your hearts.
4. Hans Urs von Balthasar, *The Glory of the Lord II: A Theological Aesthetics* (Edinburgh: T. & T. Clark, 1982), p. 14.

ferent from the scores of Christian theologians and mystics who have gone before him. But it is when we consider how this ascent occurs that we tread on more controversial territory. Is it due to the soul's powers and God-given natural abilities? Is it a sanctifying call on human life to holiness, aided by the Holy Spirit? Is it not an ascent at all but rather the descent of God to us in our sin and brokenness? Or is it the way God shares his life and benefits with us, drawing humanity to "participate" in his triune communion? This interplay between ascent and descent has not been easy for the church and has often functioned more as a grating tension than a healthy dialectic throughout Christian history.

Plato offered one solution: ascent is "natural" to the human soul, a matter of "like being drawn to like." The powerful engine driving this ascent is Plato's concept of participation, such that things "participate" in the eternal for their very existence. Housing shards of the eternal, the material sphere has an innate, "natural" longing to return to its original divine home. The Christian must reject this pantheistic description of participation outright. At the same time, however, the Christian story itself is one of ascent. It begins and ends with the revelation of a personal, triune God who calls creation to "return" to communion with him. In the Garden of Eden, humans were called the *imago Dei;* the Spirit continues this ascending vocation by making those in the church "like God" or "like Christ" (1 John 3:2; Rom. 8:29). What, then, is the engine that drives *Christian* ascent?

Calvin brilliantly synthesized the two movements of ascent and descent into one primary activity: the ongoing story of God himself with us. God has come as man to stand in for us *(descent),* and yet as man he also leads us back to the Father *(ascent).* The entire Christian life is an outworking of this ascent — the appropriate response to God's descent to us — that has already taken place in Christ. Thus, for Calvin, the only appropriate human ascent is a matter of participating in Christ. Calvin's theology of response, Christ as our response, having made the perfect response to God, vitalizes us to respond *in his response.* Ascent, then, is neither a matter of the soul's latent powers nor of conscientious Christian endeavor but of communion: it is a participation in Christ's own response to the Father, whether that be desire for God, prayer, obedience, vocation, or worship.

This hints at a different way of conceiving the divine-human relationship, such that two distinct beings are brought into a rich relationship in which their identities are not diminished but enhanced. Theological anthropology stands to be enriched precisely here, where Calvin's insistence on *participatio Christi* has radical implications for our notions of what it means to be human, what it means to be a "self," and what it means to be in relationship with God and others. Ascent functions as a concrete entry point into Calvin's doctrine of participation, enabling us to focus more specifically on the core element of participation that makes the best sense of his theology.[5]

Calvin is foremost among those who articulate this *koinōnia* relationship between God and humanity, while avoiding pantheistic overtones. This is because his articulation of participation is not due to a prior philosophical principle but flows directly from Christ's sharing in human life. Because God himself, in the person of Christ, shared fully in our humanity, human beings are able to "share," or participate, in God. What is ours has been taken on fully by him; what is his can fully become ours. Calvin reminds his readers of all the times that God makes himself the goal of human life: "I am your very great reward. . . ." "Jehovah is my portion. . . ." "I shall be satisfied with thy countenance. . . ." And then he concludes this with a discussion of participation in the divine life:

> Peter declares that believers are called in this to become partakers of the divine nature. How is this? It is because "he will be . . . glorified in all his saints, and will be marveled at in all who have believed." If the Lord will share his glory, power, and righteousness with the elect — nay, will give himself to be enjoyed by them and, what is more excellent, will somehow make them to become one with himself, let us remember that every sort of happiness is included under this benefit. (III.25.10)

This is not an external relationship of lord and liege or of friend and servant, but a relationship of sharing and mutual indwelling. Nothing less than this will satisfy Calvin, who makes both the *goal* and *means* of the Christian life to be participatory communion. This makes a vital difference in how the church conceives of sanctification, the correlation between human and divine action, and the *koinōnia*-spirituality appropriate for the Christian life.

Calvin's theology of ascent is rich with themes of participation and brings into clear focus its uniquely christological grounding:

---

5. "Ascent" also avoids the pitfalls of the word "participation," a word subject to multiple meanings and misunderstandings, while it facilitates my later discussion of Irenaeus.

Ascension follows resurrection: hence if we are members of Christ we must ascend into Heaven, because He, on being raised up from the dead was received up into Heaven that He might draw us with Him.[6]

Also from the *Institutes:*

> Thus when he said to the apostles, "It is expedient that I go up to the Father," "because the Father is greater than I," he does not attribute to himself merely a secondary deity so that he is inferior to the Father with respect to eternal essence; but because endowed with heavenly glory *he gathers believers into participation in the Father.* . . . And certainly for this reason Christ descended to us, to bear us up to the Father, and at the same time to bear us up to himself, inasmuch as he is one with the Father. (I.13.26; italics added)

Even Calvin's classic passage on the Lord's Supper and the "exchange" that happens there between humanity and Christ cannot escape mention of ascent. "This is the wonderful exchange which, out of his measureless benevolence, he has made with us; that, becoming Son of man with us, he has made us sons of God with him; that, by his descent to earth, he has prepared an ascent to heaven for us" (IV.17.2). Ascent is neither the lone journey of Jesus nor the abstracted elevation of the soul, but is the future for an embodied humanity that is copresent with Jesus and his Father.

Participation and Christianity

It is impossible to deny that the concept (and praxis) of participation is at the center of Christian faith.[7] Originating as an authoritative term from Plato's pen, it is arguably present as an idea in the Old Testament and is

---

6. *Comm. Col.* 3:1.

7. When the English word "participation" is used, we are immediately presented with a problem of ambiguity. The same term is associated with the rules of use governing Plato's *methexis,* and also those associated with the Hebraic concept of the high priest, as again with those governing the Pauline usage of *koinōnia* (which can be interpreted varyingly from both angles). As there is no "essentialist" semantic core in the use of the term, simply a set of family resemblances, I will seek to be clear about what rules apply and allow the person under discussion to define the rules of use.

sporadically integrated into the writings of the New Testament.[8] There are even scholars who argue that Paul is incomprehensible without such an understanding.[9] The apostolic fathers made increasing use of the concept as they interacted with Middle Platonism's recovery of participation, with Irenaeus taking participation wholly on board to describe the kind of relationship that humanity enjoys with the triune God. The ante- and post-Nicene fathers alike struggled to deepen the concept as they found it in the New Testament, capitulating to lesser and greater degrees to the Platonic ontology that lurked in its darker corners.[10] One need only mention Origen, Augustine, Gregory of Nyssa, Denys the Areopagite, Maximus, and Aquinas to confirm our suspicion that participation and Christianity were strange but perhaps well-suited bedfellows with a fruitful and enduring relationship.

The early Greeks had a veritable cache of words to describe group-consciousness and the notion of community-of-being that are inaccessible to us in the modern, privatized West today. (Not unsurprisingly, they had no word to describe our everyday notion of the subjective "self" or "individual.")[11] One such word in their vocabulary for which we have no equivalent is *koinōnia* ("participation"/"indwelling"/"communion"), carrying with it the overtones of sharing-in-being. This concept falls on deaf ears and blinded understandings today, especially when we try to translate it

8. Puntel looks to the *imago Dei* as predecessor for this concept in the Christian tradition (Lourencino Bruno Puntel, "Participation," in *Sacramentum Mundi: An Encyclopedia of Theology*, ed. Karl Rahner [London: Burns & Oates, 1969], p. 347). To this one might add the central notion of vicariousness in the sacrificial system.

9. Although participation is most often associated with Greek philosophy, I am here assuming the biblical scholarship of the last forty years that recognizes participation as a legitimate New Testament concept. Though Albert Schweitzer might be called the grandfather of the debate, it was E. P. Sanders who claimed Paul's theology to be centered less on justification by faith and more around "participation in Christ." For a survey of the responses to this thesis, see N. T. Wright, *What Saint Paul Really Said* (Grand Rapids: Eerdmans, 1997), pp. 11-24. Morna Hooker adds an unusual dimension to our understanding of participation in the New Testament through her term "interchange" (Morna Hooker, "Interchange in Christ," *Journal of Theological Studies* 22 [1971]: 349-61).

10. None has been better aware of the church fathers' use of this schema, while also being acutely aware of the dangerously "hypnotic power of its inner architecture," than Hans Urs von Balthasar, "The Fathers, the Scholastics, and Ourselves," *Communio* 24 (1997): 374.

11. See Collin Morris, *The Discovery of the Individual: 1050-1200* (London: S.P.C.K., 1972), chap. 1.

into almost meaningless words such as "fellowship" or "participation," or even the ambiguous "communion." These terms are meaningless in that our modern sensibilities can only approximate the notion with social images grounded at the outset in the individuality — the separateness — of its members.

When a Greek person living in the classical world experienced the world around him, he did not do so via a system of ideas about his experience but instead felt an "extra-sensory link" between what he saw and his own self.[12] "The participation of the ordinary man was a livelier and more immediate experience . . . man and nature [were linked] in a unity."[13] This was due to the *koinōnia*-consciousness of the classical world (which persisted in varying forms right up until the scientific revolution) that felt an interconnection with all of the cosmos and its human and nonhuman inhabitants.[14] It was a way of experiencing the world in immediacy, where the bounds of the self were not drawn with the stark lines so habitual to us today. Of this consciousness, Pierre Hadot says: "We have here to do with two radically different kinds of relationship to the world."[15]

So why try? Why should we reappropriate an outdated philosophical notion for spiritual theology today? Because *koinōnia* stands to address questions of contemporary culture, spirituality, and relational ontology that are so pressing for us today. It is an underappreciated resource in the Christian tradition (capturing the spirit and insight of the apostle Paul, the genius of the early Christian fathers, and the struggle of the Reformers) that carries an inherent challenge to reductionist spiritualities. George Hunsinger underscores its importance — and elusiveness — for us today:

> [W]hat makes the word *koinonia* untranslatable, and therefore a good candidate for direct appropriation into English (or any language where it may be needed), is the profound and singular connotation of "mutual indwelling." *Koinonia* . . . means that we are not related to God or to one another like ball bearings in a bucket, through a system of external

12. Owen Barfield, *Saving the Appearances: A Study in Idolatry* (New York: Harcourt Brace Jovanovich, 1965), p. 34.

13. Barfield, *Saving the Appearances*, p. 99.

14. This is documented in Barfield, *Saving the Appearances*.

15. Pierre Hadot, *Philosophy as a Way of Life*, trans. Michael Chase (Oxford: Blackwell, 1995), p. 273.

relations. We are, rather, something like relational fields that interpenetrate, form, and participate in each other in countless real though often elusive ways. *Koinonia*, both as a term and as a reality, is remarkable for its range and flexibility and inexhaustible depth.[16]

Theologians, mystics, and preachers through the ages have persistently chosen as one of their principal tools this word *koinōnia,* and they offer it to us — in an era almost crushed by religious individualism — as a life-giving gift.

But there is more. This term is at the heart of the Christian understanding of the triune God as a rich relationship not between individuals but between persons who indwell one another in a loving harmony of friendship and communion. As such, *koinōnia* is at the center of Christian theology (the study of God), anthropology (the study of ourselves), and spirituality (the Christian pattern of experience: being led by the Spirit into God's own triune communion). Edith Humphrey summarizes it this way: "The great pattern of life is the ecstasy and intimacy of God, who went out of the self to the extreme point, and so dwells among us in an intimacy we can hardly imagine."[17] This is *koinōnia*-participation, that of God himself and that which he throws open to humanity. John of Damascus describes the indescribable *koinōnia* of God thus:

> For they are inseparable and cannot part from one another, but keep to their separate courses within one another, without coalescing or mingling, but cleaving to each other. For the Son is in the Father and the Spirit: and the Spirit in the Father and the Son: and the Father in the Son and the Spirit, but there is no coalescence or commingling or confusion. And there is one and the same motion. . . .[18]

Koinōnia can guide us in a time when "God" and "spirituality" are abstracted words. It can lead us forward into reconceiving the interplay between human and divine, thus forcing further reconsideration of the nature of the self and what it means to be truly human. In a world where

---

16. George Hunsinger, *Disruptive Grace* (Grand Rapids: Eerdmans, 2000), p. 257.

17. Edith Humphrey, *Ecstasy and Intimacy* (Grand Rapids: Eerdmans, 2006), p. 4.

18. John of Damascus, "The Exposition of the Orthodox Faith," in *Hilary of Poitiers and John of Damascus,* Nicene and Post-Nicene Fathers [PNF] (Oxford: James Parker, 1898), 1:14.

"spirituality" has left the chapel for the street, if Christian spirituality is to have an identity at all, it must begin here — with *koinōnia*.

The New Testament writers use two Greek words for participation: *methexis* and *koinōnia*.[19] It is interesting that, while the more philosophical *methexis* is used from time to time (signifying to have a share in something), it is *koinōnia* (meaning to share with someone in something) that takes on a new signification under their pens. Barth summarizes the way Pauline *koinōnia* factored personal relationships into what was formerly a philosophical and cosmological conceptual tool. "In the language of the New Testament, *koinōnia* or *communicatio* is a relationship between two persons in which they are brought into perfect mutual coordination within the framework of a definite order, yet with no destruction of their two-sided identity and particularity but rather in its confirmation and expression."[20] T. F. Torrance boils this down to a categorical distinction between Platonic *methexis* and Christian *koinōnia* albeit in an emblematic way, with *methexis* as the notion of participation in the eternal realities and *koinōnia* as the notion of participation in personal relationships.[21] J. Eichler goes so far as to say that *koinōnia* is *methexis*-participation redeemed.[22]

Paul uses *koinōnia* (never *methexis*) to express the large world of the relationship with Christ and the Spirit into which humanity is beckoned. It covers a wide range of theological loci, such as Christ's sharing our humanity, our sharing his passion, glory, and ongoing eucharistic meal, and even the sharing of ourselves with one another by the Spirit.[23] "The full

---

19. Plato uses the verb *metechein* (nouns: *methexis* and *metochē*) to express the concept of "having a share in," and he uses it significantly in his notion of the individual thing to the Idea (*Phaedrus*, 253a). See Hanse, "μετέχω," *TDNT* 2:830. When Plato uses the verb *koinōnein* (noun: *koinōnia*), it has more the sense of "to share *with someone* in something which he has" and thus is more often translated in terms of fellowship than merely participation (*Republic* V.426b). Hauck says that it is peculiar to *koinōnia* that it expresses "a two-sided relation" whose "emphasis may be on either the giving or the receiving" (Hauck, "κοινωνός," *TDNT* 3:797-98).

20. Karl Barth, *Church Dogmatics*, 13 vols. (Edinburgh: T. & T. Clark, 1956-75), IV/3: 535.

21. T. F. Torrance, *Theology in Reconstruction* (London: SCM, 1965), p. 184.

22. *Metechō* is used virtually as a synonym for *koinōneō* (J. Eichler, "Fellowship, Have, Share, Participate," in *New International Dictionary of New Testament Theology*, ed. Colin Brown (Grand Rapids: Zondervan, 1975), p. 639.

23. See the overview in David L. Balás, *Metousia Theou: Man's Participation in God's*

theological import of κοινωνία will only be revealed in the Pauline letters as that most intimate union of man with God and with his fellow-men accomplished through Christ that constitutes final salvation."[24] Under Paul's hand, Greek *methexis*-participation took on personal elements of *koinōnia*-participation — "to be sharply distinguished from both [Greek] ideas and Judaism."[25]

The Johannine writings reveal an approach to participatory union with Christ like that of the Pauline Epistles, although John maintains a sharp boundary between Jesus as God's "Son" and we as his "brothers." Like Paul, his vision is that of more than fellowship, partnership, or Latin *societas*. Rather, we are taken into the divine life so that we become Christ's brothers, sharing the same Father. John does not use the term *metechein* for this, but its (more personal) equivalent, *menein*, meaning "indwelling or abiding."[26] First John most explicitly links *koinōnia* both vertically and horizontally, signifying first our communion with God and then, as a result, what we share with one another.[27] Even Peter's "partakers of the divine nature" (2 Pet. 1:4) is expressed in terms of *koinōnia*, because "we never find *metechein Christou* [to partake of Christ] or *Theou* [to partake of God] in the New Testament."[28]

Perfections According to Saint Gregory of Nyssa, Studia Anselmiana, vol. 55 [Rome: IBC Libreria Herder, 1966], pp. 6-7). Hauck breaks down Paul's usage into the "religious . . . participation of the believer in Christ and Christian blessings" (1 Cor. 1:9; Rom. 8:17); "participation in Christ . . . is achieved and experienced in enhanced form, with no dogmatic implication, in the sacrament" (1 Cor. 10:16); "the Christian participates in the detailed phases of the life of Christ" (Rom. 6:8; 8:17; 2 Cor. 7:3; Gal. 2:19; Col. 2:12; 3:1; Eph. 2:6), especially his sufferings (Phil. 3:10; 1 Pet. 4:13; 2 Cor. 1:5, 7); and "participation in the Spirit" (2 Cor. 3:13). See Hauck, "κοινωνός," *TDNT* 3:804-9.

24. John Michael McDermott, "The Biblical Doctrine of Koinōnia," *Biblische Zeitschrift* 19 (1975): 64-77.

25. J. Schattenmann, "κοινωνία," in *New International Dictionary of New Testament Theology*, p. 643.

26. John Breck, "Trinitarian Liturgical Formulas in the New Testament," in *The Power of the Word* (Crestwood, NY: St Vladimir's Seminary Press, 1986), p. 173. See also the exhaustive study by A. Feuillet, "La participation actuelle à la vie divine d'après le quatrième évangile," in *Johannine Studies* (New York: Alba House, 1964), pp. 295-308.

27. See Hauck, "κοινωνός," *TDNT* 3:807-8. See also Stephen Benko, *The Meaning of Sanctorum Communio* (London: SCM, 1964).

28. Hanse, "μετέχω," *TDNT* 2:831. "There is nothing unusual in the NT use of μετέχειν" (2.831), with all usages exhibiting the secular meaning of "to share": to share bread, to share flesh, to share a stage of development, to share the race of Israel. The only

While it has been reconfigured through the centuries in sometimes less, sometimes more helpful ways, the category of *koinōnia* (participation) has been a central means in Christian thought for reflecting on the relationship between God and humanity. In spite of the thinker who placed it on the philosophical map, participation can never be confined to a mere Platonic concept. For Christians, it expresses the reality of their experience of being drawn into the triune community and ecclesial community, by the Spirit and in the Son. How is it that Christians are said to be "in Christ" and in one another? What does it mean that one day "God will be all in all"? How are we to understand Peter's audacious promise to be "partakers of the divine nature"? In what way do we share in Christ? How do we share in the Holy Spirit? How does human agency function vis-à-vis grace? The New Testament writers and later church fathers used the concept of participation to express precisely the profound depths of this relationship between God and human beings that went beyond mere *societas*. Yet, despite Calvin's own systematic use of the word, it would appear that the term "participation" has become one that is used derisively by many Protestants, especially those who self-consciously follow Calvin.

Is this an instance of grave theological forgetfulness? Or is it the fitting end for a match that was ill suited from the very start? Those of the Radical Orthodoxy movement blame such theological forgetfulness for contemporary Christianity's inability to confront modern secular culture in constructive ways. John Milbank believes that a rediscovery of participation is at the core of his project,[29] which has been acclaimed as "the most heavyweight theological movement twentieth-century Christianity in England has produced."[30] Milbank, Catherine Pickstock, and Graham Ward together self-consciously position themselves in the tradition of Aquinas, Augustine, and Plato, taking the vital insight of these thinkers even further for a critical engagement with modern autonomy and its destructive anthropocentrism.

---

times that *metechein* is used of the relationship between humanity and God is when it is used as a noun, to denote "partaker" (μέτοχος) of Christ (Heb. 3:14) or of the Spirit (Heb. 6:4). Notably, each instance is eschatological (*TDNT* 2:832).

29. "So far, my theological project has been primarily focused upon 'participation,' but in a new way" (John Milbank, *Being Reconciled: Ontology and Pardon* [London: Routledge, 2003], p. ix).

30. From *Theology*, as quoted on the cover of Milbank's *Being Reconciled*.

The central theological framework of radical orthodoxy is "participation" as developed by Plato and reworked by Christianity, because any alternative configuration perforce reserves a territory independent of God. The latter can only lead to nihilism (though in different guises). Participation, however, refuses any reserve of created territory, while allowing finite things their own integrity.[31]

Milbank and these other theologians believe that the premodern tradition engaged in a more helpful manner with the ongoing predicament of the "one and the many." To safeguard the integrity of creatures, modernity has chosen the path that has led to its own destruction: that of defining "freedom" in terms of autonomy and distance *from* God. Instead, Radical Orthodoxy wishes to celebrate the integrity of the creaturely by returning precisely to Christianity's premodern roots in "participatory philosophy and incarnational theology, even if it can acknowledge that the premodern tradition never took this celebration far enough."[32]

Yet, through the centuries there have been other ways of sketching participation than that represented by the Plato-Augustine-Aquinas lineage, a fact that raises questions as to whether the Radical Orthodox have sufficiently engaged with the fullness of participation in the Christian tradition.[33] One such thinker has been the sixteenth-century theologian John Calvin — perhaps to the surprise of Reformed and non-Reformed alike. Calvin's doctrine of participation has its own rules, its own ontology, and its own shortcomings. Nevertheless, it is biblical, rigorous, coherent, and has a surprising amount of muscular flex for one who has been accused of being "so insistent on the separation of the human from the divine."[34] Although some see participation as a parasitic philosophy that was overcome by the Reformation, my thesis aims to tease out precisely this concept in a forefather of the Protestant tradition.

31. John Milbank, Catherine Pickstock, and Graham Ward, eds., *Radical Orthodoxy* (London: Routledge, 1999), p. 3.

32. Milbank et al., *Radical Orthodoxy*, p. 4.

33. Todd Billings points out that Radical Orthodoxy has failed to take Calvin seriously because Calvin's theology of participation does not fit into their Thomist categories. See Todd Billings, *Calvin, Participation, and the Gift* (New York: Oxford University Press, 2008), chaps. 1 and 2.

34. Patricia Wilson-Kastner, "Andreas Osiander's Theology of Grace in the Perspective of the Influence of Augustine of Hippo," *Sixteenth Century Journal* 10 (1979): 88.

Participation as a Valid Reformed Category?

Though I am concerned here with Calvin's doctrine of participation, I will indirectly explore the possible reasons for the relative neglect of this subject matter in Reformed theology.[35] Why is it that the boundaries of "truly" Reformed theology have been drawn in such a way that participation is excluded from the outset? Any number of examples can be selected, almost at random. In his book *Holiness,* which owes much to Calvin, John Webster says: "The language here — 'reconciliation,' 'fellowship,' 'relation' — is deliberate: it is not the language of participation. 'In the Lord' and 'in the Spirit' do not mean union of being between God and the Church. Their reference is not to ontological communion but to soteriology and its fruits. . . ."[36] Webster's statement reveals the ambivalence that clouds the concept of participation, and shows why so many are at pains to distance themselves from it.

Despite his debt to Calvin, Webster would be critiqued by Calvin as not going far enough:

> Thus I interpret that place of St. Paul, 1 Cor 1.9, where he says the faithful are called into the Communion (κοινωνία) of His Son: for the word Fellowship *(Consortium)* or Society *(Societas)* does not seem sufficiently to express his mind; but, in my judgment, he designates that sacred unity by which the Son of God engrafts us into His body, so that He communicates to us all that is His. We so draw life from His flesh and His blood, that they are not improperly called our food.[37]

This is the new kind of relationship between God and humanity that Calvin is exploring and advancing. We do not consort with — or enter the society of — Jesus. Rather, we "participate" — having a relationship of *koinōnia* with him. These relationships are qualitatively different from Platonic schemes of "participation" in that they are characterized by intimacy and differentiation, not consubstantiality.[38] The Trinity itself is their basis.

---

35. An excellent summary of Calvin's doctrine of participation has just recently been published (2008) by Todd Billings, whose work happily corroborates much of the research in this book (*Calvin, Participation*).

36. John Webster, *Holiness* (Grand Rapids: Eerdmans, 2003), p. 62.

37. This is from Calvin's famous letter to Martyr (8 August 1555; *CO* 15.723).

38. For a good summary of *koinōnia*-relations, see George Hunsinger, "Baptism and

Though it is commonly assumed that participation is mired in Platonic and scholastic metaphysics, I will attempt to show that Calvin's use of the term "participation" is based on a pneumatological anthropology and ontology.[39]

Calvin himself clearly draws an explicit line of continuity between the Greek noun *koinōnia* and the Latin *communio*. In defending the term *koinōnia* to Westphal, Calvin says: "[F]or I teach them that no term [κοινωνία] could better explain the mode in which the body of Christ is given to us, than the term *communion,* implying that we become one with him, and being ingrafted into him, truly enjoy his life. It is clear and certain, that this is not done naturally, but by the secret agency of the Spirit."[40] As Calvin advances above, this is a "communion" that is clearly the fruit of participating in a common reality, that "sacred unity" with the Son of God. All three words — *koinōnia, communio,* and participation — overlap in meaning but certainly move toward the signification of a "sharing" and "partaking" rather than mere external relationship. It is a present-tense activity in which humans, by the Spirit, are drawn into the life of the Son of God. We would do well at this juncture to heed Oberman's warning not to ignore how Calvin redefines terms even as he uses them.[41] Calvin's doctrine of participation has been transposed to a new key, set on a *personal* foundation; it has certainly not been obliterated.

While there are those in the West who view an association of Calvin and participation as "an undignified flight to the East," those in the East

---

the Soteriology of Forgiveness," *International Journal of Systematic Theology* 2 (2000): 248-50; "Baptized into Christ's Death," in Hunsinger, *Disruptive Grace,* pp. 253-78.

39. Billings and I differ on one important semantic issue. Billings refers to Calvin's position as "substantial participation," as opposed to more imitative theologies that leave the relationship of God and the believer at an external level. With this I wholeheartedly agree. However, I have chosen to call Calvin's position "pneumatological" or "non-substantial," because I find that the term "substantial" can hinder more than it can help, especially given Calvin's much publicized stance against Osiander and Westphal. Furthermore, I do not feel that the term "substantial" highlights Calvin's uniquely trinitarian rendering of participation, though the advantage of Billings's term is the way it takes Christ's and our concrete humanity seriously. Both Billings and I firmly ground Calvin's doctrine of participation in the Spirit, which clears up a lot of the confusion. In the end, I believe we are saying much the same thing. See Billings, *Calvin, Participation,* pp. 62-63.

40. Calvin, "Last Admonition . . . ," *T&T* 2:414 (*CO* 9.192).

41. Heiko Oberman, "The Pursuit of Happiness: Calvin between Humanism and Reformation," in *Humanity and Divinity in Renaissance and Reformation,* ed. John O'Malley (New York: Brill, 1993), p. 252.

are similarly alarmed by such an association.[42] "Since participation in the essence of God . . . is irreconcilable with the transcendentalism of the Reformed theology, it is clear that no real *participation* in God is possible."[43] This bias stems from an association of Reformed theology with a transcendentalism that is classically defined as God's simplicity, in which God transcends the fabric of contingent human existence. It is not a prejudice held only by outsiders to the Reformed tradition but by insiders as well.[44] Wilhelm Niesel's *The Theology of Calvin* exegetes all of Calvin's theology around this very Chalcedonian "radical distinction . . . impassable gulf" between God and humanity: *inconfuse, immutabiliter, indivise, insepar-abiliter.*[45] However, the burning question is whether this very line between Creator and creature inhibits participation or functions as one of its necessary ingredients. We will examine the Osiander controversy, Calvin's stance on idols, and other strongholds of Calvin's doctrine of transcendence to see whether there is something more going on besides "the inadequate grasp of divine transcendence that marks Calvin."[46]

Finally, there has been the contribution of Calvin's polemical situation that has not been taken seriously enough. Calvin perceived one of the greatest threats in his era to be the blurred distinction between God's gifts and human endowment. Given this blasphemous identification of God's action with human action, Calvin's emphasis on God's transcendence was a necessary correction. This is part of what Kathryn Tanner calls the "negative" side of the rules for coherent Christian discourse about God and the

---

42. Bruce McCormack, "The End of Reformed Theology?" in *Reformed Theology*, ed. Wallace Alston and Michael Welker (Grand Rapids: Eerdmans, 2003), p. 51. McCormack later softened this stance in McCormack, "Participation in God, Yes, Deification, No: Two Modern Protestant Responses to an Ancient Question," in *Denkwürdiges Geheimnis*, ed. Ingolf U. Dalferth, Johannes Fischer, and Hans-Peter Grosshans (Tübingen: Mohr Siebeck, 2004), pp. 347-74.

43. John Meyendorff, "The Significance of the Reformation in the History of Christendom," in *Catholicity and the Church* (Crestwood, NY: St Vladimir's Seminary Press, 1983), p. 75.

44. See the survey of the "dialectical" conception of the divine-human relationship in the Reformed tradition by Philip W. Butin, *Revelation, Redemption, and Response: Calvin's Trinitarian Understanding of the Divine-Human Relationship* (New York: Oxford University Press, 1995), pp. 15-19.

45. Wilhelm Niesel, *The Theology of Calvin* (Grand Rapids: Baker, 1980), pp. 111-13, 247.

46. Louis Bouyer, *A History of Christian Spirituality*, vol. III (London: Burns & Oates, 1969), p. 87.

efficacy of creatures. "Theologians form statements about divine sovereignty to counter improper inferences from talk about the creature's capacities. . . . A number of factors may enter into the theologian's determination of which sort of statement poses the greater danger for a Christian form of life. . . . It is proper to say that the creature is nothing in itself — without power and freedom, an empty vessel to show forth transparently the will of God — when addressing an opponent who presumes the creature is something independent of the will of God."[47] This "distance" of God from his creatures is vital if Calvin is to lay out a theology of God's intimacy *(koinōnia)* that does not absorb or consume his creatures. The high price that Calvin paid for this precision lay in the way that his jargon emphasized God's otherness, making it easy to forget that it served a deeper orientation toward the *koinōnia* of God and humanity. Karl Barth observed with surprise:

> As remarkable as it may sound when I say this about Calvin, he thinks initially not from God but from the human person and his situation. Yet the situation of *humanity* cannot be considered with any seriousness at all without thinking immediately of *God*. For what purpose is the human created?[48]

It is when we leave the combative country of the *Institutes* for the back roads of the commentaries and sermons that these things begin to surface more readily, a much-needed detour lest Calvin's polemics determine all our reading of his theology.

In conclusion, if one defines participation as a throwback to Greek metaphysics, as irreconcilable with a Reformed emphasis on God's otherness, and does not recognize the role of Calvin's polemics, then there is no such phenomenon as a "Reformed" doctrine of participation. And that, indeed, is too high a price to pay.

To this end, I will examine the participatory underpinning of Calvin's doctrine of creation (chapter 2), redemption (chapter 3), and the Christian life (chapter 4). Yet because participation — dealing as it does with how humanity and God are related — spans such a broad spectrum of topics,

47. Kathryn Tanner, *God and Creation in Christian Theology: Tyranny or Empowerment?* (Oxford: Blackwell, 1988), p. 156.

48. Karl Barth, *The Theology of the Reformed Confessions, 1923,* trans. Darrell and Judith Guder (Louisville: Westminster John Knox, 2002), p. 94.

our way into the maze will be through the conventional motif of Christian ascent (chapter 1). Once I have established Calvin's version of a Christian doctrine of participation in God with the breadth and boundaries so unique to his vision, I will be in a position to follow the implications of his doctrine upward in ascent. Yet our itinerary takes us not only downward and upward but also backward to one with a similar vision (chapter 5). Irenaeus throws Calvin's concept of participation into even sharper relief, because he uses participation to fight opposite battles. The vibrant presence of the concept in these two theologians both underscores its importance in Christian theology and allows for rich comparison.

Participation and Irenaeus

Irenaeus of Lyons stands in a similar position to Calvin, as one mediating the Platonic tradition of participation in a self-consciously Trinitarian context. Although I will make no genetic argument for their relation, I will argue for a similarity in the way in which they re-fashioned Platonic participation on the anvil of their perception of the Trinitarian relations.

Like Calvin, Irenaeus readily avails himself of the word *koinōnia* — more than eighty times throughout *Against Heresies* — to communicate the ways in which God draws humanity into his life. Throughout Irenaeus's era, Greek consciousness was bathed in the *daimones* — spirits both good and evil whose presence co-existed with humanity and in whom humanity "participated." This porous identity so typical of classical consciousness was no different for those in the early Church but it had an altogether different source: the indwelling of the believer in the mystical body of Christ. "To [the first Christians] it is quite plainly the invasion of their lives by a new quality of life altogether. They do not hesitate to describe this as Christ 'living in' them. . . . We are practically driven to accept their own explanation, which is that their little human lives had, through Christ, been linked up with the very life of God."[49] The early Christians so readily appropriated the language of participation because it offered a conceptual way into how they perceived their altered reality and worship. "Although there is no evidence that the technical-philosophical understanding of the term influenced the New Testament writers, they did use

49. J. B. Phillips, "Introduction," in *Letters to Young Churches* (London: Geoffrey Bles, 1956), p. xiv.

'participation' to express, on the one hand, human sharing in the Holy Spirit and the communion with Christ and through him God the Father, and, on the other hand, the communion between individual Christians and Christian churches within the total Christian community."[50] Where Calvin and Irenaeus form their own distinct lineage of participation (to whom, be assured, many could be added) is the way in which they use participation primarily to express the relation between the believer and the historical Son of God and, in consequence, to describe the way the believer is drawn into the triune relations. This is not a lineage that is necessarily in competition with the Plato-Augustine-Aquinas axis celebrated by Radical Orthodoxy, although its accents and corrections need to be recognized if contemporary Christianity is to benefit truly from a retrieval of participation.

During the time of Irenaeus, Plato's philosophical concept of participation maintained its appeal as an explanatory tool for the relation of particulars to the universal, offering a solution to the venerable problem of identity and difference.[51] Aristotle had vigorously critiqued this, calling it no more than a "new word," although he maintained the verb *metechein* to explain the ontological relation between the imperfect and perfect possession of a quality.[52] The Middle and Neoplatonists began to nudge participation over into the spiritual realm, using it to express the relationship between the Soul and Mind and between the Mind and the One. No longer was participation limited to a description of the relation between two radically different entities but, instead, began to express the relation between levels of the intelligible world, thus replacing ontological difference with a vertical process of identity. Balás points out that "in the later Neoplatonists, such as Proclus, it served in a more elaborate form, to structure the whole system of emanations."[53] Irenaeus stood right at the junction between Middle and Neoplatonism, deftly using participation for his Christian purposes.[54] For as Rowan Williams reminds us, participation was

50. David L. Balás, "Participation," in *Encyclopedia of Early Christianity*, ed. Everett Ferguson (London: St James, 1990), p. 692.

51. Here we enter the territory of the *sumploke eidon*, which is Plato's discussion of the "interweaving" or mutual indwelling of the forms (*Sophist* 259e, *LCL* 123:424-26).

52. See his critique in *Metaphysics* I, 987b 7-14. Participation is not easy to reconcile with causality, though Aquinas certainly tried.

53. Balás, "Encounter," p. 142.

54. For an excellent survey of participation in the Greek world and early fathers, see Balás, *Metousia*, pp. 1-14. Participation should in no way be limited to Platonism and its

"none the less understood universally in antiquity in the terms outlined by the earlier Plato."[55]

While it has been common to classify Irenaeus as "anti-philosophical" (as opposed to, say, Justin or Clement), his polemic has been increasingly appreciated for its deep grasp of and challenge to the existing philosophy.[56] "It is . . . perhaps somewhat surprising to find the idea of participation rather often in St. Irenaeus, who is usually supposed to be very little influenced by philosophy."[57] Irenaeus did not ignore philosophy but displayed a profound dexterity (and, at times, impatience) with its tools, even as he sought to exceed them. Unlike the other early Apologists, this is perhaps due to the fact that Irenaeus was not a convert from philosophy but grew up under two coinciding educations — that of classical *paideia* and of immersion in the world of Scripture.

> When I was still a boy, I knew you [Florinus] in lower Asia, in Polycarp's house. . . . I remember the events of those days more clearly than those which happened recently, for what we learn as children grows up with life and becomes part of it, so that I can speak even of the place in which the blessed Polycarp sat and taught, how he came in and went out, the character of his life, the appearance of his body, the discourses which he made to the people, how he related his association with [the apostle] John and with the others who had seen the Lord, how he remembered their words . . . and how Polycarp received from them from the eye-witnesses of the Logos of Life, and reported all things in agreement with the Scriptures. I listened eagerly even then to these things through the mercy of God which was given me, and made

---

developers; it was understood differently by many schools in the Greek philosophical tradition. See, e.g., M. Spanneut, *Le Stoicism des pères de l'église* (Paris, 1957) and J. Dillon, *The Middle Platonists* (Ithaca, NY: Cornell University Press, 1977).

55. Rowan Williams, "Analogy and Participation," in *Arius* (London: Darton, Longman, & Todd, 1987), p. 217.

56. It hardly needs to be said that the antipathy between theology and philosophy can no longer be upheld. The result was not the automatic deformation of theology (Harnack's approach) but a creative encounter. As F. Refoulé challenged long ago, early Christian theology represents something radically original that is not reducible to either a purely Hebraic or Hellenistic anterior schema.

57. Balás, *Metousia*, p. 9. For Irenaeus's encounter with Greek philosophy, see the works of Eric Osborn and Antonio Orbe. See also the important cluster of articles in *Studia Patristica* 36 (Louvain: Peeters, 2001).

notes of them, not on paper, but in my heart, and ever by the grace of God do I truly ruminate on them.[58]

Participation was a concept central to the Hellenistic philosophical schools that were themselves not simply intellectual enterprises but also a "way of life" (Hadot). As Christians began to counter this philosophy with their own "true philosophy,"[59] it was not mere correction of doctrine but a renewed way of living and being integrated completely with this revealed "philosophy." In addition to functioning as common philosophical currency, participation lent itself especially well to Christianity and its claim that humans were invited to partake of God's very life, through God's partaking of theirs.

In *Adversus haereses*, one immediately notices that Irenaeus transposes participation from between impersonals to personals. His vision is not that of the sensible participating in the intelligible, or of a mystical ascent to the simple "essence" of God but of humans participating in Christ by the Spirit. As in second-century philosophy, Irenaeus would also structure this in terms of the way that properties of the divine were communicated to the non-divine; yet these are not truly "properties" but rather personal attributes. Balás speaks of this as the transposition of "participation from a purely ontological to a personal sphere."[60] This transposition, continues Balás, was not so much the result of intentioned logic but was rather commanded by a "central intuition . . . [that of] the Christian message of God as love, a loving Communion *(koinōnia)* of Persons, creating men, and other intellectual creatures, from nothing, in order to assume them in this communion."[61]

---

58. Eusebius, *Ekklesiastike Historia*, V.20.5-7.

59. Justin Martyr was the first Apologist to commandeer the term "participation" (see *Dialogue with Trypho* 6) though in a way that is clearly indebted to Middle-Platonism. See John Behr, "The Word of God in the Second Century," *Pro Ecclesia* 9 (2000): 85-94.

60. Though stated in the context of Nyssa, the same is true of Irenaeus (David L. Balás, "Christian Transformation of Greek Philosophy Illustrated by Gregory of Nyssa's Use of the Notion of Participation," in *Proceedings of the American Catholic Philosophical Association, 1966*, ed. George McLean [Washington, DC: Catholic University of America Press, 1966], p. 156).

61. Balás, "Christian Transformation," p. 157. Breck specifically points to the doctrine of the "two hands of God," which renders knowledge of God an experiential and personal rather than theoretical encounter in Irenaeus (John Breck, "'The Two Hands of

Irenaeus was not alone in the second century when he spoke of union with God and participation in him but the peculiar *koinōnia* character of his vision is what set him definitively apart. Paul Lebeau argues that the whole of Irenaeus's theology can be condensed into the word *koinōnia*.[62]

Calvin and Irenaeus

I am not the first to notice a similarity between Calvin and Irenaeus. A century ago, Lidgett observed a common sensitivity to the believer's experience of God's fatherhood. "In Calvin," he says, "a note is struck which has not been heard since Irenaeus."[63] More recently, van Oort recognizes that "modern scholars more than once noticed that Irenaeus's theology of *Heilsgeschichte* shows striking parallels with central aspects of Calvin's theology; although a characteristic term such as *recapitulatio* is not used by Calvin, his theological conformity with Irenaeus does indeed deserve a separate inquiry."[64] T. F. Torrance, similarly, lauds Calvin's christology as "largely governed by the Irenaean doctrine of the Incarnation."[65] These observations about the common accents on God's fatherhood, recapitulation, and the incarnation take us to the heart of participation in the Son.

God': Christ and the Spirit in Orthodox Theology," *St Vladimir's Theological Quarterly* 40 [1996]: 231).

62. "The coherence of the gnostic universe was founded on the principle of incommunicability and dissociation. . . . Irenaeus's universe, as it is often noted, is a universe of unity or, more precisely, of *communion,* of communication, and of mutual exchange where each being keeps its ontological uniqueness even as they open themselves up to others" (Paul Lebeau, "Koinonia: la signification du salut selon saint Irénée," in *Epektasis* [Beauchesne, 1972], pp. 122, 124 [my translation]).

63. J. Scott Lidgett, *The Fatherhood of God* (Edinburgh: T. & T. Clark, 1902), p. 256. I thank Tim Trumper for pointing me to Lidgett's work.

64. Anachronisms aside, van Oort's point still stands in spite of the fact that Calvin did refer to *recapitulatio,* taking the term (not surprisingly) straight from the New Testament; see, for openers, his commentary on Ephesians 1:10 (Johannes van Oort, "John Calvin and the Church Fathers," in *The Reception of the Church Fathers in the West II,* ed. Irena Dorota Backus [Leiden: Brill, 1997], p. 686).

65. T. F. Torrance, ed., *Theological Dialogue Between Orthodox and Reformed Churches* (Edinburgh: Scottish Academic, 1985), p. 104. This is also the perception of Hans Scholl: see Scholl, *Calvinus Catholicus* (Freiburg: Herder, 1974), pp. 121-33. However, the similarities are probably due more to their common biblical basis (Rom. 5:12-21) than to Calvin's direct importation of Irenaeus.

Although Calvin's christocentricity is well known, it is less often grasped that Irenaeus "is the first to whom Jesus Christ, God and man, is the centre of history and faith."[66] From this shared center, both theologians work out a doctrine of the Christian life that is redolent with participation, founded on their common conviction that the life, death, resurrection, and ascent of Christ has radically changed the way we relate to God and the world.

There are risks in bringing a second-century patristic father into dialogue with a Reformation one, not least the risk of semantic distortion. For this reason, I will present Calvin in his context, paying close attention to the details of his doctrine of ascent (chapters 2–4) with little engagement with Irenaeus. Only then will I look retrospectively to Irenaeus (chapter 5), a move that recognizes the integrity of their independent historical and philosophical locations while allowing for thematic engagement. The purpose of this is to situate Calvin within the stream of patristic orthodoxy to which he belongs and to discover whether Irenaeus might have something to offer to Calvin's concept of participation. Furthermore, since Irenaeus is claimed as a father to both the Catholic and Eastern Orthodox traditions (and increasingly to the Protestant), the embryonic ecumenical possibilities are obvious as well.

I will conclude my "backward" look by bringing both theologians forward into the contemporary realm, looking at the implications of their doctrine of participation for the present day (chapter 6). What makes a comparison of Calvin and this Gallic predecessor so interesting for today is the way in which they used participation to fight opposite battles. In Calvin's time, the transcendence of God was threatened by the humanist exaltation of humanity. Irenaeus's situation could not have been more contrary, with the Gnostics compromising the goodness of humanity and creation through twisted beliefs about divine transcendence. Yet both answered their opponents with a startling vision of human participation in Christ, all the while building these anthropologies from opposite ends of the spectrum. My intent is that Irenaeus's vision would draw attention to the originality and continuity of Calvin's own concept of participation, while also providing gentle correctives as needed.

It should be quite clear that I am neither attempting to repristinate a specific era of the past nor am I constructing a pedigree of Calvin's sup-

66. Adolph Harnack, *History of Dogma*, vol. 2 (London: Williams & Norgate, 1894), p. 243.

posed sources.[67] For although Irenaeus is Calvin's seventh most frequently cited church father, Calvin was primarily "reacting to the uses that Irenaeus was put to by his adversaries."[68] Rather, I am attempting to do theology on the model of the *sanctorum communio* — the belief that we are neither isolated Christians nor objective scientists but rather within a church and stream of tradition. Barth says,

> The Church does not stand in a vacuum. Beginning from the beginning, however necessary, cannot be a matter of beginning off one's own bat. We have to remember the communion of saints, bearing and being borne by each other, asking and being asked, having to take mutual responsibility for and among the sinners gathered together in Christ.[69]

To be only a spectator of those who entered into this task of theology is to violate the nature of what they have undertaken, for theology is by nature *personal* — marked by the one who first reveals himself to us.[70] Or to put it bluntly, there is a difference between Calvin *as subject matter* and Calvin's subject matter. To give Calvin a voice is to respect not only the particularity of his time (and the particularity of revelation) with rigorous historical research, it is also to value the themes that he shares with us. It is to refuse, with Philip Butin, the false alternatives of either "confessional" or "histori-

67. Irena Backus, "Irenaeus, Calvin and Calvinist Orthodoxy: The Patristic Manual of Abraham Scultetus (1598)," *Reformation and Renaissance Review* no. 1 (June 1999): 44.

68. I have in mind here the eleven theses of A. N. S. Lane, *John Calvin: Student of the Church Fathers* (Edinburgh: T. & T. Clark, 1999), pp. 1-13. Of the three kinds of studies in relating Calvin to a predecessor, this falls into Lane's first category. "Such studies need not presuppose Calvin's being influenced by, or even acquainted with, the figure concerned. . . . The significance of such studies is usually ecumenical or polemical rather than historical" (p. 15). Nevertheless, Lane does identify Froben's 1528 Basel edition of *Adversus haereses* as that from which Calvin worked (pp. 76-77).

69. Karl Barth, *Protestant Theology in the Nineteenth Century* (London: SCM, 2001), p. 3.

70. Barth's quarrel with Harnack was a watershed of sorts for the disciplines of history and theology, which have yet to recover from the split. Harnack garnered respect for theology from a strict *historical* approach; Barth believed that this emasculated its very character as *theological*. Historical theology has come a long way since Harnack's time, and it has slowly recognized that the task of "church history" requires in itself a doctrine of the church and of history. A Christian engagement in church history requires both a strong doctrine of creation (as the place and space where God speaks) and reconciliation (as history is called into question by the one who made and is making history).

cal" theology and engage both Calvin and Irenaeus as dialogue partners for a deepened understanding of participation.[71] As Holmes quips, "The doctors are not dead and gone, but living and active."[72] If there is an attempt to "use" Calvin for this vital issue in contemporary theology, then so be it. I believe he just might have something to say.

71. Butin, *Revelation,* p. 4.

72. See Stephen R. Holmes, "On the Communion of Saints," in *Listening to the Past* (Carlisle, UK: Paternoster, 2002), p. 30.

Chapter 1

Ladders of Ascent:
A Brief History

Thee, God I come from, to thee go,
All day long I like fountain flow
From thy hand out, swayed about
Mote-like in thy mighty glow.[1]

When it comes to Calvin's concept of participation, we find ourselves with the unsurprising task of pulling apart inheritance and innovation. As much as Calvin improved on some of the excesses of medieval scholasticism, he was its rightful child and heir. The discussion in this chapter falls into three parts: (1) Greek patterns of ascent; (2) Christian appropriation of these patterns; and (3) Calvin's distinctive appropriation and transformation of this pattern, using Aquinas in particular as a foil. A brief look at the history of ascent will begin to tease out the consonance and innovations between Calvin and the developments of patristic and medieval theology. It is when we understand the uniqueness of Calvin's doctrine of ascent that we will be poised to understand his doctrine of participation and how it differed from the vision of Plato, Plotinus, and even Aquinas. And it is this basic vision that, I will argue, is not far from Irenaeus.

---

1. An example of Plotinus's "golden circle," as it was appropriated by the Christian poet Gerard Manley Hopkins, *The Poems of Gerard Manley Hopkins,* ed. W. H. Gardner and N. H. MacKenzie, 4th ed. (London: Oxford University Press, 1967), p. 189.

Greek Itineraries:
Plato's Ladder and Plotinus's Golden Circle

When early Christians attempted to understand themselves, their relationship to God, and their future, they used the tools at their disposal: words and concepts forged in the fiery minds of Greek philosophers. The Hellenistic typology of ascent was not repugnant to early Christian theologians, whose Lord had ascended into the heavens to be the "firstborn" of many brothers. Not only had rising Jewish apocalypticism paved the way for this emphasis on ascent; it was also the history of their Lord and Savior.[2] The apostle Paul, too, spoke rapturously of being "caught up to the third heaven. Whether it was in the body or out of the body I do not know — God knows" (2 Cor. 12:2). The soul's *descent* from paradise and accompanying salvation and progressive *ascent* to Christ was a way to mark the contours of the grand scheme of things: the drama of sin, salvation, and return. And yet, for a doctrine of ascent to be authentically Christian, these theologians had to wrestle with two problematic aspects of Hellenistic ascent: its underlying escapism and its ontological monism. I will begin with a description of Hellenistic cosmologies in order to lay a general framework for Christian appropriations of ascent, noting that these descriptions are only to provide general schematic accuracy sufficient to our purpose.

Plato

Plato (fourth century BCE) dominated the world of classical Greece, stamping on it his hypothesis of the soul's natural divinity and introducing the image of the ladder. Having fallen into our corrupt world of flesh, changeability, and history, the soul desires to return to its eternal homeland. "Beginning from obvious beauties he must for the sake of that highest beauty be ever climbing aloft, as on the rungs of a ladder,

2. Second Temple Judaism birthed numerous apocalypses of "ascent," and often focused on Jewish ancestors who had had such experiences (e.g., Enoch, who "walked with God; then he was no more, because God took him away" [Gen. 5:24]). The visions recounted in 1 Enoch (third century BCE) reflect a radical shift in Jewish expectation, locating the presence of God away from the Temple and now toward the heavens. See John Collins, "A Throne in the Heavens," in *Death, Ecstasy, and Other Worldly Journeys*, ed. John Collins and Michael Fishbane (New York: State University of New York Press, 1995), p. 55.

. . . so that in the end he comes to know the very essence of beauty."[3]
This strong line of demarcation between our world of appearances,
marked by instability and *becoming*, and the world of "Ideas" or "Forms"
(in *Parmenides*), marked by permanence and *being*, is pervasive throughout Plato and has had inestimable influence on the Christian tradition.
Ascent, then, factors as the path for the exiled soul out from materiality
and is accomplished by a threefold ascent of purification *(askēsis)*, illumination, and contemplative union *(theoria).*[4] Socrates' famous illustration of the chariot in *Phaedrus* describes not only the ascent of the soul
but also the previous descent into materiality. Likening the soul to
winged horses (human and divine parts) guided by a charioteer, Socrates
describes the fateful plunge of the chariot to earth, imprisoning the soul
in a physical body. "And now let us ask the reason why the soul loses her
wings!" (246D). Vice, ignorance, and a love of opinion over truth im-
prison the soul on earth for ten thousand years. However, the philoso-
pher can break the cycle by a frankly intellectual solution: nourishing his
broken wings on "the plain of truth" (248B) through contemplation and
restraining the lower elements in order to ascend once again. Here ascent and participation are clearly bedfellows, in that the soul participates
naturally in divinity and, as such, is enabled to ascend to its original
home. But perhaps even more forceful is Plato's *dis*junction between the
heavenly and the material. The soul, exiled, is no more of this world
than are the Ideas.[5]

Plotinus

Neo-Platonism, with Plotinus (third century CE) at the helm, synthesized
600 years of Platonic speculation and bequeathed to Christian philosophers even more sophisticated conceptual tools. For Plotinus, ascent functioned as the "return" from a prior departure of all reality from the One (*to
hen*). Unlike Plato's dichotomy between being and becoming, Plotinus did

---

3. *Symposium* 211C, *LCL* 166:206. See the Loeb Classical Library [hereafter *LCL*]
translation: *Plato: Lysis, Symposium, Gorgias,* trans. by W. R. M. Lamb (London: Harvard
University Press, 1984).

4. See Diotema's speech in the *Symposium* 210 A-D (*LCL* 166:200-205).

5. For an overview of Plato's oscillation between univocal participation and dualism,
see Kathryn Tanner, *God and Creation in Christian Theology: Tyranny or Empowerment?*
(Oxford: Blackwell, 1988), p. 40.

not structure his great ordering principle around a dualistic distinction between a unitive source and the fragmented reality subordinate to it. Instead, he spoke of the procession of being from the One, of like from like, in a descending hierarchy in which lower stages flow from the higher ones through emanation. This achieved systematic status in Proclus, who developed it into a nonhistorical principle of logic. He wrote of the "communion" *(koinōnia)* of all things as they exist in perpetual procession from and return to their source — a process that "must be accomplished through likeness."[6] Under Proclus's consistent treatment, procession and return became the nonsequential, interlocking movements of all causes and effects that constitute reality.

Plotinus, however, was not really a systematician, so he oscillated between procession-return as a timeless theory of reality and as a description of the soul. We will find that Augustine will follow Plotinus's individualization of the theory, while Aquinas will broaden it out into a comprehensive principle to sum up all theology (and the processions within God himself). In Plotinus, the ontological levels (three *hypostases*) that separate the soul from the One do not mediate between them as a buffer but rather are levels to which the soul is ontically assimilated as it participates to a greater and greater degree in the One.[7] "Procession" and "return" become the organizing movements around which life is understood and redirected. Plotinus claimed to have several mystical experiences with the One throughout his lifetime, such as the autobiographical passage in *Ennead* 4.8.1:

> Often have I woken up out of the body to myself and have entered into myself, going out from all other things; I have seen a beauty wonderfully great and felt assurance that then most of all I belonged to the better part; I have actually lived the best life and come to identity with the divine; and set firm in it I have come to that supreme actuality, setting myself above all else in the realm of Intellect. Then after that rest in the divine, when I have come down from Intellect to discursive reasoning, I am puzzled how I ever came down. . . .[8]

6. Proclus, *Elements of Theology*, trans. E. R. Dodds (Oxford: Clarendon, 1933), pp. 37-39. See in particular Propositions 32-35.

7. These *hypostases* are *to hen* (the One), *nous* (the intellect), and *logos* (the world-soul), which are not equal, but are a descending order of being. See *Ennead* 5.1.6.

8. *LCL* 443:397.

It is Plotinus's univocal view of reality that allows for his gradual ascent and ontic assimilation to the divine. The world is not in opposition to the divine, but rather has descended from the One and is capable of return. For Plotinus, this "return" is first a movement inward — *gnōthi seauton* — and only then a movement upward (a double movement that becomes central to both Augustine and Bonaventure).[9] The soul, finding itself on the lowest plane of being, leads "a life which takes no delight in the things of this world" and through contemplation begins to experience "liberation from the things of this world. . . ."[10] As it is purified, the soul is ontically assimilated at each enlightened higher level. "He was one himself, with no distinction in himself either in relation to himself or to other things."[11] This is Plotinian ascent — "escape in solitude to the solitary" — in which the soul's highest good is for the philosophically elite, and is an individual matter.[12]

Christian theology leaned heavily on these concepts, and it was not without temptation and crucifixion that it gradually (and not entirely) transformed them. Plato and Plotinus, whose influence is inestimable, represent the twin pitfalls of Hellenistic ascent for Christian theologians, even as they provided the necessary nomenclature.[13] Of the first, the Platonic temptation, Bernard McGinn says:

> Contemplation is only one of the historically and culturally conditioned forms in which Christian mysticism has come to birth, but it is one of the most ubiquitous and enduring.[14]

Plato's sharp disjunction between the realm of appearances and the realm of Ideas threatened to taint a typology of ascent with material suspicion, even for those who believed in a Creator. His upward itinerary, depicted by a three-staged ladder, "would shape the basic psychological structure of the following centuries."[15] Similarly, its privileging of the rational soul had the potential to stunt anthropology and, with it, sanctification.

9. Taken from the injunction inscribed above the Delphic Oracle: "Know Thyself."
10. *Ennead* 6.9.11 (*LCL* 468:345).
11. *Ennead* 6.9.11 (*LCL* 468:341).
12. *Ennead* 6.9.11 (*LCL* 468:345).
13. For example, see James Hankins's *Plato in the Renaissance*, 2 vols. (Leiden: Brill, 1990).
14. Bernard McGinn, *The Foundations of Mysticism* (New York: Crossroad, 1991), p. 24.
15. Émile Bertaud and André Rayez, "Échelle Spirituelle," *Dictionnaire de Spiritualité* 4 (Paris: Editions Beauchesne, 1961): 65, my translation.

Of the second, the Plotinian temptation, McGinn says:

The . . . master paradigm of *exitus* and *reditus,* the flowing out of all things from the First Principle and their eventual return to it, had been incorporated into Christian mysticism as early as the time of Origin. This central motif also appeared in the thought of Dionysius and through him influenced mystics in both Eastern and Western Christianity. . . . The "flowing forth" of all things from God was employed by earlier mystics primarily to express the ontological foundation for their major concern, that is, the exploration of the soul's ascent to God.[16]

The legacy of Plotinian ascent is a participatory view of reality.[17] Plotinus transposes the Platonic descent, or "fall," of the soul to embodiment into a procession of all creatures from the One. Plotinian ascent is marked less by escape than by corresponding *return.* Yet the univocal nature of such a scheme once again is challenged by Christianity's belief in a Creator who is radically *other* than his creatures. The Christian insistence on a mediator is undermined by a Plotinian ascending typology that suggests progressive, unmediated participation in divinity. In the Christian narrative, the human drama is less a matter of "like returning to like" than an act of salvation, of grace bringing unlike to participate in unlike.

All of these aspects of Hellenistic ascent continued to challenge Christian theology, even as Christian theology used descent/ascent and procession/return as a frame around which to make itself intelligible. Was this, then, the "Hellenizing of Christianity," or, in Eastern Orthodox eyes, the auspicious "Christianizing of Hellenism"?[18] There will always be theologians who deem ascent to be at cross-purposes with a theology based on the descent of God to us; similarly, there will be those who see participation exclusively as a Greek philosophical phenomenon, having no place in the New Testament. But there are others who take it seriously precisely because it has

16. Bernard McGinn, *The Flowering of Mysticism* (New York: Crossroad, 1998), p. 231.

17. This is perhaps best displayed in Pseudo-Dionysius, whose "uplifting spirituality" impacted the West in three ways: "the motif of 'procession and return,' the uplifting from the perceptible to the conceptual, and the leap beyond all concepts into the silent darkness of unknowing" (Paul Rorem, "Pseudo-Dionysius," in *Christian Spirituality I,* ed. Bernard McGinn and John Meyendorff [London: Routledge, 1986], p. 147).

18. Robert W. Jenson, "The Initial Christianizing of Hellenism," in *Christian Dogmatics I,* ed. Carl E. Braaten and Robert W. Jenson (Philadelphia: Fortress, 1984), p. 118.

been the chosen (and presumably sanctified) language of the church. Andrew Louth well notes, "And yet man *is* made in the image of God, and so these movements of ascent and descent cross one another and remain — as a fact of experience — in unresolved tension."[19] While our description of Hellenistic ascent suggests at once an escape from the world and the univocal nature of being, neither of these pitfalls need accompany an authentically Christian use of such typology (as we shall see with Calvin). Ascent has proved an invaluable category for theologians who are articulating the process of sanctification, the final "return" of all things to communion with their Creator, and participation in the One who has ascended.

Christian Journeys: Origen, Augustine, and Aquinas

I now turn to a discussion of theologians who have expressed Christian theology within a typology of ascent and/or return. We will focus on Augustine and Aquinas, two who have unquestionably left their mark on the Western (and especially late medieval) theology that Calvin inherited. Origen is interesting for our purposes as the first to arrange his theology along this formal structure and as a brief example of a theologian unable to transform such typology.

Origen

Origen's (third century) ascent-mysticism comes to us as a mixed bag. Perhaps the greatest exegete in the history of the church,[20] Origen is regarded by von Balthasar as the master of the *theologia ascendens* in that he transposed his entire cosmology, soteriology, and mysteriology into a formal structure ("attitude," von Balthasar says) of ascent.[21]

> In this everything is actually graded upwards, everything directed to the *ascensiones in corde,* everything turned upward from the concealing low-

---

19. Andrew Louth, *The Origins of the Christian Mystical Tradition* (Oxford: Clarendon, 1981), p. xiv.

20. McGinn, *Foundations,* p. 110.

21. Hans Urs von Balthasar, *Origen: Spirit and Fire* (Edinburgh: T. & T. Clark, 2001), p. 13.

liness to the radiant light of Tabor. . . . [It] is *this* Origen who entered without reserve, as it were, into the broadest ranges of the thinking of the Church. Not only did all the Alexandrians after him, not only did Pamphilius, Gregory the Wonder-Worker, Didymus, Eusebius and the Cappadocians, Jerome, Hilary, Ambrose and, through all these, Augustine accept his model of the *ascensiones in corde,* but also, mediated through these dominant figures, the little thinkers, the preachers, the people.[22]

Origen's cosmology is played out amidst the drama of fallen intellects who, in committing the first sin, "fell" into embodiment (*De principiis* 2.9). (Origen was the first to coin the word "fall" for original sin, because he regarded it as a literal fall from the higher spirit world to our lower world of materiality.) Having fallen, these intellects follow a threefold Platonic-style pedagogy to return to God: purification, illumination, and contemplative union.[23] Given this cosmic tutorial, Origen's soteriology follows suit and styles the person of Christ as the cosmic educator of these misplaced souls. (The Spirit is, not surprisingly, the Spirit of Wisdom.) In this scheme, the physicality of the Savior can be read as more or less a stage for the soul to pass by as it ascends to less and less mediated knowledge of the eternal Logos — for how could God's limitation be his ultimate expression?[24] In comparison to his near-contemporary Irenaeus, we see in this Alexandrian (and many after him) a subtle shift in accent away from the salvation of the flesh to the pedagogy of the soul.

McGinn argues that Origen's ascent "departs from Platonism both in its Christocentrism and in its biblical foundation," especially in that Origen's mystical ascent is not a Plotinian ascent in "solitude to the solitary" but is located in the mystical body of Christ, the church.[25] Furthermore, Origen rigorously distanced himself from the Platonic substructure

22. Von Balthasar, *Origen,* pp. 8-9.

23. This is woven throughout his homilies on the *Song of Songs* (1:1-12; 1:12-2:14), made particularly accessible in the translation by O. Rousseau, whose critical notes outline Origen's "Mystical Ascension" (II), "The Ladder of the Songs" (III), and "The Seven Stages" (IV).

24. "[B]ut the shadow of Christ, under which we now live among the Gentiles, that is to say, the faith of his incarnation, affords complete protection. . . . Yet the period of this shadow too is to be fulfilled at the end of the age . . ." (Origen, *The Song of Songs: Commentary and Homilies,* trans. R. P. Lawson [London: Longmans, Green, 1957], III.5).

25. McGinn, *Foundations,* p. 116.

of the soul's innate divinity. Nevertheless, Douglas Farrow rightly wonders whether Origen's scheme conjures up images of the Christian life as a reform school. He further argues: "By now it will be obvious that Origen is the real source of the idea of the general ascent of man, and of the doctrine of progress in a collective sense."[26] While this is too harsh and too general to be of much help, there is truth in Farrow's charge that Origen solidified and baptized a general Platonic template. The embodied ascension of Christ has been replaced by the ascension of the soul to higher consciousness.[27] Origen's speculation on the soul's descent led to a unique myth of descent, a fusion of Genesis 3 and the falling chariot of *Phaedrus*. His transposition of ascent into the soul's ascent *away* from the material (and even away from the humanity of Christ) bequeathed an instability to Christian reflection on ascent, for von Balthasar does not exaggerate when he says that Origen "has become invisibly all-present in Christian theology."[28]

Augustine

While variations on the soul's ascent were being played out in the East, Augustine (fourth century) imported ascent mysticism to the West. At an impressionable time in his life, Augustine landed in Milan, where Christian Neo-Platonism was thick in the air.[29] Shortly thereafter, Augustine wrote *De quantitate animae*, which analyzes a seven-step schematization of the soul's ascent to God: (1) animation (of the body); (2) sense; (3) art (abilities of the soul); (4) virtue and purification; (5) tranquility (remaining purified); (6) ingress (seeking the vision of God); (7) contemplation of God.[30] In 388, Augustine further nuanced his seven-step ascent in *De*

26. Douglas Farrow, *Ascension and Ecclesia* (Grand Rapids: Eerdmans, 1999), pp. 93 and 104.

27. Origen, *Song*, III.12.

28. Von Balthasar, *Origen*, p. 7.

29. Most likely, he was introduced to it while listening to the sermons of Ambrose (perhaps, as in Courcelle's intriguing thesis, his sermons of Holy Week, 386). Yet Augustine preferred Psalm 45 to Ambrose's eroticism; see F. Asiedu, "The Song of Songs and the Ascent of the Soul: Ambrose, Augustine, and the Language of Mysticism," *Vigiliae Christianae* 55 (2001): 313.

30. I have used the general description as summarized by Calvin, in his "Psychopannychia," *T&T* III.470. Calvin cites Augustine's *De quantitate animae* 33:70-76.

musica. Though he later abandoned this project, it is this seven-step ascent of the early Augustine that was to have the most enduring legacy in the Christian tradition: it was adopted almost wholesale by Bonaventure (in *Itinerarium mentis in Deum*) and quoted even by Calvin. This pattern was to remain an important literary device: the ladder of the gifts of the Spirit, the ladder of the seven days of creation (allegorically interpreted), the ladder of the ten degrees of humility, and the ladder of Christ.[31]

New readings of Augustine argue for a short-lived enchantment with Plotinian ascent, followed by direct engagements to subvert it. Van Fleteren charts the years 386 through 391 as the period of Augustine's attempt to ascend to a direct vision of God, followed by his commentary on Paul's *Epistles to the Romans and Galatians* (394-95), in which "the final nail is driven into the coffin of this project."[32] Cavadini goes even further, suggesting that "the *De trinitate* uses the Neoplatonic soteriology of ascent only to impress it into the service of a thoroughgoing critique of its claim to raise the inductee to the contemplation of God, a critique that, more generally, becomes a declaration of the futility of any attempt to come to a saving knowledge of God apart from Christ."[33] While this is perhaps true, it is also triumphalistic. We must not forget that Augustine set himself within the ascent tradition of which he was "a disciple as well as a critic."[34] Although he stopped speculating on the specific stages of the soul's ascent, he retained a more confessional form of a descent-ascent structure. Paul Rorem, summarizing literary analyses of Augustine's *Confessions*, charts the outline in Books 1-9 as Augustine's personal and geographic descent from God, the church, and his Christian mother, and then a return or ascent back to them and to his homeland. Augustine followed the footsteps of Plotinus rather than Proclus in that he considered this structure "not yet as an over-arching structure for God and the world, but as a parabola for an individual. When applied by the Bishop of Hippo to the pilgrimage not of Christ but of his own soul, the framework

31. See Bertaud and Rayez, "Echelle," pp. 66-67.

32. Frederick Van Fleteren, "The Ascent of the Soul in the Augustinian Tradition," in *Paradigms in Medieval Thought, Applications in Medieval Disciplines,* ed. N. Van Deusen, Mediaeval Studies, vol. 3 (Lewiston, NY: Edwin Mellen Press, 1990), p. 101.

33. John Cavadini, "The Structure and Intention of Augustine's *De trinitate,*" *Augustinian Studies* 23 (1992): 106.

34. Martha Nussbaum, "Augustine and Dante on the Ascent of Love," in *The Augustinian Tradition,* ed. Gareth Matthews (Berkeley: University of California Press, 1999), p. 63.

of procession and return as a formal outline makes a striking impact on Christian literature."[35]

Although Augustine's earlier works *(De quantitate animae* and *De genesi contra Manichaeos)* only slightly modify the pattern of the soul's contemplative ascent, he "comes to think this view of ascent unacceptable,"[36] and instead shifts to a notion of ascent as desire for God *(Confessions).*[37] This desire, rather than the soul's innate divinity, is the momentum for the soul's ascent and comes about through the tutorial of the Holy Spirit. Yet one can argue that he did not go far enough in transforming ascent in three notable ways.

First, it is a fair question to ask whether Augustine's ascent involved not only an ascent toward but also an ascent away from embodiment and physicality. Stroumsa wonders whether this fundamental shift toward ascent was aided by the "demonization of the cosmos . . . [which was] responsible for the insistence on the soul's duty to ascend to heaven."[38] Second, though Augustine's *noverim me, noverim te* linked the knowledge of God and of self together in a robust manner, this inward (and profoundly Plotinian) turn did not guard itself enough against anthropocentrism.[39] To corroborate knowledge of God by turning inward first to the home of desire, in order only then to turn upward to its object, leaves ascending desire open to multiple interpretations. In so doing, Augustine perpetuated the basic Platonic pattern of ascent, even as he critiqued it.

The third and final critique surrounds what might ironically — and anachronistically — be described as a subtle Pelagianism associated with Augustine's ascent. Although he makes the descent of God to us the fun-

---

35. Paul Rorem, "'Procession and Return' in Thomas Aquinas and His Predecessors," *Princeton Seminary Bulletin* 13 (1992): 150. See also R. J. O'Connell, "The Riddle of Augustine's 'Confessions': A Plotinian Key," *International Philosophical Quarterly* 4 (1964): 327-72.

36. Nussbaum, "Augustine and Dante," p. 62.

37. For an analysis of the parallels between Book VII of the *Confessions* and Plato's contemplative ascent in *Phaedo, Phaedrus,* and *The Banquet* (Symposium), see George Tavard, *Les Jardins de saint Augustin: Lecture des Confessions* (Paris: Cerf, 1988), pp. 25-39.

38. Guy Stroumsa, "Mystical Descents," in Collins and Fishbane, *Death, Ecstasy,* p. 147.

39. From *Soliloquies* 2.1.1. For similar statements, see *Confessions* 10.1.1 and 10.27.38. Rowan Williams argues more optimistically for Augustine's "mature reworking" of the whole theme of "entering into oneself" to find God (Williams, "The Paradoxes of Self-Knowledge in De trinitate," in *Augustine,* ed. J. Lienhard et al. [New York: Peter Lang, 1993], pp. 121-34).

damental precursor to our ascent of love, there is a lingering sense that *he* is the traveler, the one seeking God, the one desiring. While participation in God is fundamental for Augustine,[40] this eros for God is not located within Christ's response and eros for God, but within human anthropology. An interesting critique of Augustine comes from Calvin, no less, precisely here. In his *Commentary on Romans*, 5:5, Calvin notes that Augustine believes that the "love of God shed abroad in our hearts" is active — our love *for* God — rather than passive: the "knowledge of the divine love *toward* us instilled into our hearts by the Spirit of God." Ever-respectful of Augustine, Calvin concludes, "It is indeed a pious sentiment, but not what Paul means." It is no accident that Osiander often cites Augustine's interpretation of this verse to defend his own notion of divine indwelling.

Thus, paradoxically, John Meyendorff could possibly be proved right when he charges that it has been Western Christianity, not the East (despite general opinion to the contrary), that has been more influenced by Platonism precisely due to this inattentiveness to sources such as Augustine. Meyendorff argues that the church fathers were more "consistently aware of the incompatibility between ancient Greek philosophy and the gospel" due to their closeness to it.[41] One may wonder whether the generations of Western Christians who patterned their theology on the literary motifs of the early Augustine realized the extent to which he later moved away from them.[42] Regardless, "Augustine's views on the ascent of the soul, influenced directly as they were by Plotinus, Porphyry, and Ambrose and, indirectly, by Plato, held sway throughout the Middle Ages."[43]

40. See David Vincent Meconi, "The Incarnation and the Role of Participation in St. Augustine's *Confessions*," *Augustinian Studies* 29, no. 2 (1998): 61-75; Patricia Wilson-Kastner, "Grace as Participation in the Divine Life in the Theology of Augustine of Hippo," *Augustinian Studies* 7 (1976): 135-52.

41. John Meyendorff, "Greek Philosophy and Christian Theology in the Early Church," in *Catholicity and the Church* (Crestwood, NY: St Vladimir's Seminary Press, 1983), p. 46.

42. Certainly it cannot be proven, as O'Connell attempts, that there is a decisive distinction between the early ("Platonic") and later Augustine. See R. J. O'Connell, *St. Augustine's Early Theory of Man* (Cambridge: Harvard University Press, 1968); see also R. J. O'Connell, "The Plotinian Fall of the Soul in St. Augustine," *Traditio* 19 (1963): 1-35. But there should be no problem with stating the obvious: that Augustine did grow into a more Christian understanding, and away from the Neo-Platonism that had such a hand in his conversion.

43. Van Fleteren, "Ascent," p. 110.

Thomas Aquinas

When we come to the breathtaking vision of Thomas Aquinas (thirteenth century), we find many of these strands woven into his *Summa Theologiæ* of contemplative prayer and theology. The *Summa* is less a sterile intellectual apologetic, as it is often caricatured, than an invitation prayerfully to consider humanity's beginning and end, a beginning and end that are ordered wholly to God.[44] It is this rendering of the divine-human relationship on such a macrocosmic level that explains the *Summa's* continuing attraction. Readers interpret their own lives within this majestic narrative grid of our departure *(exitus)* from God in creation and our eventual return *(reditus)* to him.

For Aquinas, the contemplation of this "golden circle," as it later came to be known, is transformative. Anna Williams notes that the structure of the *Summa* "suggests [that] a unitive principle should guide all Christian theology. . . . Theologies which thus express the telos of both theology and human existence itself . . . will succeed, as Aquinas's *Summa* does, in not only speaking of theology and contemplation, but engaging in theology contemplatively."[45] Aquinas pressed participation into such a robust system that all scholastic theology after him would have to reckon with the concept. Throughout, Aquinas sought to give a nonanthropocentric account of human existence, while also identifying God as the one who desires to be with us.

If it was Augustine who bequeathed the seven-grade ascent to later generations, it was Aquinas who repristinated the Plotinian procession-return scheme, chronicling the process of creatures *from* God (*ST*, Ia, q44-119) and then the journey *to* God of reasoning creatures.[46] His *Summa* is broken down into three chronological *partes* of theology, anthropology, and, only then, christology. Aquinas lays out the rationale for his work as follows:

---

44. For an elucidation of the *Summa* as contemplative spirituality, see Anna Williams, "Mystical Theology Redux: The Pattern of Aquinas' *Summa Theologiæ*," *Modern Theology* 13 (1997): 53-74.

45. Anna Williams, "Mystical Theology Redux," p. 72.

46. Rorem argues that Aquinas's Trinitarianism — in which a procession into plurality is true not only of creation but of his doctrine of God — is of late Neo-Platonic influence, and is perhaps more influential than Augustine's infamous insistence on the logical priority of *de Deo uno* (Rorem, "Procession and Return,'" pp. 147-63).

So because, as we have shown, the fundamental aim of holy teaching is to make God known, not only as he is in himself, but as the beginning and end of all things and of reasoning creatures especially, we now intend to set forth this divine teaching by treating,

First, of God,

Secondly, of the journey to God of reasoning creatures,

Thirdly, of Christ, who, as man, is our road to God. (*ST,* Ia, Prologue)[47]

In the *Prima Pars,* Aquinas treats the doctrine of God, who is pure actuality. "[T]he first agent is pure agent acting not to get something but to communicate his own perfection and goodness . . ." (*ST,* Ia, q44, a4). Aquinas then reasons: "So God's goodness is the goal of everything. . . . God is the ultimate goal sought" (*ST,* Ia, q44, a4). Thus is creation God's own self-gift to his creatures that are "ordered towards union."[48] They participate in his goodness for their being ("being good is really the same thing as existing," *ST,* Ia, q5, a1) and long to return to this source of goodness.[49] Although Aquinas assumes that it is God who directs creatures toward their proper end, this direction is accomplished through the creature's own anthropological resource. "The fixed nature of a creature that determines how it behaves is imposed on it by God directing it to a goal, just as a determinate movement toward a target is imposed on an arrow by its archer. But the determination a creature receives from God constitutes its nature, whereas what man artificially imposes on a natural thing is coercion" (*ST,* Ia, q103, a1).[50] Aquinas clearly locates God's grace toward the creature within its natural capacity, turning grace into an anthropological asset proper to it.

In the *Secunda Pars,* Aquinas treats the flip side of procession: the creaturely return by participation. Aquinas explains this in terms of the soul's natural desire and tendency toward God, insofar as the soul is oriented to him as its final end *(reditus).* Although imprinted on creaturely reality, the *reditus* is simultaneously a goal "founded on a thing outside the

47. The quotations from the *ST* cited in the text are from the Blackfriars edition.

48. Anna Williams, "Mystical Theology Redux," p. 66.

49. "[T]his love is first in the Good itself, which is God, and from this Good it emanates into existence, and then, in its participated form in existences, it returns itself to its source which is the Good." From Thomas Aquinas, *Commentary on the Divine Names* (Marietti ed., 1950), Lecture XI, § 450 (p. 148).

50. This translation is from Thomas Aquinas, *Summa Theologiæ: A Concise Translation,* ed. Timothy McDermott (London: Methuen, 1989).

soul" (*ST*, I/IIae, q2, a7). Timothy McDermott remarks that Aquinas "envisages the life of man not merely as a journey back to man's form or nature . . . but as a journey back to the *agent* that intended that form, to the God who created man's nature."[51] Union with God is held as the supreme purpose of creation and is subsequently, as Anna Williams reminds us, "grounded in the structure of the human person."[52]

With this general anthropological pattern established, Aquinas brings in the *Tertia Pars* — and with it the realm of history. According to Aquinas, the perfection of the *Prima Pars* and *Secunda Pars* would have been complete without Christ. "Further, for the perfection of the universe it is enough for a creature to be ordered in a natural way to God as to its goal" (*ST*, IIIa, q1, a3).[53] However, sin requires intervention: Christ thus takes his place in the golden circle as one of its members, and raises human nature to "the supreme perfection" (*ST*, IIIa, q1, a6) so that it can again have the capacity to return to God.[54] This perfection is, not surprisingly, a participatory reality, "a full share in his own godhead: *God was made man that man might become God*" (*ST*, IIIa, q1, a2, quoting Augustine).[55]

The Neo-Platonic overtones of the *Prima Pars* are striking. We have seen how Plotinus structured his departure-return scheme around the *One* (*to hen*) from whom all beings proceed and participate. Aquinas accounts for the majestic scope of the procession and *telos* of the world in a similar way: "So the goal toward which all things are guided can be something outside the universe to be possessed and represented, which everything strives to share in and imitate as far as possible" (*ST*, Ia, q103, a3). As in Plotinus's program, creatures ascend to the degree that they "possess" or "share in" the being of that toward which they return. Aquinas makes the

---

51. From McDermott's "Introductory Comment," in *ST: Concise Translation*, p. 168 (italics added).

52. Anna Williams, "Mystical Theology Redux," p. 67.

53. Against this linear reading of the *Summa*, Jean-Marc Laporte, S.J., offers a concentric reading in which Christ is not "an appendix awkwardly tacked on," but the climax and point of convergence (see Laporte, "Christ in the *Summa*," *The Thomist* 67 [2003]: 231). Laporte's work richly explores the multidimensional layers of the *Summa*, but fails to deal with the deleterious results of such an ordering (in which Christ ends up being the fulfillment of human potential).

54. "[M]an needs divine assistance so as to be moved by it to act well" (*ST*, Ia/IIae, q109, a2).

55. "Factus est Deus homo, ut homo fieret Deus" (Serm. 371, 2; in Migne's *Patrologiae — Latina* 39.1660).

ontological foundation on which this is based very clear in his commentary on Dionysius's *Divine Names*: "He fills all things in such a way that nothing is bereft of his power. Dionysius adds this when he says 'lets down' [*deponitur*], which is not to be understood as some lessening, but only in that [God] pours himself into inferior things so that they can participate in his goodness."[56]

But the threat of ontological univocity (one that the Reformers felt keenly) looms large, particularly because Aquinas located this participation substantially in the depths of human *capacity*. Aquinas envisions a return to a unitive state with God, in which human nature is restored or "integrated" (*ST*, I/IIae, q109, a2-3), and is in no need of additional gifts of grace. The great achievement of Aquinas is the very majestic grandeur of the circle. God's grace precedes and concludes creaturely reality; in fact, all reality is made intelligible by it. And yet even as all things in this sacramental universe are ordered to "God," it is the undifferentiated singularity of a God who is not clearly involved in history. As Robert Jenson says, "Nevertheless, insofar as their ordering itself makes any suggestion, this must be misleading, since saving history is God's journey *with us*, not our journey away from and back to him."[57]

If Plotinus dispensed with all mediation, then Thomist anthropology, resembling as it does this Plotinian circle, is on shaky ground. The original Plotinian scheme had no need of mediation because of its sliding scale of being: all things proceeded from the One, and all things could return by participating in that which comprised part of their being. Critically, though, Aquinas did not follow Plotinus in conceiving of being as a vertical process of identity, but was held in check by his firm commitment to the Creator-creature distinction.[58] Nevertheless, he leaves his scheme open to criticism precisely here, for while there is obviously a place for mediation in Aquinas's scheme due to the Christian doctrine of sin, this can be construed more or less as mediation-as-repair. Christ comes into an already existing anthropological scheme that only needs the wheels put back

56. From the Marietti edition (1950), Lecture X, § 437 (p. 143).

57. Robert W. Jenson, *Systematic Theology I: The Triune God* (Oxford: Oxford University Press, 1997), p. 60 n. 102.

58. See William Cavanaugh, "A Joint Declaration? Justification as Theosis in Aquinas and Luther," *Heythrop Journal* 41 (2000): 265-80. Anna Williams also defends Thomas's categories of created grace and the beatific vision from any charge of ontological mixing. *Ground of Union* (Oxford: Oxford University Press, 1999).

on the cart (*ST,* IaIIae, q109, a3). Peter Wyatt presses exactly this critique of Aquinas:

> What is most striking about the golden circle is that *Pars tertia* does not belong integrally to it. The specifically christological dimension lies outside the logic of the circle. Only the movement away from God *(Pars prima)* and the movement homeward *(Pars secunda)* are essential to open and close the circuit.[59]

The implication is that, rather than being the ordering principle of the creation, Christ fixes and restores it to an original order that does not seem to require his particular history on earth to be established. Second, epistemic access to this order lies in the substance of the soul itself (a profoundly Augustinian move, if we remember that Augustine turned inward in order to find God), because Aquinas holds that the physical creation is the *counterpart* to eternal patterns. It may not be true that Aquinas himself authored the concept of the two-tier universe of medieval scholasticism, in which all of heavenly reality has an earthly analogue (despite the fact that Transcendental Thomism has often claimed this for him). However, his construal of "an inherent relation between the structure of Being and the immanent forms of the rational understanding" certainly smoothed the way to this end.[60]

Anders Nygren observes that "the religious temper of the Middle Ages can be summarily characterised by the phrase 'the upward tendency.'"[61] This tendency can be seen as the fusion of Augustinian ascent and Thomistic return. Those who inherited Augustine's seven-grade ascent are many (Gregory the Great's *Seven Steps to Spiritual Perfection,* Bonaventure's *The Mind's Ascent to God,* Ruysbroeck's *Seven Steps on the Ladder of Spiritual Love,* Teresa's *The Interior Castle,* with its seven mansions), and its other colorful variations (Guigo's *Ladder of Monks,* Richard of St Victor's *De gradibus caritatis,* Walter of Hilton's *Scale of Perfection,* Gerson's three-step *Mountain of Contemplation,* and even the twelfth-century Cistercian monastery entitled *Scala Dei*) similarly bear the mark of Augustinian desire, inwardness, and individualism. Aquinas further weighted this upward trajectory with an understanding of ascent as return, with a substantialist anthropology to boot.

59. Peter Wyatt, *Jesus Christ and Creation* (Allison Park, PA: Pickwick, 1996), p. 9.
60. T. F. Torrance, *The School of Faith* (London: Camelot, 1959), p. 1.
61. Anders Nygren, *Agape and Eros,* vol. II/II (London: SPCK, 1939), p. 397.

Given his Boethian definition of the human, Aquinas believed that the possibility of return *(reditus)* was given to human capacity.[62] This in no way was intended to short-circuit grace; rather, it depended on grace to complete the "golden circle" of which all creation took part. Yet history follows its own unexpected course. Once Aquinas located "created grace" in the soul, it began to take on a life of its own, displacing God — and sometimes more specifically, the incarnate Christ — as the source of ascent. It is this substantial view of anthropology that sanctions a consideration of the soul *in itself* and that partially explains the flowering of medieval mystical treatises on the soul and its ascent.

Calvin's Paradigm of Ascent

"Christ is the beginning, middle, and end."

Peter Wyatt has done Calvin scholarship a great favor by examining the scholastic (particularly Thomist) framework of Calvin's evangelical theology. Although Calvin wanted to distance himself from the excess of the scholastics, Wyatt emphasizes Calvin's indebtedness to medieval thought patterns and theological form. For Wyatt, Calvin's seemingly contradictory statements about redemption and creation can be partly reconciled by understanding Calvin's "evangelical" and "sapiential" (or scholastic) commitments. "In brief, the evangelical approach begins with Christ as 'God manifest in the flesh,' whose mediatorial existence becomes the crucial litmus for all theological statement. The sapiential approach begins with creation and values most highly the vision of God the Creator who is the beginning and end of all things, and whom Jesus Christ serves primarily as a redemptive agent providing the way for creatures to return to their Exemplar."[63] As part inheritor of Luther and the concerns of the *Devotio Moderna*, Calvin profoundly committed his theology to the personal and relational, particularly to the one relationship between God and humanity forged in the person of the mediator. It is

62. Aquinas (*ST* IIIa, q2, a3) directly quotes Boethius to define the human: "A person is an individual substance of rational nature [*persona est rationalis naturae individua substantia*]" (from *De Duabus Naturis* 3; in Migne's *Patrologia Latina* 64.1343).

63. Wyatt, *Creation,* pp. xxi-xxii. Wyatt is dependent primarily on Otto Pesch's distinction.

with this "evangelical" criterion that he eschews (or just ignores altogether) many medieval debates.

At the same time, Wyatt notes that the shape of the final form of Calvin's *Institutes* has much in common with "sapiential" theology, of which the primary representative is Aquinas's golden circle.[64] After the creedal structure of the 1536 version of the *Institutes,* Calvin's later editions broaden out beyond personal salvation to include the whole story of creation and its *telos* in God. While the worst of scholasticism involved excess and speculation, the best of scholasticism involved a rigorous commitment to setting salvation in its creation context. "The frame into which Calvin set his portrait of *Christus verus* is derived from the *summa theologiae* of high scholasticism and from their concern for universal intelligibility."[65] Done well, this framework goes beyond addressing what salvation is *from,* to addressing what salvation is *for,* provoking within us a grateful response of love. Calvin does not distance himself from these reflections of the "sounder Schoolmen" (III.14.11) precisely because they attempt to make sense of creation and its directedness in and to God. Rather than viewing the evangelical and the sapiential as oil and water, Wyatt believes that Calvin studies must reckon with the presence of both.[66] Calvin's evangelical project is more like pruning a tree that has grown wildly in one direction so that it will grow in another; nevertheless, it is the same tree.

A comparison of Aquinas and Calvin reveals that, while Calvin picks up on this scholastic scheme, he also fundamentally alters it. Pushing beyond Wyatt's insight, we discover that it no longer is the story of humanity's ascent to God by grace (Aquinas), or of the soul's ascent (Augustine), but of Christ's ascent.[67] Calvin refuses to tack Christ as a *tertia pars* onto

---

64. See *Institutes* II.2.4 and II.2.6. Oberman confirms that Calvin not only drew the distinction between various scholastics, but favored Thomas over others. See Oberman, "*Initia Calvini:* The Matrix of Calvin's Reformation," in *Calvinus Sacrae Scripturae Professor,* ed. Wilhelm Neuser (Grand Rapids: Eerdmans, 1994), p. 124 n. 34. See also Richard A. Muller, *The Unaccommodated Calvin* (Oxford: Oxford University Press, 2000), chap. 3.

65. Wyatt, *Creation,* p. 6.

66. But it may not be this simple. R. J. Hennessey notes that Thomas deliberately subverts the ordering of Hugh of St Victor (1090-1141 CE), who had "centered his theological work on the mystery of Christ rather than the mystery of God" ("Introduction" to *ST* 3a, in *ST,* vol. 48.xv-xx). Calvin would definitely fall more in line with Hugh than Thomas here, although we can, with Wyatt, certainly see the broad "sapiential" contours that give breadth and depth to Calvin's theological vision.

67. Aside from Hugh of St Victor, it appears that the only one to have pressed this

the Plotinian circle of creation's procession from and return to God. Instead, Christ breaks open the circle and grafts it onto himself. For Calvin, the figure of Christ has shattered any scheme that begins with creation and allows creation to be considered apart from Christ, through whom it was made and to whom it is directed. In subtly shifting Aquinas's *exitus-reditus* scheme from anthropology to Christ, Calvin challenges Aquinas's attempt at theocentrism as not going far enough. It is not Christ who fits into the procrustean bed of anthropology but we who are fitted to Christ and his ascent. In him and by his Spirit, we ascend to the Father.

Much of the basic scheme that we have seen in Augustine and Aquinas — even in Denys or Plotinus — is there. Indeed, Calvin uses the typology of ascent to bolster many aspects of his theology, not to mention his favored liturgical passage, *sursum corda* (which is similar to Origen's *ascensiones in corde*).[68] Yet in paying attention to the above test case of ascent, we begin to see just how different Calvin's use of the language is from that of the Platonic or medieval world, though Calvin's unique usage is not isolated from it. This suggests that we might differentiate Calvin (and his entire project) from that of medieval theology by the following phrase: communion, not naturalization. In Aquinas and Calvin we have two different models of participation: one is based on substantialist ontology,[69] the other on election.[70] One is a return to an original unitive state; the other involves communion with a person. Bruce McCormack sums it up as Aquinas's "tendency to understand justification as rooted in an 'ontological healing' of the soul, rather than in a more personal understanding

---

Christ pattern to such a similar structural degree was Athanasius (296-373 CE), though Calvin did not have access to his work. For more on Athanasius, see Christopher R. Smith, "The Life-of-Christ Structure of Athanasius' *De Incarnatione Verbi*," *The Patristic and Byzantine Review* 10 [1991]: 7-24. For more on Hugh, see Rorem, "Procession," pp. 157-58.

68. *Sursum corda*: lift up your hearts. See also Augustine's "On the Spirit and the Letter," chaps. 18-19, for a similar emphasis on the *sursum corda*.

69. I applaud the effort to find similarities between Aquinas and the Reformers (Cavanaugh, "A Joint Declaration?" pp. 165-80), but it is not clear that it can be done — at least in the way Cavanaugh attempts. For while Aquinas's doctrine of participation rests on the eternal processions in the triune being, Luther's rests on the justifying relationship of the historical Jesus to the Father as an act of intra-Trinitarian communion.

70. I am using "election" in a more Barthian sense to indicate the fundamental initiation and decision of God to be involved in human life, and the absolute freedom with which that self-gift is offered.

of the operations of grace."[71] This distinction is crucial but rarely perceived. Failure to make this distinction has resulted in the near loss of participation as a valid Reformed category.

John Witvliet and Christopher Kaiser have both recently paid attention to — and puzzled over — the lack of attention to ascent in Calvin scholarship.[72] Although neither comes to any conclusion, it seems that there are four probable reasons for this lacuna. First, there has been the common prejudice that ascent is anathema to the Reformation, which privileges God's gracious descent to us — not our ascent to God. As one Reformed theologian remarks, "Human beings can never raise themselves toward God and even if they could, they would not be allowed to do so, for that is the supreme sin."[73] Here ascent is assumed to be a Pelagian endeavor, the alternative to which is the path of humility and self-deprecation (arguably just as Pelagian!). This bias is the result of a general failure to differentiate between types of ascent. With his characterization of medieval Christendom's "three heavenly ladders" of merit, speculation, and mysticism, Nygren reminds us that ascent is anything but monolithic.[74] Of equal but less obvious importance is the assumption that Calvin's emphasis on depravity precludes a theology of ascent, a caricature that was perpetuated by both his followers and his opponents.[75] Third is the common prejudice that ascent is a preoccupation of Platonism, part and parcel of a mysticism not supported by Scripture and rejected by the

71. Bruce McCormack, "What's at Stake in Current Debates over Justification? The Crisis of Protestantism in the West," in *Justification*, ed. Daniel Treier (Downers Grove, IL: InterVarsity, 2004), p. 89.

72. Christopher Kaiser, "Climbing Jacob's Ladder: John Calvin and the Early Church on our Eucharistic Ascent to Heaven," *Scottish Journal of Theology* 56 (2003): 247-67; John Witvliet, "Sursum Corda: Images and Themes in John Calvin's Theology of Liturgy," in *Worship Seeking Understanding* (Grand Rapids: Baker, 2003). George Tavard submits the thesis that Calvin's later antiecumenical polemic is to blame for the oversight, but this is not borne out. For a critique of Tavard's project, see Richard A. Muller, "The Starting Point of Calvin's Theology: An Essay-Review," *Calvin Theological Journal* 36 (2001): 314-41. Otherwise, Tavard's wealth of insight into the medieval resources on ascent is invaluable.

73. Alain Blancy, "Protestantism and the Seventh Ecumenical Council: Towards a Reformed Theology of the Icon," in *Icons: Windows on Eternity*, ed. Gennadios Limouris (Geneva: WCC Publications, 1990).

74. Nygren, *Agape and Eros*, p. 403.

75. For this opinion by an unsympathetic student of Calvin, see Pierre Imbart de la Tour, *Origines de la Reforme*, vol. IV (Paris: Hachette, 1935).

Reformers.[76] The fourth reason is that only recently has attention been paid to the medieval context of Calvin's thought. While esteeming Calvin as an innovator, recent scholarship is also appreciating Calvin as an *heir* of a rich medieval mystical and theological tradition that had inestimable impact on him. Ascent is not peripheral to the primary "evangelical" thrust of Calvin's theology but is interactive with and dependent on it.

Indeed, it is fair to say that, while the opposition of Calvin to ascent is generally rejected as untenable, there has been little further research to explore Calvin's use of ascent and, more significantly, its relation to his doctrine of participation. It may come as a surprise to some that Calvin's very first Christian treatise entitled *Psychopannychia* (on the wakefulness of the soul after death)[77] is laden with themes of the soul's ascent. In this "starting point of Calvin's theology," we already see the distinctive features of his doctrine of ascent at work, particularly an acute sensitivity to doctrines that would in some way marginalize communion with God. Written in 1534, revised in 1536, and only eventually published in 1542, *Psychopannychia* has puzzled scholars for years, causing most to ignore it for its peripheral contribution (and Platonizing language). However, this document makes it clear that even in Calvin's earliest years the notion of ascent functions not as a Platonic escape from the world but as a directive toward God and union with him. This difference is fundamental. Hans Scholl remarks that already in *Psychopannychia* "the hermeneutical key, as it were, [is] the Paulinian eschatological communion with Christ."[78] This may be saying too much, too soon, but nevertheless it is a decisive theme that some would go so far as to argue would become Calvin's "central doctrine."[79]

George Tavard has done admirable work in setting Calvin's little jewel *Psychopannychia* in its proper medieval setting. Most important, Tavard

---

76. Heiko Oberman explores how the Protestant "understanding of mysticism has also been prejudiced," in his essay "The Meaning of Mysticism from Meister Eckhart to Martin Luther," in *The Reformation: Roots and Ramifications* (Grand Rapids: Eerdmans, 1994), p. 80.

77. The full treatise is found in *CO* 5.165-232, *T&T* III.413-90. It is George Tavard who has dubbed *Psychopannychia* — and entitled his own book — *The Starting Point of Calvin's Theology* (Grand Rapids: Eerdmans, 2000).

78. Hans Scholl, "Karl Barth as Interpreter of Calvin's *Psychopannychia*," in *Calvinus Sincerioris Religionis Vindex*, ed. Wilhelm H. Neuser and Brian G. Armstrong (Kirksville, MO: Sixteenth Century Journal, 1997), p. 307.

79. See Charles Partee, "Calvin's Central Dogma Again," *Sixteenth Century Journal* 18 (1987): 191-99.

points out where Calvin uses the Platonic threefold path of ascent and the Augustinian sevenfold definition of the soul. We'll begin with Calvin's use of the latter:

> Nor do I object to the illustration which [Augustine] elsewhere gives *(De Quantitat. Animae)* provided a sound and moderate interpretation be given to it, viz., that "there are many states of soul, *first,* animation; *second,* sense; *third,* art; *fourth,* virtue; *fifth,* tranquillity; *sixth,* ingress; *seventh,* contemplation: or, if you rather choose it,[80] *first,* of the body; *second,* to the body; *third,* about the body; *fourth,* to itself; *fifth,* in itself; *sixth,* to God; *seventh,* with God." . . . Even Augustine himself, I think, did not wish [to bind anyone to these], but was desirous, though in the plainest manner possible, to explain the progress of the soul: showing how it does not reach its final perfection until the day of judgment.[81]

Tavard makes the fine ecumenical point that Calvin here is not importing Augustine directly, but is doing so along the lines of the medieval mystics. This sevenfold pattern of the soul corresponds to stages of the soul's ascent, as outlined by the Victorines and Bonaventure with whom Calvin must have been familar.[82] Yet Tavard is so keen to discover in Calvin sapiential and ecumenical links to other traditions that it seems as if he has missed Calvin's original contribution. Careful attention reveals that Calvin himself is ambivalent about using Augustine's graded view of the soul. Calvin uses Augustine's typology not because he finds the sevenfold ascent to be adequate, but because he feels "induced to quote these words of the holy writer," yet never with the intention of "binding any one, or even myself, to adopt these distinctions."

Calvin's use of Augustine in *Psychopannychia* is a concession to what is his primary point — the soul's ascent as participation in Christ. When Calvin wants to talk about the soul's journey, he turns not to Augustine but to the history of Israel and of Jesus Christ:

> As Paul, in speaking of the passage of the Israelites across the Red Sea, allegorically represents the drowning of Pharaoh as the mode of deliverance by water (1 Corinthians 10:1), so we may be permitted to say that

---

80. This second pattern is typical of Bonaventure (Tavard, *Starting Point,* p. 99).
81. Calvin, "Psychopannychia," *T&T* III.470.
82. Tavard, *Starting Point,* p. 97.

47

in baptism our Pharaoh is drowned, our old man is crucified, our members are mortified, we are buried with Christ, and removed from the captivity of the devil and the power of death, but removed only into the desert, a land arid and poor, unless the Lord rain manna from heaven, and cause water to gush forth from the rock. For our soul, like that land without water, is in want of all things, till he, by the grace of his Spirit, rain upon it. We afterwards pass into the land of promise, under the guidance of Joshua the son of Nun, into a land flowing with milk and honey; that is, the grace of God frees us from the body of death, by our Lord Jesus Christ. . . . But Jerusalem, the capital and seat of the kingdom, has not yet been erected; nor yet does Solomon, the Prince of Peace, hold the scepter and rule over all.[83]

Although Calvin, as Tavard points out, is quite dexterous with medieval analyses of ascent, Calvin's main point is that the ascent of the soul is irreducibly bound up with Christ. This is not an analysis of the soul and its solitary journey toward God but its journey in Christ/Solomon, who does not yet "hold the scepter and rule over all." Our incomplete glorification is neither hamartiological nor ontological (due to creaturehood) but christological. The soul's glorification is tied entirely to Christ's. "He indeed attributes to us a hidden life with Christ our Head beside God; he delays the glory to the day of the glory of Christ, who, as the Head of the Church, will bring his members with him."[84] What is remarkable here is that despite the flurry of treatises in the 1530s on the soul and its nature,[85] Calvin turns away from the fashionable study of the soul's ascent *in se* and considers instead the church's participation in the history and ascent of Jesus Christ. With one deft move, he transposes the study of the soul from metaphysics to christology and eschatology. *Psychopannychia*, far from being an ecumenical beginning (which later goes awry, as Tavard would have it), already reveals the unique contours of Calvin's doctrine of participation.

Calvin's ascending mysticism casts a long shadow between that of the high medieval mystics and indeed that of the Counter-Reformation. For Calvin, it is only Christ's ascent that really matters to the Christian's ascent; stages of the soul's ascent hold no meaning or interest for him. It is

83. Calvin, "Psychopannychia," *T&T* III.467.
84. Calvin, "Psychopannychia," *T&T* III.465; see also *Comm. 1 John* 2:2.
85. See the chapter "The Renaissance Debate on the Soul," in Tavard, *Starting Point*, pp. 20-39.

as the schoolmen speculate on the soul's ascent (Bonaventure, Gerson) and the mystics observe the interior, private stages of the soul's ascent (Mechthild of Magdeburg, Johannes Tauler) that we notice the conspicuous absence of this in Calvin, even as his theology abounds with imagery of and a vocation to ascend. Calvin shrugs off this stylistic device like an old garment and exclusively focuses on the believer's ascent *en Christo*. In so doing, Calvin bypasses the typical discussion of the soul's stages of development with God (which often looks to subjective experience as proof of progress). Calvin's earliest Christian treatise already shows the divergence between his thought and much of medieval scholasticism, even as he attempts to build upon it and use its language. This divergence I would classify as a divergence in his concept of participation — one concept is grounded in an anthropological endowment while the other is based on the freedom of God and his desire for communion as expressed in the person of Jesus Christ.

Tavard also detects a Platonic threefold path of ascent in *Psychopannychia,* an observation that only serves to strengthen our point. Calvin borrows imagery from the Psalms of the soul progressing *ex virtute in virtutem,* from virtue to virtue, up to the vision of God "in Zion" (Zion being a common metaphor in late medieval spirituality for the beatific vision):

> What answer then will they give to David's hymn (Psalm 73), wherein he describes the *beginning, middle, and end* of the life of the blessed? He says, "They will go from strength to strength; the Lord of hosts will be seen in Zion"; or, as the Hebrew has it, from abundance to abundance.[86]

This striking allusion to the threefold way of ascent to the divine was a common pattern in the Greek philosophical tradition, absorbed by Eastern theologians (Origen, Denys the Areopagite) and Western theologians (Thomas à Kempis, John of the Cross) alike. Tavard says of the above quote, "This is the traditional threefold way of beginners into the spiritual life. . . . these stages in the spiritual life had been streamlined as the 'three ways' of purgation, illumination, and union."[87]

Tavard, again, seeking to strengthen Calvin's ties to the medieval mystical world prior to him, fails to notice how Calvin is also doing something

---

86. Calvin, "Psychopannychia," *T&T* III.441, emphasis added.
87. Tavard, *Starting Point,* p. 78.

new. Already we see in *Psychopannychia* Calvin's use of the mystical motif of ascent, but this will become more and more christological and oriented toward participation as the years progress. Twenty years after *Psychopannychia*, Calvin's commentary on the Psalms (1557) revisits the verse on the *beginning, middle, and end* of the spiritual life, but conspicuously absent is his earlier (slightly Platonic) interpretation of the "threefold path."[88] What is the definitive path for the soul's ascent? It is outlined in his commentary on Colossians 1:12 (1548), "Christ is the beginning, middle, and end."

*   *   *

Just as the fathers democratized mysticism, so did Calvin. While a rather elitist "intellectual mysticism" had been gathering force through the High Middle Ages,[89] Calvin presented an "urban mysticism" centered on the triune God's desire for us, and particularly the Spirit's role in uniting us to Christ.[90] For the average guildsman, who had no time to spend in intellectual contemplation and the uniting of the mind to God, this was indeed good news. But in bringing it down to earth, Calvin did not negate the language of the upward vector and the Christian's ascending call to greater heights of *unio cum Christo*. Even his famed emphasis on depravity (which prevents many from appreciating his mystical thrust) cannot repress the decided "upward" momentum in his theology. He simply restructured the "ladder to heaven" on quite another foundation.

For Calvin, the ladder is Christ — not in the facile explanation that "Christ is the way," but that our ascent is profoundly bound up in Christ's ascension, by our *participation in his ascent*. In one deft move, Calvin has relocated "participation" from between impersonals (the soul in the divine nature) to personals (the human being in Christ, by the Spirit). Thus, a mystical encounter is not the goal (Calvin would hardly endorse an ascent to an ecstatic state); rather, the process itself is the mystical encounter. Nor is the soul's "progress," or the believer's subjective experience as the

---

88. It is interesting that Calvin's oblique reference in *Psychopannychia* to the threefold path is mistaken: it is not from Psalm 73 as he indicates, but Psalm 84:7, as corrected in his *Commentary* of 1557.

89. For the "devotional overheating" of the High Middle Ages, see Simon Tugwell, *Way of Imperfection* (London: Darton, Longman, & Todd, 1984), chap. 14; for its elitist tendencies, see Philip Sheldrake, *Spirituality and History: Questions of Interpretation and Method*, 2nd ed. (Maryknoll, NY: Orbis Books, 1998), pp. 40-44.

90. Oberman, "Meaning," p. 85.

soul ascends, the goal (nor necessarily to be trusted as proof). It is perhaps a subjective byproduct with which some are blessed but not anything to stake one's personal *unio cum Christo* on. The mystical ascent is this deeper and deeper burrowing into Christ (always pneumatologically conceived), not our effort to do so. His ascent is our path and goal. His narrative has become our own.

Chapter 2

Creation:
The Ground and Grammar of Ascent

An asceticism and mysticism based on the natural longing for the vision of God would be anthropocentric: the standard and the goal would be derived from man himself — his longing, his eros, his self-fulfillment, in short, his own perfection. By contrast, a theocentric asceticism and mysticism would have as their point of departure man's creatureliness and its fundamental exigencies: the praise and service of God, reverential awe before the absolute Lord, and obedience to him. On this basis, all norms are to be found in God's hand from the outset. Here we can see that the way of distance and awe is the shortest way to attain to pure love. But, on the opposite side of things, whoever would jump over the level of "nature" in order to start at once with "Christian" sublimity will most likely be importing the unconscious concupiscence of nature into the highest level of reality.[1]

Because ascent has been misconstrued over the years — indeed, the metaphor has been used to devalue and escape creation for centuries — it is essential to begin with Calvin's doctrine of creation. We begin with Calvin's concept of the world as a place of communion, the "trysting place" be-

1. Hans Urs von Balthasar, *The Grain of Wheat* (San Francisco: Ignatius, 1995), p. 101.

tween God and humanity.[2] Creation is revealed to be a space overflowing with the fatherhood of God, the mediation of Christ, and the tending of the Spirit. It is only when this is established that a correct understanding of Christ's ascent, our incorporation into him, and ascent in the Eucharist can be grasped properly.

Creation, as the sphere of *koinōnia,* is the ground and grammar of an ascent that is not away from materiality but a deepened experience of communion within it. This issues forth in a concept of creation that is anything but static and impersonal. Instead, Calvin's theological vision is a dynamic interplay of God, creation, and humanity, where the creation-call on humanity and the delight and communication of God hold center stage. From the proleptic thrust of Calvin's doctrine of creation, to his projective concept of the *imago* as "toward" *(ad),* to Adam's dynamic *koinōnia* existence and then the forceful inversion of sin and the metaphor of falling (the Fall), Calvin is anything but amorphous. Communion is the groundwork of creation, the purpose of anthropology, and the *telos* toward which all creation strains.

I seek to achieve three things in this chapter: (1) to establish the christological and pneumatological framework of creation that gives rise to the possibility of participation in the first place; (2) to examine Adam's life in the garden as proof of this thoroughgoing concept of participation in Calvin's anthropology; and (3) to observe how Calvin kept the boundaries of Creator and creature distinct, even as he related them so intimately that the creature can legitimately be said to be "participating" in God's life and attributes.[3]

---

2. This phrase is taken from the commentary by Iain MacKenzie, *Irenaeus's Demonstration of the Apostolic Preaching,* trans. J. Armitage Robinson (Aldershot, UK: Ashgate, 2002).

3. Karl Popper observed (in dialogue with David Hume) that we all interpret "neutral evidence" in the light of hypotheses that cannot be verified, let alone verified "from nowhere." An "inductive" approach that seeks to articulate neutral evidence in order to draw conclusions fails to feel the force of this. Consequently, I attempt to combine the inductive and deductive approaches — the presentation of evidence together with the framework of interpretation that seems to me not simply to fit the evidence but to *interpret* it.

Eternal Mediation of the Word

"It is the proper function of the mediator to unite us to God."

The Mediator and the Communion Motif

"Participation in Christ" is not a concept that we merely stumble on in Book IV of Calvin's *Institutes,* where the typically "participationist" categories such as the sacraments and the church are to be expected. Nor do we first encounter it in Book III (participation in the sanctified life), nor even Book II (Christ's full participation in our humanity). Calvin begins his *Institutes* with a christologically and pneumatologically ordered creation, thus providing the bedrock for a Trinitarian articulation of participation and ascent. A close examination of Calvin's doctrine of mediation brings this to the surface.

Calvin's definition of mediation has a much broader range than that to which we are normally accustomed.[4] While Stancaro limited it only to "sacrifice and intercession" (based on his belief that "the son of God is mediator only as man"),[5] Calvin is quite clear that Christ's mediation did not originate with sin "but from the beginning of creation he already truly was mediator, for he always was the head of the Church, had primacy over the angels, and was the firstborn of every creature."[6] David Willis notes that "Calvin here subjects the idea of mediation to two different nuances: mediation as reconciliation and mediation as sustenance. As reconciler, the Mediator was ordained because of the Fall to restore the broken relationship between God and man. As sustainer, the Mediator always was the

---

4. In the past decade, Milbank, Pickstock, and others have rehabilitated this word in yet another direction, though it will become self-evident that Calvin keeps the concept disciplined to the strictly christological.

5. Joseph Tylenda, "The Controversy on Christ the Mediator: Calvin's Second Reply to Stancaro," *Calvin Theological Journal* 8 (1973): 154 (hereafter cited as "Stancaro II"). This is a translation of Calvin's *Ministrorum ecclesiae Genevensis responsio ad nobiles Polonos et Franciscum Stancarum Mantuantum de controversia mediatoris* (1561), found in *CO* 9.345-58.

6. Joseph Tylenda, "Christ the Mediator: Calvin Versus Stancaro," *Calvin Theological Journal* 8 (1973): 12 (hereafter "Stancaro I"). This is a translation of Calvin's *Responsum ad fratres Polonos, quomodo mediator sit Christus, ad refutandum Stancaro errorem* (1560), found in *CO* 9.333-42.

way creation was preserved and ordered."[7] Stancaro failed to see how expiation was a narrow understanding of the much more comprehensive role of the second person of the Trinity, a fact that Calvin makes clear in his 1561 letter to the Polish nobles.

> In what pertains to the matter at hand we must first see what the word mediator means. Certainly, the eternal λόγος [*logos*] was already mediator from the beginning, before Adam's fall and the alienation and separation of the human race from God. In this sense, unless we are mistaken, he is also called by Paul the first-born of all creatures; and when John says that life was in him, he indicates the mode of communication from which otherwise hidden source, the grace of God flowed to men.[8]

Refusing to collapse mediation into expiation, Calvin held the two together (the Mediator should now always be seen "together with his sacrifice") while still preserving the initial sense of the Mediator as sustainer of creation.[9] For it was only "man's rebellion that brought it about that expiation was necessary to reconcile us to God."[10] Here we see Calvin's relentless theocentrism at work, where he will allow neither human endowment nor human sin to be the starting gun for the marathon of the human race. It is God and his intent that has the first and last say: "It is the proper function of the mediator to unite us to God."[11] In this grand sweep, Calvin is positioning the forthcoming redemption (mediation-expiation) of Christ within a more comprehensive story, that of the God who intends us

7. David E. Willis, *Calvin's Catholic Christology* (Leiden: Brill, 1967), p. 70. This is the theological foundation of Calvin's doctrine of the *extra Calvinisticum* that emphasizes Christ's lordship over the universe, for "the God at work in Jesus Christ is one and the same with the God who sustains and orders the universe" (Willis, p. 6).

8. Tylenda, "Stancaro II," p. 147 (*CO* 9.349).

9. The overtones of Calvin's christological axiom *distinctio sed non separatio* are not accidental: Calvin saw these "two distinct powers which belong to the son of God: the first, which is manifested in the structure of the world and the order of nature; and the second, by which he renews and restores fallen nature" (*Comm. John* 1:5) to correspond more or less to his two natures. Calvin also gives the Spirit the first role of "sustenance" in creation (*Comm. Rom.* 8:14).

10. Tylenda, "Stancaro II," p. 147.

11. Tylenda, "Stancaro II," p. 148. Calvin describes Christ's fleshly mediation in similar terms: "And certainly he would not be a properly qualified Mediator, if he did not unite both natures in his person, and thus bring men into an alliance with God" (*Comm. Matt.* 1:23).

for communion (mediation-union). "Both angels as well as men were united to God by his grace."[12]

Although this doctrine of Christ's eternal mediation is not without its pitfalls, its purpose is to build communion into the structure of things.[13] In his doctrine of creation, Calvin refuses to envision a general relationship between the triune God and humanity. "What comparison is there between a creature and the Creator, without the interposition of a Mediator?"[14] All creation is related to God in the second person of the Trinity, who mediates creation and its *telos*. All things are created by him, created to exist in him, and created for perfect union with him ("as much as their capacity will allow").[15] This arrangement is not due to sin, but to the *en Christo* way that God relates to humanity.[16] He has not structured a universe in which life, grace, and "benefits" can be had apart from him.

The simple significance of this is that Calvin has quite clearly moved the traditional concept of "participation in God" to "participation in Christ." Christ is the Mediator not only of humanity, or "angels, but also as to the whole world."[17] This is not Plotinus's ontological emanation scheme, Denys's great hierarchy of being, or Aquinas's golden *exitus-reditus* circuit. Calvin has achieved the grandeur and intercoherence of all such schemes by reappropriating the Word's mediation of creation. The result of this is that Calvin resists the univocity of a concept of creation *within* "God," for creation is first and foremost *in* Christ, by the Spirit. Christ's mediation of creation is redolent of suggestions of incorporation and impediment, bond and boundary.

12. Tylenda, "Stancaro I," p. 12 (*CO* 9.338).

13. Is this mediator the Logos *asarkos* or the Logos *ensarkos?* Calvin is not clear. Peter Wyatt explores four tensions in Calvin's theology that result from his imprecision here: (1) the *extra-calvinisticum*, (2) Christ's mediation beyond the flesh, (3) the temporal duration of his fleshly mediatorship, and (4) predestination. "Thus, in the final ordering of the *Institutes*, the doctrine of Christ's eternal deity properly arises under the knowledge of God the Creator and in terms that convey a sense of abstraction from Christ's mediatorial ministry" (Peter Wyatt, *Jesus Christ and Creation* [Allison Park, PA: Pickwick, 1996], p. 30).

14. *Comm. Eph.* 1:10.

15. *Comm. 2 Pet.* 1:4.

16. For a complementary angle on this, see "Part II: The Trinitarian Basis, Pattern, and Dynamic of the Divine-Human Relationship," in Philip W. Butin, *Revelation, Redemption, and Response: Calvin's Trinitarian Understanding of the Divine-Human Relationship* (New York: Oxford University Press, 1995), pp. 55-94.

17. *Comm. Col.* 1:17.

The Communion Motif and the Triune Members

If we take communion to be the fundamental objective for the world that God has built (and not just a general "union," but specifically in the Mediator), Calvin's doctrine of creation opens before us with breathtaking possibility. "Now the faithful, to whom he has given eyes, see sparks of his glory, as it were, glittering in every created thing. The world was no doubt made, that it might be the theater of the divine glory."[18] All created reality, in a sense, has a Trinitarian approach to God, centered in the person of Christ. The creation of the world reveals the fatherhood of God, the mediation of the Word, and the "tending" of the Spirit.[19]

Against the mechanistic view of the Stoics (I.16.3), Calvin shows the *first member of the Trinity* to be the "foreseeing and diligent father of the family" (I.14.2) who "sustains, nourishes, and cares for everything he has made" (I.16.1). Those who "observe secondary causes in nature" need also to "ascend by them to God," for this is not so much a matter of conservation but relationship.[20] T. F. Torrance reminds us:

> Calvin was so firm upon this point that he would have nothing to do with secondary causation in theology, and inveighed against the tendency, becoming rampant in his own day, of speaking of *Nature* instead of *God,* thus *falsely transferring to nature what belongs to grace* [I.5.1; I.16.6; II.2.1, 27]. Calvin's view of creation, and of the fallen world, was deeply biblical and Hebraic in his insistence that everything created and worldly had to be related to the direct action of the gracious will of God.[21]

To merely acknowledge God's creation of the world does not go far enough, because "in this way no place is left for God's fatherly favor, nor for his judgments" (I.16.5); rather, his omnipotence is a "watchful, effective, active sort, engaged in ceaseless activity" (I.16.3). Calvin's basis for what is now termed "natural theology" is God's own ceaseless presence to

18. *Comm. Heb.* 11:3.

19. It is important to note the Trinitarian structure of mediation from the start, echoing Calvin's later distinction between efficient cause (Father), material cause (Son), and instrumental cause (Spirit) in III.14.21, and cause, matter, and effect (IV.15.6).

20. *Comm. Psalm* 65:10.

21. T. F. Torrance, "The Word of God and the Nature of Man," in *Theology in Reconstruction* (London: SCM, 1965), p. 103.

his creation, in whom it lives and moves and has its being. Paul Chung is certainly correct when he notes that, in Calvin, "[a] natural theology is not simply rejected, but integrated into a theology of the Spirit."[22]

The *Word* is at the heart of the world, defining and realizing it as a place of communion. "There are two things we must properly consider. One, that we have beginning and life through this Word. The other, that we are sustained through Him — and not only we, but all the world."[23] Calvin refers to this as the general "life energy in God's Word" that "quickens the souls of all to whom God grants participation [*participatione*] in it" (II.10.7). This is not a Platonic ontology but is the flip side of the Word's ongoing "maintaining." Nor is this participation salvific (II.10.7). Rather, it introduces an intimacy between Creator and creation in that a *person* — the Mediator — has bound himself to the ongoing life of the world. Even in the Garden of Eden, Adam received life not from God *simpliciter* but from Christ. "He was the mid-point [*medium*] between God and creatures, so that the life which was otherwise hidden in God would flow from him."[24]

Not only did life flow *from* him, but Adam's life was *in* him. "Previously, direct communication with God was the source of life to Adam; but, from the moment in which he became alienated from God, it was necessary that he should recover life by the death of Christ, by whose life he then lived."[25] Calvin makes a general point that human life is maintained only by participation in God but then he more pointedly embeds this in the Mediator. Perhaps Calvin's greatest contribution to a theology of creation is the relentless insistence and clarity with which he views humanity's relationship with the Mediator: we do not have an "in" to God, except through Christ.[26] This will become a more explicit strategy in Calvin's doctrine of reconciliation, but we can already discern a christological differentiation (pairing humanity with the mediator) at play in creation.[27]

It is Calvin's robust pneumatology that guarantees that this constant

22. Paul Chung, *Spirituality and Social Ethics in John Calvin: A Pneumatological Perspective* (Lanham, MD: University Press of America, 2000), p. 43.

23. *Serm. John* 1:1-5.

24. Tylenda, "Stancaro I," p. 13 (*CO* 9.339).

25. *Comm. Gen.* 3:22.

26. "For he who seeks to be loved by God without the Mediator gets imbrangled in a labyrinth in which he will find neither the right path nor the way out" (*Comm. John* 15:9, Torrance edition).

27. See also the findings of Butin, *Revelation*, chap. 4.

operation of sustaining and maintaining is the personal involvement of *God the Spirit*, not extrinsically upon us but in our depths. "By means of him we come to participate in God" (I.13.14).[28] Calvin assigns the Spirit both the deep things of God and the deep places of humanity: "God sendeth forth that [S]pirit which remains with him whither he pleases; and as soon as he has sent it forth, all things are created. In this way, what was his own he makes to be ours."[29] *He* is the agent of participation, bringing humanity into the deep things of God ("what was his he makes to be ours") without violating the very creation he is making ("as soon as [He] is sent forth, all things are created"). Thus participation is nuanced with communion, for the Spirit acts to affirm creation's particularity and freedom even as it is shepherded toward its *telos* of Trinitarian communion.[30] "For it is the Spirit who, everywhere diffused, sustains all things, causes them to grow, and quickens them in heaven and in earth . . . transfusing into all things his energy, and breathing into them essence, life, and movement . . ." (I.13.14). Calvin explicitly links this "deep" role of the Spirit in the first act of creation with his ongoing work, bringing forth "continually a new creation of the world."[31] However, Colin Gunton wonders whether this pneumatology overcomes the "tendency [in the Calvinist tradition] to conceive creation as externalization, as God's creation of something 'outside' himself, and so with a stress on its otherness."[32]

Gunton's concern is not to be taken lightly. For a weakened reading of Calvin's pneumatology is the culprit in not only this "excessive separation

---

28. Battles translates *sic per ipsum in Dei participationem venimus* as: "through him we come into communion with God." Beveridge translates it as: "by means of him we become partakers of the divine nature" (*CO* 2.102).

29. The Latin indicates that the translation should capitalize "Spirit" rather than keep it lowercase, as the Calvin Translation Society has rendered it. "Deus spiritum qui penes eum residet, emittit quo visum est: simulae emisit, omnia creantur. Hoc modo quod suum erat, nostrum facit" (*Comm. Psalm* 104:29, *CO* 32.96). Following this quote, Calvin protects himself from being compared with Servetus (who, he says, is mired in the Manichean error) by making it clear that this in no way encloses a portion of divinity into all living things.

30. The Spirit's presence in creation never means an inpouring of God's substance (I.15.5), nor does it carry pantheistic overtones (*Comm. Acts* 17:28).

31. *Comm. Psalm* 104:29.

32. Colin Gunton, "Creation and Mediation in the Theology of Robert W. Jenson: An Encounter and a Convergence," in *Trinity, Time, and Church*, ed. Colin Gunton (Grand Rapids: Eerdmans, 2000), p. 91. This tendency in the tradition is probably linked to Calvin's shifting language about the Spirit, which I will deal with extensively in chap. 4.

of God and the world, corresponding to Nestorianism, and . . . deism," but also fatally impacts notions of mediation.[33] Calvin consistently links the Mediator with the Spirit, indicating that an inadequate estimation of one undermines the other as well.[34] Just as the Spirit does not allow for a creation external to and separate from God, neither is the Word's mediation between externals — acting as buffer (between two things that may not come into contact) or bridge (between two distant spheres) or delegate (between two hostile parties).[35] This is much more appropriate for Arius than for Calvin. Calvin does not begin with the problem of how a transcendent God and the world are related; he begins with the truth of the Mediator, the one who functions not as a *tertium quid* or middle space between Creator and creation, but as the one in whom they are joined. In an evocative article, Rowan Williams describes mediation in terms consonant with Calvin's own comprehensive use of the term. "The Son's work is bound up precisely with the *loss* of mediatorial concepts designed to explain how the transcendent God (who is *elsewhere*) can be communicated *here*. The pivotal image of Jesus as Son radically changes the simple schema of God-and-the-world."[36] Mediation, defined as it is by the Mediator, whose "proper function [is] to unite us to God," must always be interpreted in the light of Calvin's emphasis on intimacy and communion.[37]

Mediation without Communion

So what is the relationship between heaven and earth, grace and nature? Most agree that Calvin does not speculate outside of the person of the Mediator. As the Torrance edition tantalizingly renders it, "What is the analogy [*proportio*] between the creature and Creator, without the interpo-

---

33. Gunton, "Theology of Jenson," p. 91.

34. See especially his *Serm. John* 1:1-5, in particular *CO* 47.479-80.

35. Beza tightened up the concept by distinguishing between *medius* (a thing "between two extremes") and *mediator* (a "conciliator"), applying both to Christ. See Richard A. Muller, *Christ and the Decree* (Durham, NC: Labyrinth, 1986), pp. 92-96. I agree with Beza in that *medius* does describe Christ's work *between* God and humanity, but such a concept must not then work against Christ's work of mediation that was to join, in his own person, God and humanity.

36. Rowan Williams, "Word and Spirit," in *On Christian Theology* (Oxford: Blackwell, 2000), p. 123.

37. Tylenda, "Stancaro II," p. 148.

sition of the Mediator?"³⁸ More often than not, the perception of Calvin is that there *is* no analogy; ironically, it is the view of both Calvin's advocates and opponents that this separation of human and divine is his central principle.³⁹ Pierre Imbart de la Tour laments, "Dieu et l'homme . . . Quelle antithèse!"⁴⁰ But François Wendel hails it as Calvin's theological triumph.⁴¹ What is rarely seen is that Calvin's genius is not in his separation of divine and human but in the way he distinguishes them in order to relate them properly. Their classification is for communion. Calvin here achieves with his doctrine of the eternal mediation of the Logos what Aquinas tried to do with his literary structure of procession and return. The result is not a natural harmony between nature and grace but a unique "communion motif" marked by presence and otherness. Failure to see how communion governs all of Calvin's theology of mediation has led to drastic distortions in Calvin's view of (i) creaturely reality and (ii) transcendent reality, which I will treat, respectively, below.

Does Mediation Imply Creaturely Debasement?

"The Mediator is to keep us from falling. . . ."

Calvin's treatment of the Mediator is first theo-logical: it is the mediator's function to unite humanity and God. But in considering the other side — why is creaturely reality not in itself capable of being in relationship to God without a mediator? — Calvin gives two interesting and often misconstrued anthropological reasons: insufficient righteousness and creaturely frailty.⁴² These will need some unpacking, lest they be marshaled in support of the false view that Calvin degrades creaturely reality. The test case for this is his treatment of angels: beings who have not fallen into sin, and yet who still need the Mediator in order to be united to God.

---

38. "Quae enim proportio creaturae ad Creatorem, nisi intercedeat mediator?" (*Comm. Eph.* 1:10, *CO* 52.151).

39. Perhaps the first challenge to this in a systematic way is Butin, *Revelation*, pp. 15-25.

40. Pierre Imbart de la Tour, *Origines de la Reforme*, vol. IV (Paris: Hachette, 1935), p. 69.

41. François Wendel (applying it to the two natures) calls it "a very important aspect of Calvin's theological thought, and perhaps what is most original in it" (Wendel, *Calvin: The Origins and Development of His Religious Thought* [London: Collins, 1963], p. 219).

42. *Serm. Eph.* 1:7-10, *CO* 51.295.

But the Spirit declares there, that the greatest purity is vile, if it is brought into comparison with the righteousness of God. We must, therefore, conclude, that there is not on the part of angels so much of righteousness as would suffice for their being fully joined with God. They have, therefore, need of a peace maker, through whose grace they may wholly cleave to God.[43]

Is Calvin a sin-monger here, detecting depravity even in angels?[44] Perhaps, but I think not, especially when we remember that Calvin's notion of mediation is governed by communion. The greater reason is that Calvin establishes the Mediator, rather than righteousness, as our primary bond with God. The structure of our existence, the "proper condition of creatures, is to keep close to God."[45] Not even righteousness can circumvent this primary anthropology, which relates all humanity to God in the second person of the Trinity. Calvin reacts against medieval theologies of grace because they prohibit this specific anthropology. Instead of taking creaturely (dependent) anthropology as opportunity for participation, medieval theologians took it as weakness and thus invented capacities that we do not have (II.5.9). Calvin views our anthropology as occasion for constant communion, using even our *un*fallen state as proof. Thus we see that, for Calvin, our *telos* is not moral perfection (outside the Mediator) but communion.[46] This is why redemption has surpassed creation (I.15.4): we now have the "life-giving Spirit," who enables us to participate in Christ more fully and to enjoy the Father's fatherhood (III.1.2).

This dependent anthropology is compounded by Calvin's second reason for a mediator: creaturely frailty. Unfallen creatures (and even angels)

---

43. *Comm. Col.* 1:20.

44. I am not avoiding Calvin's reference to the "vileness" of our purity. I just happen to think that this is not his point. We must not give undue weight to his constant disparagement of human natural abilities, offensive as it is to our modern sensibilities. It is the flip side of an anthropology *en Christo*, but with a rhetorical flourish — perhaps gone a bit awry. Calvin's sapiential commitments led him to spend the entire Book I of the *Institutes* reflecting not on "the miserable condition of man" but on "what he was like when first created" (I.15.1).

45. *Comm. Eph.* 1:10.

46. The parallel between this and Calvin's view of the law is striking. Just as postlapsarian obedience does not suffice to unite us to God, neither did prelapsarian obedience, "for it is not clear whether by this path [of obedience alone] we may attain eternal life" (II.7.3). Both fallen and unfallen, our *telos* is to be joined to God in Christ.

not only lack sufficient righteousness, but their lives lack "a constancy and stability."[47] Again, Calvin makes his point by using a best-case scenario: angels.

> As to angels, however, there is a question not easy of solution. For what occasion is there for reconciliation, where there is no discord or hatred? . . . It was, however, necessary that angels, also, should be made to be at peace with God, for, being creatures, they were not beyond the risk of falling, had they not been confirmed by the grace of Christ. . . .[48]

This further confirms that Calvin sees little hope for us in our nature or in any "substantial" capacity for God. As early as the 1536 *Institutes*,[49] Calvin held that even angels ("so far as they are creatures") are "liable to change and to sin, and consequently their happiness would not have been eternal. . . . Men had been lost, and angels were not beyond the reach of danger."[50] Calvin's anthropology can be easily obscured here if readers do not ask what creaturely frailty is *for*. Hidden in this passage is Calvin's definition of the creature: one whose finitude (and potential for defection) is certain but who has already been provided for, in that "Christ is already and eternally the Mediator between creatures and their Creator."[51] For all too long the negative cast of such a definition has been overplayed. When we interpret this as Calvin's pessimism about creaturely capacity, we have lost Calvin's startling vision of participation. For Calvin, even the perfect (nonfallen) creature must constantly be united to the Mediator. This is its

---

47. *Serm. Eph.* 1:7-10. Calvin links this instability to the growth that Adam and Eve were intended for in the Garden but that they cut short through their defection: "The state of man was not perfected in the person of Adam; but it is a peculiar benefit conferred by Christ, that we may be renewed to a life which is celestial, whereas before the fall of Adam, man's life was only earthly, seeing it had no firm and settled constancy" (*Comm. Gen.* 2:7). Human anthropology is grounded in creation, but like all created things, it is looking to the new creation (yet is not itself the new).

48. *Comm. Col.* 1:20.

49. "And yet even [the angels] had need of a Head, in whom they might cleave to their God" (II.12).

50. *Comm. Eph.* 1:10.

51. Wyatt, *Creation*, p. 39. Wyatt misses the positive implication for *koinōnia* of this finitude. He goes only so far as to say that our need for a mediator is due to our "potential for defection," rather than to God's more comprehensive intent of communion with us.

condition. This is its glory. "The proper condition of creatures is to keep close to God."[52]

It would be a common but basic error to hold this extrinsic, relational orientation responsible for demeaning creaturely reality itself. For Calvin, being creaturely (and, as we shall see, being *imago Dei*) is to accept gratefully our status as created — with its accompanying conditions of finitude. Adam's life in the garden was entirely dependent on this acceptance; "he could not otherwise retain it than by acknowledging that it was received from Him."[53] Although at times Calvin's rhetoric degenerates into an obsession with creaturely limitation, what needs to be remembered is this: human "lack" is part of its fundamental need for a divine partner.[54] At times this may come across as rubbing our noses in our own finitude, but it is more true to Calvin to understand that this interpretive pressure is to glory in our unique status as dependent, loved, even *participating* in God. Calvin's emphasis on creaturely frailty and sin is not to stress the distance from God but to stress that it is God who takes the initiative with us — not we with him.

Calvin's classic statement to this end is the following, which can be interpreted in two quite contrasting ways: "Even if man had remained free from all stain, his condition would have been too lowly [*humilior*] for him to reach God without a Mediator" (II.12.1). Is this a negative view of creatureliness? Or is it indicative of Calvin's attempt to forge a new anthropology in which human beings are constituted, not by themselves, but by another?[55] Despite Calvin's alleged pessimism, this is arguably his true intent. What is at stake is not creaturely honor but the Creator-creature distinction. Elsewhere, Calvin phrases it more mildly, saying that even Adam had to "depend wholly upon the Son of God."[56] Calvin can appear to be against humanness, but he is predominantly against a humanness that is defined without reference to Christ.[57] It takes careful reading to

52. *Comm. Eph.* 1:10.

53. *Comm. Gen.* 2:9.

54. Calvin's rhetoric carries him away at times: man is a "five-foot worm" (I.5.4), a "grub crawling upon the earth" (II.6.4).

55. "Nenny: ce n'est pas cela, mais il veut monstrer que nous n'avons rien qui ne depende de Dieu et en ait son ester" (*Serm. John* 1:1-5, CO 47.479).

56. *Comm. Gen.* 2:9.

57. In *Church Dogmatics* IV/1: 367, Barth criticizes T. F. Torrance for having too positive an estimation of Calvin's doctrine of the corruption of man, functioning merely as "a corollary of the doctrine of grace." Barth sensed that there was more to Calvin's pessimism than met the eye. For my critique, see chapter 6.

pull these two apart. It also takes careful reading to avoid collapsing a humanity *en Christo* into a christomonism, but rather to realize that what Calvin is attempting is to free humanity to be itself. The question of whether or not he was successful I leave until later.

Does Mediation Imply God's Distance?

In Calvin, mediation is not about the overcoming of a presupposed boundary between God and creation but about the proper way God and creation are related. However, when Calvin's emphasis on communion drops from sight, mediation has been misinterpreted either as Calvin's degradation of creaturely reality or as an excessive emphasis on God's separation from the world. We will now consider how Calvin's theology of mediation, if not governed by communion, can also lead to this false definition of God's transcendence and thus separation from the world.

Much has been made of the Reformed "mortal fear of confusing the creature with the Creator,"[58] otherwise defined as "a transcendence of abstract and negative otherness with the resultant lack of contact."[59] Does Calvin's doctrine of transcendence warrant this judgment, in which God's transcendence is the distance he keeps? Louis Bouyer goes even further, calling this

> . . . the most serious defect in his doctrine. . . . Again we come up against the inadequate grasp of divine transcendence that marks Calvin, too, as a child of his time; not because of any innovation his time produced, but because of its inheritance from the late Middle Ages. . . . God, for Calvin, could only be great in so far as man was small. His greatness was not the greatness of the infinite but the greatness of a humanly jealous God, jealous because he was only comparatively great.[60]

Bouyer is certainly right to consider Calvin's doctrine of transcendence against the background of medieval theology. Both he and Ganoczy blame this "gulf" between God and the created order on "l'influence

---

58. David Willis, *Notes on the Holiness of God* (Grand Rapids: Eerdmans, 2002), p. 114.

59. Willis, *Calvin's Catholic Christology*, p. 58.

60. Louis Bouyer, *A History of Christian Spirituality*, 3 vols. (London: Burns & Oates, 1969), 3:87, 89.

scolastique de type nominaliste . . ." with its emphasis on God's absolute power bordering on an arbitrary tyranny.[61] Oberman has already challenged this archaic view of Nominalism; but it would appear that Bouyer's real misunderstanding lies in his inability to discern the function that transcendence plays in Calvin's theology.[62] Rather than seeing it as the bastard child of Nominalism, we must view Calvin's insistence on transcendence against the background of medieval piety and its domestication of God, oriented as it was away from communion and toward manipulation.[63] God was no longer free to offer communion to his people, but "they wish to hide Him in a box, and they wish to carry Him here and there, and to play with Him as with a doll."[64]

On the philosophical front, Scotism (with its strikingly similar emphases to those within fourteenth-century devotional piety) posited that God and creatures could be brought into closer communion if the ontological divide between the two was reduced (thus threatening participation with univocity).[65] Thomism, on the other hand, while upholding the ontological divide, naturalized grace into the world (thus threatening communion). Calvin rebelled against this common misunderstanding in both piety and philosophy, by countering with God's transcendence and "glory."

Calvin fights for God's transcendence not due to some abstract Nominalist principle but for the purpose of communion. God's transcendence is not God's imprisonment over (and thus out of) the world, but rather his freedom to be present to the world. While God's transcendence is often hailed as the most distinctive mark of Reformed theology, this transcen-

---

61. Alexandre Ganoczy, *Calvin, Théologien de l'Église et du Ministère* (Paris: Cerf, 1964), p. 67. See also his *The Young Calvin* (Edinburgh: T. & T. Clark, 1987), p. 192.

62. Heiko Oberman, "*Initia Calvini:* The Matrix of Calvin's Reformation," in *Calvinus Sacrae Scripturae Professor,* ed. Wilhelm Neuser (Grand Rapids: Eerdmans, 1994), p. 119.

63. This is not to deny that Calvin uses language reminiscent of Nominalism, and that he even carried through some of its presuppositions. While this does detract from his overall theology of transcendence, it is mitigated by the ways he undermines "absolute power" with God's goodness, impartial justice, and his communion purposes. See David Steinmetz, "Calvin and the Absolute Power of God," *Journal of Medieval and Renaissance Studies* 18 (1988): 65-79; Susan Schreiner, "Exegesis and Double Justice in Calvin's Sermons on Job," *Church History* 58 (1989): 322-38.

64. *Serm. Acts* 1:9-11.

65. William Cavanaugh, "A Joint Declaration? Justification as Theosis in Aquinas and Luther," *Heythrop Journal* 41 (2000): 270.

dence — if it is to follow Calvin — must not mean external relationship to the world but the absolute freedom with which God stands in relationship to his creatures.[66] It establishes the radical noncontinuity of grace and the world. It certainly does not establish that grace and the world have nothing to do with each other! Instead, he offered the possibility of a new way to ground the Creator-creature relationship. Although it does not look promising to begin with the ontological divide between Creator and creature, it is only when this is established that participation is possible. This is Calvin's genius and what is most often misunderstood about his theological program. For we must remember that Calvin believed that it is not the divine perspective but the sinful human one to regard this ontological divide as a fearful separation.[67] From the human perspective, "we are nothing," but from the divine perspective, "how magnified"! (III.2.25).

Ironically, we can see this most clearly in what has become a classic proof for Calvin's separation of human and divine: Calvin's attack on idolatry. Calvin's infamous disregard for church music, pictures of the saints, transubstantiation, and other pictorial representations of God is commonly attributed to his belief that God is transcendent and thus "above" created reality.[68] To make matters worse, the generation that followed Calvin so feared superstition and its limitations on the sovereignty of God that they converted God's unknowability into a divine attribute.[69] It is not "what does Jerusalem have to do with Athens?" — but what does earth have to do with heaven at all? Rather, as Heiko Oberman compellingly argues, Calvin's real protest was that idols and superstition denied the pres-

66. Richard Muller also concludes that "the ontological distinction of divine from human is by no means a rigid separation" (Muller, "Christ in the Eschaton: Calvin and Moltmann on the Duration of the *Munus Regium,*" *Harvard Theological Review* 74 [1981]: 50).

67. "So greatly are we at variance with him, that regarding him as adverse to us, we, in our turn, flee from his presence" (*Comm. Gen.* 28:12). Mary Potter Engel's "perspectivalism" fails to note that it is not the divine but the human perspective that posits God "in stark contrast" — even "mutually exclusive" — to humanity (*John Calvin's Perspectival Anthropology* [Atlanta: Scholars Press, 1988], p. 2).

68. For an example of this assumption, see Carlos M. N. Eire, "John Calvin's Attack on Idolatry," in *War Against the Idols* (Cambridge: Cambridge University Press, 1986), p. 213. For Calvin's "constructive" and "implicitly trinitarian motivation" behind iconoclasm, see Philip W. Butin, "Constructive Iconoclasm: Trinitarian Concern in Reformed Worship," *Studia Liturgica* 19 (1989): 133-42.

69. Willis, *Notes,* pp. 4-5.

ence of God.[70] Calvin's exposition of the first commandment — that we have "no other gods before me" — well illustrates this. By highlighting the phrase "before my face," Calvin gives a relational analysis of the offense of idolatry, for such a phrase "makes the offense more heinous" (II.8.16). Idols allowed access to God without God, transformation without communion. They did not compromise his transcendence so much as his pledge of immanence, directing worshipers' eyes from his offer of communion to a false security carved in wood or stone. This was not Calvin's "mortal fear of confusing the creature with the Creator," but his sensitivity to the fact that communion depends on God's *freedom*.

If we remember our earlier discussion of Aquinas, his ordering of the *Prima, Secunda,* and *Tertia Partes* carried an implication about the inherent capacity of nature for grace, where created forms carried within them a natural yearning for God, a homing device of sorts. Motivated by his desire to take creation seriously as a realm of God's grace and goodness, Aquinas formed an ontology that led him to invest created forms with "vestiges" of God. Over the years, these forms — the *imago,* humanity, the soul, the sacraments — became larger than life: instead of pointing people to the God in whom they participated (and upon whom the forms depended for their very essence), they began to segregate people *from* God. They became substitutes for his presence rather than what mediated his presence. Calvin realized that for all of high scholasticism's attempts to make grace central, the result was a depersonalized grace, a grace that had no need of the person of Christ. That supreme miracle of God's freedom and grace, the incarnation, deteriorated into the basis for a claim about nature's capacity for grace. Not only was God's freedom and sovereignty curtailed, but reality stopped being an event of communion. Each instance of grace was no longer God freely choosing again and again to give himself to humanity and the created order; rather, this became a "principle" inherent in the order itself. Thus we can see that, for Calvin, God's freedom and transcendence is a necessary component of his larger relationship to the world characterized by communion.

Calvin's contest with his Lutheran opponent Osiander on this point becomes the standard fault line between the two men.[71] Their ongoing

---

70. Heiko Oberman, "The Pursuit of Happiness: Calvin between Humanism and Reformation," in *Humanity and Divinity in Renaissance and Reformation,* ed. John O'Malley (New York: Brill, 1993), p. 278 n. 80.

71. For more background on Osiander, see chapter 4 below.

battle was how to conceive of the relationships between human/divine, nature/grace, and creation/redemption. Osiander attempted to rope nature and grace together through the endowed capacity of nature to mediate the divine presence. His *imago* became just that: a necessary presupposition for God's grace. "[Osiander] asserts that man was created in God's image because he was fashioned according to the pattern of the Messiah to come" (II.12.6). It is clear that Osiander lacked Calvin's non-Platonic category of participation (communion), and it is on this ground that Calvin took his stand. Calvin used the eternal mediation of Christ as leverage, arguing that this primary mediation does not then require God to become man but rather that humanity needs to be constantly "in" God.[72] Where Osiander argued for endowment, Calvin argued for the Spirit and all that the third person entails: the free initiation of God to give himself to us and the *personal* nature of that giving (III.11.5).

Similarly, "Roman" idolatry and superstition (based as it initially was on an insight about grace's capacity to operate through nature) degenerated into a principle about nature's capacity to bear grace. Although Calvin's language about such a relationship is marked by an austerity demanded by the times, we must be able to see that he does not deny nature's intimacy with grace but rather the sacramental foundation on which it stood. Calvin desires participation, not naturalization, because he felt that the naturalization of grace would destroy communion. No longer was God's presence his free, gracious action in the Holy Spirit, but it had become an inherent possibility in creation, conceived as "endowment" or "nature." Transcendence is Calvin's way to combat this domestication of God, of which the most grievous casualty is communion.

Communion and Its Anthropological Repercussions

It is critical to note how Calvin moves the notion of Christ as "mid-point" between God and humanity from the cross, where we are accustomed to

---

72. Or, more specifically, *in Christ.* "But Osiander is always deceived — or tricks himself — in the false principle that the church would have been without a head if Christ had not appeared in the flesh. As the angels enjoyed his Headship, why could Christ not rule over men also by his divine power, quicken and nourish them like his own body by the secret power of his Spirit until, gathered up into heaven, they might enjoy the same life as the angels!" (II.12.7)

look for his mediation, all the way back into creation.[73] What Calvin is doing is weaving Christ into the pattern of creation, not as one of its properties or potentials but as its orientation.[74] In texturing creation with Christ, he avoids making Christ a static principle of creation, but rather the *person* "in whom it lives, and moves and has its being."[75] It is here that we are able to see the significance of one of Calvin's favorite titles for Christ — "first-born of all creation" — which he goes to great lengths to articulate in this participatory sense. "Hence, he is not called the first-born, simply on the ground of his having preceded all creatures in point of time, but because he was begotten by the Father, that they might be created by him, and that he might be, as it were, the substance or foundation of all things."[76]

Firstborn is not chronology but rather relational-ontology. We are "established upon Him," the result of which is an "admirable arrangement and a well-defined order which He has put into created things . . . and we can behold Him in all creatures, because he sustains all things. . . ."[77] However, this is not Platonic metaphysical ontology (where nature is ontologically continuous with divine reality), but an ontology of participation in which our beings participate in the Word for life and for our "order." Here Calvin styles his own "natural theology," marked by his fidelity to the freedom of God and resistance to any naturalization of grace. Our anthropology is bound up with participation in the Eternal Son, not because of an innate Godward movement or point of contact, but because of God's own self-gift.

What kind of an anthropology results from this? Daphne Hampson notes the revolutionary change: the Reformers tend to speak of the person "not as derived 'being,' but in terms of his modes and relations. . . . One sees

73. "He was the mid-point *(medium)* between God and creatures, so that the life which was otherwise hidden in God would flow from him" (Tylenda, "Stancaro I," p. 13, *CO* 9.339).

74. Calvin makes this point about the angels as well: ". . . secondly, because their creation ought to be viewed as having a relation to him, as their legitimate end" (*Comm. Col.* 1:17).

75. Calvin urges us to contemplate with greater diligence this general "life" in which both men and beasts participate, attributable to the persons of the Word and Spirit (*Serm. John* 1:1-5).

76. "Sitque veluti hypostasis aut fundamentum omnium" (*Comm. Col.* 1:15, *CO* 52.85).

77. *Serm. John* 1:1-5. This passage takes place in a remarkably Trinitarian context.

how profound was the break. . . ."[78] Much has been made of the Reformers' groundbreaking "relational" (as opposed to "endowment") anthropology,[79] but it is important to note how Calvin grounds our anthropology in and on Christ himself. This is not the self-directed anthropology of the scholastics nor the modern turn toward an anthropological "deposit of relationality" (e.g., Buber, Brunner, and Moltmann, to name a few). Calvin's is a profoundly dynamic and eschatological anthropology, beginning in Christ but pushing toward the day when he will be all in all.[80] The result is that Calvin is introducing relationship — another *person* — into the substructure of our ontology, making being itself relational.

This is not abandoning ontology but exchanging — to use Christoph Schwöbel's terms — an endowment metaphysics for a metaphysics of relationship.[81] Some scholars treat the Reformers' new anthropology as non-ontological, in an effort to distance themselves from the optimistic ontology that came before.[82] Kathryn Tanner realizes that part of the present misunderstanding about the role of ontology in the Reformers is due to their "negative discourse" about creaturely capacities. "The rhetorical force of that language is suitable for heading off the dangers of distortion posed by modern claims [and, indeed, medieval ones of cooperation and autonomous created powers]." But she warns:

> Interpreted, however, as providing accurate ontological descriptions, discourse according to the negative side of the rules will be "absolutized" as generally adequate apart from the need for any consideration of

---

78. Daphne Hampson, *Christian Contradictions* (London: Cambridge University Press, 2001), p. 35.

79. For a description of the anthropology of late medieval mystical theology with Luther's promotion of "faith" as the new anthropological category, see Steven Ozment, *Homo spiritualis: A Comparative Study of the Anthropology of Johannes Tauler, Jean Gerson and Martin Luther* (Leiden: Brill, 1969).

80. "Mais quoy? C'est seulement une entrée: il y faut marcher plus avant" (*Serm. Acts* 1:1-4, *CO* 48.590).

81. Christoph Schwöbel, "Christology and Trinitarian Thought," in *Trinitarian Theology Today*, ed. Christoph Schwöbel (Edinburgh: T. & T. Clark, 1995), p. 141.

82. Whereas "ontology" has for a long time been used primarily derogatorily (Raitt, Trueman) as an indication of *a priori* metaphysical ontology, others (R. Jenson, McCormack) reveal this to be no longer adequate. Rather, all theology necessarily comes with ontology: the issue is not whether one is ontological or not, but whether one is aware of the ontology with which he or she is working.

the context of its formulation. . . . Viewed as ontological descriptions, traditional statements according to the negative side of the rules become difficult to reconcile with statements according to the positive side; traditional Christian discourse lapses into incoherence.[83]

While it is true that the Reformers abandoned a medieval sacramental and metaphysical ontology, it is important to observe just how radically they changed ontology itself.[84] Calvin's emphasis on the sovereignty of God and the creature's radical dependence has the effect of redirecting ontology, but it is not an "absolutization" of creaturely incapacity (and thus "non-ontology"). Tanner calls this the "Protestant preference for an account of the effects of grace that stresses the creature's *changed relationship* with God rather than the transformation of the creature's own powers of action."[85] Despite Protestant suspicion of ontology, perhaps we could look for clues in mediation. Christ's mediation of all creation, to Calvin's purpose, destabilizes all the old views that humanity (and creation, for that matter) is complete *in se*. It is always fundamentally oriented outside itself, needing another to be complete. The "normative" human condition becomes dynamically viewed as participating in God and all his gifts. Calvin's ontology bound the person of Christ to humanity and humanity to Christ without possessing that ordering in itself.

This whole shift is described compellingly by Heiko Oberman as a move from "ontology to psychology" (perhaps clarifying these terms, with Schwöbel, as a move toward a relational ontology).[86] Oberman's point is that Calvin is moving away from anthropological language that would naturalize any part of grace and, instead, is moving toward a terminology that locates anthropology in the realm of communion with God. That is why, for Calvin, the life of the soul is "the presence of God"; hell is not a location but is the condition of living estranged from him. "Would you know what the death of the soul is? It is to be without God — to be aban-

83. Kathryn Tanner, *God and Creation in Christian Theology: Tyranny or Empowerment?* (Oxford: Blackwell, 1988), p. 155.

84. Whether or not one agrees with Professor Tuomo Mannermaa (University of Helsinki), his reclamation of "ontology" for the Reformers (Luther) has been tremendously important. For a general overview of this "Finnish school," see Carl Braaten and Robert Jenson, eds., *Union with Christ: The New Finnish Interpretation of Luther* (Grand Rapids: Eerdmans, 1998).

85. Tanner, *Creation*, p. 103.

86. Oberman, "Happiness," p. 265.

doned by God, and left to itself: for if God is its life, it loses its life when it loses the presence of God."[87] Calvin's anthropology is not oriented toward its own resources (even those given by grace), because he saw all too well that these resources quickly degenerate into that which relates God and humanity rather than the free communion of Christ by the Spirit.

The Mediator and the Garden

Having painted with fairly broad brushstrokes thus far (looking at the more abstract passages on mediation in Calvin's tracts, commentaries, sermons, and the *Institutes*), we will now look at Calvin's portrait of the Garden of Eden as specific evidence of this anthropology. In the first section I will examine the role of participation in the first humans' existence with God in the Garden of Eden; in the second section I will highlight two of Adam's characteristics — immortality and *imago Dei* — that he "owned" only by participation; and in the third I will evaluate the results of human rebellion for this existence.

Participation in the Garden

> *"Man was blessed, not because of his own good actions, but by participation in God" (II.2.1).*

Calvin uses the traditional features of the Garden of Eden to argue for the story of a humanity participating in God and whose purpose is to be near to him. "At that time, I say, when [Adam] had been advanced to the highest degree of honor, Scripture attributed nothing else to him than that he had been created in the image of God, thus suggesting that man was blessed, not because of his own good actions, but by participation in God" (*sed Dei participatione fuisse beatum,* II.2.1). Here we note the absence of the traditional list of attributes and "perfections" typical of medieval discussions of Adam; in its place is a *mode of being,* in which Adam stays near to God and participates in him for the glory that Adam himself exhibits.[88]

---

87. Calvin, "Psychopannychia," *T&T* III. 454. See also Oberman, *"Initia Calvini,"* p. 133.

88. As I have observed above, it is clear that this participation enjoyed by the first

This is a typical move for Calvin, who takes the focus off humanity *in se* and instead brings all under communion. T. F. Torrance observes: "In such a dynamic conception of man's relation to God as the Reformers envisaged, there are only two directions attributable to human existence: toward God, or away from him. . . ."[89] One might add to that observation that life in the Garden is characterized not only by right "direction" toward the Word, but living by the Word — seeking all good things *in* him, not merely *from* him. Here it is crucial to remember that Calvin's emphasis on participation is not an end in itself but is in service of intimacy and a world that has been designed specifically so that everything draws us to God. "Direct communication with God was the source of life to Adam."[90] On a deeper level, it is a fundamental characteristic of a world in which the person to whom we are drawn is also the one in whom we exist. Nothing can be had independently of him; everything is to be had in and with him.

The tree of life is central to this understanding of participation, as a "visible testimony [to Adam] that 'in God we are, and live, and move.'"[91] Calvin then continues by stabilizing this general participation specifically in the person of Christ:

> Yet I am not dissatisfied with what has been handed down by some of the fathers, as Augustine and Eucherius, that the tree of life was a figure of Christ, inasmuch as he is the Eternal Word of God: it could not indeed be otherwise a symbol of life, than by representing him in figure. For we must maintain what is declared in the first chapter of John (John 1:1-3) that the life of all things was included in the Word, but especially the life of men which is conjoined with reason and intelligence. Wherefore, by this sign, Adam was admonished, that he could claim nothing for himself as if it were his own, in order that he might depend wholly upon the Son of God, and might not seek life anywhere but in him.[92]

---

humans has not become an anthropological endowment. "Creation is not inpouring, but the beginning of essence out of nothing" (I.15.5).

89. Torrance, "Word," p. 110.

90. *Comm. Gen.* 3:22.

91. In his *Comm. Acts* 17:28 ("in him we live and move and have our being"), Calvin gives the Spirit this cosmic role. But it is to be noted that this is not so much a sanctifying role as a preserving one.

92. *Comm. Gen.* 2:9.

Without discussing Christ's mediation of creation at this point, Calvin still carries through its implications with utter seriousness: Adam "lives not by his own power" but, more specifically, "depend[s] wholly upon the Son of God," for "the life of all things was included in the Word." Here we again find Calvin's reluctance to speak in general terms; he is constantly disciplining participation to Christ. In Calvin, participation is not a principle. It is a way of living such that everything forces us to be in relationship. The flip side of this is that "our nature lacks everything that our Heavenly Father bestows" (II.2.20). The point is not the "lack," but the "bestows."

Imago Dei *and Immortality*

*"In the Old Covenant, God gave his people fellowship with himself
and thus eternal life" (II.10.8).*

The *imago Dei* functions as a focal point where Calvin works out the specifics of participation and has also functioned as a battleground for conflicting Calvin interpretation, for "it is in its teaching about the *imago dei* that Reformed theology sets forth its doctrine of the creaturehood of man and his relation to God. . . ."[93] What is this relationship between creature and Creator, human and divine? Thus far, I have been arguing for a relationship of difference governed by Calvin's concept of communion. Two scholars, Heiko Oberman and T. F. Torrance, have done much to underscore this particular view in their research on immortality and the *imago*.

In Heiko Oberman's penetrating treatment of the immortality of the soul, he shows how Calvin annexes immortality to the *imago Dei* (in his commentary on Gen. 2:7),[94] the consequence of which is to shift immortality from attribute to that which can only be had in communion.[95] Calvin does not care much for language of the "immortality of the soul"; instead, he speaks of a "participation in God, which cannot be without the blessing of eternal life" (II.10.7).[96] He then specifies this immortality in

93. Torrance, "Word," p. 102.
94. Oberman, "Happiness," p. 266.
95. Although Calvin can refer to the soul as "immortal," he immediately specifies it as a "created substance" (I.15.2), signaling its dependence on the Creator for its immortality.
96. "Erat enim solida Deo participatio, quae extra vitae aeternae bonum esse non potest" (*CO* 2.317).

pneumatological terms: Adam's body housed an "immortal spirit" (I.15.1). Furthermore, the Spirit is the "author of regeneration not by borrowing but by his very own energy; and not of this only but of future immortality as well" (I.13.14).

How are we to conceive of our partaking of the Spirit's "own energy," which results in our immortality, while avoiding any suggestion of pantheism? In his commentary on 2 Peter 1:4, Calvin protects the essence of God while still arguing that "we shall be partakers of divine and blessed immortality and glory, so as to be as it were one with God *as far as our capacities will allow* [italics added]." It is a form of participation in which God's otherness and our humanity are preserved because it is participation as communion (indicated by Calvin's nod toward pneumatological differentiation here). Just as unfallen humanity (Adam) enjoyed the "gift of immortality" (IV.14.12), so fallen humanity must "be received into communion of the Word in order to receive hope of immortality" (IV.17.8). The term "communion" *(communionem)* is significant here, signaling both a Trinitarian understanding of immortality (in the Word, by the Spirit) as well as its specifically relational context. Elsewhere, Calvin forcefully argues (II.10.8) that fellowship with God *is* eternal life, a conclusion that he is able to draw exclusively from the Old Testament as well. Given the obsession of the mid-sixteenth century with the immortal soul, Calvin's stance is remarkable. He has returned to the biblical vocabulary, discussing the soul in terms of its createdness.

Although the *imago Dei* has been treated extensively in Calvin scholarship, my purpose here is to treat it as it relates to Calvin's doctrine of participation. Rejecting the distinction between image and likeness since Irenaeus's time (I.15.2), and judging Augustine's search for the *imago* within the soul as unsound, Calvin believes that "a definition of the image of God ought to rest on a firmer basis than such subtleties."[97] Calvin begins by differentiating humanity from the animal kingdom in this way: "The likeness of God extends to the whole excellence by which man's nature towers over all the kinds of living creatures" (I.15.3); but this excellence tends to be formed in qualitative rather than quantitative terms: "And, indeed, there is nothing in which man excels the lower animals unless it be his spiritual communion with God in the hope of a blessed eternity."[98] For Calvin, what

97. *Comm. Gen.* 1:26.

98. Calvin, *A Reformation Debate: Sadoleto's Letter to the Genevans and Calvin's Reply,* ed. John C. Olin (New York: Harper & Row, 1966), p. 59.

is crucial is not merely the "endowment" of this excellence but that the excellence is turned toward God in communion. "Adam bore God's image in so far as he was joined to God" (II.12.6).

Some scholars have strongly argued — against a purely relational understanding of the *imago Dei* — that Calvin's language speaks of the image as an endowed gift (or engravings) "bestowed on man when created."[99] However, when Calvin refers to the "engravings" of the *imago* bestowed on humanity, it must be noted that he always does so in conjunction with the way in which these engravings were oriented. For example, "Accordingly, the integrity with which Adam was endowed is expressed by this word, when he had full possession of right understanding, when he had his affections kept within the bounds of reason, all his senses tempered in right order, and he truly referred his excellence to exceptional gifts bestowed upon him by his Maker" (I.15.3). This is also Gerrish's view: "To sum up: In Calvin's view, the image of God in man denotes not an endowment only but also a relationship."[100]

As we have observed in Calvin's doctrine of creation, God does not give us things that would then function without him; their very character demands communion. This is the distinctive "participation" aspect of his doctrine of the *imago Dei,* and what allows him to walk the tightrope between the two common interpretive extremes of mere "correlative" response (Torrance) and "endowment" (Faber).[101] Says Calvin: "We are no different from brutish beasts if we do not understand that the world was made by God. Why are men endowed with reason and intellect except for the purpose of recognizing their Creator?"[102] Even the unique human faculty of reason is not an end in itself, nor the preeminent mark of the *imago Dei,* but is to direct us to the Creator in recognition and gratitude.[103]

T. F. Torrance pioneers this interpretation with Calvin's use of the term "mirror," which allows Torrance to clarify Calvin's dynamic conception of the *imago.*

99. Jelle Faber, "*Imago Dei* in Calvin: Calvin's Doctrine of Man as the Image of God by Virtue of Creation," in *Essays in Reformed Doctrine* (Neerlandia, Alberta: Inheritance, 1990), p. 231.

100. B. A. Gerrish, "The Mirror of God's Goodness: Man in the Theology of Calvin," *Concordia Theological Quarterly* 45 (1981): 215.

101. T. F. Torrance, *Calvin's Doctrine of Man* (Grand Rapids: Eerdmans, 1957), p. 71; Faber, "*Imago Dei,*" p. 229.

102. *Comm. Heb.* 11:3.

103. This is underscored in B. A. Gerrish, *Grace and Gratitude: The Eucharistic Theology of John Calvin* (Minneapolis: Fortress, 1993).

Only while the mirror actually reflects an object does it have the image of that object. There is no such thing in Calvin's thought as an *imago* disassociated from the act of reflecting. He does use such expressions as *engrave* and *sculptured,* but only in a metaphorical sense and never disassociated from the idea of the mirror.[104]

Torrance well captures one side of Calvin's doctrine of participation here. The *imago* is incomplete without both God and humanity, together relating to one another. Torrance maintains: "Strictly speaking, it is God who images himself in man . . . there can be no image where there is no one beholding. . . . *Imago dei* has to do fundamentally with God's beholding rather than with man's."[105] This does not necessarily tell the whole story, as Mary Potter Engel shows in her careful study of Calvin's metaphors of "engraving" and "sculpture."[106] Chafing against Torrance's totalizing perspective, Engel advocates for Calvin a "dynamic perspectival structure," arguing that he "simply assumes the coexistence of these contradictory yet complementary views."[107] Yet this solution is not sufficient either. Engel's work is important because she highlights metaphors that often fall between doctrinal cracks; but simple faithfulness to both dynamic, competing perspectives in Calvin does not fully clarify what Calvin is doing. What is important — perhaps the most important aspect of the two (or more) perspectives from which Calvin operates — is not that they exist but how they relate to each other.

It is only when we examine these contradictory pairs in Calvin (*imago* effaced vs. *imago* preserved; *imago* dynamic vs. *imago* substantial) that we realize we are in the territory of a new way of relating human and divine. As Oberman suggests, "It has not been sufficiently noted that Calvin intended to develop a new biblical anthropology by redefining its key terms."[108] Take, for example, the way Calvin holds together two differing accounts of wisdom. In his first *Institutes* (1536), Calvin says: "That is, [Adam] was *endowed with wisdom,* righteousness, holiness, and was so clinging by these gifts of grace to God that he could have lived forever in Him . . ." (I.2, italics added).

104. Torrance, *Man,* p. 36.

105. Torrance, *Man,* pp. 35, 39, 73.

106. Engel, *Perspectival,* pp. 50-61. For Engel, these metaphors indicate that Calvin describes "the *imago* also in terms of actual qualities or endowments in human nature, that is, in terms of an inviolable constitution of human *being*" (p. 53).

107. Engel, *Perspectival,* p. 23.

108. Oberman, "Happiness," p. 252.

In a near-contemporary document, *Psychopannychia,* Calvin observes that "man, in respect of spirit, was made partaker of the wisdom, justice, and goodness of God."[109] "Endowed" with wisdom or "partaker" in God's wisdom? For Calvin, participating in God's gifts does not cut off the possibility of these gifts truly becoming our own, in our nature; but it is the only ground for them. Indeed, once Calvin establishes the proper divine perspective, he can say things such as, "Yet those good works which he has bestowed upon us the Lord calls 'ours'" (III.15.3). Also, "God, then, should make himself ours, so that all his things should in a manner become our things."[110] This signifies that the divine origin of a gift does not prohibit it from being properly ascribed to, or even becoming part of the creaturely realm.

It is only when we realize that with Calvin's insistence on Christ's mediation of creation, the division between human and divine nature is rendered inadequate — not blurred, but indeed inadequate to account for the ways in which the divine *constitutes* the human. Although I recognize that here I am not expounding, but extrapolating Calvin, it is essential to realize the ways that just such a doctrine of Christ's mediation of creation trumps incompatible notions of "divine" and "human." Humanity is only itself in relationship with God (and indeed, Calvin would go so far as to put humanity in the Son at its inception). The issue thus becomes irrelevant whether or not humanity is "endowed" with various qualities, for Calvin is not looking at humanity apart from God, but in its constant state of participation in Christ. Mary Potter Engel denies that a christological reading of the *imago* is the entirety of Calvin's view: she argues that Calvin's acceptance of "remnants" and "vestiges" of the image, even in fallen humanity, proves this. Perhaps a better approach is to note how Calvin sees *all* creation in the Mediator; thus, even the remnants are in some way being sustained by Christ and the Spirit.[111]

Torrance and Engel represent opposite sides of what has become a commonplace battle in Calvin scholarship between the "evangelical" and "sapiential" — one affirming Calvin's emphasis on God's priority (and creaturely incapacity), the other affirming Calvin's emphasis on creation and its goodness (though, truthfully, this is not as common as one would like). Against Torrance, there is not only sanctioned but necessary speech to be made about the reality of the *imago* in human life. His emphasis on the "mirror" metaphor fails in that it is a metaphor that is limited to reflection

---

109. Calvin, "Psychopannychia," *T&T* III.424.
110. *Comm. 2 Pet.* 1:4.
111. Engel, *Perspectival,* p. 62.

only, with little room for participation. It is not just God actively giving and humanity passively receiving; humanity has been called to participate in this divine image and calling. Torrance has perhaps followed Calvin too far here, rather than giving a necessary corrective. We must remember that, for polemical reasons, Calvin was at times hesitant to emphasize this "positive" role for humanity (see the conclusion in chapter 6 below). As we have seen, Calvin's instinct is always to see how creaturely reality *participates in God*, with a focus first on the Giver and only then on the gift/endowment (sometimes to the neglect of the gift). This is part of his entire orientation toward God's glory.[112] Meanwhile, an inadequate grasp of Calvin's doctrine of participation makes Engel wont to emphasize endowment over against (or simply alongside) dynamism, merely treating them as differing perspectives. In Calvin's struggle to affirm both, we find him using categories of participation that are directly tied to his doctrine of Christ's mediation of creation.

For this reason, Oberman thinks it significant that Calvin spoke of humanity as *toward* the image of God *(formatum ad imaginem Dei)*, indicating movement rather than possession.[113] As Torrance summarizes, Reformed teaching on the *imago Dei* "can be done only from the standpoint of the man renewed in Jesus Christ."[114] Calvin sees the image as both a reality in Eden (because of Christ) and a promise to come.[115]

> All men unanimously admit that Christ was even then the image of God. Hence: whatever excellence was engraved upon Adam, derived from the fact that he approached the glory of his Creator through the only-begotten Son. "So man was created in the image of God" [Gen. 1:27]; in

---

112. The warrant for this is Calvin's doctrine of the ascension and continuing priesthood of Christ, who himself restores the *imago* and represents humanity as *imago* to the Father.

113. *Comm. Gen.* 2:18.

114. Torrance, "Word," p. 102.

115. Jelle Faber explicitly denies this: "Christ was made like us for restoration; we were not made like Christ in creation" (Faber, "*Imago Dei*," p. 239). Here Faber is picking up the tail end of Calvin's argument against Osiander, where Calvin denies that "Osiander [be] allowed to infer that the first pattern of God's image was in the man Christ" (II.12.6). However, Faber fails to note that Calvin's retort to Osiander takes place in the midst of a discussion of Christ's mediation of creation. Calvin's *imago* is not collapsed into the human Jesus (à la Osiander), but neither is it complete without an eschatological movement toward and in him. For Calvin's definitive praise for the *imago Dei* in the new creation over against the old, see *Comm. Ezek.* 18:32.

him the Creator himself willed that his own glory be seen as in a mirror. Adam was advanced to this degree of honor, thanks to the only-begotten Son. (II.12.6)

Having shown that Christ has always been the "image of God" and that Adam approached this *imago*-glory "through the only-begotten Son," Calvin then shows that both creation (as its "firstborn") and the church ("as its head") have been gathered in Christ (II.12.7) from all time. Calvin's point is that Christ did not have to become human to enjoy preeminence in all things; he already *was* by virtue of his eternal mediation. Adam was not made like the human Christ, but Adam was made *in Christ* his head, the firstborn of creation.[116] Calvin saw the cosmic significance of Christ not just in creation or even in redemption, but in the fundamental participation of all reality in and through him. Desiring to invest creation with stability and glory, Calvin does so not by giving it a chronological priority over the Jesus-of-history, but by texturing it with the mediation of the eternal Word. Just as our prefallen, created state had no "firm or settled constancy" except that it was firmly in Christ, so the *imago* is "nowhere better recognized than from the restoration of [Adam's] corrupted nature" (I.15.4). As in the mediation of creation, we find Calvin constantly funneling all reality toward and into the Son, in order to establish its reality (I.15.4). Communion is the underpinning of creation.

Part of the problem is the way "creation," "nature," and "endowment" are conceived. During Calvin's time, nature was seen to possess its own self-directedness to God. Calvin never denies the significance of the created world; but he does not afford it the self-enclosedness that other philosophers and theologians did.[117] Why? Because even if nature in that model is directed toward God, it does not need God to get there. Calvin's focus on communion shifts everything from ends to means: *how* creation ends up at its goal is actually the whole point. The point is not simply that we have the *imago* or pieces of it,[118] but that the having of it is itself an act of communion. Calvin rarely

116. Firstborn is not chronology but ontology. "[He is] called the first-born . . . that he might be, as it were, the substance or foundation of all things" (*Comm. Col.* 1:15).

117. Torrance comes to the same conclusion: "This is not to deny natural theology, as such, for that would mean a denial of the natural man in his actual existence, but it does mean that a Christian theology cannot be built upon a carnal foundation . . ." (Torrance, "Word," p. 112).

118. Calvin is more than willing to speak of "vestiges" of the image, and even that all humanity is held together by this "sacred bond of union" (*Comm. Gal.* 5:14).

contemplates nature as a category in itself. It is either nature-in-communion-with-God or nature-alienated-from-God.[119] Creation is not self-enclosed but is only itself when participating in God (and as we know, Calvin never sees this as God *simpliciter*, but as in Christ, by the Spirit). In this way Calvin's declaration that the "end of the gospel [is] to hold communion with God" is truly the fulfillment of the purpose of creation.[120]

Thus far we have examined the "natural state" of humanity in the Garden of Eden and how it functions in Calvin as a clear example of communion. We have seen how Adam's life and qualities in the Garden were not given by God to be "enclosed" in Adam and take on a life of their own, but that they are held only by participation. At times Calvin can speak as if these things were endowments; other times he emphasizes their radical giftedness from God. Both are true from the perspective of participation. The tree of life has a central place because it reminds Adam and Eve that the completion that they enjoy is not their own, nor is it from the tree, but it is as they are in communion with the Word. Similarly, their immortality is a gift and is linked to the person of the Spirit. In annexing immortality to the *imago Dei*, Calvin shows that neither is part of the natural constitution of humanity, but that these are gifts to be had in communion with God. Oberman remarks that "such a way of referring to the *imago Dei* alerts us to the fact that we are here far removed from the ontological language of tradition."[121]

The Loss of Communion

> *"Would you know what the death of the soul is? It is to be without God — to be abandoned by God, and left to itself: for if God is its life, it loses its life when it loses the presence of God."*[122]

Since Calvin's view of Eden is governed by communion, we would expect the Fall to be cast in similar terms.[123] Brian Gerrish plainly sets forth Cal-

---

119. We see this clearly in his description of the Fall, where human nature became a source of confidence leading to ingratitude and the eventual loss of all the gifts of God (CO 22.36).

120. *Comm. 1 John 2:5.*

121. Oberman, "Happiness," p. 266.

122. Calvin, "Psychopannychia," *T&T* III.454.

123. I am departing from Calvin's order so that I can show how Calvin's doctrine of the Fall is heavily marked by his communion principle. In the *Institutes*, Calvin treats the

vin's view: "The doctrine of sin is not strictly about a person's moral condition but about his relationship to God."[124] Gently correcting Augustine's view of sin as concupiscence, Calvin decides that it is a sin against communion: "Unfaithfulness, then, was the root of the Fall" (II.1.4). Gerrish explains this as part of Calvin's program "to get behind human pride to the root cause of it. And what is that? He has several words for it; perhaps 'unfaithfulness' is the regulative one. But it is crucial to note that, for him, the essence of infidelity is *not listening to God*."[125] Gerrish here underscores Calvin's communion motif: the lavish abundance *and* the one prohibition in the Garden were both intended to draw Adam into communion with God, the first to a posture of gratitude, and the second to a posture of listening.[126] The tree with its prohibition was a means for God to dwell with Adam, "[f]or, unless we listen attentively to him, his majesty will not dwell among us" (II.1.4).

It was Adam's listening disposition to God that characterized his relationship with God in the Garden, not (as is sometimes supposed) an abstract moral purity. "Wherefore, the commencement of the ruin by which the human race was overthrown was a defection from the command of God. But observe, that men then revolted from God, when, having forsaken his word, they lent their ears to the falsehoods of Satan."[127] Listening, word, ears: these aural words define Adam's obedience — obedience to God's command, which Calvin defines as "trust in his person."[128] The death of the soul he equates with being "*deaf*, not hearing that living voice."[129] Adam and Eve (no less than humanity today) were to stay their course in the Garden of Eden through trusting God's character and his intent toward them. "For, indeed, their best restraint was the thoughts which entirely occupied their minds, that God is just, that nothing is

---

Fall of Adam only under Book II, "The Knowledge of God the Redeemer in Christ." Calvin does not treat humanity's sin apart from salvation.

124. Gerrish, "Mirror," p. 220.

125. Gerrish, "Mirror," p. 218.

126. T. F. Torrance documents Calvin's view of sin as ingratitude, which amounts to the reverse of an anthropology in which "Calvin practically equates the *imago* with the *actio* of gratitude" (Torrance, *Man*, p. 71 n. 6).

127. *Comm. Gen.* 3:6.

128. See the Geneva Catechism 1541, Q.7, CO 6.9. Elsewhere Calvin defines obedience as trusting in God's propitiousness (i.e., his character), not that our obedience will propitiate (III.3.2).

129. Calvin, "Psychopannychia," *T&T* III.417.

better than to obey his commands and that to be loved by him is the consummation of a happy life."[130]

Oberman rightly notes that Calvin's focus is not the loss of various "accidents," or which "natural gifts" were preserved, but rather

> Calvin is intent to follow the biblical story and vocabulary by portraying created man as "in communion with God" and fallen man as "alienated from God" . . . . When the *imago Dei* is lost, then this is not a loss in "substance" or "essence," but in orientation: since the fall man is bewildered.[131]

Calvin makes it plain that what Adam enjoyed in the Garden was primarily communion with God. When Adam defected, happiness as well as gifts were lost, not so much as a punishment but as a natural consequence of no longer participating in them. "As it was the spiritual life of Adam to remain united and bound to his Maker, so estrangement from him was the death of his soul" (II.i.5). Note the relational imagery in the earliest edition of the *Institutes*: "Moreover, he was far removed from God and became a complete stranger. From this it follows that man was stripped and deprived of all wisdom, righteousness, power, life, which — as has already been said — *could be held only in God*" (I.2, italics added). Humanity is not "stripped" of endowments in the way apples are removed from a basket, but in the way that apples die because the branch of a tree has been cut off. Adam removed himself from the source of all the benefits that he enjoyed. He no longer participated in the Holy Spirit, thus "we are despoiled of the excellent gifts of the Holy Spirit, of the light of reason, of justice, and of rectitude, and are prone to every evil. . . ."[132]

Calvin's stance on the tree of life is fascinating, giving us clues to his later treatment of the sacraments. As I have already noted, the tree served a pedagogical function to remind Adam *from whom* the life he was enjoying came. When Adam broke communion with God, the tree could no longer remind Adam that he was depending "wholly upon the Son of God" and thus became meaningless. In Book IV on the sacraments, Calvin observes:

130. *Comm. Gen.* 3:6; II.i.4.
131. Oberman, "Happiness," pp. 265-66.
132. *Comm. Gen.* 3:6. Yet there is still the presence of the Holy Spirit in the world, for if God were to completely remove his Spirit from us, we would perish (*Serm. John* 1:1-5; *CO* 47.479).

When he deprives Adam of the gift of immortality and withdraws it from him, he says, "Let him not take of the fruit of life, lest he live forever" [Gen. 3:22]. What can this mean? Could that fruit restore to Adam his incorruption from which he had now fallen? Not at all! But this is just as if the Lord had said, "Lest he enjoy vain confidence by clinging to the symbol of my promise, let that which could bring him any hope of immortality be removed from him." (IV.14.12)

In his *Commentary on Genesis, 3:22,* Calvin de-emphasizes the tree ("there never was any intrinsic efficacy in the tree") in order to emphasize its true efficacy ("Previously, direct communication with God was the source of life to Adam"). Calvin further emphasizes that God is not by necessity bound to the tree, but graciously, "out of respect to his own Institutes, connects life with the external sign, till the promise should be taken away from it."[133] Here we find an interesting convergence of themes dear to Calvin that will appear together again and again: the gracious binding of (and hence unnecessary relationship between) sign and signified and the orientation of the sacraments to communion. It is a costly destabilizing of sign and reality that Calvin felt to be worthy of his emphasis on communion, in order that God might not be "shut up" as in a prison.[134] We will explore the ramifications of this further in chapter 4.

This situation is nothing short of hell on earth, a qualitative state of misery and alienation. Fallen humanity is alienated from the Word — its source of life — and hence lives in a state of death:

We must also see what is the cause of death, namely alienation from God. Thence it follows, that under the name of death is comprehended all those miseries in which Adam involved himself by his defection; for as soon as he revolted from God, the fountain of life, he was cast down from his former state, in order that he might perceive the life of man without God to be wretched and lost, and therefore differing nothing from death.[135]

---

133. "It is indeed certain, that man would not have been able, had he even devoured the whole tree, to enjoy life against the will of God" (*Comm. Gen.* 3:22).

134. "Moreover, I call them vehicles and ladders, because symbols of this kind were by no means ordained that the faithful might shut up God in a tabernacle as in a prison" (*Comm. Gen.* 3:24).

135. *Comm. Gen.* 2:17.

William Bouwsma has opened our eyes in new ways to the relation between the culture of fear in which Calvin lived, and to his own fears of the "abyss" and "labyrinth."[136] What perhaps needs more attention is how Calvin specifically describes the Fall as a *fall into fear*. Calvin says that creation is designed so that humanity should see the goodness of God and "from it pass over to eternal life and perfect felicity." Instead, "[a]fter man's rebellion, our eyes — wherever they turn — encounter God's curse" (II.6.1). This new state of sin is the grand inversion.[137] We now misinterpret those very things "by which he would draw us to himself"; "so greatly are we at variance with him, that, regarding him as adverse to us, we, in our turn, flee from his presence."[138] Broken communion brings not just alienation but terror. "But who might reach to him? Any one of Adam's children? No, like their father, all of them were terrified at the sight of God [Gen. 3:8]" (II.12.1). Hell becomes not so much location as condition, occurring not at life's end but throughout every moment lived out of communion.[139]

*   *   *

We have seen how Calvin's conception of the Word as "foundation" of the world allows him even in the Garden to work with the notion of human participation in the divine. And yet, this is inadequate — indeed, false — as the core of Calvin's doctrine of participation. For Calvin, neither a theory of the interpenetration of the human and divine, nor an ontological principle, but a *person* determines his theology. Creation's existence is personal existence because, from the beginning, it has always been specially related to the second person of the Trinity by the Spirit. It is the mediator — the Son — whose presence establishes the world as a place of communion, and who desires a future of communion (ascent) with humanity.

Calvin's dynamic and personal conception of creation warranted an equally robust conception of sin. Humanity — living directly from the life and benefits of the Word — suddenly rejects this participatory existence

136. William J. Bouwsma, *John Calvin: A Sixteenth-Century Portrait* (New York: Oxford University Press, 1988).

137. "[L]'ordre qu'il avoit institué en la creation du monde est troublé" (*Serm. Job* 5:17-18, *CO* 33.966).

138. *Comm. Gen.* 28:12.

139. Calvin, "Psychopannychia," *T&T* III.454. See also the exploration of Calvin's "modern" views of the psychological impact of sin in Oberman, "Happiness," p. 265.

and exchanges *koinōnia* for independence and ingratitude. Refusing their specific form of createdness (an anthropology that is fundamentally oriented toward *another*), Adam and Eve attempted to bypass their "lowly estate" [*humilior*] by circumventing the only life they have — the Mediator. The Fall is a "fall" indeed, away from an existence of communion with God, which was also the ascending *telos* of creation and the very essence of their being *imago*. It is also a fall into terror.

Given this new situation of sin, how is it that humanity is going to continue its vocation of communion, its vocation to ascend? What the incarnation of God means for redemption is suddenly clear: it will be the restoration of this primary anthropology — this primary relationship — so that humanity will once again accept and revel in its status as *created*, incomplete, not-God. We will now proceed into Calvin's christology, to the man Jesus Christ, who will redeem humanity through his death and persuade them once again of God's love for them. However, this will not be mere cognitive persuasion. Jesus will be noticeably "set apart" by a sinless relationship of trust and communion with God the Father, which he reopens to all humanity through participation in his person.[140]

---

140. "[Even if men believed in the Creator] yet because they had no Mediator it was not possible for them truly to taste God's mercy, and thus be persuaded that he was their Father" (II.6.4).

Chapter Three

Christ:
The Ascending One

There can indeed be mediation by ascent, but it is not that envisioned by all the forms of the so-called christology from below. There is no ascent without the prior descent of the Son of God to our realm of sin and death, no christology from below unless the man Jesus is confessed as the mediator of creation also. And that is possible only through the gift of the Spirit, not by any other means, lest we seek to penetrate the divine incognito, the Jewish flesh of Jesus, and by so doing deprive Jesus of his mediatorial humanity. . . . The man, Jesus Christ, the mediator of salvation is first of all mediator of creation so that finally he might be eschatological mediator, recapitulating, summing up, all things in himself.[1]

In the preceding chapter on Calvin, I outlined the ground and grammar for his doctrine of ascent. I explored the general possibility for participation in the way that Calvin makes the Mediator the "foundation" of all reality, all the while making the distinction between participatory communion and a Plotinian continuity of being. More specifically, we saw how this general participation was the norm for the existence of Adam and Eve, who themselves needed the Mediator for life and all the goodness

1. Colin Gunton, "'One Mediator . . . the Man Jesus Christ': Reconciliation, Mediation, and Life in Community," *Pro Ecclesia* 11 (2002): 11.

that they enjoyed. Following this insight came the discovery that Calvin understands the Fall as a loss of participation and communion.

We now move from Christ's mediation of creation to his mediation of the *new* creation. Calvin sees with piercing clarity that, although the situation has considerably altered, the Mediator and his "office" remain consistent. The Mediator, of course, continues to play his central role between creation and the triune God, but "given the breach of the relationship from the human side, a new form of mediation is required to deal with the new and dangerous situation."[2] Calvin underscores how, throughout the Old Testament, the Word maintains this office of communion in angelic appearances: "For even though he was not yet clothed with flesh, he came down, so to speak, as an intermediary, in order to approach believers more intimately" (I.13.10).[3] Within the New Testament, the Word will continue his mediation in an even more intimate capacity in the form of his descent into full human existence: "He is near us, indeed touches us, since he is our flesh" (II.12.1).

This chapter explores the christological possibilities for participation in God, as opened up by the Spirit in the Word made flesh. Here we will review how Calvin never considers Christ in isolation from us, but rather at every possible turn specifically relates his life to us. "For this is a point we must know, that nothing was given in vain to Jesus Christ. Now He does not need it for His own use. But it is for His members, in order that all of us may draw upon His fullness and grace for grace."[4] My exposition will fall into two halves: the first examines Calvin's christological scheme of participation and how his understanding of the Trinity facilitated this; the second half explores how Calvin views the humanity of Jesus so that we can fully participate in it, following a structure of Christ's *descent* and *ascent*. Throughout, I will seek to draw out the underappreciated ontology of *koinōnia* that is integral to Calvin's thought, while also recognizing the tensions running throughout.

---

2. Gunton, "Mediator," p. 149.

3. It is his *nature* (economic function) to be the "mid-point," the one who has intimacy with creatures (I.13.10). "He was the mid-point *(medium)* between God and creatures, so that the life which was otherwise hidden in God would flow from him" (Joseph Tylenda, "Christ the Mediator: Calvin Versus Stancaro," *Calvin Theological Journal* 8 [1973]: 13; *CO* 9.339).

4. *Serm. Acts* 1:4-5.

The Bidirectional Itinerary of God

"Descending to earth, he has prepared an ascent to heaven for us"
(Institutes 1536, IV.24).

From Anthropology to Christology

Throughout the mystical writings of Calvin's contemporaries, the notion of the soul's ascent maintained its status as a primary metaphor for spiritual growth.[5] This is exemplified in the ascending poetry of Marguerite, Queen of Navarre, to whom Calvin wrote letters of spiritual and political direction.[6] In contrast to her "celestial ladders," Calvin is supremely fascinated by the contours of the descent and ascent of the Mediator:

> "And behold a ladder." It is Christ alone, therefore, who connects heaven and earth: he is the only Mediator who reaches from heaven down to earth: he is the medium through which the fullness of all celestial blessings flows down to us, and through which we, in turn, ascend [*conscendimus*] to God.[7]

What differentiates Calvin from the medieval emphasis on the "ascent of the soul" is what also differentiates him from the contemporary enthrallment with a general "ascent of humanity."[8] We recall the answers of Greek philosophy and medieval theology: ascent tended toward an anthropological principle, an ontological endowment revitalized and re-

---

5. Calvin's unique usage of "ascent" is best understood in the context of the fifteenth- and sixteenth-century obsession with the soul, evidenced by the explosion of tractates dealing with the soul's powers and "upwards" mobility. "Indeed, the soul . . . had for more than a century occupied a unique place in Renaissance literature" (George Tavard, *The Starting Point of Calvin's Theology* [Grand Rapids: Eerdmans, 2000], p. 20).

6. Paula Sommers, *Celestial Ladders: Readings in Marguerite de Navarre's Poetry of Spiritual Ascent* (Geneva: Droz, 1989).

7. *Comm. Gen.* 28:12 (*CO* 23.391). See also *Serm. Eph.* 1:10 (*CO* 51.295).

8. That the descent of Christ precedes our ascent should stop all contemporary talk of Hegelian progress in its tracks, whether it take the form given by Rahner or Hick. Calvin has only disdain for nonchristological schemes of ascent. "All who, leaving Christ, attempt to rise to heaven after the manner of the giants, are destitute" (*Comm. John* 8:19). See also *Comm. Gen.* 3:22.

stored by Christ. In a move that was radical not only for his time but also for ours, Calvin dislodges ascent from anthropology and relocates it to christology.[9] "Ascension follows resurrection: hence if we are members of Christ we must ascend into Heaven."[10]

For Calvin, a Christian's particular history with God is also the history of Jesus Christ. His descent is from the *koinōnia* of the Father, by the Spirit, resulting in nothing less than our salvation by his life and death on the cross. It is this descent that is the substitutionary aspect of his work, whereby he gives himself to us. Then the movement reverses, where Christ ascends by the Spirit to "fill all things" with this same Spirit, reigning and in union with the Father. This motion of ascent is the "participatory" aspect of his work, whereby the church is brought into Christ's return by the Spirit, offering his humanity and obedient communion to the Father. What is essential to this descending and ascending structure is that both are the movements of God. The Son is the center point for both of these Trinitarian movements, and his mission is clearly in service of the triune life and love. His mission is not that of rescue or appeasement (though it has components of those), but can only be understood as part of this larger Trinitarian movement of divine love descending to the lost and bringing them back into this same love.[11]

Here the close link between Christ's life and humanity's life reveals how we can best grasp Calvin's views on the life of Jesus with categories of participation. Jesus is clearly not an isolated figure in history who simply descends and ascends to put the wheels back on the anthropological cart. Nor is he a saintly figure for our imitation. Rather, Calvin believes that Jesus' very narrative includes the church and, as such, gives an ascending pattern to the whole of the Christian life. "Yet [John] does not simply exhort us to imitate Christ; but from the union we have with him, he proves that we ought to be like him. A likeness in life and deeds, he says, will prove

---

9. Yet this dislocation is primarily a move *for anthropology.*

10. *Comm. Col.* 3:1.

11. As such, descent and ascent magnify both the Trinitarian communion and the Trinitarian economy. Butin reminds us that this is no "abstract trinitarian principle," but is Calvin's relentless application of the Trinitarian economy to human salvation (Philip W. Butin, *Revelation, Redemption, and Response: Calvin's Trinitarian Understanding of the Divine-Human Relationship* [New York: Oxford University Press, 1995], p. 184). Richard Muller further notes that it is the movement from humilation to exaltation that governs Calvin's historical and economical christology (*Christ and the Decree* [Durham, NC: Labyrinth, 1986], p. 33).

that we abide in Christ."[12] It is Jesus' ascent back to the Father into which humanity is included and which completes the economic mission of the second person of the Trinity. Ascent thus becomes the metaphor that governs the entire Christian life — a life marked by a "return" to God and inclusion in the triune life of love. "We are the sons of God because we are endowed with the same Spirit as his only Son."[13]

This ascent, however, comes at no small price. Crucifixion is at the nexus of descent and ascent. Our participation in Christ's ascent and return to the Father is not based on similarity — a "like returning to like" — but on our alterity from God. The only basis for humanity's ascent is the *mirifica commutatio*:[14]

> This is the exchange which out of his measureless goodness he has made with us: that, receiving our poverty unto himself, he has transferred his wealth to us; that taking our weakness upon himself, he has strengthened us by his power; that having received our mortality he has given us his immortality; that, descending to earth, he has prepared an ascent to heaven for us; that, becoming Son of man with us, he has made us sons of God with him. (*Institutes* 1536, IV.24)

The earliest edition of the *Institutes* sounds this theme clearly, and Calvin barely altered it for his final edition. Our call to participate in Christ is one that begins in a costly exchange that he makes with us. Even as ascent is "natural" to humanity (in that communion is God's creation-purpose for us), it is also profoundly "unnatural." Guilt had to be pardoned, sin had to be paid for, rebellion had to be quashed. His participation in our descent is the sole basis of human participation in his ascent: "We understand that all these things could not be brought about otherwise than by his cleaving to us wholly in spirit and body" (IV.17.9).

---

12. *Comm. 1 John* 2:6; see also IV.15.5.

13. *Comm. Gal.* 4:6.

14. Like Luther and his "fröhliche Wechsel," Calvin found the patristic notion of the "wonderful exchange" with us a powerful expression of our redemption and ensuing new life in Christ. It first appears in the Epistle to Diognetus (c. 170-300 CE): "O sweet exchange! O unsearchable operation!" (*Diog* 9.2, *ANF* I.28).

Trinitarian Matrix for Participation

Calvin's ability to reconceptualize participation and thus the manner of human ascent began in his doctrine of the Trinity. Two years before the publication of Philip Butin's *Revelation, Redemption, and Response,* Christoph Schwöbel rightly protested that Calvin's Trinitarian break-throughs had been radically underestimated, remaining "without decisive implications for [his] theology, apart from supporting [his] christological doctrines."[15] Butin's work has begun to turn the tide. Although Calvin is loath to dwell on the Mediator's procession or intra-Trinitarian relation-ship ("Let us then willingly leave to God the knowledge of himself" [I.13.20]), Calvin always points us to the Trinitarian economy: how the Trinity works to bring us to itself. This is anything but the functionalism of "creator, redeemer, and sustainer."[16] Nor is it a simplistic dichotomy be-tween the immanent and the economic Trinity. Rather, it is a robust the-ology of the communion, cooperation, and interrelationship between Fa-ther, Son, and Holy Spirit for the salvation and sanctification of humanity.

It is here that Calvin's overlap with the patristic fathers (and especially Irenaeus) becomes apparent. If Irenaeus's breakthrough was to distinguish the members of the Trinity according to their economic activity, Calvin is attempting to know the Trinity once more through the story of the econ-omy.[17] This story is nothing less, as Butin asserts for Calvin, than the *instantiation* "of what we can know of God's intra-Trinitarian relation-ships."[18] The result is a crucial reorientation away from the standard read-

15. Christoph Schwöbel, "The Triune God of Grace: The Doctrine of the Trinity in the Theology of the Reformers," in *The Christian Understanding of God Today,* ed. James Bryne (Dublin: Columba, 1993), p. 51.

16. For this "division of labor" in the High Middle Ages, see Gerald Bray, *The Doctrine of God* (Downers Grove, IL: InterVarsity, 1993), pp. 202-4. For its reappropriation in contemporary theology, see the critique by Geoffrey Wainwright, "The Doctrine of the Trinity: Where the Church Stands or Falls," *Interpretation* 45 (1991): 117-32.

17. "[Irenaeus's] means of describing the Trinity became known as economic trini-tarianism" (William Rusch, *The Trinitarian Controversy* [Philadelphia: Fortress, 1980], p. 7). In so doing, Calvin is correcting late medieval Nominalism with its total separation between God's acts and being.

18. Calvin believed that epistemological access to the "immanent" Trinity was to be had only through the "economic" story of God's relationship with humanity. This does not prohibit reflection on the intra-Trinitarian relationships, but it certainly gives a proper entry point to them (Butin, *Revelation,* pp. 74, 39-42).

ing of Augustine on the Trinity and thus away from some of the traditional "Latin" emphases that had marked Western theology for
centuries.[19] As Schwöbel points out, this freed Calvin to take up the "important insights of the trinitarian logic developed by the Cappadocians."[20]
Calvin's commitment to the unique distinctions between the members of
the Trinity (as revealed in the economy) opened to him a new way of relating Father, Son, and Spirit. Gerald Bray summarizes it this way:

> Calvin held to a doctrine which said that the three persons were co-
> equal in their divinity and united with each other, not by sharing an im-
> personal essence, but by their mutual fellowship and co-inherence —
> the Cappadocian doctrine of *perichōrēsis* in God, applied at the level of
> person, not essence. . . .
>
> The freedom of personal relationships in the Godhead obviously
> means that any hint of causality latent in the terms "generation" and
> "procession" must be carefully avoided. . . . [Although Calvin admits
> that the person of the Son has his beginning in God], what he means is
> that everything the Son is and does must be understood with reference
> to the Father, because that is the way the Son understands himself —
> not because he is ontologically dependent on the Father as the only true
> *autotheos*.[21]

This explains Calvin's distinctive orientation in christology toward the
dynamic person of Christ (rather than abstract natures), because God's
"divine" being is no longer an abstraction for Calvin but is rather inter-

---

19. Despite the many caricatures of East and West (most notably by De Regnon
himself), it can simply be said that the East persisted in highlighting Irenaeus's "economic trinitarianism," while the West tended to follow Augustine's *opera trinitatis ad
extra indivisa sunt*. Calvin did not deny Augustine's maxim (I.13.25), but it is not adequate to describe Calvin's Trinitarian theology either. Butin helpfully points out the
Eastern *and* Western characteristics in Calvin's doctrine of the Trinity (Butin, *Revelation*, pp. 44-45).

20. Schwöbel, "Triune God of Grace," p. 51. For a general overview of what
"Cappadocian" specifically entails, see Butin, *Revelation*, pp. 42-45. I also agree with the
general, rather than specific, observations of T. F. Torrance, "Calvin's Doctrine of the
Trinity," *Calvin Theological Journal* 25 (1990): 165-93; see also Torrance, "The Doctrine of
the Holy Trinity in Gregory Nazianzen and John Calvin," in *Trinitarian Perspectives*
(Edinburgh: T. & T. Clark, 1994), pp. 21-40.

21. Bray, *Doctrine of God*, pp. 202, 204.

preted in light of the divine activity in the world and the relations this reveals. Thus, Calvin does not begin his soteriology with the "necessity" of the two natures (II.12.1) but with what has become recognizably one of the most pivotal features of his unique christology: he explores the person and work of the Mediator.[22] In the words of Oberman, this amounts to a "shift of accent from a natures-Christology to an offices-Christology, converging towards a Mediator-theology."[23] Likewise, Calvin's pneumatology is not characterized by the traditional discussion of the power or potential of "grace," but is saturated in *personal* discourse about the Holy Spirit.

With this dual emphasis away from bare natures to the person, and away from improper speculation on the immanent to the economic Trinity, Calvin was poised to rethink Jesus' life in terms of relationships rather than substance or natures. Perhaps most radically, Calvin began to rethink Jesus' earthly relationship to the Father. Here Calvin shifts the commonly conceived connection between Christ and the Father from shared substance to include the person of the Holy Spirit. Unlike Aquinas and much of medieval theology that looked to the hypostatic union to provide Jesus with the divine qualities needed for his mission,[24] the Spirit becomes the key player in the descent and ascent of Christ.[25] This is the fruit of Calvin's movement away from an Augustinian Trinitarianism, which rendered the three members of the Godhead functionally indistinguishable. As a result, Calvin pioneered a Trinitarian model based on the mutuality of the work of the Son and Spirit.[26]

22. Jill Raitt, "Calvin's Use of Persona," in *Calvinus Ecclesiae Genevensis Custos*, ed. Wilhelm Neuser (New York: Lang, 1984), p. 286.

23. Heiko Oberman, "The 'Extra' Dimension in the Theology of Calvin," *Journal of Ecclesiastical History* 21 (1970): 60.

24. For an overview of Aquinas's position, see Gary Badcock, "The Anointing of Christ and the *Filioque* Doctrine," *Irish Theological Quarterly* 60 (1994): 241-58.

25. Modern theologians have shaken even more fruit from this pneumatological tree. It has not been until recently that theologians (von Balthasar, Congar, Barth, R. Jenson, Weinandy) have begun to insist that the Holy Spirit is crucial for Jesus' *sonship* — his eternal relationship that is also constituted by time. Calvin obviously does not go this far, but his persistent attempt to constitute Jesus' humanity by the Spirit is perhaps a forerunner of this recent attempt to constitute his divinity in the same way. Calvin is pushing past the notion that the hypostatic union is all that Christ needs, and instead is beginning to recover the relevance of the Holy Spirit as the one who enables the humanity of Jesus (conception), his obedient relationship to the Father, his anointing, his suffering, death, and resurrected life.

26. "It is a mistake to imagine that the Spirit can be obtained without obtaining

This is a significant departure from medieval ontology, where abstracted "essence" is determinative for the person. Calvin here moves from Christ's divine quality to his specific *mode* of relationship: in the Spirit to the Father. Christ's sinless birth, for example, was not due to his divine nature or to Mary's virginity, but "because he was sanctified by the Spirit" (II.13.4). Neither did the hypostatic union afford Jesus any supernatural privileges, but the Spirit gave such "divine" characteristics as holiness and righteousness in a fully human manner.[27] Even more radically, Calvin somewhat limits the "special" access that Jesus has to the Father, noting instead that his access is what is also offered to the rest of humanity — the Holy Spirit. "The Son of God became man in such a manner, that God was his God as well as ours."[28] Similarly, even the love of the Father that Jesus enjoyed was not the "divine love" that he had had from the beginning; instead, it was a humanly received love, by the Spirit, so that it could then be available to us.[29]

To summarize, we see two significant innovations in Calvin's doctrine of the Spirit. First, he has shifted the primary bond between the human Jesus and the Father from divine substance to the divine person of the Spirit. This opens up a new realm for the Spirit's operation in the life of Jesus, where the Spirit has its own particular mission from the Father in conceiving, anointing, and empowering Jesus' mission.[30] In effect, Calvin's approach here redeems us from confused readings of Chalcedon: rather than two naked natures coexisting without mingling, Calvin treats the whole person of Christ, who, by the Spirit, is kept truly human and truly divine.[31] The Holy Spirit represents a new way of being *in relationship* —

Christ; and it is equally foolish and absurd to dream that we can receive Christ without the Spirit" (*Comm. Eph.* 3:17).

27. "Therefore he does this for us not according to his divine nature but in accordance with the dispensation enjoined upon him" (III.11.8).

28. *Comm. Eph.* 1:17.

29. *Comm. John* 15:9. Were it to be the eternal divine love, then Calvin fears that Christ could not make it available. See the section below entitled "Qualifications."

30. It took one hundred years for the Puritan John Owen to develop this further, when he argued that it is the Spirit who enables Jesus to be and do his particular mission on earth while also mediating freedom to him.

31. Historically, a strict Chalcedonian emphasis on the two natures tended to obscure the Holy Spirit — an accusation that cannot be leveled at Calvin. This is why we could argue that Calvin used the doctrine of the two natures *hermeneutically* (McCormack, *For Us and Our Salvation: Incarnation and Atonement in the Reformed Tra-*

the joining of two unlikes in a relationship of particularity and yet union. Second, and as a result, Calvin is enabled to shift the bond between God and humanity from a more Platonic view (based on an ontological similarity between divine and human) to the person of the Holy Spirit.[32] Once again, an abstract "similarity" or "point of contact" is subverted for a person, anchoring human participation only in God himself, beginning with the self-gift of God to us in the person of the Spirit.

The Descent of Jesus: His Earthly Humanity

"Besides, he was anointed for our sake, in order that we may all draw out of his fatness. . . ."[33]

This innovative pneumatology needs to be seen as central to Calvin's commitment to participation. The Spirit becomes the one who guarantees that everything Christ does is in a *humanly* appropriate mode. Why? Because Calvin is profoundly convinced that it is only if Jesus is thoroughly human that we (as human) can participate in him. In the Geneva Catechism (1542), Calvin rather cavalierly ignored the significance of the life of Christ.

Q: "Why do you go immediately from His birth to His death, passing over the whole history of His life?"

A: "Because nothing is said here about what belongs properly to the substance of our redemption."[34]

Later, he rectified this in the *Institutes* 1559: "He has achieved [salvation] for us by the whole course of his obedience" (II.16.5).

---

dition [Princeton, NJ: Princeton Theological Seminary, 1993]) and that it was not his starting point in constructing his christology. Rather, it functioned to give a picture to creaturely integrity even as it comes in contact with the divine.

32. In numerous different settings, Calvin consistently draws on the Spirit as the uniting factor: "the Holy Spirit is the bond" (III.1.1); "the bond of this unity" (III.11.5); "this spiritual bond" (III.11.10); "the Spirit truly unites things separated in space" (IV.17.10).

33. *Comm. Heb.* 1:9 (Torrance ed., *CO* 55.18).

34. T. F. Torrance, *School of Faith* (Eugene, OR: Wipf and Stock, 1996), p. 13; *CO* 6.25.

Although Calvin is not as imaginative (or perhaps naïve) as Irenaeus in seeking out a one-to-one correspondence between Jesus' lived life and our humanity, both are convinced that our salvation is bound up not only in the death but the life — specifically the obedience — of Christ. "Our Lord came forth as true man and took the person and name of Adam in order to take Adam's place in obeying the Father" (II.12.3). Calvin's continued commitment to funnel all our present reality through Christ gives his narrative of the historical Jesus a unique twist. As he retells the small idiosyncratic events of the life of a man fifteen hundred years earlier, there is an understood performative connection between those events and the believer's present. Is Christ baptized for his own sake? No, he is baptized for us. Is he called "beloved" because the Father has loved him since the beginning of time? Are his acts of obedience isolated instances of law-keeping? No, they are all for us: "Nor has Christ any thing, which may not be applied to our benefit."[35] As such, the humble life of Jesus of Nazareth is not a self-enclosed story, at least not in Calvin's version. It does not intrude into the present in the sense that it is a moral pattern for us to follow, but because it was lived deliberately for us to share in by the same Spirit available to both Jesus and us.[36] Every event in Jesus' life was done with the intent that humanity be able to draw from it and be made new by it.

The strength of Calvin's convictions led him to affirm that Christ was fully conscious of this throughout his life. Wallace points out how often Calvin quotes Christ saying that "for their sakes I sanctify myself," indicating Christ's awareness of his life as for others.[37] Calvin says in his commentary on John 17:19:

> "And for their sakes I sanctify myself. . . ." It is, because he consecrated himself to the Father, that his holiness might come to us; for as the blessing on the first fruits is spread over the whole harvest, so the Spirit of God cleanses us by the holiness of Christ, and makes us partakers of it. Nor is this done by imputation only, for in that respect he is said to

---

35. *Comm. Heb.* 7:25.

36. "[Paul] not only exhorts us to follow Christ [in mortification]. But [the apostle] also takes hold of something far higher, namely, that through baptism Christ makes us sharers in his death, that we may be engrafted in it" (IV.15.5); see also *Comm. Heb.* 5:9.

37. Calvin "seldom fails to quote [John 17:19] whenever he speaks about sanctification" (Wallace, *Christian Life*, p. 13).

have been made to us righteousness; but he is likewise said to have been made to us sanctification (1 Cor 1:30), because he has, so to speak, presented us to his Father in his own person, that we may be renewed to true holiness by his Spirit.

Christ does not say, "For their sakes I sanctify *them*"; rather, he says, "I sanctify *myself*" — revealing that our sanctification is not given abstractly to us but only as we participate in his person. If Adam and Eve had constantly to "depend wholly upon the Son of God" and received blessing only "by participation in God" (II.2.1),[38] we now see Calvin characterizing this participation with the actions and movements of the historical Son of man.[39]

The following two subsections will highlight two avenues through which Calvin explores the fullness of Christ's humanity: Jesus' flesh and Jesus' obedience. Why is it so critical to Calvin that Jesus experience everything in a humanly appropriate way? Because Calvin's doctrine of participation rests on our fully human participation in the fully human One. The Spirit comes to the fore in these sections because, if the one who preserves the humanity of Christ is also given to us, then our participation in Christ will also preserve and enhance our humanity. Simultaneously, both sections allow close scrutiny of where Calvin's pneumatology is ambiguous, open to competing interpretations as revealed in the history of Reformed theology.

Jesus' Flesh: The Place for Our Participation

Calvin resolutely held that creatureliness had its own appropriate forms of enjoying the divine life — of receiving, appropriating, and becoming the things of divinity.[40] If God intended to share his life with us, and humanity was created for communion (indeed, "by means of [the Spirit]

38. *Comm. Gen.* 2:9.

39. This, of course, fundamentally rests on Paul's correlation between Adam and Christ. As early as 1534-36, Calvin says, "The whole controversy turns on a comparison between Adam and Christ" ("Psychopannychia," *T&T* III.456).

40. For a survey of Calvin's references to enjoying, participating in, and "becoming divine," see Carl Mosser, "The Greatest Possible Blessing: Calvin and Deification," *Scottish Journal of Theology* 55, no. 1 (2002): 36-57.

we come to participate in God," I.13.14), then Calvin believed that this did not need to happen at the expense of creatureliness. This is the supreme significance of the earthly life, or "flesh," of Christ: Christ's participation in our condition (his relating to God in creaturely appropriate ways) allows us to participate in God in creaturely appropriate ways as well.

This is where Calvin's doctrine of Christ's "flesh" comes into play, as the location where all his benefits are stored. Christ's flesh functions as a synecdoche for his true humanity — the whole life of the Mediator lived for us — and thus is seen to be the locus of human salvation. "[Since the flesh of Christ] is pervaded with fullness of life to be transmitted to us, it is rightly called 'life-giving.' . . . For there he is properly speaking not of those gifts which he had in the Father's presence from the beginning but of those with which he was adorned in that very flesh wherein he appeared" (IV.17.9). Here Calvin is referring to the humanly acquired and thus the humanly appropriate qualities of Christ, which he refers in shorthand to being located "in his flesh" or "in his human nature . . . so that from it we may all draw."[41] Elsewhere, Calvin makes clear that "the flesh of Christ is not *per se* vivifying"; rather, we are to understand by "flesh" a fully human life in which the Spirit invites us to participate.[42]

Qualifications

Are we perhaps streamlining Calvin's language more than we should? Calvin himself can oscillate between using "flesh" to indicate the material "stuff" that Jesus assumes, and at other times referring to Jesus' full humanity, sustained by the Spirit. Although it is clearly this latter pneumatological category that is our "access" to God (because in it Christ has won salvation for us in a humanly appropriate way), Calvin's language can pull in quite the opposite direction. This has issued in three critiques of Reformed soteriology, as seen in Calvin's following remark:

> For as the eternal Word of God is the fountain of *life* (John 1:4), so his flesh, as a channel, conveys to us that *life* which dwells intrinsi-

---

41. *Comm. Heb.* 2:11.

42. "Quia nec per se vivifica esset caro Christi, nec vis eius ad nos usque nisi immensa spiritus operatione perveniret" (Letter to Martyr, 8 August 1555, *CO* 15.723).

cally, as we say, in his Divinity. And in this sense it is called life-giving, because it conveys to us that life which it borrows for us from another quarter.[43]

First, Calvin's talk of the "flesh" can be viewed as usurping territory that is properly that of the Spirit, by implying that his bare flesh is somehow in and of itself powerful. When Calvin claims that "the flesh of Christ is like a rich and inexhaustible fountain that pours into us the life springing forth from the Godhead into itself" (IV.17.9), the Spirit seems superfluous. Elsewhere Calvin is more precise: "the bond of this connection is the Spirit of Christ [who] is like a channel through which all that Christ himself is and has is conveyed to us" (IV.17.12). Calvin's inconsistent pneumatology here has led McCormack to the conclusion that Calvin's theology is riddled with a residual "Platonic ontology of participation," which he negligently picked up from early church fathers, specifically Cyril.[44] McCormack is wary of an interpretation of Christ's flesh that would then need "cleansing" of the "disease" of sin. Far preferable is Calvin's own notion of Christ's "life-giving" flesh, which is not an abstract nature that he fixes. Rather, he is the head and we are the members: participation in him by the Spirit, not nature, is how we are healed.[45] Calvin always fares better when he sticks to the Pauline notion of headship rather than the more Platonic image of fountain *(Timaeus)*.

Second, Calvin's talk of Christ's flesh as "channel" can give the impression that the blessings we receive are channeled from a higher place, betraying — ever so slightly — an inclination to shy away from the material realm as the genuine realm of salvation history. The implications are that God is here not acting *as* man but *through* a man.[46] Third, as the Me-

---

43. *Comm. John* 6:51.

44. Bruce McCormack, "What's at Stake in Current Debates over Justification? The Crisis of Protestantism in the West," in *Justification,* ed. Daniel Treier (Downers Grove, IL: InterVarsity, 2004), p. 105.

45. *Comm. John* 17:19.

46. I recognize that Calvin is simply making a comment on Christ's office as the Mediator, but to then speak of him as a "channel" de-emphasizes participation in his person and causes a focus more on the things that are being channeled. It is also quite conceivable to read into this the Augustinian dictum — *per Christum hominem ad Christum deum* — where Christ's flesh is only for the purpose of leading us to his divinity.

diator accumulates life and blessings for us, Calvin can so emphasize that these occur in his human nature that this nature can take on a status of its own — functioning as a buffer between humanity and God.[47] Calvin's Christ begins to look, as David Coffey puts it, suspiciously like "a mixture of divine being and human being, like oil and water."[48] Recognizing Calvin's vigorous pneumatology will keep all readings of Christ's "flesh" consistent, moving beyond any interpretations of the flesh as a point-of-contact to the humanity of Christ as threshold-of-communion.

These all point to tensions in Calvin's pneumatology that we have also observed in his theology of creation, where invitations to a robust reading of the Spirit alternate with possibilities for more functional readings. Often, Calvin simply is not clear: in his portrait of Christ, does the Spirit merely insert us into the flesh of Christ, where life, benefits, and all sorts of treasure are stockpiled for us? Or does the Spirit actually help us participate in the whole Christ, living in the eschatological promise of the new creation? These are real problems to be reckoned with in Calvin, ones that will press all the more to the fore as we approach his magisterial outworking of adoption and the Eucharist (chapter 4).

Jesus' Obedience: The Shape of Our Participation

Having established the full humanity of Christ as shaped and sustained by the Spirit, Calvin pursues a new question. What shape does human life take when it is shaped by — or participates in — the Word of God? There are two aspects of Christ's life that are worthy of note, both as a direct result of Calvin's pioneering pneumatology: the shape of human agency and the shape of obedience.

First, as the fully human one, Jesus was endowed with human agency by the Spirit. "As musical sounds, though various and differing from each other, are so far from being discordant that they produce

47. This is a danger of which Colin Gunton did not fully take account, especially in his endorsement of John Owen's Reformed christology and pneumatology.

48. David Coffey, "A Proper Mission of the Holy Spirit," *Theological Studies* 47 (1986): 245. Elsewhere, Calvin emphasizes that we participate in Christ's person — human and divine (III.11.8-9): "Mesmes il est et Dieu et homme en nous" (*Serm. Luke* 2:1-14, *CO* 24.966).

sweet melody and fine harmony; so in Christ there was a remarkable example of adaptation between the two wills, the will of God and the will of man, so that they differed from each other without any conflict or opposition."[49] Here Calvin attempts to acknowledge freedom in a human subject, for, in the person of Christ, we find a man who is neither an extension of the divine will nor autonomous from it. Whether Calvin is entirely successful is another issue (for Christ can only give freedom to humanity from within the notion of election); regardless, Calvin correctly displaces freedom from an anthropological endowment and relocates it to the realm of the Spirit. "Without the Spirit man's will is not free" (II.2.7). Calvin views Christ as held by the Spirit in such a way that he was able to respond to God freely, with human agency falling under a category of *participation.* "He wills to work in us . . . that [we] may actually so walk" (II.3.10). Philip Butin summarizes Calvin's intent, and perhaps even his genuine achievement: "For Calvin, God's gracious action in us can also and at the same time via the Trinity be an authentically human response."[50]

Second, Jesus' earthly life of obedience is framed in terms of love for the Father and response by the Spirit. This is significant in that Jesus' obedience is seen less as Herculean feats of will power (or an extension of his divine clout) and more as communion — his Spirit-led love for the Father as enacted in every aspect of his life. From the pen of Calvin, Christ's righteousness took on human shape: "Now someone asks, How has Christ abolished sin, banished the separation between us and God, and acquired righteousness to render God favorable and kindly toward us? To this we can in general reply that he has achieved this for us by the whole course of his obedience" (II.16.5). This was a critical move for Calvin to make, lest Christ's righteousness be seen as his *divine* righteousness and thus be exclusive of human participation. It was Osiander who made the critical mistake of believing that righteousness was conferred upon us by the "Deity of Christ." Calvin explains: "I showed, on the contrary, that salvation and life are to be sought from the flesh of Christ in which he sanctified himself, and in which he consecrates Baptism and the Supper."[51]

---

49. *Comm. Matt.* 6:10 (trans. Lucien Richard, *The Spirituality of John Calvin* [Atlanta: John Knox, 1974], p. 133).

50. Butin, *Revelation,* p. 76; for his entire analysis, see pp. 76-82.

51. Calvin, "True Partaking . . . ," *T&T* II.554.

Yet Calvin insists on not only the humanly appropriate form of Jesus' righteousness, but also its content:

> He came forward of his own accord, to offer the Father the sacrifice of obedience. . . . We are thus taught that he was subjected to death, because he wished it to be so; that he was crucified, because he offered himself.[52]

Because Calvin considers the entire life of Christ as essential for our salvation, he rejects a view of righteousness as God's abstract "justice" and instead focuses on the right-relatedness of the Son to the Father: "As if he could atone for our sins in any other way than by obeying the Father!" (II.16.12).

Calvin makes it clear that only love motivates true obedience, and Christ's obedience is no exception. As T. F. Torrance summarizes, it is of the "positive righteousness of His obedient and loving Life lived in perfect filial relation to the Father from the cradle to the grave."[53] Calvin is eloquent about this in his exegesis of Christ's baptism. Observing that some of his contemporaries held to the legal explanation that, "since Christ had voluntarily subjected himself to the law, it was necessary that he should keep it in every part," Calvin replies, "But I prefer a more simple interpretation. . . ." In an imaginary dialogue with John the Baptist, Calvin has Jesus explain that, while everyone's calling is different, each calling still requires that we render simple, relational "obedience to God the Father."[54] Christ's baptism was not primarily a legal necessity but rather faithful filial obedience. Human obedience, too, follows the same contours. In his commentary on Hebrews 11:7, Calvin places obedience as a subset of communion with God; it is the flower, not the root of the sanctified life. It is unbelievers who are marked by servile obedience and "behave like hirelings" (III.2.12). Calvin dismisses their obedience as not only insufficient but devilish.

Even in his discussion of Christ's death, Calvin brings Christ's loving obedience to the fore as a lens through which to view the substitutionary

---

52. *Comm. Matt.* 17:1. Also from the *Comm. Heb.* 5:8: "[F]or he was abundantly willing to render to his Father the obedience. . . ."

53. T. F. Torrance, "Justification: Its Radical Nature and Place in Reformed Doctrine and Life," *Scottish Journal of Theology* 13 (1960): 232.

54. *Comm. Matt.* 3:13.

and forensic aspects of the atonement. Calvin contends that "even in death itself his willing obedience is the important thing" (II.16.5).[55] This reveals that Christ's obedience did not make him fit for sacrifice but that, for the first time, the right-relatedness of God is lived out in human form. Gerrish notes that "Calvin reads Christ's story in consistently filial terms — even where the text hardly warrants it. He is so sure that Christ's affliction was the affliction of an obedient son that he has him cry out on the cross: 'Father, father, why have you forsaken me?' (The text says, 'My God, my God . . .')."[56]

Thus, it is not the "death" itself that saves, but the *person* of the Mediator. It is his life of obedience and his sin-scattering death into which we are brought to participate, and only as such is his death salvific. "By our participation in it," Calvin says, "his death mortifies our earthly members so that they may no longer perform their functions" (II.16.8). Calvin takes the New Testament emphasis on guilt, acquittal, and substitution[57] as central to his doctrine of the atonement, because the Mediator's work must be unique and unrepeatable.[58] However, to highlight substitution without participation is dangerous, because it becomes just that: a work that has become separate from and efficacious without the person.[59] The danger is further compounded by whether or not Christ's substitution is interpreted as penal substitution or mediatorial

55. See also *Comm. John* 10:18; *Comm. Isa.* 42:1.

56. *Institutes* 1536, II.15. B. A. Gerrish, *Grace and Gratitude: The Eucharistic Theology of John Calvin* (Minneapolis: Fortress, 1993), p. 61.

57. It is significant that "acquittal" is consistently put in the context of the Father's initiative, not appeasement ("The Father destroyed the force of sin when the curse of sin was transferred to Christ's flesh," II.16.6) and the Son's initiative as well ("we must not understand that he fell under a curse that overwhelmed him; rather — in taking the curse upon himself — he crushed, broke, and scattered its whole force. Hence faith apprehends an acquittal in the condemnation of Christ, a blessing in his curse," II.16.6).

58. "Christ's grace is too much weakened unless we grant to his sacrifice the power of expiating, appeasing, and making satisfaction" (II.17.4). Colin Gunton adds, "Not that there are no punitive elements in Calvin; it is in any case difficult to contend that there are none in scripture. But in some way that we shall have to explore the offense that there must be in any genuine theology of the cross is located in the wrong place by the federal scheme" (Gunton, "Aspects of Salvation: Some Unscholastic Themes from Calvin's Institutes," *International Journal of Systematic Theology* 1 [1999]: 254).

59. Turretin is an example of a Reformed theologian who embraced Calvin's rich themes of substitution (perhaps even outshining Calvin) but who did not incorporate Calvin's themes of participation.

substitution.[60] As Gunton says of Calvin, "Jesus' life and death are there not to perform some external substitution, but yet to take our place in such a way that we are truly brought to God."[61] Jesus' death is not mere punitive justice for sin but for the purpose of life — the promise for a new way of being with God. "For in [his flesh] was accomplished the redemption of man, in it a sacrifice was offered to atone for sins, and an obedience yielded to God, to reconcile him to us; it was also filled with the sanctification of the Spirit. . . ."[62]

Much ink has been spilled over the content and character of Calvin's atonement theology, perhaps the most recent example being Timothy Gorringe's *God's Just Vengeance*. In it, Gorringe claims that behind the *Institutes* looms an "Absolute Monarch, whose power had been theorized by Machiavelli. It is in this way that he fundamentally conceives of God. . . . Where Anselm conceives sin as failing to render God his due, for Calvin the point is that God has given us the law, which we have defied, thus meriting eternal death."[63] This represents perhaps the most widespread caricature of Calvin, whose dour atonement theology is rivaled only by his dour personality.

Gorringe has overlooked much of the atonement theology of Calvin that would undermine this portrait, most grievously the entire section entitled "The work of atonement derives from God's love; therefore it has not established the latter" (II.16.4). In this section, Calvin most pointedly shows that God is not conditioned by Christ to love us, "For how could he have given in his only-begotten Son a singular pledge of his love to us if he had not already embraced us with his free favor?" (II.16.2) Instead, redemption is brought about by the perichoretic cooperation of Father *(causam)*, Son *(materiam)*, and Spirit *(effectum)* (IV.15.6). Any penal ele-

---

60. "Mediatorial substitution" is akin to the letter of Hebrews, where the Mediator comprises two relationships: (1) God relating to the world by taking on its sin and giving it his righteousness; and (2) humanity relating to God by becoming obedient to the will of the Father and fulfilling its created purposes of remaining in faithful communion with the Father. These alternatives have been laid out by Christoph Schwöbel, "Reconciliation: From Biblical Observations to Dogmatic Reconstruction," in *The Theology of Reconciliation,* ed. Colin Gunton (Edinburgh: T. & T. Clark, 2003), p. 24.

61. Gunton, "Mediator," p. 152.

62. *Comm. John* 6:51. The sentence ends thus: " . . . and at length, having vanquished death, it was received into the heavenly glory."

63. Timothy Gorringe, *God's Just Vengeance* (Cambridge: Cambridge University Press, 1996), pp. 136, 139.

ments in Calvin's atonement theology are held in check by this governing Trinitarian structure, lest they run riot and resemble Gorringe's caricature of Calvin.

Pace Gorringe, Calvin's emphasis on sacrifice is both biblical and psychological ("trembling consciences find repose only in sacrifice," II.16.5) and does not merely interface with sixteenth-century punitive justice. Perhaps most surprisingly to those of Gorringe's opinion, Calvin affirms that it is the sinful human perspective that interprets God as, "so to speak, hostile to us . . ." (II.16.2). Heiko Oberman constantly reminds us that Calvin's view of sin is uniquely psychological for his time.[64] Calvin is concerned for the "trembling consciences" of his parishioners and identifies sin to be projecting characteristics of wrath and anger (II.12.1) onto God. Gorringe's terrifying "Absolute Monarch" is the vista from the summit of sin, not grace.

To be fair to Gorringe, Calvin is handicapped by his own inconsistencies and his attempts at sixteenth-century "pop" psychology. First, Bruce McCormack points us to the places where Calvin undermines himself by falling into the language of death as the satisfaction of God's righteousness.[65] This forensicism, isolated from Calvin's equally rich themes of participation, is bound to distort and be destructive along the lines that Gorringe outlines. Second, Calvin does not believe truly that God is our "enemy," but he does conjecture that human psychology needs a good dose of fear to be driven to true gratitude (II.16.2). This does not bear out in human experience, of course, as Calvin himself attests (III.3.2, 20)!

It is Calvin's focus on the person of Christ in a Trinitarian framework that keeps his soteriology, while rich with forensic imagery, from becoming functional with "apersonal models of legal exchange."[66] It is union with Christ that leads to the "wonderous exchange" (*mirifica commutatio*, IV.17.2) with our Savior, justifying *and* sanctifying us as we are continuously united to him.[67] According to George Hunsinger, the courtroom

64. Heiko Oberman, "Subita" (1993).
65. Bruce McCormack, *For Us and Our Salvation: Incarnation and Atonement in the Reformed Tradition*, ed. David Willis-Watkins (Princeton, NJ: Princeton Theological Seminary, 1993), p. 28.
66. Christoph Schwöbel, "Christology and Trinitarian Thought," in *Trinitarian Theology Today*, ed. Christoph Schwöbel (Edinburgh: T. & T. Clark, 1995), p. 137.
67. "[T]aking the weight of our iniquity upon himself (which oppressed us), he has clothed us with his righteousness. . . ." That this exchange is to be read in a

metaphor is potentially misleading, especially when dissociated from union with Christ, the very context it was intended to serve. "In the *Institutes*," argues Hunsinger, "Calvin made clear that for him the matter of imputation was participationist not forensic."[68] Calvin's "forensic" doctrine of the atonement centers on our being counted righteous *en Christo*, not simply as legal declaration but as the righteous one in whom we are incorporated in mystical union (III.17.8).

In *Calvin's Doctrine of the Christian Life*, Wallace summarizes how the contours of Christ's whole life are for the church's participation. By means of hundreds of quotations, Wallace underscores how Calvin's conception of the Christian life is dependent on a participatory union with Christ, rather than imitation:

> The basic principle in Calvin's thinking on this matter is that what has already happened to Christ the Head can be regarded and legitimately spoken of as having already happened to those who are members of His body by virtue of the union effected by faith. What is possessed by Christ is also already the possession of those who are in Christ.[69]

For Calvin, Christ's death and resurrection are clearly the life-pattern for the Christian believer, for whom they take the form of mortification and vivification. "Both things happen to us by participation in Christ. For if we truly partake in his death . . . that corruption of original nature may no longer thrive. If we share in his resurrection, through it we are raised up into newness of life to correspond with the righteousness of God" (III.3.9). Calvin is adamant, though, that this is not merely an example for us to follow, for "we are not only invited through the example of the risen Christ to strive after newness of life; but we are taught that we are reborn into righteousness through his power" (II.16.3). It is precisely here that Calvin's doctrine of participation holds so much promise: we are not only "invited through the example" of Christ to respond to him; we are

---

participationist way is evident also from the fact that the exchange of iniquity for righteousness is only one of many things we receive from our participation in Christ's humanity. Also listed are our becoming sons of God with him, our ascent with him, immortality, strengthening by his power, and receiving his wealth.

68. From an unpublished manuscript by George Hunsinger (2005), "Calvin's Doctrine of Justification: Is It Really Forensic?" p. 7.

69. Ronald S. Wallace, *Calvin's Doctrine of the Christian Life* (Grand Rapids: Eerdmans, 1961), p. 82.

reborn into him. Christ is not the promise of the new creation; he *is* the new creation.

Qualifications

Here again we find an interesting tension: so concerned is Calvin to maintain the human dimension of Jesus' life that he can go too far, refusing to acknowledge when Christ's human qualities are also reflections of divine ones. In reacting against outlandish speculation on the immanent Trinity, Calvin can separate the immanent from the economic in such a way that it threatens to empty Christ's obedience of its content.

> *As the Father hath loved me.* He intended to express something far greater than is commonly supposed; for they who think that he now speaks of the sacred *love* of God the Father, which he always had toward the Son, philosophize away from the subject; for it was rather the design of Christ to lay, as it were, in our bosom a sure pledge of God's *love* toward us.[70]

Calvin here defaults to the *pro nobis* aspect of Christ's relationship with the Father, understandable given his intense focus on the mediator. Kept in the context of the triune relations, Calvin could have asserted both its content as reflective of the eternal love of the Father for the Son, as well as its implications for the human Jesus. Christ's obedience, in turn, could have been seen as both a call on his life as human as well as a reflection of his divine person, having the same character but a different outworking, the result of which might have been that Christ's obedience is never naked obedience but obedience *as a Son.*

Without this important anchor, Christ's obedience can be easily appropriated by human ideas of moral behavior. Bruce McCormack notes that the tradition that followed in Calvin's footsteps tended to portray the redemptive significance of Christ's obedience almost exclusively as law and satisfaction of its demands: "Unfortunately, the prominence of law in the conception resulted in an abstracting of law from the *graciousness* of the divine willing and action, thereby construing the efficacy of Christ's work in terms of *merit.*"[71] The term "merit" comes from Calvin's own pen

---

70. *Comm. John* 15:9.
71. McCormack, *For Us,* p. 24.

(II.17), probably in an effort to enter a significant debate of his time (and, using the language, wrest it back for his purposes).[72] But in so doing, Calvin has opened the door to a conception of a righteousness detachable from the person of Christ ("merits" that are acquired for us) and detachable from his love for the Father. It is a short step to seeing Christ's obedient life as a commodity for us, to be applied to us *without* our participation in the person of Christ. One scholar has used this very discussion of merit to suggest that, for Calvin, "salvation requires the application of Christ's merit to oneself."[73] It is no secret that much of John Wesley's theology was in reaction to this abstracted version of righteousness which was used, as Wesley described, to "justify the grossest abominations."[74]

When obedience is separated from adequate Trinitarian reflection, an ambiguous relation to the law develops. Although Calvin frames Christ's obedience to the law primarily in terms of his obedience to the Father, this can be subverted for a relationship of divine and human law, where "the principle of obedience to the divine law"[75] constitutes personal sanctification. No longer is the Christian life framed in terms of communion; but Beardslee defends "the forgiven sinner, [who] measuring his life by the Law . . . seeks a society in which the substance of the Law is operative for all."[76] When read rightly, Calvin's emphasis on law-keeping stands squarely within his understanding of union with Christ and participation in the divine life. The work of Todd Billings, *Calvin, Participation, and the Gift*, demonstrates Calvin's understanding of the law as God's gracious invitation for the Christian voluntarily to love God and neighbor.[77] It is as they participate in Christ — the Law's fulfillment — that Christians can

72. In so doing, he is attempting to destabilize Anselm's satisfaction theory by attributing the adequacy of Christ's merit to "God's good pleasure" (II.17.1), as well as to challenge the mistaken notions of merit put forth by Laelius Socinus.

73. Joseph Wawrykow, "John Calvin and Condign Merit," *Archiv für Reformationsgeschichte* 83 (1992): 82.

74. From John Wesley's 1792 pamphlet "Thoughts on Christ's Imputed Righteousness," in *Works* 10.312; cited by Gary Badcock, *Light of Truth and Fire of Love* (Grand Rapids: Eerdmans, 1997), p. 107.

75. John W. Beardslee III, "Sanctification in Reformed Theology," in *The New Man: An Orthodox and Reformed Dialogue*, ed. John Meyendorff and J. C. McLelland (New Brunswick, NJ: Agora, 1973), pp. 132-48, esp. p. 145.

76. Beardslee, "Sanctification," p. 145.

77. Todd Billings, *Calvin, Participation, and the Gift* (New York: Oxford University Press, 2008).

once again experience the delight intended for them in creation. However, history has demonstrated that when obedience is vacated of participation, it is most often seen through Sinaitic categories.[78]

Regarding these "deep problems that the Reformation left unsettled in its own ranks," George Hunsinger laments the "openings that Calvin unwittingly left to moralism [as] the Reformed tradition subsequently developed."[79] Yet if Christ's primary expression of righteousness on earth is maintained (as Calvin elsewhere does) as his unswerving communion with the Father, then human salvation is both by this obedient communion and for communion. Only when this is brought to the fore can a moralistic account of Christ's life diminish and, with it, a corresponding moralistic account of the Christian life.

The Ascent of Jesus: His Continuing Humanity

"Christ did not ascend to heaven in a private capacity."
(Commentary on John 14:2)

Participation in Christ is not merely made possible by the Ascension but takes on Christ's own ascended shape of return to communion with the Father: for he "has entered into heaven and He bears us there."[80] Over the years, the Ascension has been used to justify the presence of the church (Augustine), the defectiveness of the body (Origen), Mary as the ladder to heaven (Bernard), the local presence of Christ in the elements (Aquinas), as well as its exact opposite (Zwingli).[81] Jesus' ascent has figured prominently in Calvinist scholarship as well (perhaps most notoriously used to club Lutheran sacramentology over the head!). Yet there was more in as-

78. Gorringe (*God's Just Vengeance*) believes that it is a theology of penal atonement (such as Calvin's) that is to blame for the rising emphasis in eighteenth- and nineteenth-century Britain on law, offenses against which were "satisfied" by just (and often cruel) punishment. He would perhaps do better to examine this ambiguity within Calvin as to what is the *content* of obedience and law. It is interesting to note that both penal atonement and obedience-as-law-keeping arise from inadequate Trinitarian reflection.

79. George Hunsinger, "A Tale of Two Simultaneities: Justification and Sanctification in Calvin and Barth," *Zeitschrift für Dialektische Theologie* 18 (2002): 316, 324 n. 10.

80. *Serm. Acts* 1:6-8 (*CO* 48.618).

81. For a survey of how the ascension has been interpreted throughout the ages, see Douglas Farrow, *Ascension and Ecclesia* (Grand Rapids: Eerdmans, 1999).

cent than its implications for the Lord's Supper. For Calvin, the Ascension has three main functions: first, it threw open the realm of pneumatology and, with it, the historical possibility for human participation in God; second, it represented the future of the Christian as *koinōnia:* to be with God, in Christ; third, it functioned as a protective measure to keep God from being manipulated or "pulled down" to our sphere of idolatry and superstition.

He Ascended to Fill All Things

Calvin magnificently draws out the consequences that Jesus, our head, has ascended. This is not only to display his power and authority,[82] or to subdue all "pride and loftiness,"[83] but because we are to be incorporated in him and to participate in his every movement. "In a word, Christ did not ascend to heaven in a private capacity, to dwell there alone, but rather that it might be the common inheritance of all the godly, and that in this way the Head might be united to his members."[84] When Jesus ascended into heaven, creation was definitively re-headed, re-*capitulated*,[85] and this miracle of the Spirit is the foundation for our participation.[86] "Whence also, Paul being witness, he ascended into heaven that he might fill all things."[87] Although Calvin reminds us that Christ always "filled" everything,[88] this is a filling in a new way, because it is the glorified Jesus who now fills everything "by the power of his Spirit."[89] This is not a principle of unity that ties humanity to the cosmos, nor is it a reinstated Platonic

---

82. *Comm. Ps.* 47:5; *Comm. Ps.* 68:18; *Comm. John.* 16:10, 28; *Comm. Eph.* 4:10.

83. *Comm. Ps.* 47:5.

84. *Comm. John* 14:2.

85. "The meaning [of "recapitulation"] appears to me to be, that out of Christ all things were disordered, and that through him they have been restored to order" (*Comm. Eph.* 1:10).

86. "Therefore the Spirit is He who makes Christ abide in us, who sustains and nourishes us, and fulfills all offices of the Head [*omniaque capitis officia impleat*]" (Letter to Martyr, 8 August 1555, *CO* 15.723).

87. *Comm. Gen.* 28:12.

88. "But this did not prevent him, while filling heaven and earth with his divine essence, from wearing his flesh in the womb of his mother, on the cross, in the sepulcher" (Calvin, "Last Admonition . . . ," *T&T* II.385).

89. *Comm. Eph.* 4:10.

ontology; rather, it is a human who is now the center of the restoration of the fallen cosmos.[90] We come full circle from the one who mediated our creation to the one who now, at the right hand of the Father, is mediating all things in the full power of the Spirit.

When Calvin writes that "from the Ascension our faith receives many benefits" (II.16.14), what is most striking are their Trinitarian implications. The first benefit is that he has entered heaven "in our flesh, as if in our name," bringing the elect in some sense already into the presence of the Trinity. For Calvin, Jesus' true "flesh" in heaven functions just as it did here on earth: as a way of securing our fully human participation in God. Jesus represents a creature fully in the dimension of God: the resurrection did not change his physicality into a spiritualized reality, but it was indeed transposed, "becom[ing] different from what it was before" (IV.17.14). If Christ has been lifted into heaven and is, as human, enjoying full communion with the Father and Spirit, then in some way "we have an entrance to heaven in common with him."[91] It should be noted here that Calvin's theology follows the Gospel of John in that descent and ascent are not exclusive of one another but are interwoven, for Christ's Ascension is the manifestation of the eternally humiliated one.

This crucified one is the key to our ascent. In his person we do not see the absorption of the human into the divine *(distinctio sed non separatio!),* but the ultimate *telos* of our humanity fulfilled. This is why, for Calvin, humanity's ascent is never becoming less human or creaturely (for Calvin's doctrine of the creature has always had room for our "growth," or ascent), but becoming truly human in this *man.*[92] The order of redemption began with his physicality and descent. His obedience consisted in this very acceptance of his creaturely status: of being a man, whose obedience and even miracles were not on the order of supernature but of the Spirit, so that his entire experience of life and death could include our created limitations as well. With the sending of the Spirit at Pentecost, this man's history was made ours for participation. Ascent is primarily Christ's, yet his mission was to include us in his ascending return to the Father. Union with God is only through his body, his humanity, his

90. Calvin states that the restoration of Christ relates not only to us "but to all creatures" (*Serm. Eph.* 1:10).

91. *Comm. John.* 3:13. From this first benefit, Calvin's doctrine of adoption receives its ontological basis.

92. This growth only occurs as we acknowledge our "lowly status."

"weakness." Ascent is with him and is "up" to his physicality, where he lives and reigns with the Father.

Second, as both head and *priest*, Christ's very presence is an intercession,[93] "for it belongs to a priest to intercede for the people, that they may obtain favor with God."[94] Calvin's Trinitarian theology prevents him from envisioning this as would "those [who] err very grossly, who imagine that Christ falls on his knees before the Father to pray for us."[95] Rather, Calvin is captivated by this image of the human one, at the side of the Father, continually representing humanity to the Father and "bear[ing] our names before God to show that He has us in His heart."[96]

Third, the Ascension helps us to not "confine our attention to ourselves" but to remember that our identity is now elsewhere. "Thus, we look to our Head Who is already in heaven, and say, 'Although I am weak, there is Jesus Christ who is my strength. Although I am full of all miseries, Jesus Christ is in immortal glory and what He has will some time be given to me and I shall partake of all his benefits. . . .'"[97] This is not so much the displacement of the self but the enlargement of the self, such that the circumference of our identity now involves another person. For Calvin, the Christian sense of the self is forever bound up with another — Christ — and it is this reality that redefines our self-understanding.

Calvin's fourth and final "benefit" of the Ascension is the Spirit himself, though he understands that the Spirit governs all of these benefits.[98] The Spirit is given by Christ so that we can fully enter into Christ — the one who "fills all things in every way." Calvin does not attribute our participation in Christ to a function of his divine being (that automatically fills all things), for to do so would shortcut *koinōnia*. It is the Spirit who brings us into a God-saturated life through his engrafting us into the human, ascended Christ, who is in the presence of the Father.

---

93. *Comm. John.* 16:10; *Serm. Acts* 1:6-8; *Comm. Heb.* 9:11.

94. *Comm. Heb.* 7:25.

95. *Comm. 1 John* 1:21.

96. *Serm. Acts* 1:6-8 (*CO* 48.618). Calvin relates this to the high priest of Israel, who "carried on his head the names of the children of Israel . . . although he entered all alone, yet it was for all."

97. *Serm. Acts* 1:6-8 (*CO* 48.619).

98. This comes across, not surprisingly, in his famous letter to Peter Martyr (8 August 1555), in which the Spirit is not only the one who makes Christ dwell in us, but is also the one who brings us into Christ in a spirituality that "draws us upwards" (*CO* 15.723).

Holy Spirit: Rethinking Presence

Why is it that Calvin cherishes Jesus' departure as "one of the chiefest points of our faith"?[99] It seems strange that Calvin's supreme doctrine of our communion with Christ should rest on Christ's departure, his physical absence from us. For it is no secret that Calvin was adamant that Jesus' ascent to heaven was in the flesh, and continues at the right hand of God the Father in *human form*. Both Calvin and Thomas Aquinas took Jesus' Ascension with utter seriousness, but they drew opposite conclusions from it.[100] Calvin was not willing to rethink human nature/physicality simply on the basis of Christ's Ascension; too much was at stake to do that.[101] Even Christ's glorified body, changed as it is, still has the physical limitations of a human body, "contained in space, [having] its own dimensions and its own shape" (IV.17.29).

Where Calvin was unwilling to rethink human nature and embodiedness, he was willing to rethink presence. He accomplished this not by the usual Gnostic spiritualization (a charge he leveled at his opponents, who did not take Christ's embodiment seriously enough [IV.17.29]), but by making the bodily presence of Christ the realm of the Holy Spirit:[102] "For thus they leave nothing to the secret working of the Spirit, which unites Christ himself to us. To them Christ does not seem present unless he comes down to us. As though, if he should lift us to himself, we should not just as much enjoy his presence!" (IV.17.31). Calvin saw the Spirit's work as that of transposition: taking what was the realm of physicality and moving

99. *Comm. Acts* 1:9.

100. See George Hunsinger, "The Bread that We Break: Toward a Chalcedonian Resolution of the Eucharistic Controversies," *Princeton Seminary Bulletin* 24 (2003): 242-46.

101. Calvin's reasons for this were that, if Christ did not still possess a fully human nature and body, then (1) we (as human) could not participate in him (III.11.8); (2) there would be no human presence with the Father (II.16.14); (3) our salvation *by flesh* would be overthrown (IV.17.32); (4) the Second Coming would be unnecessary (IV.17.27); (5) there would be no miraculous restoration/translation of our bodies (III.25.7).

102. Through the resurrection, the Spirit has created an ontologically different form of human existence. "For Paul very well teaches that believers eagerly hasten to death not because they want to be unclothed but because they long to be more fully clothed [2 Cor. 5:2-3]" (III.9.5). Christ's physical properties do not change into spiritual ones, but they change. "But, say our opponents, if there is conversion, one thing must become another. If they mean that something becomes different from what it was before, I assent" (IV.17.14).

it to the Trinity's domain. "The Holy Spirit did descend from heaven to this end; whereby we learn that the distance of place doth no whit hinder Christ from being present with those that be his at all times."[103] Here Calvin is not allowing the Spirit to be the scapegoat for a thoroughly unsatisfactory doctrine of presence. The Spirit is not a spiritualized mode of Christ; rather, the Spirit is the person in whom we now have access to the embodied Jesus. As Farrow says, "By looking to the Spirit — not as a substitute for Jesus but as a link to him — Calvin displayed a keener sense of the interpersonal, trinitarian dimensions of human existence *coram deo*."[104] In arguing for Jesus' embodied presence in heaven, Calvin is not withdrawing him, as if behind closed doors, but rather is making him "everywhere" available. "Nevertheless, I willingly confess that Christ is ascended that he may fulfill [fill] all things; but I say that he is spread abroad everywhere by the power of his Spirit, not by the substance of his flesh."[105] This access is through communion, the Trinitarian mode of being with God: by the Spirit, in and to the embodied Son, who himself is in the presence of the Father.

With the ascent of Jesus and the descent of the Spirit, participation as *communion* became a historicized possibility. Calvin's frustration is at its outer limit when he wrestles with those who take this historical watershed lightly — whether it be Westphal, Osiander, or even "the apostles [who were] desiring the carnal presence of Christ" back in Christ's own day.[106] During Jesus' earthly ministry, the apostles could imitate, replicate, and enjoy the comfort of his presence; but this fell far short of communion and participation in him. At one point Calvin even goes so far as to lambaste the disciples for glorying only in Christ's descent "as if nothing more were needed," as though they considered themselves "rich with a single gold piece."[107] "'You ought to have rejoiced,' he says, 'because I return to the Father,' for this is the ultimate object at which you ought to aim."[108] With Christ's presence "transposed" into the realm of the Spirit, it becomes a category of communion. It is for this reason that Calvin makes the "carnal presence" of Christ and "communion" in the Spirit mutually exclusive al-

---

103. *Comm. Acts*, Argument.
104. Farrow, *Ascension and Ecclesia*, p. 176.
105. *Comm. Acts* 1:9; see also *Institutes* IV.6.10 and II.16.4.
106. *Comm. Acts* 1:11.
107. *Comm. John* 16:28.
108. *Comm. John* 14:28.

ternatives, where the carnal presence is the unmediated presence — that which we can hold and have without the Spirit.[109] Both are forms of "presence," but in one, we take matters into our own hands, so to speak, by grasping Christ without the Spirit; in the other, we have communion with Christ — only in the Spirit.

Upward Spirituality

Of all that may be said about Christ's Ascension in Calvin, the most over-looked has been how Christ's ascent functions as the interpretive grid for the ongoing Christian life. "Our redemption would be imperfect if he did not lead us ever onward to the final goal of salvation" (II.16.1). That goal, I am arguing, can only be described as Calvin's vision for our *koinōnia* with the Father, through Christ, in the Spirit.

Calvin refers to this eschatological hope of communion as "heaven," shorthand for the place where the Father dwells.

> Thus when he said to the apostles, "It is expedient that I go up to the Father," "because the Father is greater than I," he does not attribute to himself merely a secondary deity so that he is inferior to the Father with respect to eternal essence; but because endowed with heavenly glory he gathers believers into participation in the Father. . . . And certainly for this reason Christ descended to us, to bear us up to the Father, and at the same time to bear us up to himself, inasmuch as he is one with the Father. (I.13.26)

This calls for a spirituality that, in Calvin's (and Paul's) language, is oriented "toward the goal of the upward call" (III.25.1). Because our "hope rests in heaven," Calvin exhorts "the godly . . . with eyes fast fixed on Christ [to] wait upon heaven," thus displaying the truth that "where our treasure is, our heart is" (III.25.1). "Heaven" is to be understood in terms of the fulfillment of our communion with Christ; for even Plato, Calvin notes, understood union to be man's highest good! (III.25.2).

Simultaneously, Calvin recognizes that the key to God's communion with humanity is God's transcendent freedom. It is in this second sense

---

109. "Surely, the coming of the Spirit and the ascent of Christ are antithetical" (IV.17.26).

that Calvin's emphasis on heaven and ascent must be understood. If "people dare limit the operations of God, according to their own pleasure, [to render him], as it were, shut up within bars of wood or iron," then Calvin would combat this with a resurrection of the biblical imagery of heaven.[110]

> When they place God in heaven, they do not confine him to a certain locality. . . . In short, they put the universe under his control; and, being superior to every obstruction, he does freely every thing that may seem good to him.[111]

Calvin is acutely aware that this is not a "dwelling among the spheres . . . nor is it literally a place beyond the world, but we cannot speak of the kingdom of God without using ordinary language."[112] Heaven is a qualitative place, made so by God's otherness. "I am rather inclined to refer it to heaven, conceiving the meaning to be, that the ways of God rise high above the world, so that if we are truly desirous to know them, we must ascend above all heavens."[113] Paul's injunction to the Colossians to "seek those things that are above" (Col. 3:1) directly informs this understanding of ascent as an epistemic act of obedience in which our notions of God are informed by God's own presence. Calvin's emphasis on our "ascent to heaven" comes with the notion of God's closeness and otherness, of communion with him and his transcendence. Yet neither can God's transcendence — his otherness — be used to "shut [him] up in heaven . . . to remove him to the greatest distance. . . ."[114] Heaven represents God's freedom *from* human manipulation and *for* communion.

Hence, Calvin will emphasize time and again that we are to be drawn up to God rather than dragging him down to us — whether it be in the Lord's Supper, idolatry, or carnal ways of conceiving of God. Yet it is not only that we must ascend to Christ (and not he to us), but that our whole lives are now reoriented and repersonalized by our communion with the Son of God. "For our affections must ascend to heaven, or otherwise we would not be at all united to Jesus Christ."[115] The command "lift up your hearts" is

---

110. *Comm. Ps.* 78:41.
111. *Comm. Ps.* 115:3.
112. *Comm. Eph.* 4:10.
113. *Comm. Ps.* 77:13.
114. *Comm. Ps.* 14:1; see also 7:17; 9:11; 10:6; 24:8; 36:11; 75:7; 102:19.
115. *Serm. Acts* 1:1-4 (*CO* 48.596).

not so much a command against tying God to the things of this world as it is a command to live out of our new identities, which are bound up with the person of the Son. This ascent is not a command laid on our shoulders, but it is bound up with our participation in our "forerunner's own ascent."[116] "He raises us upwards by transforming us into his own image."[117]

If Calvin's doctrine of transcendence is not about God's distance from us but his freedom from our carnal images of him and the unconditioned nature of grace, then why has it been so misunderstood? This is where Calvin's preference for spatial imagery tends to break down. In order to confront the utter majesty and otherness of God, one must be willing to "withdraw from the world. We must ascend above earth and heaven when we think of this Word."[118] Perhaps Calvin's primary weakness is that his language of earth and heaven is usually cast in terms of mutual exclusivity, giving a sense that the "upward call" is not so much that their "eyes are turned to the power of the resurrection" in the here and now (III.9.6), but rather the abandonment of the here and now.[119]

Although Calvin emphasizes that heaven is *spatio* instead of *loco*, the overall effect can leave a lingering taste of Platonism in the mouth.[120] Colin Gunton reminds us that it is only when we hold together Christ's mediation of both salvation and creation that we can avoid "risk[ing] a reversion to the very Gnostic, or near-Gnostic, equation of the person with the soul which has so dogged our tradition, and is near to the surface in Calvin."[121] We are at times uncertain whether it be the carnal or the *mate-*

116. *Comm. Heb.* 6:20.

117. *Comm. Gen.* 17:22.

118. *Serm. John* 1:1-5, *CO* 47.472.

119. Despite Calvin's rhetoric, Lucien Richard notes that Calvin's ascent is not based on "contempt for the world" and helpfully contrasts him with Thomas à Kempis's more world-denying spirituality. See Lucien Richard, *The Spirituality of John Calvin* (Atlanta: John Knox, 1974); see also Charles Partee, "Soul and Body in Anthropology," in *Calvin and Classical Philosophy* (Leiden: Brill, 1977), pp. 51-90.

120. Oberman notes: "To be sure, we should bear in mind that Calvin attempted to tone down the emphasis on locality by writing in 1543 'spatio' instead of 'loco' in the central formulation of this issue: 'Atqui haec est propria corporis veritas, ut spatio contineatur' (*Inst.*, IV.17,29; *OS.*, v. 386, 6f). In the final version of the *Institutes*, the French translation of 1560, this entire sentence is omitted!" (Oberman, *"Extra,"* p. 49 n. 1). For Calvin's rejection of the medieval "container" notion of space for a more relational one, see T. F. Torrance, *Space, Time and Incarnation* (London: Oxford University Press, 1969), pp. 30ff.

121. Gunton continues: "If Christ is mediator of salvation only, there is a twofold

rial that is to be left behind, lest one be reprimanded, as were the two women who sought him at the tomb.[122] He also speaks of this ascent as a "faculty of the soul," describing it in typical dualistic (Platonic) imagery of vision and sight.[123] Even though it is a "spiritual" ascent, Calvin would have done well to bind this more explicitly and consistently to the person of the Holy Spirit. "[Jesus] again exhorts Nicodemus not to trust to himself and his own sagacity. . . . For to ascend to heaven means here 'to have a pure knowledge of the mysteries of God, and the light of spiritual understanding.'"[124]

John Witvliet notes that "the pervasive imagery of ascent and descent raises the specter of unwanted dualism in Calvin's thought."[125] This danger, however, is implicit in the theology of all who came before Calvin and used this formal literary device. Calvin will head off its worst dangers by placing the human, *enfleshed* Jesus at the right hand of the Father, and by calling us upward, not to an immaterial contemplation of him, but to a communion with him by the Spirit. "'Christ,' says he, 'calls us upwards to himself.'"[126]

*   *   *

We have seen how Calvin carefully thinks through the implications of Jesus' full humanity in order that the latter's life might invite our full human participation in it. This results in a new — even radical — place for the Spirit in the life of Christ, whose union with the Father is not primarily of essence but communion. Because of the central role of the Spirit, Jesus' obedience was not so much a response *to* God as it was his living out his Sonship — his triune identity — in human form, with Calvin highlighting communion as one of the chief marks of Christ's life and death. At the

---

price to pay. We run the risk of breaking his link with Israel and of making his work [of] salvation out of the world rather than along and with it" (Gunton, "Mediator," p. 154).

122. "Therefore, the women did wrong in satisfying themselves with having nothing more than the half of his resurrection, and desiring to enjoy his presence in the world" (*Comm. Col.* 3:1).

123. *Comm. 1 Tim.* 6:16. It is important to remember that Calvin does not flirt with Cartesian dualism, but with Platonic dualism. For similar themes, see *Comm. Acts* 17:24.

124. *Comm. John* 3:13.

125. John Witvliet, "Sursum Corda: Images and Themes in John Calvin's Theology of Liturgy," in *Worship Seeking Understanding* (Grand Rapids: Baker, 2003), p. 136 n. 27.

126. *Comm. Col.* 1:2.

same time, we saw how Calvin's reaction to Nominalist speculation also hindered him from considering the ways that Jesus' life naturally reflected (in a humanly appropriate way) his eternal relationship with the Father. We can argue that this left the door open to precarious understandings of his obedience as meritorious rather than grounded in communion.

Calvin's pioneering pneumatology inaugurates a new form of human participation in the triune life of God. The Spirit created — in the life, death, and resurrection of the Son — a real possibility for humanity to share in the love of the triune God. The Son, as the head and center of a new creation, ascended that he might "fill all things" in a wholly new way. His absence now signaled that "presence" is firmly grounded in the Spirit. As humanity's ascent is only to be found in its ascended head, it is brought not only into the shape of his life but also its direction — by the Spirit, in the Son, to the Father.

Chapter Four

The Spirit:
The Eucharistic Ascent

It is an all too abbreviated and misleading formula that says, God descends that man might ascend. Just as it is an all too short saying (that does not express what is decisively Christian) that says, God became man that man might become God. First of all, what applies here is Paul's dictum: *Qui descendit, ipse est et qui ascendit* ["the very one who descended also ascends"]. Man does not so much effect the countermovement to Christ — even with grace. Rather, he is a Christian only in exact imitation of Christ's movement. The law of Christ is the law of the one Christ: head and body.[1]

Just as "the religious temper of the Middle Ages [can] be summarily characterized by the phrase 'the upward tendency,'"[2] Calvin, too, spoke of the Christian life in terms of *ascent,* but he placed the "upward tendency" on a new footing. For Calvin, humanity's ascent is solely a participation in Jesus, whose bidirectional mission summarizes soteriology: "The situation would surely have been hopeless had the very majesty of God not descended to us, since it was not in our power to ascend to him" (II.12.1). Here Calvin uses "ascent" to denote the intended "direction," or *telos,* of

1. Hans Urs von Balthasar, "The Fathers, the Scholastics, and Ourselves," *Communio* 24 (1997): 361.

2. Anders Nygren, *Agape and Eros,* vol. II/II (London: SPCK, 1939), p. 397.

humanity. It is a word that summarizes the call to creatures to be in communion with God; as such, it encapsulates the Christian life.

In this chapter I will allow Calvin's Trinitarian structure of descent and ascent to guide our discussion of the concrete specifics of the Christian life, beginning with the triune descent to us and our inclusion in this "return," or ascent, by the Spirit, in the Son, to the Father. Therefore, this chapter will fall into three parts: (I) it will show that humanity's ascent is *by* the Trinity (discipleship); (II) it will show that humanity's ascent is *into* the Trinity (adoption); and (III) it will show that humanity's ascent is embodied and sacramental (Eucharist).

Discipleship

"These, I say, are the most auspicious foundations upon which to establish one's life . . ." (III.6.3).

In chapter 3 I noted the way in which Calvin structured Jesus' Ascension both to signal the historical opening of participation *en Christo* and to seal the church's future as communion. "As God he is the destination to which we move; as man, the path by which we go. Both are found in Christ alone" (III.2.1). The descending and ascending structure that Jesus' life took is to be the shape of the Christian life as well. Accordingly, one would expect this bidirectional emphasis to be found of both Christ and of humanity, as the following selection of Calvin's writings reveals:

From the embryonic *Institutes* (1536):
We confess that he, sent by the Father out of divine kindness and mercy, descended to us to take on our flesh, which he joined to his divinity. . . . What then? The matter was hopeless if the very majesty of God would not descend to us, since it was not in us to ascend to Him. And so God's Son became for us Immanuel, that is, God with us. (II.12)

From the Old Testament commentaries (Genesis, 1550-54):
If, then, we say that the ladder is a figure of Christ, the exposition will not be forced. For the similitude of a ladder well suits the Mediator, through whom ministering angels, righteousness and life, with all the graces of the Holy Spirit, descend to us step by step. We also, who were

not only fixed to the earth, but plunged into the depths of the curse, and into hell itself, ascend even unto God. . . .[3]

From the New Testament commentaries (John, 1553):
For how shall any mortal man ascend to the height of God, unless he be raised on high by the hand of his Son? God in Christ condescended to the mean condition of men, so as to stretch out his hand. . . .[4]

From the polemical writings (*Ultima Admonitio ad Westphalum*, 1557):
For we must remember that our Lord descends to us, not to indulge our body, or keep our senses fixed on the world, but rather to draw us to himself, and hence the preamble of the ancient Church, Hearts upward, as Chrysostom interprets.[5]

From the Sermons (Ephesians 4:10, 1558):
Now that Jesus Christ has shown us the way, and that by many afflictions he has entered into the Kingdom of heaven, that he has entered into life by way of death, that he was raised on high after he placed himself so low. . . . When we see this, we know — in the first place — how precious our souls were to the Son of God such that he desired to be abased for us, and we treasure the gospel, by which such a good is communicated to us, knowing that if the Son of God had not descended to us, there would have been no other way for us to approach God his Father. . . . And thus, being under the tyranny of Satan and sin, how could we aspire to what is on high, without Jesus Christ drawing us there? It was necessary in the first place for him to descend here below.

This sampling of quotations illustrates how pervasively Calvin regards ascent as where the Father is, and thus as entailing communion. Ascent has nothing to do with human potential. Nor does it have to do with pagan divinization (though it bears close family resemblance to early Christian doctrines of *theosis*). Instead, Christ's mission can only be understood in this larger context of bringing humanity back into the communion that he enjoys with the Father.

Yet, quite extraordinarily, even as Calvin makes humanity's ascent an

3. *Comm. Gen.* 28:12.
4. *Comm. John* 8:19.
5. Calvin, "Last Admonition . . . ," *T&T* II.443.

impossibility without Christ, so he makes Christ "incomplete" without humanity's ascent. Calvin binds Christ's descent to human ascent, revealing that his descent to earth (our salvation) is not the completion of the process but only half of it. We express only one side of the matter when we consider what Christ has done; we must also consider his bringing humanity to share in it. For the fact that Christ has done things *for us* in no way empowers the Christian life. In a rather dramatic statement, Calvin calls Christ "mutilated" if his descent *to us* does not also result in our ascent back to the Father:

> "For the Father is greater than I" . . . . [A]s it has not been granted to us to reach the height of God, Christ descended to us, that he might raise us to it. "You ought to have rejoiced," he says, "because I return to the Father"; for this is the ultimate object at which you ought to aim. By these words he does not show in what respect he differs in himself from the Father, but why he descended to us; and that was, that he might unite us to God; for until we have reached that point, we are, as it were, in the middle of the course. We too imagine to ourselves but a half-Christ, and a mutilated Christ, if he does not lead us to God. . . . Let us therefore learn to behold Christ humbled in the flesh, so that he may conduct us to the fountain of a blessed immortality; for he was not appointed to be our guide, merely to raise us to the sphere of the moon or of the sun, but to make us one with God the Father.[6]

These are strong words. The descent of Christ to crucifixion and death is pivotal, but it does not exist for its own sake. It is not a settling of accounts, but is oriented toward another movement to bring humanity "up" to the Father as sons in him — "one with God the Father." Calvin will even go so far as to say that "until He is united to us, the Son of God reckons himself in some measure imperfect. What consolation is it for us to learn that, not until we are along with him, does he possess all his parts, or wish to be regarded as complete!"[7] Here Calvin shows that it is not the arduous ascent of the individual soul but a radical new model for the church, by which the triune God takes it upon himself to ensure human ascent.

6. *Comm. John* 14:28.

7. *Comm. Eph.* 1:23. Calvin balances this with the notion of aseity: "His wish to be filled, and, in some respects, made perfect in us, arises from no want or necessity; for all that is good in ourselves, or in any of the creatures, is the gift of his hand."

Calvin was at pains to sketch out the Trinity's role in humanity's ascent in order to show that the Christian life is not response *to* God but inclusion *in* God. Just as the God-to-human trajectory was a triune endeavor, so the human-to-God trajectory is the same.[8] The descent of God first matches human descent into misery and is "into hell itself,"[9] but it is no different from the triune movements of grace toward humanity that have marked the divine-human relationship from the beginning.[10] It is the "negative" side of christology, in which God descends to redeem a brokenness that is beyond repair; but it is always a movement initiated by the love of the Father, enacted by the Son, and enabled by the Spirit. The ascent of God is similarly the "positive" side of christology, in which, by the Spirit, the Son gathers believers into himself to return to communion with the Father. The fact that the Trinity governs both of these movements has far-reaching implications for the outworking of discipleship. When this is not attended to — when ascent becomes a response to Christ rather than a participation in Christ — then the implications for Christian discipleship are devastating.

Calvin saw with piercing clarity that an exclusive focus on the descent of Christ resulted in stultified views of the Christian life, usually construed ontologically, sacramentally, or ethically — which I will deal with respectively below. In scholastic theology, we saw how this ascent had to be ordered to an ontology that explained ascent in terms of human continuity with the divine. For how else could this impossible "ascent" be accomplished?[11] Heshuius and others represent the second, sacramental kind, where the relationship of hu-

---

8. For an exposition of the Trinitarian ordering of the human-to-God trajectory, see Philip W. Butin, *Revelation, Redemption, and Response: Calvin's Trinitarian Understanding of the Divine-Human Relationship* (New York: Oxford University Press, 1995), chap. 6.

9. *Comm. Gen.* 28:12.

10. I might also add that with this economic-Trinitarian emphasis, there tends to be an automatic narrowing of the traditional gulf between divine and human because the Trinity is not cast in terms of metaphysical attribute (which often is construed simply as the opposite of what is human, immortal, invisible), but in terms of economic activity (that instead presupposes God's action, revelation, and incarnation). We do not know him except "as he is toward us" (I.10.2). Furthermore, in this grand scheme of the economic — perhaps best characterized as the descent and ascent of God — sin cannot take on an exaggerated episode (notwithstanding Calvin's celebrated depictions of it).

11. Ozment shows how this is the basic pattern for both Tauler and Gerson as well (Steven Ozment, *Homo Spiritualis: A Comparative Study of the Anthropology of Johannes Tauler, Jean Gerson and Martin Luther* [Leiden: Brill, 1969]).

manity to Christ is construed through the medium of grace. This fell far short, Calvin believed, of Trinitarian participation in Christ, but it was an instance where the elements threatened to substitute for *koinōnia*.

The moral philosophers represent the third unsatisfactory way of relating Christ to humanity. Calvin knew that, regardless of how much Jesus had accomplished on the cross, humanity still could not respond appropriately to such a cataclysmic event. The Christian life could never be a matter of mere grateful response to Christ's descent. Yet this is precisely the system that the philosophers perpetuated.

> Now let those persons who think that moral philosophy is duly and systematically set forth solely among philosophers find me among the philosophers a more excellent disposition. They, while they wish particularly to exhort us to virtue, announce merely that we should live in accordance with nature. But Scripture draws its exhortation from the true fountain. (III.6.3)

Humanity's ascent to the Father is not as the moral philosophers envisioned, by "virtue" and "nature," but could only be framed in terms of the Spirit bringing humanity to participate in *Christ's* ascent. His ascent is the first fruits of the human return to communion with the Father, for "we are Christians proceeding from him, as rivulet from a fountain."[12] Without taking participation in Christ's ascent seriously, the moral philosophers left the human-to-God trajectory to the realm of human response, thus ridding it of *koinōnia*.

Calvin sketches out the alternative to the moral philosophers in a passage redolent of participation, lyrically beginning with our adopted *(en Christo)* status and only then its "ethical" outworking. In a rapid succession of six exhortative sentences, Calvin first lays out the triune God's activity that is the impetus and power for human response, and only then dwells on our corresponding activity:

> Ever since God revealed himself as Father to us . . .
>> Ever since Christ cleansed us . . .
>> Ever since he engrafted us into his body . . .
>> Ever since Christ himself, who is our Head, ascended into heaven . . .

12. *Comm. Heb.* 1:9.

Ever since the Holy Spirit dedicated us as temples to God . . .

Ever since both our souls and bodies were destined for heavenly incorruption and an unfading crown. . . . These, I say, are the most auspicious foundations upon which to establish one's life. One would look in vain for the like of these among the philosophers, who, in their commendation of virtue, never rise above the natural dignity of man. (III.6.3)

Clearly, Calvin is pushing for a participation he feels is little understood. He makes much this same point in his commentary on 1 John 2:3, where he makes it clear that our "becoming like Him, for we shall see Him as He is" is "taken from the effect, not from the cause." Calvin explains that the apostle "does not teach us, that we shall be like him, because we shall see him," but it is our becoming like him (which is only by participation) that enables us to see. The only "foundation" for the Christian life is not so much what Christ has done *for us*, requiring our response, but rather the triune God's own activity into which we are included. Calvin responds: "The apostle does not say that He was sent to help us attain righteousness but Himself to be our righteousness" (III.15.5).

In later Reformed theology, ascent once again tended toward the realm of moral response, where the Spirit aids individuals to meet the demands of the Christian life, usually through imitation and obedience.[13] This "ascent," however, does not capitalize on Calvin's insight that descent and ascent are both movements of God. In his Ascension Sermons, Calvin speaks of the ethical implications of the Ascension of Jesus:

We must leave our earthly members, which separate us from Him, and we must be raised on high. How? In true chastity, in sobriety, in true charity, in temperance, in diligence, in patience, in every other virtue. These are the wings to raise us to heaven. . . .[14]

If Calvin were to have stopped here, there would have been a problem. However, he immediately clarifies the foundation for this: ". . . although properly speaking we need not have wings to fly there, or ladders to climb

---

13. For a contemporary example, see Robert A. Peterson's chapter on "Christ our Example," in *Calvin's Doctrine of the Atonement* (Phillipsburg, NJ: Presbyterian and Reformed Publishing Co., 1983), pp. 77-82.

14. *Serm. Acts* 1:1-4 (*CO* 48.596).

there; but that Jesus Christ leads us there and raises us by the graces which He distributes, as those which I have named."

Early on, Calvin deliberately inverts Luther on this very point. In Luther's *Praefatio* to his Latin works (1545) he describes his exegetical breakthrough as realizing that God's righteousness is to be grasped *by faith*. Calvin contradicts this, noting that Luther's emphasis on the responsive faith of the believer *to Christ* should instead be construed as the "'active' faithfulness *of God* as the stable foundation of salvation."[15] Luther's accent shifted the emphasis of salvation from Christ's shoulders to our own, which is no small theological detail.[16] Contemporary scholar Carlos Eire shows little sensitivity to Calvin's radical reformation of this very point when he describes Calvin's doctrine of worship as "a human act. . . . Any human motion in the material sphere that is intended as worship, or carries with it any reverence toward divinity, is an attempt to cross over from one sphere to the other, to communicate."[17] Eire's perspective does not reflect Calvin well but does a good job of reflecting much sentiment about Calvinism that is entirely devoid of participation, where God is described as in another sphere and the burden of ascending to him is left to humanity in the form of acts of "worship." Instead, Calvin proposes radical and "auspicious foundations" (III.6.3) for humanity's ascent: *koinōnia* with Christ, which is our spiritual worship.

Adoption

"Adoption . . . is not the cause merely of a partial salvation, but bestows salvation entire. . . ."

Ascent, then, clarifies the orientation of the Christian life and the means by which we go. "Christ, for this reason, is said to send the Spirit from his

15. See Calvin's exegesis of Ps. 7:18 (CO 31.87) and Ps. 22:31 (CO 31.237 B), and its exploration by Heiko Oberman, "*Initia Calvini:* The Matrix of Calvin's Reformation," in *Calvinus Sacrae Scripturae Professor,* ed. Wilhelm Neuser (Grand Rapids: Eerdmans, 1994), p. 134 n. 74.

16. This critique needs qualification in light of recent Finnish work on Luther's doctrine of participation. Suffice it to say that Calvin purposely distanced himself from Luther here, which is to make an important point about Calvin, not Luther, at this juncture. Nevertheless, I find Calvin's emphasis on participation to be oriented more to the realm of human sanctification, whereas Luther's is more toward Christ-personalism.

17. Carlos M. N. Eire, "John Calvin's Attack on Idolatry," in *War Against the Idols* (Cambridge: Cambridge University Press, 1986), p. 213.

Father (John 16:7) to raise us, by degrees, up to the Father."[18] But ascent does not go far enough; it describes the *telos* of humanity — communion — but not the type. It is only when we begin to scrutinize Calvin's Trinitarian metaphor of adoption that we perceive its ability to tie much of Calvin's theology together.

Humanity's Ascent into the Triune Communion

Quite remarkably, adoption has been overlooked by the Reformed tradition as one of Calvin's most significant doctrines. As Robert Webb says, "The evangelical doctrine of adoption . . . has received but slender treatment at the hands of the theologians. It has been handled with a meagerness entirely out of proportion to its intrinsic importance, and with a subordination which allows it only a parenthetical place in the system of evangelical truth."[19] But for many reasons (not least of them its prolonged internment in the *ordo salutis*), adoption has not been probed for its rich resources and boundaries that it offers to a doctrine of participation in God. Only recently has Calvin been rediscovered as a theologian par excellence of the Trinity, and with this reinvigorated understanding comes a renewed appreciation for the familial metaphor of adoption.[20] Through it, Calvin expresses not just the fact of salvation but its character, which is marked by knowing God's fatherhood and by becoming sons in the Son, able to cry *Abba* (II.14.5).[21]

If the effect of Adam's sin is that "no one now experiences God as Fa-

18. Joseph Tylenda, "Christ the Mediator: Calvin Versus Stancaro," *Calvin Theological Journal* 8 (1973): 16.

19. From *The Reformed Doctrine of Adoption*, quoted in Tim Trumper, "The Theological History of Adoption I: An Account," *Scottish Bulletin of Evangelical Theology* 20 (2002): 4.

20. Philip Butin points to Karl Barth as pioneer of this controversial reclamation (Butin, *Revelation*, p. 5). For a history of the handful of theologians who have defended the significance of adoption (those of the Dutch Second Reformation, the Puritans, Erskine, McLeod Campbell, Candlish and Crawford, and others), see Trumper, "Theological History of Adoption I," pp. 4-28.

21. Because Calvin does not see the Son's relation to the Father as a mere picture, but an ontological reality for our participation, it is clear that inclusive language would burn the bridge on which Calvin stands. See also the discussion by Jane Dempsey Douglass, *Women, Freedom, and Calvin* (Philadelphia: Westminster, 1985), pp. 8-9.

ther" (I.2.1), Calvin envisions the saved life as "tast[ing] his fatherly love, [we are] drawn to love and worship him in return" (I.5.3). Calvin remarks that, even throughout the Old Testament, God "willed, through expiations and sacrifices, to attest that he was Father" (II.9.1), thus giving "testimonies of his mercy and fatherly favor . . . to the patriarchs of old" (II.9.2). With the advent of Christ, Christian faith is described as an experience of God's fatherhood (III.2.30) as did prophets of old; but now "we can more richly enjoy it" (II.9.1). It is quite remarkable just how far Calvin goes to equate faith, not with belief or knowledge *(cognitio)* alone, but with recognizing God's fatherhood.[22]

> Therefore God both calls himself our Father and would have us so address him. By the great sweetness of this name he frees us from all distrust, since no greater feeling of love can be found elsewhere than in the Father. Therefore he could not attest his own boundless love toward us with any surer proof than the fact that we are called "children of God." (III.20.37)

God's fatherhood functions here as a beautiful metaphor for the human experience of God in salvation and the move from fear to trust. Gerrish observes: "At every critical turn in his progress through the principal matters contained in the Christian philosophy, he invokes the child-father relationship with an acuteness that fully justifies Warfield's verdict: in the Reformation era Calvin was preeminently the theologian of divine fatherhood."[23]

However, this does not begin to plumb Calvin's doctrine of adoption that goes beyond metaphor. He begins by describing Christ as "the bond whereby God may be found to us in fatherly faithfulness" (III.2.32), a reality for even the patriarchs who were called "sons of God" only *en Christo*.[24] Why? Because only the one who is the Son has a right to call the Father, "Father."[25] This is not merely a term of endearment but a term that de-

---

22. Faith's object is not a doctrine but the person Jesus; therefore, it is itself a relationship of *koinōnia*. As Wilhelm Kolfhaus says, "faith is, for Calvin, union with Christ" (Kolfhaus, *Christusgemeinschaft bei Johannes Calvin* [Neukirchen: Moers, 1939], p. 37).

23. Gerrish, *Grace and Gratitude*, p. 27.

24. "Were not the holy patriarchs of old also held to be among the sons of God? Yes — relying upon this right ["sons of God through Christ"], they called upon God as Father" (II.14.5).

25. "Yet this ought to be unwaveringly maintained: to neither angels nor men was

scribes an ontological reality and an immanent relationship within the god-head.[26] For "to this name [Son] only Christ has a right, because he is by nature *the only Son of God;* [yet] he communicates this honor to us by adoption, when we are engrafted into his body."[27] Calvin is fighting here for a notion of sonship that is not metaphorical but requires participation, "[f]or here it is not a matter of figures, such as when atonement was set forth in the blood of beasts. Rather, they could not actually be sons of God unless their adoption was founded upon the Head" (II.14.5). There are those who would treat this adoption along the lines of a change in the "status" of the recipient. Yet Calvin himself pursues the language much further than this.

Quite extraordinarily, Calvin pictures the relationship within the immanent Trinity as open to humanity. Our justification is not only acceptance by God but our inclusion in a specific relationship through the economic action of God.[28] We remember that, in Calvin's definition of the Trinity, the names Father, Son, and Spirit refer to an immanent relationship (and thus personal communion) rather than segregated economic function.[29] Even as we find Calvin hesitant to speculate on these triune relationships, it is clear that these relationships are what drive his notion of adoption.[30]

God ever Father, except with regard to his only-begotten Son" (II.14.5). "[I]t is quite unfitting that those not engrafted into the body of the only-begotten Son are considered to have the place and rank of children" (II.6.1).

26. Gerrish takes most of the paternal and filial references in Calvin to be metaphorical (since they do not refer to "eternal begetting"). In so doing, Gerrish dilutes God's paternity to a metaphorical benevolence, and empties the significance of the immanent Trinity for the economy. If there is any metaphorical "accommodation" to human capacity in Calvin's use of the term "Father," it is an accommodation, Calvin says, in allowing human fathers also to appropriate such a glorious title, rather than in God's own paternity himself (*Serm. 1 Tim. 9, CO* 53.13).

27. *Comm. John* 3:16.

28. Calvin's doctrine of adoption is connected to justification (I.10.1), sanctification (III.6.3; *Comm. Rom.* 8:14), election (III.25.4), the *imago Dei* (III.11.6; III.11.8), and the *historia salutis* (II.7.1-2; II.10). It was the continental theologian Francis Turretin who subordinated adoption to justification in the *Theological Institutes* (Turretin, *Opera,* II.585), dispossessing adoption of its true character for many years to come.

29. "By these appellations . . . is signified their mutual relationships" (I.13.19). Calvin's differentiation of the triune members has less to do with separating functional spheres (creation, redemption, consummation) than with their perichoretic unity in all activity (IV.15.6; *Comm. John* 6:57).

30. In a discussion of the Trinity, Calvin remarks that "he is shown to us not as he is

To comprehend aright what was intended by saying, that Christ and the Father are *one,* we must take care not to deprive Christ of his office as Mediator, but must rather view him as he is the Head of the Church, and unite him with his members. Thus will the chain of thought be preserved, that, in order to prevent the *unity* of the Son with the Father from being fruitless and unavailing, the power of that *unity* must be diffused through the whole body of believers. Hence, too, we infer that we are *one* with the Son of God; not because he conveys his substance to us, but because, by the power of his Spirit, he imparts to us his life and all the blessings which he has received from the Father.[31]

Christ's union with the Father is neither private achievement nor a direct result of his divinity; rather, it is for us, for our participation. Butin calls this nothing less than Calvin's "bold inclusion of believers in the *perichoresis* of the divine life through their participation in Christ by the Holy Spirit."[32] If "neither has Christ any thing, which may not be applied to our benefit; for he has been given to us by the Father once for all on this condition, that all his should be ours," then this even includes his union with the Father.[33] "He does not speak simply of his Divine essence . . . he is called *one,* as regards his mediatorial office."[34] This is, we remember, because Calvin is always concerned that the Mediator experience things in a humanly appropriate way; otherwise, as human, we could not participate in them. What is so impressive about Calvin's doctrine of mediation is that he unfolds it to its fullest possible implication: this is our salvation life, the communion of Father and Son, made available for our participation by the Spirit.

It is in his analysis of the baptism narrative, however, that Calvin's language is most striking: time and again he pushes the point that Christ was not declared as the "beloved" as intra-Trinitarian commentary but also *for us.* "It was rather the design of Christ to lay, as it were, in our bosom a sure

---

in himself, but as he is toward us" (I.10.2). While the immanent Trinity will always be "incomprehensible" (I.11.3) to us, it still expresses itself toward us. Hence adoption is a manifestation "toward us," as a "comprehensible" revelation of the incomprehensibility of the Trinity.

31. *Comm. John* 17:21.

32. Butin, *Revelation,* p. 43. Differentiating between the mystical and the hypostatic unions would strengthen Butin's point.

33. *Comm. Heb.* 7:25.

34. *Comm. John* 17:21.

pledge of God's love toward us."[35] Thus, Christ's baptism — his declaration of being the "beloved Son" — specifically becomes the "pledge of our adoption," whereby we may "boldly call God himself our Father."[36] We find Calvin taking his cue from Jesus' own communion with God by the Spirit, a relationship that is unique but also is held out to the church as a tangible picture by which to understand union with God. Calvin notes that Jesus' filial submission

> was accompanied by this announcement [of *Beloved*], in which he was offered to us by the Father, that we may rely on this pledge of our adoption. . . . The designation of *Son* belongs truly and naturally to Christ alone: but yet he was declared to be the Son of God in our flesh, that the favor of Him, whom he alone has a right to call *Father*, may be also obtained for us.[37]

Calling God "Father" is directly linked to our being engrafted in the only one who has a "right" to Sonship.[38] For "it is indisputable that no one is loved by God apart from Christ: 'This is my beloved Son,' in whom dwells and rests the Father's love. And from him it then pours itself upon us, just as Paul teaches: 'We receive grace in the beloved'" (III.2.32). From this we see that general truths about a relationship with God, that God loves humanity, or that we are his children are no longer generalities to Calvin but specific to Christ's own relationship with God that he shares with us.[39] Justification is not only our free gift of righteousness and pardon, but of relationship. And this is not into some general relationship, but one or-

---

35. *Comm. John* 15:9.

36. *Comm. Matt.* 3:17. Here Calvin links Christ's baptism with adoption; elsewhere, he links the sacrament of baptism with adoption. "Baptism must, therefore, be preceded by the gift of adoption, which is not the cause merely of a partial salvation, but bestows salvation entire, and is afterwards ratified by baptism" (Calvin, "True Method of Obtaining Concord . . ." *T&T* III.275; this is the second half of the full treatise in *CO* 7.545-674, *T&T* III.189-239/240-343).

37. *Comm. Matt.* 3:17.

38. Calvin elsewhere makes the important distinction that God is not just *my* Father but *our* Father (*Institutes* III.20.38).

39. For God's love of believers and its relationship to the declaration of Christ's belovedness, see III.2.32; *Comm. John* 5:20, 17:23; *Comm. Eph.* 1:5. For the title of "children" and its relationship to Christ's being called the beloved "Son" at his baptism, see IV.15.1 and *Comm. Matt.* 3:17.

dered to the Son's own human experience of communion with God — his sonship, our adoption.

Breadth and Boundaries to Participation

Calvin's notion of adoption renders more precise the concept of "participation in God." It is entirely christologically disciplined, a move that — surprisingly perhaps — both closes doors and opens them. Due to the shakeup in Lutheran scholarship by the new Finnish research,[40] some strands of Reformed theology have tended to be on guard against notions of participation in God.[41] Adoption, however, carries radical implications for participation in the divine life while also assuaging traditional Reformed fears (i.e., loss of distinction between Creator/creature and neglect of the atonement). "What," asks Calvin, "is the goal of our adoption which we attain through him, if it is not, as Peter declares, finally to be partakers of the divine nature (2 Pet. 1:4)?"[42]

To begin with, adoption naturally includes within its definition important boundaries to a concept of participation in the divine life. We can see this most clearly when we contrast Calvin's doctrine of adoption with Luther. Throughout his writings Luther displayed a preference for the model of nuptial union, saying (as quoted by R. Jenson):

> "Faith . . . unites the soul with Christ, as bride with her bridegroom. From this marriage it follows . . . that Christ and the soul have everything together: what Christ has belongs to the believing soul and what the soul has belongs to Christ" (Luther, *WA* 1, 20, 25). This claim is not intended as rhetoric or trope but as a proposition about an ontic actuality.[43]

40. Carl Braaten and Robert Jenson, eds., *Union with Christ: The New Finnish Interpretation of Luther* (Grand Rapids: Eerdmans, 1998).

41. See *Westminster Theological Journal* 65, no. 2 (2003), which devotes half of its issue to this concern, with articles by Paul Metzger (pp. 201-14), Mark Seifrid (pp. 215-30), Carl Trueman (pp. 231-44), and Robert Jenson (pp. 245-50).

42. "Quis enim finis est nostrae adoptionis, quam per ipsum consequimur, nisi tandem participes simus divinae naturae, sicut testatur Petrus?" (*CO* 9.351), in Joseph Tylenda, "The Controversy of Christ the Mediator: Calvin's Second Reply to Stancaro," *Calvin Theological Journal* 8 (1973): 148.

43. Robert W. Jenson, *Systematic Theology II: The Works of God* (Oxford: Oxford University Press, 1999), p. 295.

Unlike Luther, Calvin does not use the *communicatio idiomatum* of Christ and the soul as the model for our integration into the divine life. (Nor does he use the two natures of Christ to inform human relationship to God.)[44] Calvin is comfortable with many metaphors of union (head and members, vine and branches, marriage, Eve's formation from Adam), but upon examination they evoke a participation that is firmly Trinitarian: that is, they involve the Spirit who mediates Christ's humanity to us. Aquinas, likewise, has a rigorous Trinitarian theology of human adoption into the divine life, which (as described by Bruce Marshall) is "to receive a share in the one, natural, eternal and person-constituting relationship of the Son to the Father — a share in his inner-divine *filiatio*, his own sonship or 'begottenness.'"[45] Yet here we find the *unio mystica* on the verge of dissolution into the *unio hypostatica*, a scenario with which Calvin would be quite uncomfortable, we can be sure.[46] While Aquinas used the inner perichoretic life of the Trinity as the model, Calvin stuck to the biblical economy and limited participation to our inclusion into Jesus and his vicarious humanity, full stop.

For Calvin, the only way to protect creaturehood was to have union with a *triune* God, whose own differentiation makes room for human particularity. Therefore, the goal becomes not mere union with the divine, but communion — an experience of differentiation as well as love. Human ascent is into sonship, but never as the Son. "As to the second clause, in which he says that he *ascends to his Father and our Father,* there is also a diversity between him and us; for he is the Son of God by nature, while we are the sons of God only by adoption."[47] Characteristically, Calvin insists

---

44. To use Calvin's famous quote that Christ's "divinity and our human nature might by mutual connection grow together" (II.12.1) to support anything other than a general statement about God and humanity is careless. It is not Calvin's model of human participation in the divine.

45. Bruce Marshall, "Action and Person: Do Palamas and Aquinas Agree About the Spirit?" *St Vladimir's Theological Quarterly* 39 (1995): 391. I owe this citation to George Hunsinger.

46. *Comm. John* 14:20. I am using Hunsinger's language: "Two possible mistakes need to be avoided here. One is to reduce the *unio hypostatica* downwards into the *unio mystica*. This is the typical mistake of modern liberal theology. The other moves in the opposite direction by dissolving the *unio mystica* upwards into the *unio hypostatica*. This is the typical mistake of various high sacramental ecclesiologies" (George Hunsinger, "The Dimension of Depth: Thomas F. Torrance on the Sacraments of Baptism and the Lord's Supper," *Scottish Journal of Theology* 54, no. 2 [2001]: 166 n. 14).

47. *Comm. John* 20:18; see also *Institutes* II.14.5.

that humans will never fully "know what is the sacred and mystical union between us and him, and again between him and the Father." But Calvin does say that we will enter it: ". . . but that the only way of knowing it is, when he diffuses his life in us by the secret efficacy of the Spirit."[48] Calvin here differentiates between the *unio mystica* ("mystical union between us and him") that is mystically connected to (but not identical with) the *unio hypostatica* ("between him and the Father"), giving even further clarity by making the Spirit the agent of this union. If Chalcedon does indeed inform Calvin's christology and anthropology, then even a radical interpretation of adoption certainly passes the test. Even as we participate in a form of the divine being — communion — creaturely integrity is preserved because Christ himself sanctified in his person a specifically human form of communion with the divine. Human "sonship" in Calvin is a critical boundary-marker, signifying that we are not directly ushered into the unity experienced between Father and Son eternally, but rather into Jesus' human expression and experience of that communion.

Therefore, adoption gives precision to "participation in God" by keeping it firmly tied to participation *en Christo*, by the Spirit. And yet this is not a statement to diminish the reality of participation in the divine; rather, it highlights a radical participation in the divine that simultaneously secures creaturehood. Calvin makes it clear that Christ's humanity is not to protect believers from things divine, but to help believers participate in exactly these things. "But we shall not be satisfied with having Christ, if we do not know that we possess God in him. We must therefore believe that there is such a unity between the Father and the Son as makes it impossible that they shall have anything separate from each other."[49] Just as the Spirit preserved the humanity of Christ, enabling all that he did to be a truly *human* expression and experience, so the Spirit brings humans to participate "indirectly" in the triune communion, in a fully human manner in the Son. This is why Calvin can be so radical as to say, "As Christ is one with the Father, so we are one with Him."[50] Wendel calls this an "even more peculiar text" in that it is in contradiction to the "whole position taken up by Calvin."[51] This is a characteristic Reformed

48. *Comm. John* 14:20.
49. *Comm. John* 17:10.
50. *Serm. 1 Sam.* 2:27-30 (*CO* 29.353).
51. François Wendel, *Calvin: The Origins and Development of His Religious Thought* (London: Collins, 1963), p. 237.

response, where the boundaries of Calvin's doctrine of participation are perhaps more underscored than its corresponding breadth. It is often overlooked that, in Calvin, the Trinity provides for both. One need not fear fusion with a triune God.

A Necessary Excursus

This brings us to the heart of the debate between Calvin and Osiander. In the late 1540s, a reformer came onto the scene who did more than merely stir the theological waters. Calvinists, Lutherans, and others united in a common front against Andreas Osiander, whose theology of justification and participation in God threatened to sink the Reformation boat. While this is most often cited as a debate about "external" pardoning (the declaration of righteousness) versus the "internal" infusion of righteousness, my hope is to show that it is a critical debate between two conceptualities of participation. Calvin's solution to the problem demands close attention.

As historical irony would have it, Osiander and Calvin battled a mutual enemy: an abstract, forensic view of righteousness. In this view (often associated with Melanchthon, justifiably or not),[52] righteousness was given to sinners not through union with Christ but was "imputed" in a mechanistic fashion.[53] In such a scenario, there lurked the danger that the

---

52. If there is to be a difference between Luther and Melanchthon, it would be the decisive one of *attitude* that in more than one way impacted content. Melanchthon's theology tends to be flavored by an extreme mechanistic causality as opposed to Luther's Christ-personalism. (Hunsinger makes this same distinction by quoting Melanchthon's "God makes us righteousness, for Christ's sake" versus Luther's "Christ *is* our righteousness.") For the thesis that Melanchthon's forensicism was influenced by Nominalism, see Stephen Strehle, "Imputatio iustitiae: Its Origin in Melanchthon, its Opposition in Osiander," *Theologische Zeitschrift* 50 (1994): 205. Hunsinger traces the development of forensicism from Melanchthon to Quenstedt in his unpublished manuscript entitled "Calvin's Doctrine of Justification: Is It Really Forensic?" (2005), pp. 1-7.

For a general overview contrasting Melanchthon and Luther, see Robert Kolb, "'Not Without the Satisfaction of God's Righteousness': The Atonement and the Generation Gap between Luther and His Students," in *Archiv für Reformationsgeschichte, Sonderband*, ed. Hans R. Guggisberg and Gottfried G. Krodel (Gütersloh, Germany: Gütersloher, 1993), pp. 136-56; Mark A. Seifrid, "Luther, Melanchthon, and Paul on the Question of Imputation," in *Justification*, ed. Mark Husbands and Daniel Treier (Downers Grove, IL: InterVarsity, 2004), pp. 137-52; and Robert Jenson's response in *Westminster Theological Journal* 65 (2003): 248-49.

53. Imputation is not necessarily forensic in character, although it has long been cen-

completion of Christ's work *pro nobis* could be accomplished without Christ himself. Justification could occur by divine fiat, riding on Christ's merits and activities in the past. Christ no longer was the substance of our righteousness, but merely paved its way.

This alarmed both Osiander and Calvin. Osiander charges:

> They teach [doctrines] colder than ice, that we are accounted righteous only on account of the remission of sins, and not also on account of the righteousness of the Christ dwelling in us by faith. God is not indeed so unjust as to regard him as righteous in whom there is really nothing of true righteousness.[54]

Osiander believed that Christ's justification was robust enough to make sinners truly righteous and, as opposed to declaratory imputation, was dependent on the presence of Christ. Yet in Osiander's scheme, this was the presence of the *divine* Christ, whose human work on the cross played little or no role. Calvin notes that the divine, eternal Christ "overwhelms and fills" the believer with Logos-righteousness "by the infusion both of his essence and of his quality" (III.11.5).[55] Osiander could only envision a participation in righteousness that was infused righteousness, such that our

---

tral to a forensic interpretation of justification, so much so that it is difficult to pull the two apart. A few definitions are in order. Strictly speaking, "imputation" involves the "gifted" character of our righteousness, underscoring that it comes only from God and not from ourselves. "Forensicism," as the primary framework in which one understands justification, holds God's "declaration" of our righteousness to be the mechanism by which we become righteous. It sees the courtroom (with a judge, a convicted sinner, and a sentence) as the closest metaphor to understanding how God's declaration of "innocent" could become true of the subject. When imputation and forensicism are brought together, it is this *legal* pronouncement of innocence (in the face of the law's condemnation) that is "imputed" to us. However, imputation (God's gift of righteousness) does not necessarily occur through the mechanism of a juridical declaration but can also occur through union with Christ.

54. Quoted in Reinhold Seeberg, *Textbook of the History of Doctrines*, trans. Charles E. Hay (Philadelphia: Lutheran Publication Society, 1905), p. 370.

55. For this, Osiander leaned on an Augustinian insight that grace and its effects (e.g., righteousness) are due to the presence of Christ within us. See Patricia Wilson-Kastner, "On Partaking of the Divine Nature: Luther's Dependence on Augustine," *Andrews University Seminary Studies* 22 (1984): 113-24; see also Wilson-Kastner, "Andreas Osiander's Theology of Grace in the Perspective of the Influence of Augustine of Hippo," *Sixteenth Century Journal* 10 (1979): 72-91.

humanity became continuous with (or replaced by!) Christ's divinity. For Osiander, it is this "participation" that is justifying and sanctifying, where God's verdict of "righteous" rests on a prior reality within the believer.

Like Osiander, Calvin wanted a justification tightly bound to the *person* of Christ. He observes:

> We do not regard [Christ] as outside of and distant from us, in such a way that His righteousness is imputed to us in mechanical fashion, but we put Him on and are made members of His body, and He has deemed us worthy to be united with Him. . . . (III.11.10)

This cannot be boiled down to Calvin's fight for the "imputation" of righteousness over against Osiander's substantial "impartation," or even Calvin's thoroughgoing "forensicism" versus Osiander's "participation." For Calvin, justification involved elements of all of these things. Calvin's primary concern is a correct doctrine of union and participation: *how* it is that we are incorporated into Christ and his benefits.[56] Melanchthon represented one unsatisfactory way, where the "external" elements of his doctrine of imputation well nigh separated Christ from the believer. Osiander represented the other, where the "internal" transformation brought about by Christ seemed to be at the expense of his free gift of pardoning righteousness.

The nub of the issue, for Calvin, was pneumatological. "[B]ut because [Osiander] does not observe the bond of this unity, he deceives himself. Now it is easy for us to resolve all his difficulties. For we hold ourselves to be united with Christ by the secret power of his Spirit" (III.11.5). In a surprising gesture, Calvin goes so far as to point out his agreement with Osiander; but then he clarifies the terms on which this agreement can be had, namely, humanity's present participation in the *human* Jesus' righteousness, by the Spirit. "That righteousness of which Christ makes us partakers with himself is the eternal righteousness of the eternal God —

---

56. Hunsinger shows that both justification and sanctification are participatory categories. Imputed righteousness — the result of "putting on Christ" — retains an important forensic aspect that is once-for-all. It corresponds to the first half of Calvin's distinction between possessing *(possidere)* Christ and all that is his and partaking of *(participare)* Christ. Imparted righteousness — being "engrafted into Christ" — is the continuous state of participating in Christ and communion. Christ alone holds these two benefits within himself. See George Hunsinger, "A Tale of Two Simultaneities: Justification and Sanctification in Calvin and Barth," *Zeitschrift für dialektische Theologie* 18 (2002): 318.

provided Osiander accept the firm and clear reasons that I have brought forward" (III.11.9).

What Osiander lacks is twofold: an appreciation for the ongoing presence of Christ's humanity as our only access to participation in God and for the Spirit's work to continually put us into this humanity. By "spurning this spiritual bond," Osiander "forces a gross mingling of Christ with believers" (III.11.10). Whereas Osiander worked in substantial categories, Calvin worked in Spirit categories, "not by an inflowing of substance, but by the grace and power of the Spirit . . . who surely works in us without rendering us consubstantial with God" (I.15.5). By pinpointing Osiander's low appreciation of the Holy Spirit as the culprit, Calvin is able to make a critical distinction between participation-as-infusion (what I generally refer to as "Platonic participation") and participation-as-*koinōnia* (what I generally refer to as "Trinitarian participation").

Rarely is Osiander's Trinitarian theology saddled with the blame for his heterodox doctrines, but this is precisely where one should look (not least because Calvin countered Osiander with a Trinitarian response). Osiander's theology bears the mark of Augustinianism taken to the extreme, where the members of the Trinity are virtually undistinguishable. In his *On Justification,* Osiander reasons according to the unity of the divine nature: since the Word dwells in us, so must "also the Father and the Holy Spirit dwell in us" (III.11.5), so Calvin reports. Therefore, justification means nothing less than the indwelling of an undifferentiated godhead. Yet, as both Calvin and Irenaeus intuited, a doctrine of participation in God is a threat to creaturehood when it lacks Trinitarian differentiation.[57] With such a singular view of God, Osiander's doctrine of participation could in no way be an instance of *koinōnia* and communion — the bringing together of two "unlikes" in a relationship of mutual indwelling — but rather of sameness. As Calvin intuited, such a doctrine of indwelling is actually a *threat* to creaturehood. Not surprisingly, Wilson-Kastner shows that Osiander's doctrine of participation was more akin to the Platonic concept of the many and the one, in which "the relation of finite reality to the absolute is that it depends on and derives its being from the one."[58] Calvin, on the other hand, ordered his concept of participation to

57. On the Trinitarian structure of Calvin's response to Osiander, see Butin, *Revelation,* pp. 70-71.

58. Wilson-Kastner, "Andreas," p. 84. Wilson-Kastner displays a more limited understanding of the Greek church fathers when she compares Osiander favorably to them.

the activity of the triune members: being brought by the Spirit to share in the Son, to the glory of the Father. Osiander repristinated classical — as opposed to Christian — participation, and this is where Calvin makes his stand against Osiander.

Calvin's distinct alternative to Osiander's "inflowing of substance" grew directly from his appreciation of the Spirit's relationship to the humanity of Christ. Without the Holy Spirit as the central player, Calvin knew that the humanity of Christ would drop to the sidelines in favor of a more "spiritualized" and "immediate" relationship to the divine. It was this that characterized Osiander, who could quite cavalierly sidestep all of Jesus' human work of atonement, because who needed that when the righteousness *(asarkos)* could be had to hand? Central to Osiander's theology, as laid out in his 1551 "About the One Mediator Jesus Christ and the Justification of Faith," was a sharp distinction between the work of the human and divine Christ. As human, Jesus' earthly work of atonement remains in the past; only in this historical capacity was he our "reconciliation." As God, Jesus' divine work is in the present as he mediates his divine grace to humanity by dwelling within them — or "justifying" them. Osiander's treatment of Christ is a classic test case for how he sees a human subject in the presence of the divine. Jesus' obedience was not a human expression of God's righteousness, but a replacement of his own righteousness entirely with divine *ousia*. Jesus' humanity was not preserved by the Holy Spirit, but rather overwhelmed by the divinity within him. As usual, the anthropological apple does not fall far from the christological tree. What happens to Christ's humanity also happens to us. For just as the human Jesus of Nazareth was infused with divine essence, so the believer is physically indwelt by the divine Christ.

Calvin, on the other hand, could not "tear Christ to pieces" (III.11.6) by separating his person from his work.[59] Righteousness — indeed, divine righteousness — was available to faith but only mediated through Christ's human work (III.11.7) of expiation and obedience. It was not a matter of siphoning off some divine property, but was the Spirit's miraculous work to incorporate us into the Savior (II.11.10). To emphasize this point, Calvin calls Christ's flesh this "fountain of righteousness" (III.11.9), offered to faith so that it results in a humanly appropriate righteousness that neither

---

59. For more on this theme, see the research on the "Christ torn to pieces" by Mark Garcia, *Life in Christ: Union with Christ and Twofold Grace in Calvin's Theology* (Carlisle, UK: Paternoster, 2008).

overwhelms nor remains outside of us.[60] "We are united to the Son of God by a bond so close, that we can find *in our nature* that holiness of which we are in want."[61] The Holy Spirit is critical here, as the one who mediates the human, crucified, ascended life of Jesus to us.

It is one of the ironies of theological history that the Osiander debate has come to be seen as the triumph of forensic imputation — over against participation. In response to this much-perpetuated misunderstanding, Todd Billings reveals that Calvin holds together (while distinguishing) pardon and indwelling as essential aspects of union with Christ and the *duplex gratia*.[62] Calvin's response to Osiander was not extrinsicism but *koinōnia*, a carefully articulated relationship between humans and the humanity of Christ, by the Spirit. Our righteousness is not "by imputation only, for in that respect he is said to have been 'made to us righteousness'; but he is likewise said to have been 'made to us sanctification' (1 Cor. 1:30), because he has, so to speak, presented us to his Father in his own person, that we may be renewed to true holiness by his Spirit."[63] In this wide world of *koinōnia*, imputation has a central place by being the direct result of *unio cum Christo*, a distinctly participative category. Hunsinger summarizes it this way: "For Osiander mystical union led to infusion; for Calvin, to imputation."[64]

Here, in Calvin's discussion of justification, the same rigorous boundaries are at work as in his doctrine of adoption. In both, the Holy Spirit al-

60. Osiander was never able to account for a humanly appropriate righteousness (either Christ's or ours) but only divine righteousness. Strehle explains that this is the result of the "qualitative distinction between God and man" that Osiander maintained throughout his works, expressed by the simple axiom *in Deum non cadit accidens* — God alone possesses his attributes and does not share them. In this stark dualistic scheme, there is no room for human participation in the divine qualities as human. Even Christ's human righteousness is discounted in this scheme (Strehle, "Imputatio," p. 210).

61. *Comm. Heb.* 2:11 (emphasis added). This is very much Bruce McCormack's understanding when he remarks that Christ's obedience goes beyond cleansing to "(more positively) the establishing of a divine-*human* righteousness" (Bruce McCormack, *For Us and Our Salvation: Incarnation and Atonement in the Reformed Tradition*, ed. David Willis-Watkins [Princeton: Princeton Theological Seminary, 1993], p. 23).

62. Billings's work does much to overthrow the perceived antithesis between forensic importation and participation in Calvin, for "importation is inextricably tied to union with Christ: believers come to 'possess' Christ and his righteousness." Billings, *Calvin, Participation, and the Gift: The Activity of Believers in Union with Christ* (New York: Oxford University Press, 2008), p. 15; see also pp. 57-61.

63. *Comm. John* 17:19.

64. Hunsinger, "Calvin's Doctrine of Justification," p. 16.

lows true participation in the very life of God — which is the *humanity of Christ* — while acting as a safeguard against substantial participation. This is not Platonic participation (dependent on continuity of being) but a participation that allows two different beings to share in the lives of each other, by the Spirit.

Anthropological Implications

What this demands is a new appreciation of Calvin's theological anthropology. At the very least, this debate reveals that ontology matters. Quite simply, the differing notions concerning participation of Calvin and Osiander are based on conflicting ontological commitments. To say that Calvin relies on the Holy Spirit as the mediating person for participation (rather than Osiander's univocity of being) does not indicate that one has ontological commitments while the other does not.[65] Rather, Calvin is forging what Jenson calls the new "Reformation ontology," which is well encapsulated in his theology of adoption.[66] This led him far beyond a Platonic doctrine of "participation in the divine realities" to one that had to factor in the personal nature of the triune members and transformational communion with them.

The ontology that allowed Calvin to develop his notion of Trinitarian participation — our adoption — also allowed him to steer clear of the opposing extremes of mechanistic imputation and fusion. For despite their opposing theologies, both Melanchthon and Osiander fell prey to an "ontology [that] is inconsistent with the gospel as understood by the Reformers."[67] This is where Calvin's commitment to Christ's ascent also reveals his ontological commitments; for he consistently used ascent to redirect our attention away from ourselves (even our salvation) and to Christ, "who is seated in the heavenly realms." It was less a spatial statement than it was one pertaining to theological anthropology. Calvin envisioned the lives of the elect as so engrafted into Christ that they could

---

65. Wilhelm Niesel is one who perpetuates a detrimental split between soteriology and ontology — as if to imply that salvation does not have profound ontological ramifications! He observes: "[The *unio mystica*] is not a doctrine of being (ontology) but a doctrine of salvation (soteriology)" (Niesel, "Union with Christ," in *Reformed Symbolics* [Edinburgh: Oliver & Boyd, 1962], p. 185).

66. Robert W. Jenson and Eric W. Gritsch, *Lutheranism: The Theological Movement and its Confessional Writings* (Philadelphia: Fortress, 1976), p. 65.

67. Jenson and Gritsch, *Lutheranism*, p. 65.

never again be considered independent of Christ, or he of them. Rather, it is the shared reality — having one's being-in-another — that now defines the church's existence.

> Yet more: we experience such participation in him that, although we are still foolish in ourselves, he is our wisdom before God; while we are sinners, he is our righteousness; while we are unclean, he is our purity; while we are weak, while we are unarmed and exposed to Satan, yet ours is that power which has been given him in heaven . . . ; while we still bear about with us the body of death, he is yet our life. (III.15.5)

While Osiander was preoccupied with whether the individual subject was really righteous, Calvin no longer looked to the bounds of the person to define truth about the person. This new "Reformation ontology" did not begin with the human being as a substance prior to all community, but it began with the truth of the person-in-Christ: the adopted child of God. The problem was not so much *what* Osiander was looking for, but *where*. Bruce Marshall helpfully calls this the "extrospective" rather than "introspective" glance.[68] But it is probably best encapsulated by Calvin's contemporary, Peter Martyr Vermigli: "It is possible to say that we are more perfectly in Christ than He is in us."[69] The extrospective glance does not leave us unchanged; rather, it changes where we look for evidence of our transformation. For Calvin, the locus (and evidence) of salvation is not in ourselves, but elsewhere. This explains why Calvin uses the metaphor of "engrafting" *(insero)* so frequently: it decenters the human and instead highlights the human-in-Christ. It elicits more of a participatory consciousness that is centered on the Other, which is key to Calvin's spiritual anthropology.[70]

What can it mean that those in the family of God "live" in another? Or as Calvin is so fond of saying, that we are "engrafted" into Christ — even into his righteousness, even into his sonship? A reevaluation of the

68. Bruce Marshall, "Justification as Declaration and Deification," *International Journal of Systematic Theology* 4 (2002): 16.

69. *Defensio* 752, quoted in Joseph C. McLelland, *The Visible Words of God* (Edinburgh: Oliver and Boyd, 1957), p. 148.

70. Despite the fact that he is hesitant to call this "participation," this is the point made so eloquently by John Webster, *Holiness* (Grand Rapids: Eerdmans, 2003), p. 83: "The Christian's sanctity is in Christ, in the Spirit, not *in se*; . . . it is a matter of the *externality* of the *sanctitas christiana*, the saint being and acting *in another*."

centrality of participation as the heart of Calvin's soteriology cannot help but affect our notion of the bounds of the self. Calvin makes it clear that Jesus' life is brought to bear on believers not so much in the modern style of cause and effect, but of being included in this life through participation. Calvin sets this down in one of the most lyrical passages of the *Institutes:*

> We are not our own: let not our reason nor our will, therefore, sway our plans and deeds. We are not our own: let us therefore not set it as our goal to seek what is expedient for us according to the flesh. We are not our own: in so far as we can, let us therefore forget ourselves and all that is ours.
>
> Conversely, we are God's: let us therefore live for him and die for him. We are God's: let his wisdom and will therefore rule all our actions. We are God's: let all the parts of our life accordingly strive toward him as our only lawful goal. . . . But the Christian philosophy bids reason give way to, submit and subject itself to, the Holy Spirit so that the man himself may no longer live but hear Christ living and reigning within him. (III.7.1)

This is not only a soteriological reality but also an anthropological one. Using marriage as an illustration, Calvin goes so far as to say that, as the husband and wife become one person, so we become as "one person" with Christ. "To use a common phrase, they shall constitute one person; which certainly would not hold true with regard to any other kind of relationship. . . . 'We are bone of his bone, and flesh of his flesh' (Gen 2:23); not because, like ourselves, he has a human nature, but because, by the power of his Spirit, he makes us a part of his body, so that from him we derive our life."[71] This is not the autonomous person whose powers have been actualized by the forgiveness and resurrection of Christ; instead, this is the birth of a new creation: the person-in-Christ. Adoption interweaves these strands beautifully, in that "sonship" is only derived from the Son. And as Calvin makes clear, this new anthropology is distinctly the realm and work of the Holy Spirit. For it is the "power of the Spirit, by which we are born again in Christ, and become new creatures."[72]

---

71. *Comm. Eph.* 5:30-31.
72. *Comm. John* 7:39.

Adoption and the Role of the Holy Spirit

It is curious that Calvin does not even mention the Holy Spirit in the title of Book III. This is a telling omission, because Book III describes the new environment in which Christians live, where the Spirit is not an aid to but the quality of this new *koinōnia* existence. Calvin does not mention the Spirit because the latter is not the objective focus but the constitutive reality of the Christian. He is the personal presence that constitutes the life of reconciliation, specifically in the shape of adoption. Calvin emphasizes this aspect in his reference to the Spirit, who is first the "spirit of adoption":

> First, he is called the "spirit of adoption" because he is the witness to us of the free benevolence of God with which God the Father has embraced us in his beloved only-begotten Son to become a Father to us; and he encourages us to have trust in prayer. In fact, he supplies the very words so that we may fearlessly cry, "Abba Father!" (III.1.3)

The Holy Spirit is the "place" where all this happens. Calvin insists over and over that his work is to bring us into an experience of fatherhood similar to what is enjoyed by the Son. Most to the point, Calvin underscores "'participation in the Spirit,' without which no one can taste either the fatherly favor of God or the beneficence of Christ" (III.1.2).

While we often find an emphasis on the Spirit's role to empower Christian living, Calvin moves his emphasis to the realm of identity: just as Jesus' relationship to the Father is constituted by the Spirit, so we are given the same Spirit who constitutes our new relationship with the triune God and hence our new identity. Butin summarizes Calvin: "In short, the bond of Christ's relationship with God the Father is identical to the bond of the believer's relationship with God the Son, because in both cases that bond is God the Holy Spirit."[73] Although making plenty of room for how the Spirit illuminates minds and empowers obedience, Calvin leans heavily on the Spirit's work as the one who confirms our being and only then our doing.[74] He is "first" called the Spirit of adoption in that he re-

---

73. Butin, *Revelation*, p. 83.

74. I. John Hesselink's rehabilitation of the Holy Spirit in Calvin is weakened by his emphasis on individual pietism. Calvin consistently sublimates isolated instances of "extraordinary leading of the Spirit" (*Comm. Matt.* 9:20) to the Spirit's primary work of help-

minds us over and over of the new relationship that is now an ontological reality. Calvin emphasizes this repeatedly: "[T]he Spirit testifies to us that we are children of God. . . ."[75] He "persuade[s] our hearts that we are children of God" (III.13.4).

> Paul declares that those very ones "who are led by the Spirit of God are the sons of God . . ." (Rom. 8:14). And these men would have it that those who are children of God are moved by their own spirit, but empty of God's Spirit. Paul teaches that God is called "Father" by us at the bidding of the Spirit, who alone can "witness to our spirit that we are children of God (Rom. 8:16)." (III.2.39)

As the one who continually reminds us of the new relationship that is reconstituting our very being, he cries out this relationship for us by putting in our mouths the very words that Jesus prayed. Praying "Abba," therefore, is more than a cry of distress and becomes a confirmation of the filial relationship into which we have been brought.[76] Calvin notes that "the Apostle intended shortly to show that the final end of our adoption is, that what has in order preceded in Christ, shall at length be completed in us."[77]

Adoption best captures the richness of Calvin's vision. "Adoption . . . is not the cause merely of a partial salvation, but bestows salvation entire."[78] Here Calvin rejects an understanding of salvation that only concerns itself with acquittal and guilt, instead underscoring salvation as inclusion into a family. The category of adoption reminds the church that its primary profession is to *be* sons and daughters, and that ethics — no different from the church's triune identity — also flows from this participation in God. Obedience takes on the cast of expressing our filial love for

---

ing the church to live into its filial identity. "[Incidents] like this must not be made into a common rule," says Calvin, for all God's children "are endowed with the Spirit of adoption" (*Comm. Acts* 14:9). See I. John Hesselink, "Governed and Guided by the Spirit," in *Reformiertes Erbe*, ed. Heiko Oberman (Zurich: Theologischer Verlag, 1993), p. 168.

75. *Comm. Rom.* 8:16.

76. "But because the narrowness of our hearts cannot comprehend God's boundless favor, not only is Christ the pledge and guarantee of our adoption, but he gives the Spirit as witness to us of the same adoption, through whom with free and full voice we may cry, 'Abba, Father'" (III.20.37).

77. *Comm. 1 John* 2:2.

78. Calvin, "True Method . . . ," *T&T* III.275.

the Father,[79] sanctification becomes living more deeply into this identity as children,[80] prayer is a right because he is Father,[81] and freedom rather than fear marks those who are "sons."[82] Even more than the breadth of categories it embraces, adoption gives them their proper orientation to communion. Salvation can never be a transaction in this scheme but becomes our inclusion into a form of God's own communion — our adoption. We know God's fatherhood when we participate in Jesus' relationship with him, as child and Father. Ferguson argues that Calvin "does not treat sonship as a separate *locus* of theology precisely because it is a concept which undergirds everything he writes."[83] As such, Ferguson is unique, but not at all misguided, in his desire to see "sonship as an organizing principle for understanding salvation" in Calvin.[84]

Spirit as "Bridge" vs. Agent of Participation

If this is indeed the scope of intention in Calvin's doctrine of adoption, then we must not only make note of its relative omission in the history of Reformed scholarship, but we must also ask why? Some claim that its neglect is due to the fact that the Reformers had their "hands too full";[85] others say it was because Luther's emphasis on justification began to usurp other distinctive Reformed doctrines;[86] still others, more helpfully, link it

79. "[S]uch children ought we to be, firmly trusting that our services will be approved by our most merciful Father, however small, rude, and imperfect these may be" (III.19.5).

80. "[T]he Spirit testifies to us that we are the children of God" (*Comm. Rom.* 8:16); "resembling their Heavenly Father in righteousness and holiness, they prove themselves sons true to their nature" (III.18.1).

81. "[W]e dare call upon him as Father, while he deigns to suggest this sweetest of names to us" (III.20.14).

82. *Institutes* III.19.2-5.

83. Sinclair B. Ferguson, "The Reformed Doctrine of Sonship," in *Pulpit and People,* ed. William Still, Nigel Cameron, and Sinclair Ferguson (Edinburgh: Rutherford House, 1986), p. 82.

84. Ferguson, "Sonship," p. 86.

85. Candlish, *Fatherhood of God* (Edinburgh, 1869), p. 192, quoted in Tim Trumper, "The Theological History of Adoption II: A Rationale," *Scottish Bulletin of Evangelical Theology* 20 (2002): 181.

86. George Hendry says: "There has sometimes been a tendency in Protestant thought, especially in the Lutheran church, to lean too heavily on the doctrine of justification. . . . For when God extends his grace to us in Jesus Christ, he not only releases us

to the rise of juridical categories (between the seventeenth and nineteenth centuries) and then to the vacuous notions of adoption that replaced them (in the nineteenth and twentieth centuries, primarily of the universal "fatherhood" of God and "brotherhood" of man).[87] Yet even in the present-day rehabilitations of adoption, there persists a predominantly "flat" notion of adoption that seldom attempts to link it to the triune communion. I would like to explore the possibility that such a narrowing can be traced to the existence in Calvin of two competing interpretations of the Spirit, mirrored in the larger tradition of the West, that alternately neglect or foster deep appreciation for adoption.

Historically, the West has struggled to personalize the Holy Spirit. Robert Jenson chronicles the depersonalization of the Spirit from the time of Augustine, through the medieval era (when the Spirit became "grace"), and into the Reformation, when attempts were made to *re*-personalize the third person of the Trinity.[88] Yet despite this radical return to Spirit-discourse, there persisted in the Reformers a difficulty in imagining how exactly the Spirit differed from the Father and Son. Often the Spirit came to be little more than a chronological extension of the Son's work, the means to the christological end set forth by the Father. Walter Kasper singles this out as one of the primary failings in the theological imagination of the West:

> The abstractly metaphysical mode of thought of Latin Trinitarian doctrine has led to failure to recognize the personal rôle and freedom of the Spirit in sacred history. Most theologians have ascribed the work of sanctification and indwelling of the Spirit to the Holy Spirit *only by appropriation;* only a few . . . have by dint of considerable intellectual efforts spoken of a personal indwelling (not just by appropriation) of the Spirit.[89]

---

from our guilt, he also receives us into his family" (Hendry, *The Westminster Confession for Today* [Richmond, VA: John Knox, 1960], p. 141, quoted in Trumper, "Theological History II," p. 182).

87. See Trumper, "Theological History I," pp. 17, 27.

88. Robert W. Jenson, "Pneumatological Soteriology," in *Christian Dogmatics II*, ed. Carl E. Braaten and Robert W. Jenson (Philadelphia: Fortress, 1984), pp. 125-42.

89. The quote continues: ". . . the Spirit in his bond with Christ, and in rendering present the person and work of Christ, does not enslave man under an alien law, but sets him free, does not put him in leading-strings by rigging him out with recipes and time-

Rowan Williams homes in on this ambiguity by showing that theologies of the Spirit have either presented the Spirit as crossing distance between God and creatures or, on the other hand, bringing the creature into participation in the triune life.[90] In the first picture, the Spirit "bridges" the things of God with the creature (often information or benefits); in the second, the Spirit *is* the life of God who acts "in and with" rather than just "on" the creature. These two pictures of the Spirit, prevalent in the West, are also distinct interpretive possibilities in Calvin.[91]

"In the twentieth-century," Eugene Rogers notes of these two interpretations of the Spirit, "Calvin scholars have nicely illustrated this divide."[92] Yet this should not be too surprising, as we have already noted how this very tension runs through Calvin himself. In chapter 2 above, we found that the Spirit's distinct role in creation is to bring the "deep" things of God to his creation, while simultaneously noting a tendency in the tradition to read a more "external" relationship of God to his creation. In chapter 3, we found that Christ's "true humanity" alternated between highlighting the Spirit's role (as the one who maintained his creaturely integrity and who constituted his experience of sonship) and sublimating the Spirit's role (where Christ's "flesh" usurps the territory of the Spirit). Even though Calvin sought to curb pneumatological reductionism, his theology still wavers between seeing the Spirit as the one who constitutes the experience of Christ and seeing the Spirit as the one superadded onto a completed picture of Christ — who received the Spirit "not so much for his own sake, as for the sake of others."[93] Between these alternatives, adoption has a clear home in the former (Spirit as "participatory reality") but is almost entirely lost when the latter (Spirit as the link, or "bridge," to God) is emphasized.

---

tables to consult, but releases him into the air of freedom. . . . His function is, therefore, not merely to render Jesus Christ present, but to make him present as filled by the Spirit" (Walter Kasper, *Jesus the Christ* [London: Burns & Oates, 1976], pp. 258-59).

90. Rowan Williams, "Word and Spirit," in *On Christian Theology* (Oxford: Blackwell, 2000), pp. 105-27.

91. These distinct possibilities overlap with Hunsinger's observation of Calvin's two options for salvation: what takes place in the perfect tense (receiving and participating in a completed process) or the present + perfect tense (supplementing and completing a process) (Hunsinger, "Dimension," p. 157).

92. Eugene Rogers, "The Mystery of the Spirit in Three Traditions: Calvin, Rahner, Florensky or, You *Keep* Wondering Where the Spirit Went," *Modern Theology* 19 (2003): 245.

93. *Comm. Matt.* 3:16.

Calvin struggled, somewhat successfully, to give the Spirit a genuine mission in the life of Christ; and we find this same struggle at play as he attempts to relate the Spirit to the life of the church. Calvin certainly does not deserve Bouyer's criticism that he "refused to recognize any light of the Holy Spirit within us other than as manifested in an understanding of the true meaning of the Scriptures."[94] Yet many of Calvin's most stalwart followers limit the Spirit to just that, revealing a reductionist tendency in interpretations of Calvin's pneumatology.[95] For where it goes unnoticed that the Spirit does not just point to the human Jesus' work but somehow has an essential part in his mission, it is easy to cast the Spirit's present role in similarly passive, bridging categories. Unfortunately, Calvin does not smooth the way when he gives Book III the title "The Way In Which We Receive the Grace of Christ: What Benefits Come To Us From It, and What Effects Follow." This phraseology can easily appear to subsume the Spirit *under* the person of Christ, as a linear, impersonal extension of his work and his benefits. Neither does Calvin's discussion of Christ's "merit" help things,[96] nor his emphasis on "imputation" when abstracted from his context of participation.[97] And this is where Calvin's language can be most ambiguous, inviting both notions of the Spirit as "bridge to" Christ's benefits and also of the Spirit as "participatory reality in" these benefits.

Even when Calvin does speak of the "benefits" in a dangerously abstract way, he consistently clarifies in other places that these are participatory realities, not objects:

> By these words he means that we receive the Spirit in order that we may enjoy Christ's blessings. For what does he bestow on us? That we may be washed by the blood of Christ, that sin may be blotted out in us by

94. Louis Bouyer, *A History of Christian Spirituality*, vol. III (London: Burns & Oates, 1969), p. 87.

95. Wilhelm Niesel, *The Theology of Calvin* (Grand Rapids: Baker, 1980), pp. 28-39.

96. See chapter 3 above.

97. Richard Gaffin observes that "a definite liability attaches to this expression. 'Alien' suggests what is remote, at a distance; it can easily leave the impression of an isolated imputative act, without a clear relationship to Christ and other aspects of salvation. . . . A different tone is heard in Calvin" (Gaffin, "Biblical Theology and the Westminster Standards," *Westminster Theological Journal* 65 [2003]: 178). Imputation, for all its once-for-all accents, can easily slight the Spirit's work as new eschatological fulfillment.

his death, that our old man may be crucified (Rom. 6:6), that his resurrection may be efficacious in forming us again to newness of life (Rom. 6:4); and, in short, that we may become partakers of his benefits.[98]

For the most part, Calvin keeps the "benefits" of Christ tightly bound to his person, so that only when we are brought to participate by the Spirit in the "being" of Christ do we then experience the "meaning" (benefits) of Christ. "Such is the determination of God — not to communicate himself, or his gifts to men, otherwise than by his Son."[99] Calvin pointedly clarifies that this goes above and beyond "imputation only" to a real sharing, signaling that we are to be brought to participate in him, not to appropriate him (or his benefits) for ourselves.[100]

In Reformed scholarship, there has been of late a rise in interest in *unio cum Christo* as part of a move toward recovering Calvin's original emphasis on communion and *koinōnia*. Yet even this apparently encouraging trend only underscores the pervasive flatness that lurks around interpretations of Calvin's pneumatology. William B. Evans's critique of nineteenth-century scholarship still applies: *unio cum Christo* is still "at best only a formal statement" and can still lead to radically differing interpretations within Reformed theology.[101] One temptation hidden within this new resurgence of "union" is that it can degenerate into a transaction of benefits between the believer and Christ. In this view, the finished work of Christ leaves no room for the Spirit except as the one who points to Jesus' work in his absence, or who acts as the bridge between the believer and Christ's available benefits. Thorough student of Calvin that he is, even François Wendel makes such an assumption:

> In a good many passages, indeed, the Holy Spirit plays the part of an obligatory mediator between Christ and man, just as the Christ is the mediator between God and man. And in the same way that Jesus Christ is the necessary instrument of redemption, so is the Holy Spirit the no

98. *Comm. John* 16:14.
99. *Comm. Col.* 1:19.
100. *Comm. John* 17:19. Calvin's Trinitarian emphasis kept his doctrine of the imputation of righteousness from degenerating into the abstraction that it became.
101. "There is no single 'Reformed doctrine of union with Christ,'" he writes. "In the context of nineteenth-century American Reformed theology, one must distinguish the 'federal union' of Hodge, the 'organic union' of Nevin, and the 'moral union' of New England" (Evans, "Imputation," p. 443).

less necessary instrument by means of which this redemption reaches us, in justification and regeneration.[102]

Wendel's observation highlights the image of the Spirit as the one who crosses the distance between God and creatures, bridging humanity with various "benefits." In calling the Spirit the "instrument by means" of which the things of Christ come to us, Wendel maintains a flat notion of Spirit rather than recognizing him as the one "through [whom] we come into communion with God" (I.13.14). This flattening trend is crystallized by Jae Sung Kim in a work entitled "*Unio Cum Christo:* The Work of the Holy Spirit in Calvin's Theology": Kim concludes that "the Spirit can cross the gap between God and man."[103]

From such restrictive interpretations, it is a short step to "union with Christ" as latent natural theology, where communal life with God is enclosed in a utilitarian process by which we receive the benefits of Christ. Ceasing to reflect God's *koinōnia*-reality, union becomes the response to a prior human need for the commodities of salvation. It is Dietrich Bonhoeffer who reminds us that Calvin's emphasis on the benefits of Christ can go one of two ways. He cites Melanchthon's famous maxim, *Christum cognoscere est beneficia eius cognoscere* ["to know Christ is to know his benefits"],[104] and notes that "theology has often apostatized here."[105] For whether or not Melanchthon's maxim already indicates the modern predisposition toward a functional christology, it certainly opens up the possibility for a split between the being and meaning of Christ.[106] The

102. Wendel, *Origins*, pp. 239-40.

103. Jae Sung Kim, "*Unio Cum Christo:* The Work of the Holy Spirit in Calvin's Theology" (Ph.D. diss., Westminster Theological Seminary, 1998), p. 144.

104. *Loci Communes*, 1521, *CR* 21.85. This tendency could also be read into Calvin: "By these words we are taught that then only do we know what Christ is, when we understand what the Father hath given to us in him, and what benefits he brings to us" (*Comm. John* 4:10).

105. Dietrich Bonhoeffer, *Christology* (London: Collins, 1966), p. 48.

106. Christoph Schwöbel comments: "The contrast between meaning and being is in this way understood as an expression of the relationship of the work and person of Christ, and it is claimed that the work of Christ, soteriology, is the only legitimate access to Christology whereas metaphysical reflection on his being, his person can only lead us to inadequate notions of God and salvation" (Schwöbel, "Christology and Trinitarian Thought," in *Trinitarian Theology Today*, ed. Christoph Schwöbel [Edinburgh: T. & T. Clark, 1995], p. 118).

danger here is that the *beneficia Christi* can be used to bolster a functional soteriology in which an anthropocentric obsession with the meaning and work of Christ is all that matters.[107] The Spirit is then incorporated into this transaction between God and humanity, as simply the one who is the bridge that links us *to* the things of Christ rather than as the one to bring us *into* Christ and the *koinōnia* that he has inaugurated in his person. And this, Bonhoeffer reminds us, "ends in a repudiation of any christology."[108]

What is at stake, I have been arguing, is a correct interpretation of Calvin's view of the Spirit, whose work must not be understood merely as the appropriation of the *beneficia Christi* but as their fulfillment within us. For when pneumatology slips from identity (in him) to appropriation of Christ's commodities (by him, through him), then the benefits of Christ become commodities to be possessed. It is a short step to adoption as a stage to be passed through,[109] or, worse, as a solely forensic declaration indicating that one's status has been changed. When it is discussed within this context, adoption — not surprisingly — becomes flattened into a legal transaction between two individuals, à la Griffith: "Adoption is forensic: it establishes the sinner with the status of son."[110] This notion of adoption is representative of that functional trend in christology that would use Christ for its own ends — to gain salvation, legal adoption, or the benefits of Christ.[111] Here the primary "benefit" of Christ — that is, adoption —

---

107. Rowan Williams reminds us that to know only Christ's benefits is to introduce "some human standard" by which to evaluate the work of Christ — an observation proved only too true by the variety of ways in which Christ's "obedience" has been interpreted (Williams, "Barth on the Triune God," in *Karl Barth: Studies of his Theological Method,* ed. S. W. Sykes [Oxford: Clarendon, 1979], p. 166).

108. Bonhoeffer, *Christology,* p. 48.

109. Although it is primarily the Westminster Confession that should be thanked for keeping adoption as a live Reformed category, it confines adoption to chronology: justification, then adoption, then sanctification. The resulting impression is not that of an entrance into a new, triune form of communion, nor indeed membership in a family, but of individuals passing through various stages in their Christian life.

110. Howard Griffith, "'The First Title of the Spirit': Adoption in Calvin's Soteriology," *Evangelical Quarterly* 73, no. 2 (2001): 147. Griffith's quote may be helpful toward understanding the "for us" aspect of adoption, but it drops the "in us" entirely out of the picture. Of course, we cannot merit our adoption, but does this automatically make it forensic?

111. Only when humans cease to use Christ for their own ends — even salvation — can they properly fulfill their creation purposes of the glorification of God. "It is not very

has been radically severed from Christ's own person as Son and has been used by humanity to achieve a goal beyond him. Christ is thus made an instrument of a process rather than the person in whom adoption is found. Correspondingly, the benefits of Christ often become detachable from the person of Christ, to be transferred to us by the Spirit without fundamentally bringing us into the Spirit's new domain. This is the unmistakable tone of the recent article in which the author asks, "Is There a Reformed Way to get the Benefits of the Atonement to 'Those Who Have Never Heard'?"[112]

Calvin himself exposes this contemporary tendency toward a functional Christology when he observes that "they sought in Christ something else than Christ himself."[113] Ganoczy echoes this, showing that Calvin's christology is fundamentally rooted in pneumatology: "This does not mean that the Spirit functions as the one who enables us to taste the benefits of Christ; that is, in a quasi-instrumental manner. Rather, the third person of the Trinity brings the being of God into the heart of the human person."[114] On at least three occasions Calvin rejects prepositions that would make Christ merely instrumental for our salvation and instead proposes what can only be seen as a pneumatological solution: the Spirit's work to bring the church to live *in* Christ:

From his *Commentary* on Romans:
But I prefer to retain the words of Paul, *in Christ Jesus,* rather than to translate with Erasmus, [*alive to God*] *through Christ Jesus;* for thus the grafting, which makes us one with Christ, is better expressed (6:11).

---

sound theology to confine a man's thoughts so much to himself, and not to set before him, as the prime motive of his existence, zeal to illustrate the glory of God. For we are born first of all for God, and not for ourselves. As all things flowed from Him, and subsist in Him, so, says Paul (Rom. 11:36) they ought to be referred to Him" (Calvin, *A Reformation Debate: Sadoleto's Letter to the Genevans and Calvin's Reply,* ed. John C. Olin [New York: Harper & Row, 1966], p. 58).

112. R. Todd Mangum, "Is There a Reformed Way to Get the Benefits of the Atonement to 'Those Who Have Never Heard'?" *Journal of the Evangelical Theological Society* 47 (2004): 121-36.

113. *Comm. John* 6:26. I thank George Hunsinger for directing me to this reference.

114. Alexandre Ganoczy, "Observations on Calvin's Trinitarian Doctrine of Grace," in *Probing the Reformed Tradition,* ed. Elsie Anne McKee and Brian G. Armstrong (Louisville: Westminster John Knox, 1989), p. 99.

From his *Commentary* on 1 Corinthians:

The phrase *in ipso (in him)* I have preferred to retain, rather than render it *per ipsum (by him)*, because it has in my opinion more expressiveness and force. For we are *enriched in Christ,* inasmuch as we are members of his body, and are engrafted into him: nay more, being made one with him, he makes us share with him in everything that he has received from the Father (1:4).

From his *Commentary* on 2 Corinthians:

It is in the same manner, assuredly, that we are now *righteous in him* — not in respect of our rendering satisfaction to the justice of God by our own works, but because we are judged of in connection with Christ's righteousness, which we have put on by faith, that it might become ours. On this account I have preferred to retain the particle ἐν ("in"), rather than substitute in its place *per* ("through"), for that signification corresponds better with Paul's intention (5:21).

Clearly, Calvin is pushing for a profound participation of the church-in-Christ that is the realm of the Spirit. He refuses the notion that *by* or *through* Christ our reality has been altered; rather, our reality is only altered as we dwell *in* him — by the Spirit. Butin's sensitivity to Calvin surfaces here, as he argues that "for Calvin, pneumatology and Christology are two sides of the same coin."[115] From this it becomes clear that the only way to remedy a functional christology is a full rendering of a participatory pneumatology.

This alternative is found in Calvin's "deep" version of adoption, where the Spirit's role is to remind the church of its identity, continuing to bring it out of itself to live a life of love and communion with God. The Spirit continues the work of Christ, but only in such a way that his "work" is construed as sonship, freeing the elect to cry, "Abba." Of this model, Rowan Williams notes: "The Spirit's witness is not a pointing to the Son outside the human world, it is precisely the formation of 'Son-like' life in the human world; it is the continuing state of sharing in the mutuality of Father and Son; it is forgiven or justified life . . . if the Spirit interprets anything, it is neither Father nor Word, but . . . the relation of Father and Son; and he interprets it by re-creating, translating it, in the medium of

---

115. Philip W. Butin, "Two Early Reformed Catechisms, the Threefold Office, and the Shape of Karl Barth's Christology," *Scottish Journal of Theology* 44 (1991): 210.

human existence."[116] Thus the Spirit does not appropriate the benefits of Christ *for* the elect; rather, he fulfills them *in* the elect. He does not point to Jesus' work in his absence, but "through him we come into communion [*sic per ipsum in Dei participationem venimus*] with God" (I.13.14). The full notion of adoption flourishes in this context, for it is "participation in the Spirit," without which no one can taste either the fatherly favor of God or the beneficence of Christ" (III.1.2).

The Eucharistic Ascent

"That is why the sacraments are compared to the steps of a ladder. . . ."

Nowhere is Calvin's emphasis on ascent more celebrated than in his theology of the Lord's Supper. And that for good reason: the Reformed faith began as a unique eucharistic approach. It is ascent that set apart the Reformed tradition from the very beginning.[117] Now we shall see how Calvin displaces the eucharistic debates from a wrangle over substance to one defining the true nature of participation. Once again, Calvin gives a clear place for substance only by transposing it into the realm of the Spirit. Whether this erodes substance or actually grounds it is a question that I hope to answer.

Ascent is Calvin's antidote to eucharistic idolatry. The sacraments are "steps of a ladder" that lead us up to the whole Christ, rather than fixating our eyes on "different parts" of him, adoring him "in this place and that."[118] The problem with medieval sacramentalism, in Calvin's opinion, is that it reversed the direction of the ladder.

We must note that when God declares himself to us, we must not cling to any earthly thing, but must elevate our senses above the world and

116. Williams, *On Christian Theology*, p. 120.

117. For background on the eucharistic controversies of the sixteenth century, see the many essays by Brian Gerrish and Joseph Tylenda, and the more general one by William Cavanaugh, "Eucharistic Sacrifice and the Social Imagination in Early Modern Europe," *Journal of Medieval and Early Modern Studies* 31 (2001): 585-605. I regret that Wim Janse's research had not yet been published at the time of the submission of this book and thus has not been assimilated into this chapter.

118. *Comm 1 Cor.* 11:24.

lift ourselves up by faith to his eternal glory. In sum, God comes down to us so that then we might go up to him. That is why the sacraments are compared to the steps of a ladder.[119]

It is God's prerogative to come down; we must go up. "He descends to them, therefore, not to occupy their minds with a gross superstition, but to raise them up by degrees to spiritual worship."[120] Calvin sees the sacraments as part and parcel of this primary move of grace, in which God's movement toward us enables our communion, or ascent, to him. "By them he stretches out his hand to us, because, without assistance, we cannot ascend to him."[121] When this primary downward movement is ignored, an idolatrous one usurps it, "pull[ing God] down from his throne; for his Majesty must be brought into subjection to us, if we would have him to be regulated according to our fancy."[122]

But Christ's Ascension — so critical for Calvin's eucharistic doctrine — was not simply an antidote to idolatry. Neither did it mark Calvin's cumulative endorsement of Chalcedon. Rather, it functioned to reconfigure human reality in terms of God's reality, cementing human participation in the divine. If a human life has been brought "up" into God without change or confusion, and our "partaking" of his very humanity is raising us up into God's triune *koinōnia*, then we see just how essential the Eucharist is as a confirmation of Calvin's doctrine of participation.

Sacraments, Spirit, and Participation

Although many assume that Chalcedon was the motivating force behind Calvin's doctrine of the Lord's Supper, it is more appropriate to see it as providing the boundaries for Calvin's primary intention: the Eucharist as proof of a *koinōnia* held out to humanity now, without change or confusion. Similarly, Calvin's doctrine of the Spirit — so essential for this participation — is often cheapened as Calvin's antidote to ubiquitous notions of the ascended Christ. Instead, and more positively, much of Calvin's eucharistic theology turns on his prior realization that a truly human par-

---

119. *Serm. 2 Sam.* 6:1-7.
120. *Comm. Exod.* 16:36.
121. *Comm. Gen.* 2:9; see also *Comm. Ps.* 84:3.
122. *Comm. Ps.* 78:41.

ticipation in God must happen in a truly human way.[123] It is not so much the enemy of ubiquity per se, or the Chalcedonian boundary that forced Calvin's hand, but the risk to the "concrete humanity of Jesus, including his bodily specificity and self-identity, which he retains for the sake of priestly ministry to his church and as a divine affirmation that finite creaturely being can be the recipient of eternal life."[124] The fundamental fact of Christ's continuing embodiment bodes well for similarly embodied creatures, who are brought into his perfection of creaturely reality and temporality.[125] The Lord's Supper, far from merely acting as a defensive doctrine against other eucharistic mishaps, is Calvin's doctrine of participation worked out to its furthest end.

As early as the 1536 *Institutes*, Calvin intuits that the Lord's Supper is not so much a debate about the nature of the "real presence" as it is about the "rules" for participation in Christ:

> If this force of the sacrament had been examined and weighed as it deserved, there would have been quite enough to satisfy us, and these frightful contentions would not have arisen which of old, and even within our memory, have miserably troubled the church, when men in their curiosity endeavored to define how Christ's body is present in the bread. . . . But those who feel thus, do not pay attention, in the first place, to the necessity of asking how Christ's body, as it was given for us, became ours; how his blood, as it was shed for us, became ours. But that means to possess the whole Christ crucified, and to become a participant in all his benefits. Now, overlooking these highly important matters, in fact neglecting and well-nigh burying them, our opponents fight over this one thorny question: How is the body devoured by us?[126]

---

123. This builds on Niesel's interpretation of Calvin's Chalcedonian christology. But I am attempting to show that it was a guiding principle for Calvin, rather than the goal of his theology. It gave boundaries to his robust doctrine of participation.

124. Douglas Farrow, "Between the Rock and a Hard Place: In Support of (something like) a Reformed View of the Eucharist," *International Journal of Systematic Theology* 3 (2001): 178.

125. We do well to remember that, for Calvin, communion controls the direction of our participation: the Spirit brings us up to where Christ is. Calvin is against anything that would attempt to bring Jesus down to us ("breaking him into pieces," III.11.6, 16.1) or multiply his body ("this is to lacerate the body") rather than bringing us up into God and his *koinōnia* life (Calvin, "True Partaking . . . ," *T&T* II.515).

126. 1536 *Institutes* IV.27.

Calvin puts this into practice in his 1549 *Consensus Tigurinus,* where he begins not with a word about the sacraments but with Jesus Christ and the nature of our participation in him.[127] He moves from the (I) goal of the church being to lead us to Christ; through to (II) Christ as the interpretive center of the sacraments; to (III and IV) the nature of Christ's human life lived for our participation; and finally, to (V) our union and participation in him. What these examples move us toward is a realization that what frames Calvin's discussion of the Eucharist is his doctrine of our participation in God, specifically in Christ's humanity. "In the same way are we to judge concerning participation. . . . Indeed, if the power of the mystery as it is taught by us, and was known to the ancient church, had been esteemed as it deserves for the past four hundred years, it was more than enough to satisfy us" (IV.17.33).

Any complete exposition of Calvin's eucharistic theology would point out that the sacraments assure one of a true participation in Christ, but are not the only means of participation. Their participation "participates," shall we say, in the larger participation of the church in Christ, contributing to a larger reality without controlling or creating it. Calvin consistently sticks to his proper order of interpretation: from the *reality* of participation ("[n]ow that sacred partaking of flesh and blood . . . Christ pours his life into us") to the *means* of it ("the Supper"); the means of participation never creates the reality (IV.17.10).[128] In chapter 3, we saw how Christ's flesh signified his entire life lived on our behalf, for our participation. This is the primary "partaking of his flesh and blood" from which the eucharistic celebration takes its meaning — "but rather it is on this condition that we are sharers of His body and His blood."[129] Christ's de-

127. The full text of the *Consensio mutua in re sacramentaria ministrorum Tigurinae ecclesiae . . .* can be found in *CO* 7.735-44; the English translation is found in *T&T* II.212-20.

128. "[F]or the analogy of the sign applies only if souls find their nourishment in Christ — which cannot happen unless Christ truly grows into one with us, and refreshes us by the eating of his flesh and the drinking of his blood" (IV.17.10). "[I]n [this Sacrament] they have a witness of our growth into one body with Christ such that whatever is his may be called ours . . ." (IV.17.2).

129. "This is also why the holy table is made ready for us, so that we may know that our Lord Jesus, having descended here below and having emptied Himself of everything, was not, however, separated from us when He ascended into His glory in heaven. But rather it is on this condition that we are sharers of His body and His blood" (*Serm. Luke* 2:1-14, *CO* 46.966).

scent (his participation in our situation) is the condition for our ascent, defined in this passage as our participation in the "holy table."

The Ascension of Jesus signaled clearly to Calvin that the eucharistic question had to involve both substance and the Spirit. For this reason, the bread and wine must be allowed to maintain their creaturely character as meal, as testimony not only to the incarnation but also to the integrity of human nature in general. And yet, as testimony to the work of the Spirit, these very elemental things are taken up, transfigured, brought nearer to their intended end by their very participation in the triune *koinōnia*.[130] It is the Spirit whose ministry has always been to bring the things of God and the created order together in full participatory relationship, not by acting as a bridge but by reconfiguring (and indeed restoring) creation in terms of God's communion.

> But, in order that we may be capable of this participation, we must rise heavenward. . . . It seems incredible, that we should be nourished by Christ's flesh, which is at so great a distance from us. Let us bear in mind, that it is a secret and wonderful work of the Holy Spirit, which it were criminal to measure by the standard of our understanding. . . . Allow [Jesus] to remain in his heavenly glory, and aspire thou thither, that he may thence communicate himself to thee.[131]

This is the eschatological dimension of the Lord's Supper, which continues to bring us from the old creation into the new. The Spirit brings us into God's reality, not him into ours. As Douglas Farrow says, "It is *we* who require eucharistic relocation."[132] Forgoing the usual complaints about the spatial nature of this scheme, Calvin's point is that God controls our eucharistic participation, and that the nature of this participation is *koinōnia*. The Lord's Supper thus becomes a transforming event for creaturely reality — ours, not Jesus' — for to be brought into *koinōnia* with the triune God is an ontologically shattering event.

The risen Lord is the promise of, and the only path toward, our participation in God while the Spirit is the element of differentiation.

---

130. For more on this, see Jeremy Begbie, "Repetition and Eucharist," in *Theology, Music, and Time* (Cambridge: Cambridge University Press, 2000), p. 171.

131. *Comm. 1 Cor.* 11:24.

132. Douglas Farrow, *Ascension and Ecclesia* (Grand Rapids: Eerdmans, 1999), p. 177.

I frankly confess that I reject their teaching of the mixture, or transfusion, of Christ's flesh with our soul (IV.17.32). . . . In the same way we are to judge concerning participation, which they do not recognize unless they swallow Christ's flesh under the bread. Yet a serious wrong is done to the Holy Spirit, unless we believe that it is through his incomprehensible power that we come to partake of Christ's flesh and blood. (IV.17.33)

The Spirit is the one who allows two differing qualities to participate in one another, in what George Hunsinger calls "*koinōnia*-relations."[133] This is what Calvin feels is the crux of his insight against Osiander (III.11.10), Heshusius,[134] and Westphal.[135] "For as to his communicating himself to us, *that* is effected through the secret virtue of his Holy Spirit, which can not merely bring together, but join in one, things that are separated by distance of place, and far remote."[136]

Sign and Symbols

For this pneumatological reason, Calvin can argue that the sacraments actually communicate *and* cause what they signify: "It would be extreme madness to recognize no communion of believers with the flesh and blood of the Lord" (IV.17.9). Calvin gives the sacraments the dual function of testifying to that reality while also being the "means of participation" in it. "Now that sacred partaking of his flesh and blood, by which Christ pours his life into us, as if it penetrated into our bones and marrow, he also testifies and seals in the Supper — not by presenting a vain and empty sign, but by manifesting there the effectiveness of the Spirit to fulfill what he promises" (IV.17.10). Just as the sermon is an "apocalyptic event" in that it brings the congregation into the presence of the Word,[137] so the Lord's

133. See George Hunsinger, "Baptism and the Soteriology of Forgiveness," *International Journal of Systematic Theology* 2 (2000): 248.

134. "[H]ow will [Heshusius] escape the charge of having thus blundered? For if there is any eating which is not spiritual, it will follow that in the ordinance of the Supper there is no operation of the Spirit" (Calvin, "True Partaking," *T&T* II.520).

135. "If no operation of the Spirit were here interposed, Westphal might justly boast that he is victor . . ." (Calvin, "Last Admonition . . . ," *T&T* II.387).

136. *Comm. 1 Cor.* 11:24.

137. Heiko Oberman, "Reformation, Preaching, and *Ex Opere Operato*," in *Christian-*

Supper takes its effectiveness from the *koinōnia* of Christ, not the abstracted "benefits" of Christ.[138] This is because the Spirit does not bring us information but rather brings us into the new eschatological reality of Christ.

Where Calvin's emphasis on participation begins to become obscured is when he rather uncritically brings in the Augustinian language of the "inward" and "outward,"[139] the "invisible" and "visible,"[140] and the "internal" and "external."[141]

> Let them hear Augustine, whom they pretend to regard as a saint. "Visible sacraments were instituted for the sake of carnal men, that by the ladder of sacraments they may be conveyed from those things which are seen by the eye, to those which are perceived by the understanding." (IV.19.15)[142]

By using Augustine's strong bifurcation between "spiritual" and "visible" reality (what is the invisible beneath this visible sacrament? what is the promise beneath this outward sign?), Calvin tries to redirect the church from idolatrous grasping to *koinōnia* with God. But in casting out one demon, Calvin invites seven others. Heron puts his finger precisely on the "fundamental problem to be faced by any approach to the Eucharist via the category of 'sign': there is always the danger that the two sides thus correlated, the physical and spiritual, visible and invisible, may appear to fall apart — or, what is little better, to be held together only in a quite arbitrary fashion."[143]

---

ity Divided, ed. Daniel Callahan (New York: Sheed & Ward, 1961), p. 225. I might also mention that Calvin's view of receiving the Word in preaching is a true participation, just as is the Lord's Supper. That is the basis for his definition of the church: as any place where the Word is preached and the sacrament administered.

138. *Comm. 1 Cor.* 1:24. Indeed, this is the central rediscovery of the Reformation, that Christ's person and work are inseparable.

139. "[H]e inwardly fulfills what he outwardly designates" (IV.17.5).

140. "[A] visible sign is given us to seal the gift of a thing invisible" (IV.17.10).

141. The title of Book IV begins: "The External Means . . ."

142. Beveridge translation. Calvin is quoting Augustine's *On Diverse Questions* 43: "Sacramenta (inquit) propter carnales, visibilia instituta sunt: ut ab iis quae oculis cernuntur ad ea quae intelliguntur, Sacramentorum gradibus transferantur" (Migne, *Patrologiae — Latina* 40.28).

143. Alasdair Heron, *Table and Tradition* (Edinburgh: Handsel Press, 1983), p. 73. T. F. Torrance also notes this potential for interpreting the relationship between sign

It is only Calvin's strong pneumatology that is a possible solution against arbitrariness.

Despite the threat of dualism inherent in his vocabulary, Calvin attempts to hold them together in the unified world of the Spirit, who does not lead us "up and away" to the things of God, but is himself *their condition.* "We are truly made partakers of the proper substance of the body and blood of Jesus Christ . . . [which] is made effectual by the secret and miraculous power of God, and that the Spirit of God is the bond of participation, this being the reason why it is called spiritual."[144] Calvin devises no ephemeralized, docetized Christ but a true feeding on his "substance," which is made possible when we are raised "heavenward" in the dimension of the Spirit. "But with this partaking of the body, which we have declared, we feed faith just as sumptuously and elegantly as those who draw Christ himself away from heaven" (IV.17.32). But this happens only under certain circumstances:

If we refuse not to raise our hearts upwards, we shall feed on Christ entire, as well as expressly on his flesh and blood. And indeed when Christ invites us to eat his body, and to drink his blood, there is no necessity to bring him down from heaven, or require his actual presence in several places, in order to put his body and his blood within our lips. Amply sufficient for this purpose is the sacred bond of union with him, when we are united into one body by the secret agency of the Spirit.[145]

In all of these passages, participation in the Spirit is what gives significance and substance to the sign. Despite his reliance on Augustine, Calvin's pneumatology enabled him to avoid most of the Neo-Platonist dangers that colored Augustine's own sacramental theology.[146] For when

---

and signified through the light of Platonic dualism. See T. F. Torrance, *Theology in Reconciliation* (Grand Rapids: Eerdmans, 1975), p. 129.

144. Calvin, "Short Treatise . . . ," *T&T* II.197, §60.

145. Calvin, "True Partaking . . . ," *T&T* II.516.

146. When one overlooks Calvin's pneumatologically and christologically structured doctrine of participation, it is all too easy to accuse him of mere Platonic dualism, as does Kilian McDonnell: "Calvin's use of the theme of the two worlds is so extensive that it amounts to a borrowing of a structure. . . . Plato's concept of participation is to be seen with even greater clarity in Calvin's doctrine of the sacraments. The sacraments are outward signs of that invisible good will which God has toward us. They give invisible truths

Calvin is working in categories of participation, flesh does not war with spirit, nor visible with invisible, nor sign with signified. A "bridge" notion of the Spirit, however, would prove deadly to this robust pneumatological dynamic — one that Calvin seems to invite by his notion of the sacraments as "ladder to God."

The Temptations of Ascent

The ambiguity hidden in Calvin's image of the ladder (and, for that matter, in his entire vocabulary of ascent) is that a ladder leads one to another place. What is not clear from Calvin's language is whether the physical truly participates in the spiritual, or whether the physical leads one away from itself and up to the spiritual. Three eucharistic temptations result from such imagery: symbolism, inwardness, and altruism.

Concerning the first temptation, the visible church and its sacraments can be rendered superfluous when compared to their "higher spiritual meaning," with the Spirit acting as bridge between these mutually exclusive spheres.[147] Calvin here walks a very fine line between separating and altogether rupturing their connection, making him all too susceptible to a symbolism that he vigorously denied. Hunsinger too notes how Calvin "failed to see clearly at the same time that in and with the bread and the cup Christ is really present to the church, through the very same Spirit, in the vicarious humanity of his body and blood."[148]

This leads to the second temptation, pinpointed by Bucer in 1549, that a primary focus on Christ's location *in heaven* could not only invalidate things here below, but could lead to an individualized ascent of the soul.[149]

---

to man under a visible sign" (McDonnell, *John Calvin, the Church, and the Eucharist* [Princeton: Princeton University Press, 1967], pp. 34-35).

147. We have already seen (in chap. 3 above) this tendency in his treatment of Christ's flesh, which at times participates in the Spirit to give us life, and other times is a channel, bringing the things of divinity "from another quarter" (*Comm. John* 6:51). Even the title of Book IV borders on this dualism: "The External Means or Aims by Which God Invites Us Into the Society of Christ and Holds Us Therein."

148. Hunsinger, "Dimension," p. 175.

149. Although Bucer saw eye to eye with Calvin on the *Consensus Tigurinus* (1549), he questioned the necessity of the "upward glance" as its foundation. "Let them not make a new article of faith concerning the certain place of heaven in which the body of Christ is contained" (Bucer's *Letter to Calvin*, 14 August 1549, *CO* 3.352).

As a result, it has been difficult for some to interpret Calvin's substantial union as little more than a "cognitive plus" or "mere psychological process."[150] As Douglas Farrow observes, "This helps to explain why the marks of inwardness are everywhere present in Calvin's sacramental writings, belying (if that is not too strong a word) the 'true partaking' he nonetheless believed and preached. It helps to explain why some find it easy to reduce his eucharistic teaching to the *sursum corda*, that is, to the invitation to 'feed on Him in your hearts by faith and with thanksgiving,' as the prayer book has it."[151] For although this primary focus on Christ's location in heaven invited radical reflection on the Spirit, Farrow accuses Calvin of being "not radical *enough*" in working out the full implications of the Ascension.[152]

Only when Calvin's eucharistic ascent is kept in check by his other pneumatological leaning — the doctrine of the Spirit as participative reality — is there possibility for the visible church truly to be the sine qua non of salvation. Otherwise, the eucharistic mystery involves only the individual and his or her inward feelings of piety. Heron, too, sees this as a failure, as well as latent potential, in Calvin's doctrine of the Spirit.

> It may well be that this weakness is bound up with a common tendency to ignore or underplay the place and role of the Holy Spirit, and to reduce him to a merely historical influence or inward power flowering from Christ through the church and through history. It is the Spirit as the "third moment" in the life of God who is supremely involved in the eschatological outworking of God's reconciling and redemptive act in Jesus Christ. . . . Here Calvin's stress upon the role of the Spirit in the Eucharist is of capital significance, though Calvin himself did not pursue it so far as we may need to do today.[153]

It seems as though Calvin was able to articulate a robust doctrine of participation that is oriented *upward*, but his mistrust of the physical realm

---

150. Bouyer, *History*, p. 91.

151. Farrow, *Ascension and Ecclesia*, p. 179.

152. "Calvin handled the dialectic of presence and absence almost exclusively in spatial terms, and to that extent in a *non*-eschatological fashion" (Farrow, "Between," p. 181).

153. Heron, *Table and Tradition*, p. 154. See also T. F. Torrance, "The Paschal Mystery of Christ and the Eucharist," in *Theology in Reconciliation* (Grand Rapids: Eerdmans, 1975), pp. 106-38.

left him tongue-tied over its *downward* implications for the material realm (whether in the form of the sacraments, the church, or elements of our humanity).[154] "For we must remember that our Lord descends to us, not to indulge our body, or keep our senses fixed on the world, but rather to draw us to himself, and hence the preamble of the ancient Church, Hearts upward, as Chrysostom interprets."[155] The irony is that Calvin's emphasis on Jesus' bodily absence — the very thing intended to ensure our creatureliness — suggests a flight from the physical realm altogether.

The third temptation posed by the "ladder" is Calvin's celebration of the divine gift, to the oft-perceived exclusion of human participation in it. "There is as much difference between this sacrifice [in the mass] and the sacrament of the Supper as there is between giving and receiving" (IV.18.7). The strength of this outlook is obvious: Calvin securely protects the gratuity of Christ's gift in that we do not manhandle him and feed on him, but rather offer ourselves *to him* "to be fed with such food" (IV.17.32). Yet "receiving" the Lord's Supper does not necessarily lead to passivity, as many have assumed, but can itself be a form of participation. Todd Billings argues, in response to the accusations of certain Radical Orthodox theologians, that "receiving" for Calvin is not passivity but the proper order of things: first, Christ offers his life and vicarious humanity to us. Then, with him as our priest, we can offer ourselves back to the Father (II.15.6).[156] Thus Calvin's Supper is not a propitiatory sacrifice but a "sacrifice of gratitude" (IV.18.13) that is inseparably connected with love, equity, justice, and "all the duties of love" (IV.18.16).[157] But while Calvin's emphasis on "receiving" does not eliminate our participation, it is — as William Cavanaugh warns — "in danger of becoming mere altruism."[158] This insight is well-grounded, particularly if our "sacrifice of gratitude" is construed as our response to Christ rather than our place with Christ in his self-offering to the Father. When this occurs, our

154. In other places Calvin will speak of Christ's descent "by the Spirit" by which "he himself lives in us," using near-paradoxical qualifications. See Ronald S. Wallace, *Calvin's Doctrine of the Word and Sacrament* (Edinburgh: Scottish Academic Press, 1995), p. 208.

155. Calvin, "Last Admonition . . . ," *T&T* II.443; see also *Serm. 2 Sam.* 6:1-7.

156. For more, see T. F. Torrance, "Legal and Evangelical Priests," in *Calvin's Books*, ed. W. H. Neuser (Heerenveen, Netherlands: Groen, 1997), pp. 73-74; Gerrish, *Grace*, pp. 152-56; and Wallace, *Word and Sacrament*, pp. 214-16.

157. Todd Billings, *Calvin, Participation, and the Gift* (New York: Oxford University Press, 2008), chap. 4.

158. Cavanaugh, "Eucharistic," p. 598.

self-sacrifice is in danger of no longer participating in Christ's self-gift but imitating it.

Calvin's great strength lay in his rich and consistent emphasis on the necessity of human participation in Christ. His weakness lay in his inability (or polemical reticence?) to reflect on the fittingness of the material realm for just such a relation. This reticence resulted in a suspicion of material things as unable to bear the weight of spiritual reality. That the Spirit does not lead us "up and away" to God but creates in material things God's divine reality is something from which Calvin tends to shy away.

This is illustrated in Calvin's pragmatic and conflicting instructions to churches regarding the Lord's Supper. Calvin adamantly endorses the physicality of the Lord's Supper, instituted as it was by God "as our weakness requires" and for our edification.[159] In Calvin's logic, physical people need physical assurance. In fact, "the practice of all well ordered churches should be to celebrate the Supper frequently" (especially given that mass was usually received once yearly [IV.16.44]).[160] Yet what Calvin gives with his right hand he takes away with his left: "Since the infirmity of the people is still such that there is danger that this holy and excellent mystery might be brought into contempt if it were celebrated too often . . . it has seemed good to us that the Holy Supper should be celebrated once a month."[161] Quite the contrary to his above reasoning, the weakness of human physicality does not require physical things but justifies a very limited use of them. Four years after this ordinance, Wallace notes that Calvin "further gave in to the weakness of human nature" by agreeing to a celebration pared down to only four times a year![162] In neither scenario is the Lord's Supper a physical tribute to the goodness of the physical world and the Spirit's role of creating communion in the world but acts as either condescension to, or even a temptation toward, the flesh.

159. Specifically, "visible signs" are needed as our weakness requires (Calvin, "Short Treatise . . . ," *T&T* II.171, §15).

160. Calvin, "Short Treatise . . . ," *T&T* II.179, §29.

161. In the "Articles concernant l'organisation de l'église," 1537 (*CO* 10a.7).

162. From "Les Ordonnances ecclésiastiques," 1541 (*CO* 10a.25). Both of these citations are discussed in Wallace, *Word and Sacrament*, p. 253. It is interesting to note that the Anabaptists applied this same reasoning ("infirmity of the people . . . this excellent mystery might be brought into contempt") to prohibit infant baptism.

*   *   *

At its low point, and especially when interpreted through the lens of a flat pneumatology, Calvin's doctrine of the Lord's Supper leads us "up" to a spiritual reality that is extrinsic to the material realm. At its height, Calvin's eucharistic theology is no different from that anthropology for which I have been arguing: communion in the Lord's Supper is not a human activity but the Spirit's means of grounding and reconstituting our very being. As such, the Eucharist is an extension of that all-radical, all-transforming communion we share, by invitation, with the Trinity. For communion with the risen Jesus can never be anything but material and mediated by creaturely things.

Chapter Five

The Ascending Vision of Irenaeus

Irenaeus' four untidy problems (image and likeness, sin and fall, breath and spirit, flesh and spirit) show that human life depends on participation in God. . . . Participation defines Irenaeus' account of the life which will grow to all eternity. . . . Salvation presupposes creation and ends in participation.[1]

For the gnostics, there is no "participation" but only a unique spirit-nature. The gnostic conception of "natures" excludes the economy of grace: there is neither gift nor participation. For Irenaeus, on the other hand, there is a communion (κοινωνία) between Spirit and flesh.[2]

At this point, my in-depth analysis of Calvin opens outward to dialogue with an early church father. Known for his influential development of *koinōnia*, Irenaeus is a key figure who is considered the fountainhead of both Roman Catholic and Eastern Orthodox traditions. Despite their differences, christology for Irenaeus *and* Calvin serves this theological an-

---

1. Eric Osborn, *Irenaeus of Lyons* (Cambridge, UK: Cambridge University Press, 2002), pp. 230, 216.
2. Ysabel de Andia, *Homo vivens* (Paris: Études augustiniennes, 1986), pp. 223, 335 (my translation).

thropology of *koinōnia:* the human vocation of union with the triune God. As a result, they both place ultimate significance on the Spirit as the one who draws the human into this ascending relation of *koinōnia,* such that human anthropology (and spirituality) can never be considered from an autonomous point of view. The strategic importance of chapter 5 is the historical credibility that it gives to a Christian rendering of *koinōnia,* especially as it is articulated in a context as far removed from Calvin's time as we are from Calvin today. Furthermore, precisely because of the different nature of the attack on creation during his time, Irenaeus can deepen Calvin's reflections on the relationship between *koinōnia* and the cosmos. Both Calvin's creaturely "pessimism" and Irenaeus's creaturely "optimism" have their place in an understanding of Christian participation; indeed, their differences highlight the defining force of the doctrine across varying centuries and polemical challenges to the church.

In 177 CE, when Irenaeus departed for Rome, the lives of many hung in the balance. His mission was to deliver a letter from imprisoned Christians awaiting martyrdom, one of whom was the bishop of Lyons. In his absence, things grew worse: Gaul was increasingly persecuted, the bishop was martyred, and the church was decimated. Upon his return, he stepped into the blood-soaked position of bishop of Lyons to shepherd a church battered from without and within. Despite all appearances, however, the greatest threat to Irenaeus's flock was a small group of Christian insiders who claimed mystical enlightenment concerning the true story of God and humanity. Masterfully interweaving the Christian story with their own myths of gods and universes, this group of Gnostics spun a near-seamless narrative that spoke of Christ, the Scriptures, the Holy Spirit — all things inclusive of the Christian story — yet swallowing it into their own.[3]

The early Gnostic zeitgeist can be seen as a response to the accumulating hunger for spirituality in the second century. The Greco-Roman empire had inherited a world bathed in a consciousness of *daimones,* spirits both good and evil whose presence coexisted with humanity and was con-

---

3. I use "Gnostics" here, very loosely, to signify the groups that Irenaeus specifies: Valentinians, Marcionites, Marcosians, followers of Ptolemy, etc. In general, scholars agree on the reliability of Irenaeus's description of the Gnostics (even after the discoveries at Nag Hammadi), though Irenaeus is more or less responsible for the invention of a unified Gnostic front, complete with heretical lineages. Although Elaine Pagels has tried to discount Irenaeus's reliability, Robert Grant has countered this in his review of her two books (1973, 1975) in *Religious Studies Review* 3 (1977): 30-35.

tinuously felt. These spirits were on hand to lend wisdom, to nurture various personal traits such as courage, and to dabble with one's fate. For example, Homer's warriors are depicted as suddenly overcome or carried away by the energy of a god.[4] One paid tributes to the gods not so much for the hope of external blessing but for the far more radical hope of being guided and/or possessed by the *daimon* itself. Centuries later, Plato was to attribute much of Socrates' inspiration to his *daimon,* for "when it came time for action, he trusted in his own *daimon,* as he also trusted in the *daimon* of his interlocutors."[5]

The Stoics began to reverse all this: they launched a process of secularization that replaced personal spirits with a cosmic consciousness.[6] Their concept of *oikeosis* (self-autonomy) strongly challenged the porous identity of late classical consciousness. In place of what Klaus Berger has termed "the permeable self" came a "Stoic" sense of self-reliance and self-sufficiency.[7] "It is foolish to pray for this when you can acquire it from yourself. We do not need to uplift our hands towards heaven, or to beg the keeper of a temple to let us approach his idol's ear, as if in this way our prayers were more likely to be heard. God is near you, he is with you, he is within you."[8] Seneca's famous resolve *not* to pray typifies the increasing aspirituality of the first century, the climate in which Gnosticism seeded itself so effectively.

The message of these "evangelists" within his own church that seemed to goad Irenaeus most was one of the descent and dissolution of creation. The Gnostic experienced life as a foreigner, alienated from his or her true spiritual home because of being physically incarcerated in flesh and earth. With such antipathy to the created realm, a Gnostic creator could only be cast as having been "either careless, or inferior, or [paying] no regard to those things which took place among His own posses-

---

4. See "Plato's Self-Mastery" in Charles Taylor, *Sources of the Self: The Making of the Modern Identity* (Cambridge: Harvard University Press, 1989), chap. 6.

5. Pierre Hadot, *Philosophy as a Way of Life,* trans. Michael Chase (Oxford: Blackwell, 1995), p. 164.

6. This consciousness was characterized by "the feeling of belonging to a whole which goes beyond the limits of [one's] individuality" (Hadot, *Way of Life,* p. 273).

7. Klaus Berger, *Identity and Experience in the New Testament* (Minneapolis: Augsburg Fortress, 2003), chap. 2.

8. From Seneca's letter to Lucilius (XLI: *On the God within us*), *Ad Lucilium Epistulae Morales* I, trans. Richard M. Gummere (London: Heinemann, 1918), *LCL* 77:273.

sions" (*AH* II.2.1), declares Irenaeus. Irenaeus was struck by a world that was, rather than spiraling downward into fragmentation and disintegration, ascending by its nature — set on a course by the Spirit for "growth and increase" (*augmentum et incrementum, AH* IV.11.1), intimacy and perfection. To the Gnostic world of incommunicability and dissociation, of radical dualism and isolation, Irenaeus spoke the unthinkable and impossible: *koinōnia* — participation, relationship, communion.[9] That word occurs more than eighty times in *Adversus haereses* alone, and it most characterizes Irenaeus's counternarrative of ascent.[10] "And to as many as continue in their love towards God, does He grant communion [*koinōnian*] with Him. But communion with God [*koinōnia*] is life and light, and the enjoyment of all the benefits which He has in store" (*AH* V.27.2).

In contrast to Calvin's structure of the *Institutes* (1559), whose chapters are broadly divided into the perichoretic spheres of Father, Son, Spirit, and church, *Adversus haereses* follows no systematic structure. Yet, despite the apparent lack of method,[11] *Adversus haereses* marches to a distinctly Trinitarian rhythm.[12] The descent of the triune God to humanity and the reverse procession back to himself forms what Irenaeus calls the Trinitarian "symphony of salvation" (*consonantiam salutis*, IV.14.2). The processions within God overflow into God's mission to humanity (*AH* V.18.2), forming the grand narrative of the God whose terminus is not humanity but God himself.[13]

9. Paul Lebeau analyzes five elements of "dissociation" and "incommunicability" that permeate Gnostic thought: that within the Supreme God himself; between spirit and matter; between time and eternity; between human beings; and between knowledge and moral action (Lebeau, "Koinonia: la signification du salut selon saint Irénée," in *Epektasis* [Paris: Beauchesne, 1972], pp. 122-23).

10. D. Bruno Reynders, *Lexique comparé du texte grec et des versions latine, arménienne, et syriaque de l'Adversus Haereses de saint Irénée,* Corpus Scriptorum Christianorum Orientalium, vol. 141 (Louvain: Imprimerie orientaliste, 1954), V.75; VI.58.

11. Mary Ann Donovan calls the recent defense of the literary and theological unity of *AH* IV the "single most striking contribution" to an appreciation of Irenaeus's maligned methodology. She surveys Bacq, van Unnik, Schoedel, and Perkins over against the older critique of Harnack, Bousset, Loofs, and even Quasten (Donovan, "Irenaeus in Recent Scholarship," *Second Century* 4 [1984]: 221-27).

12. See Andia, *Homo vivens,* pp. 139-43.

13. I have borrowed the term "terminus" from Khaled Anatolios, "The Immediately Triune God: A Patristic Response to Schleiermacher," *Pro Ecclesia* 10 (2001): 172.

Descent: Father — Son — Spirit

[This is the order, the rhythm, and the movement by which a formed and *created* humanity becomes the image and likeness of the uncreated God]: the Father planning everything well and giving His commands, the Son carrying these into execution and performing the work of creating, and the Spirit nourishing and increasing what is made, but man making progress day by day, and ascending towards the perfect, that is approximating to the uncreated One. (*AH* IV.38.3)[14]

Ascent: Spirit — Son — Father

This is the gradation and arrangement of those who are saved, and that they advance through steps of this nature: also that they ascend through the Spirit to the Son, and through the Son to the Father. (*AH* V.36.2)

Humanity's return to God is the inverse of the primal Trinitarian movement. The Trinity initiates this movement, constitutes this movement, and is the final resting place for humanity. Descent and ascent are the actions of the same God who is both humanity's genesis and terminus. Already within the broad overarching structure of *Adversus haereses*, we find the creature's Trinitarian participation in God to be central to Irenaeus's theological vision and his rebuttal of the Gnostics.

The ascent of humanity is manifestly *theo*-logical anthropology. As Adhémar d'Alès says, "[N]ot only does all the initiative belong to God, but all the effort as well."[15] This progressive growth is wholly the work of God. Mary Ann Donovan rightly notes its distinctiveness:

> Irenaeus's approach is through description of the divine activity in the economy rather than through description of the stages of mystical ascent to God. The result in either case is union with God: Irenaeus's concern is with the divine role in effecting this union. . . . This principle distinguishes the Irenaean position from platonic, Gnostic, and later patristic teaching on the ascent of the soul.[16]

14. Brackets indicate my translation of the original Latin: "Per hanc igitur ordinationem et hujusmodi convenientiam et tali ductu factus et plasmatus homo secundum imaginem et similitudinem constituitur infecti Dei . . ." (*SC* 100[2]:954).

15. Adhémar d' Alès, "La doctrine de l'Esprit en S. Irénée," *Recherches de Science Religieuse* 14 (1924): 533, my translation.

16. Mary Ann Donovan, *One Right Reading? A Guide to Irenaeus* (Collegeville, MN: Liturgical Press, 1997), p. 118.

This is the specific angle of Irenaean ascent: it is God's slow and steady activity to bring humanity fully into its created *telos*, which is to be fully alive in the Spirit. The command to "grow and increase" has been written into human anthropology as a positive element of being, with the source of the progress not from within but without: "Shall not this then be lawful for God, since He is ever willing to confer a greater degree of grace upon the human race, and to honour continually with many gifts those who please Him?" (*AH* IV.9.3). So exactly how does Irenaeus weave the story of God and humanity into an anthropological ascent that keeps this *koinōnia* at the fore?

As Ysabel de Andia has shown in her classic study of Irenaean anthropology, the answer is not an easy one. She divides Irenaean anthropology into three distinct narratives of progress: the economic, the christological, and the pneumatological.[17] Irenaeus weaves these three strands throughout *Adversus haereses* to form the grand tapestry of his anthropology; all three strands are different expressions of ascent. Accordingly, this chapter bears a tripartite structure as it narrates Irenaeus's distinctive vision on ascent and participation.

The three ascents will be as follows: (I) *The ascending economy of Adam* is the journey of creation into ever-greater levels of *koinōnia* (participation) in God. It is the story of humanity formed by the pedagogy of God throughout the different stages ("economies") of salvation, with a specific focus on the dynamic call of creation "from lesser things to those greater ones which are in His own presence . . ." (*AH* II.28.1). (II) *The ascending economy of Christ* follows how Irenaeus weaves anthropology into the history of Christ — the second Adam — who recapitulates all of creation and restores humanity to its true integrity as capable of receiving the Spirit. (III) *The ascending economy of the Spirit* reveals humanity's progression to be taken ever deeper into the life of the Spirit for its adoptive "filiation" and preparation for the face-to-face vision of the Father.

The Ascending Economy of Adam

"God indeed makes, but man is made."

In this first ascent, Irenaeus begins with the lens of creation. He looks at its origins, its ontology, and its goal in order to prove that salvation is not

17. Andia, *Homo vivens*, p. 22.

out of the world but in it. The ascent of creation does not carry us beyond creation; rather, its establishment is more and more in the realm of God. Like C. S. Lewis's vision in *The Great Divorce*, it is as the humans "ascend" in holiness that they are able to endure and enjoy the firmness and solidity of creation, rather than be wounded by it. The problem is not creation, but that the ghostly humans are not sustantial enough. The Gnostics, however, sketched out a fantastic ascent of an entirely different ilk. "They [the Valentinians] keep circling about those things which are below, going as far as the first and second Ogdoad, and because they unskillfully imagine that, immediately after the thirty Æons, they have discovered Him who is above all things Father, not following out in thought their investigations to that Pleroma which is above the three hundred and sixty-five heavens, which is above forty-five Ogdoads" (*AH* II.16.4).[18] Theirs was an intellectual ascent that repudiated the created order and yet whose scope, Irenaeus wryly notes, did not extend much further than the end of their nose.

Despite the bravado of a resolutely dualist system, Gnostic salvation can take place only when the differences between God and the world are erased: one is saved by virtue of the divinity that one already has. As Kurt Rudolph says, "The gnostic is already redeemed, although the completion of the redemption is still outstanding."[19] In such a system, one's spiritual nature determines everything. In the case of the Gnostics, there could be no participation, but only a solitary "spiritual nature."[20] Thus, ironically, there is much to be said for understanding Gnosticism as an essentially monistic system.[21]

Irenaeus realized that this was a distinction that humanity could not afford to lose, for it "wounded men unto death" (*AH* IV.Pref.4) by eliminating the possibility of union with God. Union, Irenaeus knew, was not based on same substance (Plato) but on difference and grace. To accept the Gnostic myth was nothing short of receiving a "mortal wound." Irenaeus charged the Gnostics with "homicide" (*AH* III.16.8) because they

18. For more on this particular sect, see C. Markschies, "Valentinian Gnosticism: Toward the Anatomy of a School," in *The Nag Hammadi Library After Fifty Years*, ed. J. D. Turner and A. McGuire (Leiden: Brill, 1997), pp. 401-38.

19. Kurt Rudolph, *Gnosis* (San Francisco: Harper & Row, 1977), p. 115.

20. Andia, *Homo vivens*, p. 223.

21. For a similar interpretation of Gnostic "monism," see William R. Schoedel, "Topological Theology and Some Monistic Trends in Gnosticism," in *Essays on the Nag Hammadi Texts*, ed. M. Krause (Leiden: Brill, 1972), pp. 88-108; see also Schoedel, "Gnostic Monism and the Gospel of Truth," in *Rediscovery of Gnosticism* (Leiden: Brill, 1980), pp. 379-90.

distorted the distinction between God the Creator and humanity his creation. Although many know Irenaeus for his devastating case against Gnosticism, few understand the latter's real danger as a cosmology that threatened participation in the divine life.

Irenaeus responded, not by correcting Gnostic dualism between humanity and God, but by delineating even more radically between them.

> And in this respect God differs from man, that God indeed makes, but man is made [*Deus quidem facit, homo autem fit*]; and truly, He who makes is always the same; but that which is made must receive both beginning, and middle, and addition, and increase (*AH* IV.11.2).[22]

The phrase "God makes, man is made" is critical for understanding the shape of Irenaeus's rebuttal of the Gnostics, because it replaced their dualism with an even more inviolable distinction. Von Balthasar notes that "this difference cuts so deep that the other, Greek distinction between spirit and matter totally pales in comparison."[23] It seems a strange countermove — to emphasize the difference between God and humanity to those who already saw nothing in common between spiritual and physical — but Irenaeus recognized this as being a saving distinction. Joseph Caillot rightly pronounces Irenaeus's insistence on difference "as grace, a way of union."[24]

Deus facit: *God Makes*

Before portraying the ascending economy of Adam, we must first explore Irenaeus's ontology, which is encapsulated in the phrase *Deus facit, homo fit*.[25] As a direct challenge to Gnostic ontology, Irenaeus grounds human

---

22. *SC* 100(2): 500.

23. Hans Urs von Balthasar, *The Glory of the Lord II: A Theological Aesthetics* (Edinburgh: T. & T. Clark, 1982), p. 64.

24. Joseph Caillot, "La grâce de l'union selon saint Irénée," in *Penser la foi*, ed. Joseph Doré and Christoph Theobald (Paris: Cerf, 1993), pp. 394-95.

25. I have elsewhere expanded on the significance of the phrase *Deus facit, homo fit* (Julie Canlis, "Being Made Human: The Significance of Creation for Irenaeus's Doctrine of Participation," *Scottish Journal of Theology* 58 [2005]: 434-67). By beginning with God, not humanity, Irenaeus gives God a freedom from the necessity of creating the world, while creation is gifted with an unprecedented differentiation from God. This

ascent not on human potential, let alone some immanent facet of our nature, but on God's transcendence — a transcendence conceived not according to Greek categories of distance but informed by creation and incarnation. Irenaeus's radical distinction differentiates humanity from God precisely by relating it to God. The genius of such a scheme is that it allows for coherent discourse about the divine and nondivine in a noncontrasting relationship, conceived as fundamentally different, but mutually affirming. Kathryn Tanner confirms that "divine transcendence, according to Irenaeus, does not exclude but rather allows for the immanent presence to creatures of God in his otherness."[26] The difference between God and humanity is not primarily one of substance or distance but of making and made, giving and receiving. Irenaean transcendence bespeaks a God who "contains all things" and is therefore related to everything in an equally direct manner — *because* God is the Creator and "origin of all things."[27] Therefore, humanity does not have a form of existence or an "ontology" except as enclosed-in-God. They are joined in relationship, even as they are utterly different.

Then Irenaeus moves in to characterize the nature of the God who makes, since this will give definition to the ascent. Humanity does not ascend by impersonal *gnosis* but by costly love:

> For thou dost not make God, but God thee. If, then, thou art God's workmanship, await the hand of thy Maker which creates everything in due time; in due time as far as thou art concerned, whose creation is being carried out. Offer to Him thy heart in a soft and tractable fashion . . . lest by becoming hardened, thou lose the impressions of His fingers. (*AH* IV.39.2)

Humanity is not just "made," but is *being made* by a personal Creator, whose hands stay close to humanity from the beginning of creation to its

---

construction of transcendence is in total contrast to Gnostic cosmology, which reads God off of the world (projecting his distance-transcendence), and instead suggests an extreme of divine involvement with the world.

26. Tanner, *God and Creation in Christian Theology: Tyranny or Empowerment?* (Oxford: Blackwell, 1988), p. 56.

27. "He contains all things, but He Himself can be contained by no one" (*AH* II.30.9, see also *AH* II.1-5; IV.3.1; IV.19.2). For further discussion, see William R. Schoedel, "Enclosing, Not Enclosed: The Early Christian Doctrine of God," in *Early Christian Literature and the Classical Intellectual Tradition* (Paris: Beauchesne, 1979).

completion. Creation is a masterpiece of the entire Trinity: "Now man is
. . . formed after the likeness of God, and moulded by His hands, that is,
by the Son and the Holy Spirit to whom also He said, 'Let Us make
man.'"[28] Yet the work of the two hands is not complete on the sixth day of
creation, but they persevere in their creative work throughout the history
of humanity and the history of each person, so involved as to leave finger-
prints. Although "never at any time did Adam escape the hands of God"
(*AH* V.1.3), Irenaeus allows for the fact that some humans will reject the
hands.[29] Humanity is not an extension of the hands, but neither is its destiny complete without them. Union and participation in the life of God
becomes God's intent for humanity, the clue that makes sense of creation
at all.

Nevertheless, Irenaeus takes us deeper, beyond a relationship of mere
creation. Human ascent is part of its nature as "created" *(homo fit)*, but the
God overseeing this ascent is not only Creator but triune. For what purpose did the hands set to work on the world? "In the beginning, therefore,
did God form Adam, not as if He stood in need of man, but that He
might have some one upon whom to confer His benefits" (*AH* IV.14.1).[30]
Humanity arrives at the scene of a world absolutely full — overflowing —
with communion and worship. In *Epideixis* 10, Irenaeus paints a picture of
a universe in which the Son and Spirit, at the pinnacle of creation, offer
the divine worship. Von Balthasar remarks that "this universe of adoration
is inherently Trinitarian."[31] So the "benefits" for which humanity is created is this Trinitarian universe of adoration.

In one of Irenaeus's most revealing discussions of creation, he uses
John 17 (Jesus' plea to share the divine glory with humanity) as a commentary on Genesis 1, allowing us a glimpse of the vast scope of his vision of
creation. By situating creation squarely in the midst of Jesus' high priestly
prayer to share the divine glory, we see that the creation purposes of God
are to share the divine glory with humanity — a glory that is nothing less
than the triune *koinōnia*. Irenaeus begins with a portrait of the eternal

28. *AH* IV.Pref.4. Note the resonance with Job 10:8: "Your hands shaped me and
made me."

29. This subversion is cast in typically relational terms: "He inflicts that separation
from Himself which they have chosen . . ." (*AH* V.27.2).

30. Here, by grounding his doctrine of creation firmly on the bedrock of grace and
abundance, Irenaeus anticipates in a delightful way the doctrine of aseity (and avoids
many of its later pitfalls because of his doctrine of the two hands).

31. Von Balthasar, *Glory II,* pp. 61-62.

glory shared between the Father and Son: "For not alone antecedently to Adam, but before all creation, the Word glorified His Father, remaining in Him; and was Himself glorified by the Father, as He did Himself declare, 'Father, glorify Thou Me with the glory which I had with Thee before the world was.'" Then, in a surprising move, Irenaeus turns Christ's glory (conceived in these strikingly personal terms) outward, "not vainly boasting of this, but desiring that His disciples should share in His glory" (*AH* IV.14.1). "Glory," as Irenaeus reads the Old and New Testaments, is the Trinitarian communion of "fatherhood-sonship in the Spirit."[32] It is this for which humanity was created, and — as one would expect — the work of redemption is that humanity, once again, "may be capable of receiving the glory of the Father [*capax gloriae Patris*]" (*AH* V.35.2). Irenaeus closes *AH* IV.14.1 by reflecting that we, like the disciples, flock to Christ as eagles to a carcass, "participating in the glory of the Lord, who has both formed us, and prepared us for this, that, when we are with Him, we may partake of His glory."

It is only now that we are fully situated to appreciate the depth of Irenaeus's polemic against Gnosticism. Far from excessively cataloguing or caricaturing Gnostic cosmologies, Irenaeus is taking on these very cosmologies simply because their framework prohibits participation. Says de Andia, "The gnostic universe offers no communion, because there is no participation. The only relation between substances or natures is one of consubstantiality."[33] Human participation in God can only function in a world in which divine and human are not opposed but related by God's love: *Deus facit, homo fit.* The Gnostics' hands were tied by their own cosmological conjecture. Gnostic dualism, by denying the full contingent relationship between humanity and God, had to compensate with an overspiritualization of humanity "by means of a mythological synthesis of same-quality being of Creator and creature."[34] Oscillating between exclusion and fusion, Gnostic anthropology can best be

32. See Andia, *Homo vivens,* chap. 1. This is also at the heart of Thierry Scherrer's thesis, which reveals glory to be "*koinōnia* trinitarie, relation de paternité-filiation dans l'Esprit" (Scherrer, *La Gloire de Dieu dans l'oeuvre de Saint Irénée* [Rome: Gregorian University Press, 1997], p. 291).

33. "The gnostic universe offers no communion, because there is no participation. The only relation between substances or natures is one of consubstantiality" (Andia, *Homo vivens,* p. 169).

34. Iain MacKenzie, *Irenaeus's Demonstration of the Apostolic Preaching,* trans. J. Armitage Robinson (Aldershot, Hants: Ashgate, 2002), p. 46.

seen as schizophrenic.[35] In neither scenario can the human *as human* participate in God *as God*. Without the relationship of *koinōnia*, humanity either must be divinized to the loss of creatureliness or must cease to exist entirely, "lest man, falling away from God altogether, should cease to exist" (*AH* IV.20.7).

Irenaeus rallied for that deepest distinction between God and humanity — that of maker and made, giving and receiving — in order that God and humanity could progress toward one another in deeper and deeper *koinōnia*. For Irenaeus, the secret was not in "a casting away of the flesh, but by the imparting [*communionem/sugkoinōnian*] of the Spirit" (*AH* V.8.1).[36] Irenaeus fought for a sphere in which flesh is neither antithetical to — nor subordinate to, nor changed into — spirit, but in which flesh participates in the Spirit for its integrity, salvation, and fulfillment. For Irenaeus, this ascent was not just a matter of right theology, but manifestly a way of being and worshiping.[37]

Homo fit: *Humanity Is Made*

> *"And in this respect God differs from man, that God indeed makes, but man is made [Deus facit; homo fit]; and truly, He who makes is always the same; but that which is made must receive both beginning, and middle, and addition, and increase." (AH IV.11.2)*

Before examining Irenaeus's ascending anthropology, we saw him lay down bedrock in the form of the Creator-creature distinction. In clear contrast to the Valentinians, who "projected [man] onto the screen of heaven in order to fascinate him and, professedly, to redeem him by the

---

35. Of course, there is no single "Gnostic anthropology," but even within individual schools there is contradiction. Even Plotinus complains about how the Gnostics gathered their information from various and even competing sources (*Ennead* 2.9.6).

36. *SC* 153:94.

37. Irenaeus was not simply combating false knowledge with true knowledge, but knowledge with worship (*AH* II.26.1), speculation with Eucharist (*AH* IV.18.5), a "-logy" with an "-urgy." To call this a "counter-myth," as William P. Loewe does, is to miss what Irenaeus was doing; it also fails to communicate Irenaeus's staunch commitment to tradition over against innovation (Loewe, "Myth and Counter Myth: Irenaeus's Story of Salvation," in *Interpreting Tradition*, ed. J. Kopas [Chico, CA: Scholars Press, 1984], pp. 39-54).

contemplation of this magnified image of himself," Irenaeus knew the only appropriate place to begin was with God *(Deus facit)*.[38] Yet, instead of taking him further from the pressing Gnostic concerns about humanity, this brought Irenaeus right to the heart of things: to safeguard God *is* to safeguard humanity; to unmake God *is* to unmake humanity. For the Gnostics could not accept what Irenaeus knew about the nature of God's relationship with humanity, namely, that God has bound himself to humanity in such a way that anthropology is the inverse of theology, not its opposite.

Viewed through this lens of creation, human ascent is most often referred to as "growth" by "Him who made, established, and still nourishes us" (*AH* III.10.3). Creation's ongoing growth is the corollary of God's ongoing creation. Growth is not a deficiency but is inextricably linked to the way God has structured creation for participation, not autonomous completion.[39] Gustaf Wingren penetrates straight to the heart of this:

> God and man are not the same. God is the only Creator. The function of creation never passes to man. Man is receptive, and remains such — he is involved in the process of growth. But man's destiny and true being are precisely to grow, i.e., to receive from a source which lies outside man. If this function of growth or receptivity cease, man's humanity also ceases. Man can only be man according to his own nature in communion with God. . . .[40]

Creation only ascends as it receives: this is its vocation and that for which it was created. This is why "thankfulness," for Irenaeus, is a distinctly anthropological category rather than an ethical one.[41] It is consent to a life of participation and growth in God and thus is constitutive of being rather than an attempt to find a source of life in ourselves. "For the receptacle of His goodness, and the instrument of his glorification, is the man who is

---

38. Von Balthasar, *Glory II*, p. 33; Clement of Alexandria makes a similar observation of the Greek teacher Theodotus in *SC* 23:78.2.

39. One must be sure to clarify that it is finitude that causes us to look to the Creator for our very beings, not dependence in and of itself (which would be slavery, or pantheism). Our radical "dependence" on God is what gives us our very freedom before God.

40. Gustaf Wingren, *Man and the Incarnation* (Edinburgh: Oliver & Boyd, 1959), p. 210.

41. Irenaeus consistently links gratitude to growth: *AH* III.25.4; III.20.2; IV.11.2; IV.38.4.

grateful to Him that made him; and again, the receptacle of His just judgment is the ungrateful man . . ." (*AH* IV.11.12). It is an entire orientation, an obedient correspondence as those who are made to the one who makes. Human precariousness is the mystery of God's binding himself to our existence. Those who are ungrateful "transgress the law of becoming" and refuse to become human (*AH* IV.38.4).[42]

So into what would God have Adam grow? Into genuine human existence. Genesis 1–3 marks not the pinnacle of humanness but its foundation (*AH* IV.38.3). Everything in Irenaeus's description of Adam and Eve points to the incompleteness of their state. Yet this incompletion is not a matter of God's incapacity but rather the intimacy of the *Deus facit, homo fit* arrangement.

> For neither does God at any time cease to confer benefits upon, or to enrich man; nor does man ever cease from receiving the benefits, and being enriched by God. For the receptacle of His goodness, and the instrument of his glorification, is the man who is grateful to Him that made him. . . . (*AH* IV.11.2)

The "perfection" of Adam and Eve's life in the Garden lay not in any attributes that they possessed but on their constant state of receiving from God. Survival was not inherent in their being, but they were filled both with God's life ("breath") and his attributes ("immortality").[43]

This is the picture of a sumptuous life, exuberant in its physical and spiritual wholeness that comes from the prodigality of God. Yet it is not the ecstasy of *methexis* but of *koinōnia*,[44] for the Garden's excellence is marked by communion with the Word:[45] "He would walk and talk with the man pre-

---

42. Translation by von Balthasar, *Glory II*, p. 63.

43. Of immortality, Irenaeus says that this came from the "excelling power of this Being, not from [their] own nature" (*AH* V.2.3). This specific reference to immortality is linked also to the Eucharist; immortality in both the garden and the Eucharist underscores that immortality for Irenaeus is always a property of God that is given for our participation. The benefits and fruits of the tree of immortality are tied to Adam's intimacy with the Word, for "the friendship of God imparts immortality to those who embrace it" (*AH* IV.15.4). See also John Zizioulas, *Being as Communion* (Crestwood, NY: St Vladimir's Seminary Press, 1985), pp. 80-82.

44. See pp. 5ff. of my introduction, above.

45. The presence of the Word in the garden, "prefiguring the future," is good warning that Irenaeus's three ascents (of Adam, Christ, and the Spirit) are constantly being

figuring the future, which would come to pass, that He would dwell with him and speak with him, and would be within mankind, teaching them righteousness" (*Epideixis* 12).[46] The initial state in the Garden is the beginning of a life of participation in God's very life, a *koinōnia* that is progressive and will build muscle and sinew into humanity. Full *koinōnia* is a glory that Adam cannot stomach from the outset, for "even if he had received the Spirit, he could not have contained [*capere*] it" (*AH* IV.38.2). Farrow brings us to the heart of Irenaean ascent: "The 'imperfection' is this: The love for God which is the life of man cannot emerge *ex nihilo* in full bloom; it requires to grow with experience."[47] This "infancy" suggests not flawed or sinful existence, but merely the unfinished nature of God's *koinōnia*-project and the radical depth of the possibilities for communion with him.

Simultaneously, this humanization is also called "ascension into God" (*AH* III.19.1).[48] And it is here that Irenaeus's core contribution to theological anthropology can still be felt. For Irenaeus, creatures by their very definition must participate in God's life. "For he formed him for growth and increase, as the Scripture says: 'Increase and multiply'" (*AH* IV.11.1). Human nature is not a given but a phenomenon, something "embedded in time" and thus requiring the "growth" or ascent of the two hands.[49] Therefore, submission to the Creator-creature differentiation *is* ascension into God, says Irenaeus. "But by preserving the framework thou shalt ascend to that which is perfect" (*AH* IV.38.2). His definition of "creature" includes inbuilt direction toward the Creator:

---

woven and interwoven together, and are not to be taken independently. The garden is painted as a provisional place, for Irenaeus never intended a process of growth without the Word. As Daniélou remarks, "the mediation of the Word would still have been necessary for their journey from the Garden to heaven" (Jean Daniélou, "Histoire des origines Chrétiennes," *Recherches de Science Religieuse* 58 [1970]: 152).

46. Only in this context does the prohibition not to eat of the tree make sense (*Epideixis* 15). Far from serving as an arbitrary test of obedience, it functioned as an opportunity for Adam to stay in communion with the *voice* of the Word. "For Adam it is said, 'Hear ["Ηκουσεν] the voice of the Lord God'" (*AH* V.17.1). De Andia reminds us that the etymology of the Greek verb "to obey" (ὑπακούω) gives an auditory connotation: it is "to hear" (ἀκούω) and then to put oneself under (ὑπα) the voice (Ysabel de Andia, *Homo vivens*, p. 100 n. 60).

47. Douglas Farrow, "St. Irenaeus of Lyons: The Church and the World," *Pro Ecclesia* 4 (1995): 348.

48. Translated by *ANF* as "promotion," though the Latin is *fraudantes hominem ab ea ascensione quae est ad Deum* (*SC* 211:372); see also *AH* III.20.2; IV.20.7; IV.33.4.

49. Von Balthasar, *Glory II*, p. 66.

For he who holds, without pride and boasting, the true opinion [*veram gloriam*] regarding created things and the Creator, . . . shall also receive from Him the greater glory of promotion, looking forward to the time when he shall become like Him who died for him . . . [the One who] might accustom man to receive God, and God to dwell in man, according to the good pleasure of the Father. (*AH* III.20.2)

The Creator-creature line, that deepest of all distinctions, can be held fast while the two still approximate each other by the very nature of the creature's definition (which still allows for and mandates reception, or "growth"). "But man receives advancement and increase towards God. For as God is always the same, so also man, when found in God, shall always go on towards God" (*AH* IV.11.2). The creature participates in the Creator not in defiance of its definition but in fulfillment of it. Irenaeus insists that, in humanity's ascent, "neither is the substance nor the essence of the creation annihilated (for faithful and true is He who has established it) . . ." (*AH* V.36.1). Iain MacKenzie echoes that: "Humanity's perfection is the realization of the created estate; it is not as the perfection of God. . . ."[50]

The Ascent of Creation: Deification

Growth is the essence of Irenaeus's doctrine of "deification," a rather anachronistic label given that the term was not coined until Gregory Nazianzen (fourth century CE).[51] Deification is indeed a useful concept to capture the noncompetitive relationship between creature and Creator so central to Irenaean ascent, as are other phrases, such as "ascension/promotion into God" or the created "approximating the Uncreated" (*AH* IV.38.3). These are central arrows in Irenaeus's anti-Gnostic defense. But they remain *deconstructive* concepts — tearing down the Gnostic a priori of the radical incompatibility between heaven and earth — rather than the *constructive* ones he seems to prefer, such as the use he makes of adoption.

50. MacKenzie, *Demonstration*, p. 69.
51. Irenaeus is viewed by many as the originator of the concept because of the formula of "exchange" that has become associated with him, "the Word of God, our Lord Jesus Christ, who did, through his transcendent love, become what we are, that he might bring us to be even what he is himself" (*AH* V, Pref.).

As Carl Mosser observes, Irenaeus takes up a thorough defense of the language of "gods" (Psalm 82) because of his opponents' claims.[52]

Irenaeus is dexterous with the term "god," as was typical of second-century linguistic usage,[53] and he accused the Gnostics of misunderstanding growth.[54] For they "cast blame upon Him, because we have not been made gods from the beginning, but at first merely men, then at length gods" (*AH* IV.38.4). The Gnostics wanted nothing to do with the contaminated material sphere, and they indicted God for his catastrophic mistake of creating material rather than spiritual beings. Irenaeus countered with a defense of deification, the ultimate validation of creation's mandate to grow:

> How, then, shall he be a God, who has not as yet been made a man? Or how can he be perfect who was but lately created? How, again, can he be immortal, who in his mortal nature did not obey his Maker? For it must be that thou, at the outset, shouldest hold the rank of a man, and then afterwards partake of the glory of God. For thou dost not make God, but God thee [*Non enim tu Deum facis, sed Deus te facit*]. (*AH* IV.39.2)[55]

Irenaeus does not scorn the Gnostic desire to be divine, just as he did not scorn the content of Satan's promise to Adam and Eve.[56] Rather, Irenaeus

---

52. Carl Mosser, "The Earliest Patristic Interpretations of Psalm 82, Jewish Antecedents and the Origin of Christian Deification," *Journal of Theological Studies* 56 (2005): 30-74.

53. The broad semantic range of the word "god(s)" is certainly taken for granted by Irenaeus (idols — *AH* III.6.3; god-like qualities in a human — *AH* III.19.2). For the general usage of this term throughout the Greco-Roman world, see George M. Schurr, "On the Logic of Ante-Nicene Affirmations of the 'Deification' of the Christian," *Anglican Theological Review* 51 (1969): 97-105. Going even further, Carl Mosser notes that Irenaeus's use of parallelism between Ps. 82:6, 7 "suggests that the conceptual synonymy between immortality and 'godhood' was not confined to the Greco-Roman world but was found in ancient Israel as well" (Mosser, "Earliest Patristic Interpretations," n. 22).

54. The various Gnostic sects displayed a startling impatience, desiring perfection from the start. Irenaeus believed that this revealed a complete misunderstanding of God's power, which manifested itself through his choice of *weak* things (*AH* III.20; V.3).

55. *SC* 100(2): 966.

56. It is not Adam's desire for incorruptibility that is the problem, but that Adam is tempted to have it without participation: "supposing that the incorruptibility which belongs to him is his own naturally . . . as if he were naturally like to God" (*AH* III.20.1). The Latin does not personify the evil to be Satan, but rather man's own pride (*SC* 211:386).

becomes hot under the collar when becoming "gods" is promised *too early,* that is, to those who were too small to receive it. "Irrational, therefore, in every respect, are they who await not the time of increase. . . . Such persons know neither God nor themselves" (*AH* IV.38.4). Their temptation is to impatience, grasping for the ends without the *koinōnia* means. This "hatred of grace," as Vladimir Lossky calls it, is the total overthrow of the *Deus facit, homo fit* relationship because it disrupts the primary relationship of giving and receiving.[57] "For, while promising that they should be as gods" (*AH* III.23.1), Satan "beguiled Eve, by promising her what he had not himself . . ." (*AH* IV.Pref.4). Satan promised what God intended, while Eve's sin was in not waiting for it to be given to her.

Irenaean deification is not about possessing godness per se, but it is about receiving all that God desires to give and being "grown" by God such that we can actually receive. As an essential defense of Irenaeus's ascending anthropology, the polemical focus of deification is certainly not about a specific result (and this is where most Irenaean interpreters go too far — but that would be the Gnostic mistake), but about a *process* of staying under the two hands of the Creator.

> Offer to Him thy heart in a soft and tractable state, and preserve the form in which the Creator fashioned thee, having moisture in thyself, lest, by becoming hardened, thou lose the impressions of His fingers. . . . But if thou, being obstinately hardened, dost reject the operation of His skill, and show thyself ungrateful towards Him, because thou were created a mere man, by becoming thus ungrateful to God, thou hast at once lost both His workmanship and life. For creation is an attribute of the goodness of God but to be created is that of human nature. (*AH* IV.39.2)

As long as God continues to give and humanity receives, the Creator-creature distinction will be preserved, even as humanity "grows" to become more and more like God. Even in the eschaton, we continue to receive, as testimony to our created state and to God's eternal abundance. "Man should always possess something towards which he might advance" (*AH* IV.20.7). This, Irenaeus argues, has been God's plan from the beginning: to create man imperfectly in order to confer perfection on him, a

---

57. Vladimir Lossky, *Orthodox Theology: An Introduction,* trans. Ian and Ihita Kesarcodi-Watson (Crestwood, NY: St Vladimir's Seminary Press, 1989), p. 82.

perfection that is envisioned as mature *koinōnia:* "the new heaven and the new earth, in which the new man shall remain continually, always holding fresh converse with God. [These] things shall ever continue without end" (*AH* V.36.1).

We conclude by noting that Irenaean deification refers to the radical nature of God's gift, and it functions less as an anthropological than doxological concept. Humanity is set on a course of ascent *(homo fit)*, but for Irenaeus this is a statement manifestly about God *(Deus facit)*, his primacy, and his gifts:

> But learning by experience that we possess eternal duration from the excelling power of this Being, not from our own nature, we may neither undervalue that glory which surrounds God as He is, nor be ignorant of our own nature, but that we may know what God can effect, and what benefits man receives, and thus never wander from the true comprehension of things as they are, that is, both with regard to God and with regard to man. (*AH* IV.2.3)

Those who would improperly justify their own ascending theology by means of referring to Irenaeus's "deification" language are certainly out of line.[58] For there must be an acknowledgment not only of the *fact* of Irenaeus's noncompetitive relationship between divine and human, but also of the *how*. "If, however, we must speak strictly, we would say that the flesh does not inherit, but is inherited . . ." (*AH* V.9.4). Ironically, deification is one of Irenaeus's proofs of the integrity of the Creator-creature *(Deus facit, homo fit)* relationship. The gift is never "naturalized" into humanity. It is less about our appropriation of God than of his appropriation of us. "He has established with the Word the whole world, . . . and to the whole world He has given laws, that each one keep to his place and overstep not the bound laid down by God . . ." (*Epideixis* 10).

---

58. See, for example, John Hick, *Evil and the God of Love* (London: Macmillan, 1985), pp. 217-21. The past two centuries have been marked by theories of the destiny of humanity and its inevitable evolutionary march toward self-transcendence. Yet Hegel's talk of the divinizing Infinite Spirit should sound off-key to any reader of Irenaeus. Irenaeus does not pipe a tune of progress, but a participatory relationship of communion with God. Growth is not cultural evolution, but *koinōnia*. Neither is it appropriate to deny deification in Irenaeus, as does David Cairns, who rejects the doctrine due to his static notions of anthropology (Cairns, *The Image of God in Man*, rev. ed. [London: Collins, 1973], p. 103).

* * *

In conclusion, let us recapitulate the first strand in the Irenaean tapestry of ascent, that of Adam/creation. Although Irenaeus's controlling theme of "God makes, humanity is made" was forced on him by Gnostic claims, he transformed it into the axis on which his counterworld turned. In going far beyond the simplistic opposition between matter and spirit, Irenaeus nullified (or transcended) it. For Irenaeus agreed with the Gnostics that the fate of humanity was at stake. Yet, by blurring the Creator-creature demarcation, they were in effect eliminating participation in God. It was a form of "homicide" (*AH* III.16.8) because it denied the very basis of their being: God and his creative commitment to them.

Now we can see why Irenaeus could not just counter Gnostic heresy with Christian theology. He had to first dismantle Gnostic cosmology brick by brick (*AH* I and II) before rebuilding a Christian framework that could bear the weight of participation (*AH* III through V). "The flesh, therefore, is not destitute of participation in the constructive wisdom and power of God. But the power of Him who is the bestower of life is made perfect in weakness — that is, in flesh . . ." (*AH* V.3.3). The only divine-human relationship conceivable to the Gnostics was a self-canceling one. For Irenaeus, such a competitive relationship between Creator and creature was not only insupportable, it was the elimination of life. What was needed was not a Gnostic change in creatureliness but instead a deepened understanding of the creature. Terminology such as "ascension into God" (*AH* III.19.1) captures the largeness of Irenaeus's vision for the perfection of humanity qua humanity, but it can never be severed from his equal emphasis on the deepened personal *koinōnia* that is this ascent. He says that the "Father . . . bestowed the faculty of increase on His own creation, and called him upwards from lesser things to those greater ones which are in His own presence . . ." (*AH* II.28.1).

The Ascending Economy of Christ

He did "ascend to the height above, offering and commending to His Father that human nature which had been found."

When seen through the ascending economy of Adam, Irenaeus expresses the *telos* of humanity as "ascension into God," or in terms of the "created approximating the Uncreated," or of "men becoming gods" (section I).[59] These metaphors are all related to the Creator-creature distinction, where Irenaeus undertakes to prove that created things are not excluded from the divine life by focusing on the compatibility of flesh/Spirit, created/Uncreated, gods/God. But when Irenaeus desires to describe the quality of this ascent, he gives precision to participation through Trinitarian metaphors such as adoption (section II) and adoptive filiation (section III). Creation is indeed "fitted" for growth, but this goes far beyond creation's own compass. It is now the "two hands" that are the content of this growth.

We will now follow the story not of Adam but of the Second Adam, whose ascending narrative gathers humanity into his own. Irenaeus masterfully weaves human anthropology into the history of Jesus, whose recapitulation restores to humanity its ascent ("faculty of increase"). This, we will discover, is sketched in terms of receiving the Spirit.

Gnostic Descents and Ascents

Descent and ascent played a pivotal role in the Gnostic myths of redemption. Therefore, it comes as no surprise to find Irenaeus challenging their skewed sense of direction.[60] Each sect played a variation on a common theme, which was the confusion of the descending and ascending missions of the Son and Spirit.[61] From these inadequate notions of Jesus' descent and ascent they drew inadequate notions of their own, with noetic "ascent" functioning as a primary Gnostic metaphor for salvation.[62] Irenaeus reports: "This, then, is the true redemption . . . that their inner man may as-

59. References are, respectively: *AH* III.19.1; IV.38.3; IV.39.2.

60. Gnostic speculations on descent and ascent are a syncretized version of Hellenic procession and return motifs, with a savior to boot. Osborn distills the four phases of the Gnostic redemptive myth: extension, dispersion, concentration in a savior, and return to unity through the savior (Eric Osborn, "Irenaeus: God as Intellect and Love," in *Prayer and Spirituality in the Early Church, I,* ed. Pauline Allen et al. [Brisbane: Australian Catholic University Press, 1998], p. 176).

61. Irenaeus specifically pinpoints this error in the following Gnostic "heretics": Marcus in *AH* I.14.6, 15.3; Marcosians in *AH* I.21.3; Simon Magus in *AH* I.23.1; Saturninus and Basilides in *AH* I.24.4, 5; Carpocrates in *AH* I.25.1; Ophites and Sethians in *AH* I.30.3, 14; Valentinians in *AH* II.20.3; III.11.3.

62. *AH* II.22.3; 20.3; 30.5, 7.

cend on high in an invisible manner, as if their body were left among created things in this world, while their soul is sent forward to the Demiurge" (*AH* I.21.5). This intellectualized ascent corresponds to the ascent of the Gnostics' savior, who is "an incorporeal power, and the *Nous* of the unborn father." He transfigured Simon of Cyrene into his likeness, so that the Jews crucified Simon while Jesus, "standing by, laughed at them . . . and thus ascended to him who had sent him, deriding them, inasmuch as he could not be laid hold of, and was invisible to all."[63] Even Paul, who "ascended to the third heaven," is claimed for their own, though Irenaeus wryly notes that the Valentinians surpass Paul and go straight for the "seventh heaven," though they fall short of the apostle's "high degree of perfection in the love of God" (*AH* II.30.7).

The "descent" portrayed in Gnostic redemption myths disemboweled the incarnation, while "ascent" docetized the resurrection. Irenaeus combats these fictitious transpositions with the descent and ascent of two hands of God, in his efforts to thwart Gnostic spiritualizing of the Son. As Farrow notes of this conflation, "Theirs is a one-hand theology, built around a synthetic spirit-Christ."[64] Likewise, Irenaeus fought for the double ascent of the Spirit and Son in a historical, conjoined mission back to the Father to rebuke docetized readings of the atonement or ascension.[65] For, "although they certainly do with their tongue confess one Jesus Christ," their doctrine "departs from Him who is truly God" over precisely this issue of his descent and ascent, says Irenaeus (*AH* III.16.6).

The Descent and Ascent of the Son of God

Irenaeus diagnosed the Gnostic problem as a failure of the imagination — a vision of God that was too confining and thus precluded their accep-

---

63. *AH* I.24.4, the interpretation of Saturninus. The Valentinians were equally convinced that Jesus did not suffer, but they constructed this in terms of the descent of two Christs. Irenaeus replies, "The impassible Christ did not descend upon Jesus, but that He Himself, because He was Jesus Christ, suffered for us; He . . . who descended and ascended" (*AH* III.18.3).

64. Douglas Farrow, "The Doctrine of the Ascension in Irenaeus and Origin," *ARC* 26 (1998): 39.

65. Of the Gnostic savior, Farrow observes: "The descending and ascending saviour was not a particular man, then, but rather the primal or universal man, the idea of Man" (Farrow, "Doctrine of Ascension," p. 35).

tance of the descent of God into our temporal and material existence. On the other hand, any reader of Irenaeus notices immediately that he does not suffer from this ailment. We see this magnificently displayed in Irenaeus's christological reading of the Old Testament (the "Scriptures"), which he takes as indisputable testimony to humanity's ongoing pursuit by both of the hands. Jesus' descent is that for which the Word and the Spirit have been preparing through their many direct encounters with the patriarchs and prophets — "it being customary from the beginning with the Word of God to ascend and descend for the purpose of saving those who were in affliction" (*AH* IV.12.4). The Spirit, too, has been in and amongst his creation, raising "up prophets upon the earth, accustoming man to bear His Spirit [within him], and to hold communion with God. . . . Thus, in a variety of ways, He adjusted the human race to an agreement with salvation" (*AH* IV.14.2). Von Balthasar well captures the significance of these descents: "The economy of salvation is the training of man by God to encounter the God-man."[66] These visitations were continually pressing toward the culmination of God's purpose, whereby the two hands would actually *enter* humanity.

. . . *ex virgine natum Filium Dei* (AH III.16.2)

What is at stake over the "descent" of Jesus is the issue of his true humanity, that truly great miracle that "baffled" (*AH* V.21.2) both the Gnostics and Satan, the latter believing more readily in his divinity than his humanity. Thus Mary became the first of many battlefields for orthodoxy. The Gnostic sects had ingenious ways of grappling with the human-divine identity of Jesus: some said that Christ "passed through Mary just as water flows through a tube" (*AH* I.7.2); others said that "Jesus was merely a receptacle of the Christ, upon whom the Christ, as a dove, descended" (*AH* III.16.1). "But," Irenaeus replies, "according to the opinion of no one of the heretics was the Word of God made flesh" (*AH* III.11.3). It is noteworthy that Irenaeus does not place sole significance on Mary's humanity, but deems the Spirit to be decisive as well: "So too Christ's body is made by the Spirit" (*Epideixis* 71).[67] Here, as in creation, we find

66. Von Balthasar, *Glory II*, p. 87.
67. "Christi corpus a Spiritu eius factum est" (*SC* 406:184, trans. Joseph Smith). Elsewhere, Irenaeus attributes the "forming" of Jesus to *both* hands (*AH* V.1.3). For further discussion, see Anatolios, "Immediately," p. 176.

that the Spirit is the one who does not spiritualize creation but ensures its true nature (*AH* III.22.1), even the true humanity of Christ. We also encounter the first in a series of "pneumatic installments" in the life of Christ, where the uniqueness of Christ is marked by the presence of the Spirit in his life and redemptive ministry.

Mary's virginity is of utmost importance to Irenaeus, not because of the associated notions of chastity and sinlessness, but for striking up a parallel between the First and Second Adam. Guided by Romans 5:19, Irenaeus further attempts to work out how the details of Jesus' life relate to our salvation:[68]

> Not despising or evading any condition of humanity, nor setting aside in Himself that law which He had appointed for the human race, but sanctifying every age, by that period corresponding to it which belonged to Himself. (*AH* II.22.4)

As such, it was vitally important that Jesus' generation be similar to Adam's. "For as by the disobedience of one man who was originally moulded from virgin soil, the many were made sinners and forfeited life; so was it necessary that, by the obedience of one man who was originally born from a virgin, many should be justified and receive salvation" (*AH* III.18.7). Jesus' true "descent" into our world of fallen flesh and history is an identification, in a sense, with the descending turn the world has taken since Adam's sin. It is only because of his genuine descent that his ascent will have the implications for material reality that qualify this as a redemption *of* the world, not out of it. Donovan observes that "the recapitulation is so important that the possibility of God modeling Christ anew from fresh mud, as it were, is excluded."[69]

This is no Irenaean fetish, a primitive hunt to find a one-to-one correspondence between Jesus and humanity, but rather the reflection of a theologian who believed that God entered the world to re-create it.[70]

68. "For just as through the disobedience of the one man the many were made sinners, so also through the obedience of the one man the many will be made righteous" (NIV).

69. Donovan, *One Right Reading?* p. 87.

70. Undergoing all the stages of the human life cycle ("for this reason he became an infant, because we were infants, so he might bring us to adulthood" [*AH* IV.38.2]), Jesus not only contains all of human experience, but all nations and generations prior to Him as well (*AH* III.22.3). Irenaeus can push the parallelism too far, imagining that Jesus actu-

Irenaeus's Jesus is not a Gnostic "receptacle" but a man pressed up against humanity — limb to limb, flesh to flesh, face to face — gathering all of creation into his own humanity in order to heal and save. But what is the basis for this supreme connectedness?

> For the Creator of the world is truly the Word of God: and this is our Lord, who in the last times was made man, existing in this world, and who in an invisible manner contains all things created, and is inherent in the entire creation, since the Word of God governs and arranges all things; and therefore He came to His own in a visible manner, and was made flesh, and hung upon the tree, that He might sum up all things in Himself. (*AH* V.18.3)

As mediator of creation, the Son has not descended to something foreign but has come to his own (*AH* V.2.1). The head of the original creation is the head of the new. M. C. Steenberg muses on this mutuality: "Irenaeus presents a deeply holistic typology wherein type and antitype are connected in a real and ontological manner, such that the activities of either one intimately affect the existence of the other."[71] Steenberg's observation is incisive but would benefit from deeper reflection on the two-staged headship of Christ over creation.[72] As head of the first creation, "Christ Jesus . . . gathered together [*recapitulans*] all things in Himself." As head of the new creation, "He is man, the formation of God; and thus He took up [*recapitulatus*] man into Himself . . . thus summing up [*recapitulans*] all things in Himself . . . as well as constituting Himself Head of the Church, He might draw all things to Himself at the proper time" (*AH* III.16.6).[73]

---

ally lived into ripe old age in order to sanctify all experiences of humanity (*AH* II.22.4-6), though we do not find him overly concerned about Jesus sharing the female experience!

71. M. C. Steenberg, "The Role of Mary as Co-Recapitulator in St Irenaeus of Lyons," *Vigiliae Christianae* 58 (2004): 130.

72. It is for lack of attention to this headship that Irenaeus became known for having a "physical" rather than "ethical" view of redemption. John Lawson follows Harnack in dismissing Irenaeus's views on human nature, calling Christ "the point of infection when divine-humanity propagated itself through the race" (John Lawson, *The Biblical Theology of Saint Irenaeus* [London: Epworth, 1948], p. 157). What defines human "nature" is not a static substance but humanity's relationship to its creator (*Deus facit, homo fit*). Christ's recapitulation of this nature was in restoring this primary relationship rather than some physical-mystical injection of his nature into our own.

73. *SC* 211:312-14.

For Irenaeus, recapitulation did not have so much to do with undoing wrong (though that it certainly did), but rather was an assertion of the Lordship of Christ over all reality, and thus of the unanimity of creation and redemption.

. . . unctus est a Patre Spiritu (AH III.9.3)

It was the descent of the Word into physicality that was Irenaeus's first battle. His second was to establish the Holy Spirit as the true protagonist of the baptismal descent. While the Gnostics speculated on all manner of *aeons* who descended onto Jesus (resulting in his docetization), Irenaeus maintains that it is none other than the Holy Spirit. "For Christ did not at that time descend upon Jesus, neither was Christ one and Jesus another: but the Word of God . . . was anointed by the Spirit from the Father [and] was made Jesus Christ" (*AH* III.9.3).

The significance is twofold — for Christ's humanity and for the human race. First, and quite remarkably, Irenaeus insists that Jesus genuinely needed the baptism of the Spirit for his mission.[74] "Inasmuch as the Word of God was man . . . in this respect did the Spirit of God rest upon Him, and anoint Him to preach the Gospel to the lowly" (*AH* III.9.3).[75] Rather than turning to his "naked" divine power, Jesus turns to the Spirit to carry out the divine mission appointed to him. In so doing, Jesus is choosing to live as a creature and submit, once again, to the *Deus facit, homo fit* distinction.

Here we have the heart of Irenaean recapitulation and the key to human ascent. Irenaeus notes that it is not only God's becoming human

---

74. A. Orbe, "El Espiritu en el bautismo de Jesus (en torno a san Ireneo)," *Gregorianum* 76 (1995): 663-99. See also the discussion in Daniel A. Smith, "Irenaeus and the Baptism of Jesus," *Theological Studies* 58 (1997): 626-29.

75. Irenaeus is no adoptionist. Irenaeus holds the Spirit to be essential to the Son's mission, but not to his divinity. To this end, Irenaeus speaks of the sevenfold gifts given to the Son for precisely this mission (*Epideixis* 9). He is not "approaching here a view held by his Gnostic opponents," as Daniel Smith argues, thus underestimating how much Irenaeus allows the Spirit truly to constitute the divine-human person of the Son (Smith, "Irenaeus and the Baptism of Jesus," p. 632). At the other extreme, neither can we follow Gustaf Wingren, who undermines the role that Irenaeus assigns the Spirit in the life of Christ. "But Jesus' life is a life of undestroyed humanity only because God dwells in Him. . . . Jesus has become pure man, i.e., He has become victor, by reason of His divinity" (Wingren, *Man and the Incarnation*, p. 136).

that is needed for our salvation, "but also that a human being would give himself to God" (*AH* III.18.7).[76] Anatolios corroborates this, observing that, in Irenaeus, it is "not simply generic divinity, God-stuff, that is being joined to humanity in Christ," but rather that Jesus, "as Son of the Father, is a Godward God."[77] In recapitulation of Adam's refusal to grow, Jesus is the man who has surrendered to his createdness — receiving at every moment what he needs from the Father — and thus fulfilling his calling as human.[78] In his person, creation is reoriented once again to growth and ascent.

Second, the Spirit not only empowers the human Jesus' mission, he *is* Jesus' mission. Jesus is the one who is reseeding the human race with the Spirit. In a startling succession of agrarian images, Irenaeus likens the cross to a plow whose purpose is to "cleanse his land." By this "mechanism fixed with pins," Christ's crucifixion "has reclaimed the savage earth" and made it ready for planting and "the gathering in of the produce in the last times" (*AH* IV.34.4). Having been "cleansed" and "reclaimed" in the person of Christ, humanity is now ready once again to receive the Spirit. "Wherefore [the Spirit] did also descend upon the Son of God, made the Son of man, becoming accustomed in fellowship with Him to dwell in the human race . . ." (*AH* III.17.1). Irenaeus envisions this transforming dynamic as Jesus remaking a home in humanity for the Spirit, by "accustoming" the Spirit to his former dwelling and making it inviting once again. Irenaeus is distinctive in the history of theology for making the Holy Spirit an essential component of human being, augmenting Paul's tripartite division to "body, soul, and *Holy* Spirit" (*AH* V.6.1). Christ's mission, therefore, is indeed a recapitulation, given that Irenaeus sees Adam's sin as a rejection of the Spirit with dire consequences for human anthropology.[79]

It is imperative to note that Jesus does not do this *for* or *to* humanity, but he is the locus where it all happens. Humanity's past, present, and future are funneled into the person of the Son. "These things He recapitu-

76. "Et facere ut et Deus adsumeret hominem et homo se dederet Deo" (*SC* 211:366); translation by Donovan, *One Right Reading?* p. 84.

77. Anatolios, "Immediately," p. 173; see also Hart, "Irenaeus," p. 161.

78. *Epideixis* 15; *AH* III.20.1.

79. For Irenaeus, the soul does validate the body, but the soul serves the body in receiving the Spirit (*AH* III.18.2). For how this engaged with Gnostic anthropology, see Roger Berthouzoz, *Liberté et grâce suivant la théologie d'Irénée de Lyon* (Paris: Cerf, 1980), pp. 95-102.

lated in Himself . . ." (*AH* V.20.2). Iain MacKenzie notes how theologies of redemption usually fall short of Irenaeus's understanding, for "redemption is not a transaction of which Christ is the agent; He is redemption embodied. . . . Humanity attains its redemption by participation in Him."[80] But it would be a mistake to miss, as MacKenzie often does, Irenaeus's pneumatological basis for this. Farrow leads the way: "If Jesus is head of the human race from Adam to the last generation, if indeed he is lord of all creation, it is as and because the Spirit lends to that creation a perichoretic form of existence which is centered on him."[81] This is the crucial insight of Irenaeus's doctrine of participation that remains firmly pneumatological, not only christological.

> Wherefore also the Lord promised to send the Comforter, who should join us to God. For as a compacted lump of dough cannot be formed of dry wheat without fluid matter, nor can a loaf possess unity, so, in like manner, neither could we, being many, be made one in Christ Jesus without the water from heaven. (*AH* III.17.2)

To this end, Orbe provocatively speaks of Christ as the "virtual man" on account of creation, and as becoming the "actual man" by the Spirit.[82] The Spirit — as the agent of Christ's own transformation — comes to produce the same life within us, by putting us "into Christ," who in turn gives us the gift of this selfsame Spirit. Christ recapitulates all for us, but we are not merely linked to, or included in, this completed recapitulation. Rather, the recapitulation is the inauguration of life once again in the Spirit, and so itself is the introduction to a dynamic way of being with and in God.

Thus the anointing of Jesus Christ stands out as a fundamental moment in human history. "Therefore did the Spirit of God descend upon Him . . . so that we, receiving from the abundance of His unction, might be saved" (*AH* III.9.3). Christ's primary mission is to receive and give the Spirit — or, as Farrow summarizes, "to draw the Spirit into man and man

---

80. MacKenzie, *Demonstration*, p. 181.

81. Douglas Farrow, *Ascension and Ecclesia* (Grand Rapids: Eerdmans, 1999), p. 60.

82. A. Orbe, *La Uncion del Verbo*, Estudios Valentinianos, vol. III (Rome: Gregorian University, 1961), p. 633. This is corroborated by Anatolios, who perceives in Irenaeus that "if the Son is the Godward God, the Spirit is the one who actualizes the Godward stance of the Son as a human communal Godward stance" (Anatolios, "Immediately," p. 176).

into the Spirit, that man might truly become a living being."[83] In Jesus, the "new human," we discover a specifically Trinitarian way of being human:

> These things, therefore, He recapitulated in Himself: by uniting man to the Spirit, and causing the Spirit to dwell in man, He is Himself made the head of the Spirit, and gives the Spirit to be the head of man: for through Him (the Spirit) we see, and hear, and speak. (*AH* V.20.2)

By paying attention to Christ as the locus of where this all begins, Irenaeus not only defines the human as one receiving the Spirit but also reveals the vocation of humanity to be progression in the Spirit. Jesus' anointing both underscores and fulfills his humanity: though part of Christ's very humanness was bound up in his conception *by* the Spirit, he himself needed to progress *in* the Spirit to baptism and beyond. Ysabel de Andia calls this the ". . . progressive pneumatization of his flesh — conceived by the Spirit, anointed by the Spirit, resurrected by the Spirit."[84]

For Irenaeus, these "pneumatological installments" are snapshots in Christ's career, giving us glimpses into a dynamic pneumatological life of communion with God in the Spirit. The debate about whether Irenaeus believed that Christ received all he needed at conception — or later, at baptism — appears wrongheaded, for the Spirit is not a quantitative but a distinctly qualitative element in the life of Christ.[85] Christ grows in *koinōnia* — in love for the Father in the Spirit — just as all humanity is intended for this very growth. Anatolios relates the significance of the baptism this way: "The descent of the Spirit upon Jesus is the event whereby the divine fellowship between the Son and the Spirit is extended to humanity through the humanity of the Word made Incarnate."[86] It is only Irenaeus's robust Trinitarianism that takes seriously the Spirit as the dynamic of the Christian life that makes this possible. "For in the name of Christ is implied, He that anoints, He that is anointed, and the unction itself with which He is anointed" (*AH* III.18.3).[87] And as Irenaeus reminds

---

83. Farrow, *Ascension*, p. 60.

84. Ysabel de Andia, "La résurrection de la chair selon les Valentiniens et Irénée de Lyon," *Les Quatre Fleuves* 15-16 (1982): 67.

85. For the details of this debate, see Daniel Smith, "Irenaeus and the Baptism of Jesus," pp. 631-34.

86. Anatolios, "Immediately," p. 175.

87. See also *AH* III.9.3. I disagree with Smith's interpretation: "Irenaeus did not ap-

us, Jesus' baptismal anointing is nothing less than a preparation for Pentecost (*AH* III.17.1).

> *. . . et in carne in caelos ascensionem dilecti*
> *Iesu Christi Domini nostri.* (AH *I.10.1*)

In his study of Irenaeus and the Ascension, Douglas Farrow observes that Irenaeus orients the creation mandate to "increase and multiply," not to creation, but to Pentecost. In a striking quotation, Irenaeus charts the slow growth of humanity through creation to servitude, to freedom, to sonship, and to full participation in God. This, he says, is the fulfillment of the creation mandate: "For He formed him for growth and increase, and the Scripture says: 'Increase and multiply'" (*AH* IV.11.1). Here we see Irenaeus grounding the human vocation in creation but consistently orienting it to the future — in the Pentecostal abundance and fruitfulness of the Spirit.

> By allowing the Ascension and Pentecost to serve as a commentary on Genesis 1, [Irenaeus] further develops his thesis that it is of the essence of man to advance towards God. Freedom in and for this advancement — understood as an actual increase of being which flows from a common participation in the communal life of God — becomes for him the *conditio sine qua non* of human existence.[88]

By tying human growth to Christ's Ascension, Irenaeus shows that no account of anthropology can make only side reference to Christ. Nor can any account of Irenaean growth put itself forward as an unbroken ascension since the time of the Garden of Eden (Hick, R. Brown). The growth of humanity does not properly begin in the Garden of Eden, but in the other garden — Gethsemane. And for this reason, as Farrow reminds us again and again, Irenaeus does not put forward a general "ascent of man" but rather the *ascent of the one man*.[89]

---

pear to conceive of the Spirit as a distinct person, but rather as the Spirit or power of the Father, or (in the case of the conception) as the divinity of the Son" (Smith, "Irenaeus and Baptism," p. 624).

88. Farrow, "St. Irenaeus," pp. 347-48.

89. There are those who would pit Irenaeus against himself (Harnack, R. Brown, F. Altermath), arguing that recapitulation (a return) is at odds with his creation theology of growth (an advance). This is clearly only a problem for those who read into Irenaeus evolutionary rather than pneumatological definitions of "growth." Henri Lassiat analyzes

Irrespective of sin, there never was any "growth" without the two hands. Von Balthasar is truly perceptive here: "The last chapter [Christ] does not take its lead from the first [Adam], but the other way round, as the true art of storytelling demands. So the physical world is the promise of the supernature which is to follow. . . ."[90] What is the supernature of which von Balthasar hints? It is the new form of human existence broken open by the Ascension: that of living by the Spirit in the presence of the Son and Father. Creation, even from the start, is oriented toward the new creation.[91]

Jesus' Ascension serves as the final nail in the coffin of Gnosticized ascent: "And still further, some affirm that neither their soul nor their body can receive eternal life, but merely the inner man . . . which they decree as being the only thing to ascend to 'the perfect'" (*AH* V.19.2). Jesus' physical ascent was not the ultimate rejection of the material world but its validation as the reinstated home of the Spirit (*AH* IV.18.5). He "ascend[ed] to the height above, offering and commending to His Father that human nature [*hominem*] which had been found, making in His own person the first-fruits of the resurrection of man" (*AH* III.19.3). By bringing human nature to the presence of the Father, he is not merely "man" in heaven, but man as fully possessed by the Spirit. This is the trump card that Irenaeus plays to prove that the goal of God's economy is not the spiritualized man, but the en-Spirited Man who then gives this very Spirit to humanity.[92] "And the third article is the Holy Spirit . . . who *in*

---

the semantic range of ἀνακεφαλαίωσις *(recapitulatio)*, revealing that it carries both a sense of "return" and also "fulfillment/perfection," depending on the meaning assigned to the preposition ἀνα and the subsequent substantive κεφαλή (Lassiat, *Promotion de l'homme en Jésus-Christ d'après Irénée de Lyon* [Paris: Mame, 1974], p. 283 n. 8). Eric Osborn points out that the term was primarily a literary one in the second century (Osborn, "The Logic of Recapitulation," in *Pléroma: Salus carnis, Homenaje a Antonio Orbe*, ed. Eugenio Romero-Rose [Santiago de Compostella, Spain: Aldecoa, 1990], p. 321). Thus it would not be improper for us to read into the term the notion of Christ as the "summary" of Scripture as well.

90. Von Balthasar, *Glory II*, p. 73.

91. Because the substance of *caro* is integral to Irenaean anthropology, it is not destroyed — as Origen would have it — but resurrected. The resurrection thus manifests salvation (rather than constitutes it), in that in the resurrection we see that flesh is once again in the dimension of the Spirit (*AH* IV.31.2; *Epideixis* 72, 73).

92. Irenaeus follows John's Gospel, which posits the Ascension as the *condition* for Pentecost: "Up to that time the Spirit had not been given, since Jesus had not yet been glorified" (John 7:39, NIV).

the end of time has been poured forth in a new manner upon humanity . . ." (*Epideixis* 6).

In rather dated language, d'Alès calls this "a heavenly reality: his humanity, fully penetrated by the Spirit of God, having become the life-
giving Spirit."[93] This is unfortunate in that it draws attention away from
Christ's deified humanity qua humanity-in-full-communion-with-God
and to a more physical notion of substance-penetrated-by-Spirit. We
must avoid this for two reasons. First, it downplays the notion of Christ's
ongoing priesthood in that it emphasizes the physical species at the right
hand of the Father rather than Jesus as the human who perfectly gave
himself to the Father (*AH* III.18.7), and incorporates us into his Our Father prayer. "Wherefore," Irenaeus continues, "he passed through every
stage of life, restoring to all communion with God." Second, a focus on
Christ's "deified humanity" can, despite all intentions, de-emphasize the
koinōnia that is the reality of his completed mission.[94] Irenaeus makes
clear that Christ's Ascension is for humanity's *telos*, which, because it is
Trinitarian, is always personal: "He has also poured out the Spirit of the
Father for the union and communion of God and man, imparting indeed
God to men by means of the Spirit, and, on the other hand, attaching men
to God by His own incarnation, and bestowing upon us at His coming
immortality durably and truly, by means of communion with God . . ."
(*AH* V.1.1).

In the Ascension, the drama between the Spirit, Christ, and humanity
is an unceasing dance. Christ's Ascension is in many ways the culmination
of a human life lived in the Spirit. He does not leave off being human in
the Ascension, but he enters a fuller form of human existence more perfectly in harmony with the Spirit — which has been creation's vocation all
along. Having ascended, he enters his state of glory, "to gather all things
into one," and to return this very Spirit back on all creation that they
might enter this perichoretic existence (*AH* I.10.1). "Thus does he attribute the Spirit as peculiar to God, which in the last times He pours forth
upon the human race by the adoption of sons . . ." (*AH* V.12.2). The Spirit

93. "[A] heavenly reality: his humanity, fully penetrated by the Spirit of God, having
become the life-giving Spirit" (Alès, "L'Esprit," p. 516).

94. I follow Torrance's caution here: "To be concerned with the Spirit, to know him,
to be acted on by him, is immediately to be concerned with the Being or *ousia* of God the
Creator. That, as I understand it, is the import of the patristic notion of *theosis* or 'deification'" (T. F. Torrance, *"Spiritus Creator,"* in *Theology in Reconstruction* [London: SCM,
1965], p. 214).

that he sends is not a general spirit of progress but, much more pointedly, the "Spirit of adoption" who brings humanity into this cruciform and filial form, that in him they might return to the Father.[95] Ascent takes on sharp definition as adoption.

The Ascent in Christ: Adoption

Humanity's ascent is not an unbroken progression from the Garden, but it requires serious intervention.[96] Accordingly, "growth" is not an adequate metaphor on its own for Irenaean anthropology because it does not take sufficient account of the Son and Spirit. Singled out as a lone strand in Irenaeus's anthropological tapestry, a theology of "growth" in Irenaeus can stray into anthropologies that look more like an apotheosis of humanity. For it is not just that creation is suitable for growth (as Irenaeus had to first convince the Gnostics), but that this growth has ultimately occurred *in the Son.* This is Irenaeus's "true art of storytelling" in action, as von Balthasar calls it, where the "first chapter" of growth actually takes its lead from the last.

It is no coincidence that Irenaeus portrays the goal of humanity's ascent to be the Father — the grand terminus of human growth that is a relationship (called the "face-to-face" or "paternal" vision). If we are to arrive at such a destination, it is only as sons and in his person, "the Spirit truly preparing man in the Son of God, and the Son leading him to the Father" (*AH* IV.20.5). The Son and Spirit are equal players in this ascent, with adoption taking place through the Son (*AH* II.11.1), and the Spirit

95. Yet, as his battle with the "heretics" makes clear, this does not amount to wholesale universalism. Even though subjective appropriation is not an issue with which Irenaeus is concerned, Norman Russell points out that all the patristic fathers worked with a distinction between ontological participation and dynamic/personal participation in the Son (Russell, "'Partakers of the Divine Nature' [2 Peter 1:4] in the Byzantine Tradition," in *ΚΑΘΗΓΗΤΡΙΑ,* ed. J. M. Hussey [Camberley, UK: Porphyrogenitus, 1988], pp. 51-67).

96. Humanity's ascent has been reconfigured into God's ascent — and that at a costly price (*Epideixis* 31). It involves the *re*-creation of the sixth day. The Son of man "underwent His sufferings upon the day preceding the Sabbath, that is, the sixth day of the creation, on which man was created; thus granting him a second creation by means of His passion . . ." (*AH* V.23.2). See Trevor Hart's defense of Irenaeus's strong conception of sin (Hart, "Irenaeus," pp. 165-66, 173-74).

getting us accustomed to this new status as sons. An attention to the "exchange" motif in Irenaeus, precisely this adoptive exchange, keeps his ascending anthropology in its proper context.

Despite recognizing that Irenaeus had the first "exchange formula," Irenaean scholarship shows little consensus as to its nature. The formula of exchange that has become associated with him — "the Word of God, our Lord Jesus Christ, who did, through his transcendent love, become what we are, that he might bring us to be even what he is himself" (*AH* V.Pref) — is but one of many.[97]

> For it was for this end that the Word of God was made man, and He who was the Son of God became the Son of man, that man, having been taken into the Word, and receiving the adoption, might become the son of God. (*AH* III.19.1)

What is being exchanged is not humanity for divinity (a common misreading of the Irenaean exchange), but an alienated humanity for a *koinōnia*-humanity.[98] Note carefully that humanity is not just given this altered relationship *ex nihilo*, but receives it only as "having been taken into the Word." Adoption is being taken into the Son, his progress, his ascent to the Father. Irenaeus never encapsulates humanity's future as becoming gods except to put down Gnostic dualism, and then he consistently clarifies this future in Trinitarian terms (adoption, image and likeness, filiation, incorruptibility, and the like).[99] The significance of this is that it gives growth a decided slant toward *koinōnia*, which becomes strikingly clear in Irenaeus's exegesis of Psalm 82.

---

97. "Son of God" — *AH* III.10.2; "receive the adoption" — *AH* III.16.3; "adoption of sons" — *AH* III.18.7; "accustom man to receive God" — *AH* III.20.2; "accustomed to eat and drink the Word of God . . . [and] to contain in ourselves the Bread of immortality, which is the Spirit of the Father" — *AH* IV.38.1, to name a few.

98. Mosser reminds us that it was not only nineteenth- and twentieth-century protestant liberals (Harnack, Inge) who mistook the Irenaean exchange, but currently Mormon scholarship has taken on this formula as evidence for its doctrine of eschatological polytheism (Carl Mosser, "Mormonism and the Christian Doctrine of Deification" [Th.M. thesis, Fuller Theological Seminary, 2002], pp. 262-66).

99. Thierry Scherrer attests that "'sonship' and 'divinization' are equivalent terms for Irenaeus" (Scherrer, *Gloire*, p. 129). Adoptive sonship, though, keeps us from the monism of Hellenistic divinization, because adoption is *by* the Spirit, *in* the Son (and through his flesh!), *to* the Father.

It is a common assumption that the early fathers grounded deification on Peter's comment about becoming "partakers of the divine nature." However, 1 and 2 Peter were not accepted as part of the canon until the fourth century. A biblical theology of "deification," therefore, was not dependent upon this text but rested upon an antecedent Jewish exegetical tradition of Psalm 82, combined with Pauline notions of divine sonship. In the face of the Valentinian claim to a divine anthropology and plurality of deities, Irenaeus does not shy away from these verses but instead reappropriates them for *koinōnia*:

> And again, "God stood in the congregation of the gods. He judges among the gods." He refers to the Father and the Son, and those who have received the adoption; but these are the Church. . . . Who is meant by God? He of whom He has said, "God shall come openly. . . ." But of what gods does he speak? Of those to whom He says, "I have said, 'Ye are gods, and all sons of the Most High.'" To those, no doubt, who have received the grace of the "adoption, by which we cry, *Abba*, Father." (*AH* III.6.1)

Here Irenaeus shows his opponents that those who are "gods" are those who have been *adopted*, having been brought to share not in a divine substance but in divine *sonship*. Furthermore, the allusion to Romans 8:14-16 places the "divine property" of sonship squarely in the Spirit's realm.[100] Clearly, what is "deifying" about the exchange is not the sort of species that humanity becomes, but the divine origin of the gift: sonship.[101] Adelin Rousseau believes that the cry of *Abba* epitomizes full

---

100. Although some would read the legal nature of the Greco-Roman world into early conceptions of adoption, Irenaeus clearly takes his cue from the world of Scripture: the self-chosen opening of God and his inner relationships. See J. M. Scott, who argues against adoption (υἱοθεσία) as only a legal metaphor in Paul (Scott, "Adoption, Sonship," in *A Dictionary of Paul and his Letters*, ed. Gerald F. Hawthorne and Ralph P. Martin [Downers Grove, IL: InterVarsity, 1993], p. 16).

101. "Without exception, in the earliest extant postbiblical Christian interpretations of Psalm 82:6, the most significant phrase is the declaration to divine sonship, not the declaration of godhood. The psalm was read as a descriptive summary of salvation history. The declaration to sonship was considered a prophecy of the Johannine and Pauline notions of being begotten and adopted as children of God and being raised in glory. Because of the synonymous parallelism within the verse, the patristic writers were happy to apply the word "gods" to glorified believers, but this was done on the basis of Paul's

participation in divine life: "One would not be betraying the thought of the Bishop of Lyons by saying that, for him, the adopted sons are truly — though by grace and participation — that which the Father and Son are by nature."[102] This becomes more apparent in Irenaeus's second quotation of Psalm 82 against the Ebionites (*AH* III.19.1), in which he also explains "gods" in terms of adoption, and adoption as being "taken into the Word." This is not an acquired gift or a "formal" effect of grace, but participation in the Holy Spirit, who leads us into the triune *koinōnia* of Father and Son.

Adoption is equally an ethical progression. Thierry Scherrer notes that Irenaeus characterizes the work of sanctification as the glory of adoption, where the Spirit engraves the very traits of the Son on the church.[103] It is not the abstract fulfillment of a moral code but seeing the marks of the Son in humanity that delights the Father, "so that by means of his resemblance to the Son, man might become precious to the Father" (*AH* V.16.2). Irenaean ethics are adoption ethics: the church's actions now flow from love and familial confidence, for "the children possess greater confidence [than the servants] . . ." (*AH* IV.13.2). Irenaeus reminds us that, though humanity's former slavery was self-imposed (*AH* IV.15.1), God has entered our situation, broken our bondage, and himself bestows the proper ethical response:

> Granting to men largely and without grudging, by means of adoption, to know God the Father, and to love Him with the whole heart, and to follow His word unswervingly. . . . But He has also increased the feeling of reverence; for sons should have more veneration than slaves, and greater love for their father. (*AH* IV.16.5)

The very shape of the ethical life is communion, in which ethics spring from the altered sphere of *koinōnia* that is given to humanity. Irenaeus clearly gives participation priority in ethics: he begins not with an ethical injunction but by reminding us that we received "in addition the Son of God, that man too might be a partaker [*particeps*/μέτοχος] of God." Only then does Irenaeus extrapolate that thus "our walk in life required to be

---

teaching that believers would be raised to incorruptibility and immortality (1 Cor. 15)" (Mosser, "Earliest Patristic Interpretations," p. 73).

102. From Rousseau's commentary in *SC* 210:254.

103. Scherrer, *Gloire*, p. 131.

more circumspect . . ." (*AH* IV.28.2). If it is from the posture of sonship that actions are truly ethical, then all ethics is personal encounter, arising as it does from participation in the Son.[104] We have been brought from slaves to sons in this great recapitulatory "operation of liberty," which "implies that a more complete subjection and affection towards our Liberator has been implanted within us" (*AH* IV.13.3).

Ethics springs from the fact that humanity now has the affections of adoption. Iain MacKenzie calls this a "double-demonstration," first of the Son and then of *sons*, "who witness to this by their words and acts which point to Christ as the substance and circumference, the center and the horizon, of their proclamation. . . . Any such disjunction would mean that they had become something else. 'Demonstration' as applied to the activity of the faithful, is the stamp, the impression, the likeness, of the Word made flesh upon them. By their words and action, the Word made flesh is perceived; through them He is made audible and visible and therefore demonstrated."[105]

* * *

Irenaeus's christology is an exposition also of the Spirit: the Spirit who conceived Jesus, anointed him, and then was given in Pentecost to the world through him. Equally, this Spirit puts humanity into Christ. Both the God-to-human and the human-to-God directions are prominent in Irenaeus's christology. Salvation is both God's reaching out to humanity and the recapitulation of the human response to God. To participate in this response to God is to become sons, to be liberated into a new way of relating to God such that we act like and begin to look like sons as well.

Likewise, Irenaeus's christology has radical anthropological ramifications. Adam's sin was to reject being human, opting instead for an experiment of autonomy and instant growth. In Farrow's pithy phrase, sin sent humanity "into reverse."[106] Jesus' recapitulation of this grave disordering not only restored human anthropology but its *koinōnia*-existence. The de-

104. The Platonizing tendencies in Justin's ethics (imitation of God's perfections, *Apol.* I.10.1, II.4.2) have been overcome in Irenaeus, who even interprets Jesus' Sermon on the Mount in terms of slaves/sons (*AH* IV.13.3). For Justin's ethics, see Gerhard May, *Creatio ex Nihilo* (Edinburgh: T. & T. Clark, 1994), p. 128.

105. MacKenzie, *Demonstration*, p. 36. He is playing, of course, on the title of Irenaeus's *Epideixis*, which is translated as "demonstration," or "proof."

106. Farrow, *Ascension and Ecclesia*, p. 51.

scent of the Spirit on Christ thus becomes central to Irenaeus's defense of human anthropology against the Gnostics who "set aside" the Spirit, thus "imbibing a poison" (*AH* III.17.4). "In Christ there was a restoration of the true human nature, not an external addition of 'grace' to an otherwise autonomous human existence."[107] This is no mere return to the beginning, but "a new starting point."[108] Humanity's true ascending vocation is returned to it, yet with ascent amassing greater Trinitarian clarity. Restored ascent is now christologically conceived and pneumatologically defined. In the words of Wingren, "to be in Him is to be at home in humanity's true being."[109]

The Ascending Economy of the Spirit

"The Holy Spirit . . . the ladder of ascent to God"

Now we see the three anthropological strands discerned by de Andia coming together. The economic ascent of humanity is part of its very createdness, for God never stops giving to his creation, nor does his creation cease receiving (I). The christological ascent of humanity is tied up in its forerunner: his ascent heralds not the withdrawal of God from the sphere of creation, but its entry into God. Jesus' ascent marks the total overthrow of Satan's dominion, which was to tear flesh apart from Spirit (II). Now we grasp the third pneumatological strand: having fully received the Spirit, Jesus' flesh becomes the pivot of the Spirit who is poured out on all humanity, "the Holy Spirit, the earnest of incorruption, the means of confirming our faith, and the ladder of ascent to God" (*AH* III.24.1).

107. John Meyendorff, "Humanity: 'Old' and 'New' — Anthropological Considerations," in *Salvation in Christ: A Lutheran-Orthodox Dialogue,* ed. John Meyendorff and Robert Tobias (Minneapolis: Augsburg, 1992), p. 62.

108. Pierre Évieux, "Théologie de l'accoutumance chez saint Irénée," *Recherches de Science Religieuse* 55 (1967): 54.

109. Wingren, *Incarnation*, p. 154.

The Human Protagonist

Under the lens of creation, all was taken from the necessary theocentric standpoint: God makes, humanity is made. God gives, humanity receives. Under the lens of the Spirit, though, things are different. Irenaeus takes great liberties to highlight this recapitulated creature and the Spirit's marvelous work of transformation. This is not only a deliberate snub of Gnostic dualism; it is perhaps the most remarkable aspect of Irenaean anthropology, where he uses flesh to prove God.

> ### Adversus haereses III.20.2
> The glory of the human being is God; and the receptacle of the operation of God and of all God's wisdom and power is the human being.[110] Just as the physician is proved by his patients, so is God also revealed through men.

> ### Adversus haereses IV.20.7
> For the glory of God is a living man; and the life of man consists in beholding God.

> ### Adversus haereses V.36.3
> One "Father . . . one Son . . . one human race also in which the mysteries of God are wrought."

Chastising Gnostic inability to differentiate in Scripture between mere "flesh" and the miracle of "flesh receiving the Holy Spirit" (*AH* V.8.1), Irenaeus proclaims that flesh is not the antithesis of the Spirit but is his magnum opus. God receives glory not by dissolving his creation but by raising precisely this substance to his own sphere of union and communion. In the words of Orbe, "making contemplation of Himself the life of human *caro*, now inchoative, finally total through the five senses."[111] While shame of human weakness gave rise to Gnostic spin doctors, Irenaeus announced the pe-

---

110. "Gloria enim hominis Deus, operationis vero Dei et omnis sapientiae eius et virtutis receptaculum homo" (*SC* 211:388). The English translation is by Mary Ann Donovan, *One Right Reading?* p. 85, which is a vast improvement on the *ANF* rendition: "For the glory of man [is] God, but [His] works [are the glory] of God; and the receptacle of all His wisdom and power [is] man."

111. Orbe, "Irenaeus," p. 414.

culiarity of the Christian God, who ties his glory to the perfection of weakness. "The flesh, therefore, is not destitute [of participation] in the constructive wisdom and power of God. But . . . the power of Him who is the bestower of life is made perfect in weakness — that is, in flesh . . ." (*AH* V.3.3). Those who are "spiritual" are only so "because they possess the Spirit of the Father, who purifies man, and raises him up to the life of God" (*AH* V.9.2).

If situating the human at the center was essential for his polemic against the Gnostics, it was the Ascension that gave Irenaeus theological grounds to do so. The Ascension of Jesus clinches the process that had begun with his birth: that of returning the Spirit to the flesh of humanity. Thus the human body — that former place of death — becomes the very locus of God's activity and presence (*AH* V.19.2), for we have access to God's Spirit in no other place. Human flesh now takes center stage in the ongoing Irenaean drama. It is this aspect of Irenaeus that von Balthasar believes to be so inaccessible to the Protestant tradition:

> This whole economy proclaims the pure goodness of the God who guides it. In comparison, any kind of spiritualizing does violence to man and in the end takes its revenge by turning into a new legalism. It does so because spiritualising of every stamp despises the *naturalia praecepta* and has to replace them with purely positive ones. This has been confirmed time and again by the history of the Church and of dogmatics, and it is also the reason why Irenaeus' basic attitude cannot be assimilated by true Protestantism. The ancient Greek idea, also sanctioned by the Bible, of God's "lack of envy," the idea that God is not jealous of created nature, but is able to guide it gently and, where necessary, even to crucify it, is dear to Irenaeus.[112]

But this is precisely Irenaeus's gift to the whole church. Forced by the Gnostics to reckon with the goodness of nature, Irenaeus perceives the "goodness" of creation to be precisely its *inscape:* "the Son and the Spirit, by whom the world is held in continuing relation to God the Father."[113] Thus Irenaeus is freed to build a "christology on the concept of man,"[114]

---

112. Von Balthasar, *Glory II*, p. 80.

113. I borrow Colin Gunton's spin on Gerard Manley Hopkins's famous term (Gunton, *The One, the Three, and the Many* [Cambridge: Cambridge University Press, 1993], p. 55).

114. Oscar Cullmann, *The Christology of the New Testament* (London: SCM, 1963), p. 189.

and to prove the "Trinity . . . by the history of mankind" because the foundation is one in which the Trinitarian *koinōnia* of God upholds this relational universe (*AH* V.18.2).[115] For even with the human being at center stage, this is still humanity under the two hands. Irenaeus remains steadfast in his focus on God, God's gifts, God's sustenance — even as he celebrates humanity's appropriation of these things.[116]

Thus it comes as no surprise that Irenaeus centers the entire divine drama on the singular stage of humanity. This is the central mystery of the *Deus facit; homo fit* drama, in which God's giving and humanity's receiving provide the suspense for all acts of the play. Taking its cue from Greek tragedies, Gnostic drama took place in the aeons and pleromas irrespective of humanity, whose fate was long settled by these cosmic events. Humanity was given no script but only had a part to sing in the chorus of "nature" — depending on which of the three natures one possessed.[117] Instead, Irenaeus scores the gradual ascension of humanity, free to accept their creation-call to perfection under the tutelage of the two hands.

> For by means of the very same hands through which they were moulded at the beginning, did they receive this translation and elevation. For in Adam the hands of God had become accustomed to set in order, to rule, and to sustain His own workmanship, and to bring it and place it where they pleased. (*AH* V.5.1)

And where is this "place" that the two hands are pleased to "translate" and "elevate" humanity? It is the *state* of being in full reception of the Spirit, such that the creation purposes of God are completely fulfilled.[118] The

---

115. J. Quasten, *Patrology*, vol. 1 (Utrecht: Spectrum, 1962), p. 294.

116. At times Irenaeus focuses on the gift, other times on the giver. But this should never tempt us to separate them, for they are "inseparable" in Irenaeus, says Adhémer d' Alès ("L'Esprit," p. 530).

117. It is no accident that Irenaeus aimed Paul's tripartite anthropology specifically against the tripartite anthropology of the Gnostics (*AH* I.6.1), who divided humans not into three parts, but into three classes: the spiritual substance (already divine), the material substance (incapable of receiving anything divine), and animal substance (halfway between, inclining either to the material or spiritual). See n. 79 above in this chapter.

118. The context of the discussion is of the "ascensions" of Enoch and Elijah, who are representatives of humanity's ascent "in the substance of the natural form . . . thus pointing out by anticipation the translation of the just." Irenaeus then makes clear that the "just" are humans "such as have the Spirit" (*AH* V.5.1).

goal of the two hands is humanity's full participation in God and his benefits (*AH* IV.14.1), which Irenaeus often describes as humanity being grown
so that it can "contain God" or "bear God."

"The Holy Spirit . . . the ladder of ascent to God" (AH III.24.1)

The whole Irenaean history of salvation can be seen through this slow
process by which humanity is "little by little accustomed [*assuescentes*] to
receive and bear God" (*AH* V.8.1). To follow in the footsteps of this verb
"to accustom" (*assuesco* occurs twenty-four times in *Adversus Haereses*) is to
catch sight of Irenaeus's unique ascending anthropology, stretched out as
it is over a chronological frame.[119] We will also follow how often the
Latin word *assuesco* is paired with its goal — *capere et portare Deum* — creation being accustomed to receive and bear God.[120]

In the Ante-Nicene Fathers *(ANF)* English edition of *Adversus
haereses, capere* is translated as "to contain" or "to receive." Its nuances are
that of the relationship of two objects, one of which is being obtained by
the other. In this specific context, humanity is being "little by little accustomed" to contain, receive, take, or — as Houssiau thinks is most proper —
to "seize" that which it is not.[121] The connection to Irenaeus's doctrine of
participation is unmistakable, not least the fact that the root word of participation, *particeps*, is *pars* + *capere*, the "sharing in" a part. The other word
that Irenaeus uses is *portare*, translated as either "to bear" or "to sustain."
Von Balthasar says: "*Portare* ranges between the dignity and suitability for
receiving the weight of a burden, the burden of God, the responsibility of
carrying it with oneself, of carrying it to the end. . . ."[122] Its nuances are that
of *capere* extended over a long period of time: not only have the two objects
been reconciled *(capere)*, but they are now in a long-term relationship with
one another such that humanity is said to sustain *(portare)* this state of participation in God. All three members of the Trinity are at one time or another said to be grasped by humanity in this way.[123]

119. Évieux, "Théologie," p. 7.
120. *AH* V.8.1, *SC* 153:92.
121. Houssiau feels that "to seize" is superior to "to contain," especially given that
Irenaeus's polemic against the Gnostics was about their mistaken belief that God was
"contained within bounds, but does not contain" (*AH* IV.3.1).
122. Von Balthasar, *Glory II*, p. 56.
123. *Portare* — God (*AH* V.8.1; *SC* 153:92); the Spirit (*AH* IV.14.2; *SC* 100[2]:542);

Seized by the Son: Accustoming

Even in the Garden, Adam needed "accustoming" to be able to receive the full gifts of the Spirit, for he was "neither accustomed nor disciplined to perfection" (*AH* IV.38.1).[124] Here Irenaeus is not speaking of an aesthetic or moral perfection; rather, he insists upon "terming those persons 'perfect' who have received the Spirit of God" (*AH* V.6.1). As we noted of Christ's progressive reception of the Spirit, the Spirit is not a quantifiable object for Irenaeus, but a quality of life as deeper *koinōnia* with God. Full *koinōnia* is a glory that Adam cannot stomach from the outset, for "even if he had received the Spirit, he could not have contained [*capere*] it" (*AH* IV.38.2). Though the full module of "accustoming" was to happen within the pleasant bounds of the Garden, Adam instead refused the Holy Spirit.[125] The "longsuffering" God (*AH* III.20.1) then changed course, and the divine drama continued unabated on the stage of history throughout different "economies."[126]

> Thus it was, too, that God formed man at the first, because of His munificence; but chose the patriarchs for the sake of their salvation; and prepared a people beforehand, teaching the headstrong to follow God; and raised up prophets upon earth, accustoming [*accuescens*] man to bear [*portare*] His Spirit, and to hold communion with God. (*AH* IV.14.2)[127]

---

capere — God (*AH* V.8.1; *SC* 153:92); the Father (*AH* III.20.2; *SC* 211:392); the Word (*AH* V.36.3; *SC* 153:466); *continere* — the Spirit (*AH* IV.38.1; *SC* 100[2]:948).

124. This is not physical infancy, as Orbe observes, but that Adam and Eve were in a state of *non-perfection*. "Ils étaient une humanité commançante" (summary by Daniélou, "Histoire," p. 151). John Hick's interpretation borders on the evolutionary/naturalistic when he speaks of this "immature creature who was to undergo moral development and growth," viewing growth as the accumulation of experience rather than deepened participation in Trinitarian communion (Hick, *Evil and the God of Love*, pp. 220-21).

125. Adhémar D'Alès notes that for Irenaeus the Spirit was given in a precarious way in the Garden. Drawing from 1 Cor. 15:45, Irenaeus links the Spirit to the "breath of life," whereas the Second Adam gives the "life-giving Spirit." The gift of the Spirit, "the constitutive element of the perfect human," becomes a stable gift in Christ (Alès, "L'Esprit," pp. 511-13, 529).

126. οἰκονομίας (*AH* III.23.1; *SC* 211:445). Irenaeus here has Marcion specifically in mind, as he shows that the Old and New Testaments are different economies of the same symphony of salvation.

127. *SC* 100(2):542.

Here humanity, in the Jewish nation, is once again being "accustomed" to the purpose for which it was created — participation in God: "to bear His Spirit and to hold communion with God."

Although the first Adam "could not [*capere*] him," those in the Second Adam are brought to their created *telos* through the slow but steady accustoming of the two hands. This exchange is accomplished by a double accustoming: God's accustoming himself to humanity, and humanity's becoming accustomed to God.[128] Jesus' mission is expressed precisely in these terms:

> Giving humanity the power to contain [seize — *capere*] the Father, the Word of God who dwelt in man became the Son of man that He might accustom [*adsuesceret*] man to receive God, and God to dwell in man, according to the good pleasure of the Father. (*AH* III.20.2)[129]

This is the descent of Jesus: in his humanity, creation is once again accustomed and enlarged to receive the things of God. The Spirit's mission resonates with this theme, as he then takes this christological accomplishment and kneads it into the rest of humanity.[130]

> Wherefore [the Spirit] did also descend upon the Son of God, made the Son of man, becoming accustomed [*adsuescens*] in fellowship with Him to dwell in the human race, to rest with human beings, and to dwell in the workmanship of God, working the will of the Father in them, and renewing them from their old habits into the newness of Christ. (*AH* III.17.1)[131]

Participation (bearing/seizing/containing God) is a two-sided miracle, and we find both sides clearly outlined above. First, humanity is destined for a deep and enduring relationship of participation in God and in his divine gifts. Although this is wholly "unnatural" to humanity, God desires to bring humanity *(assuesco)* to the place such that it can bear the weight of

---

128. Évieux, "Théologie," p. 24.

129. *SC* 211:392.

130. It is important to note the anti-Gnostic polemic here: the Spirit descends not immediately to ascend again, but to "learn" to stay with and in humanity. Furthermore, he does not come to a particular "spiritual" man or to a spiritual class of humanity, but to all.

131. *SC* 211:330.

his glory. Exchange, therefore, stands at the center of Irenaean participation. It is only the "descent of God" and his self-accommodation to humanity that allows for humanity to become accustomed, in Christ, to the things of God, thereby "ascending" to the Father.

Yet this is not the end of the story, for participation has two sides, and Irenaeus loves to examine it from the underside as well. It is not only a divine gift to humanity, but a human experience embedded in time: "God's temporal art."[132] Because Irenaeus sees all of materiality — flesh, history, time — under the two hands, he is able to take history seriously as the Spirit's genuine canvas. Therefore, the Spirit's descent has an ontic component: he bequeaths to humanity a new form of existence whereby it can "bear" *(capere et portare)* even the things that are not natural to it. The gifts are not bestowed on a mute and fixed human nature; rather, nature is reconfigured under the impact.[133] Both the gift and capacity become pneumatologically conceived. To this end, Irenaeus speaks of our being "contained or seized" *(capere)* by the Son in order that we might "seize him" in return.

> And they are not able to search out the wisdom of God, by means of which His handiwork, confirmed and incorporated with His Son, is brought to perfection; that His offspring, the First-begotten Word, should descend to the creature, that is, to what had been moulded, and that it should be contained [*capiatur,* "seized"] by Him; and, on the other hand, the creature should contain [*capiat,* "seize"] the Word, and ascend to Him, passing beyond the angels, and be made after the image and likeness of God. (*AH* V.36.3)[134]

While Irenaeus implies a radical participation here — "seizing the Word" — this ascent is under the strictest of controls: it is not the creature on its own who participates in, or "bears God." It is the creature, the human, who bears God. Iain MacKenzie reminds us: "This progress is essentially the Word's first and foremost. It is ours by participation in the progress of

---

132. Von Balthasar, *Glory II*, p. 70.

133. *Koinōnia* orders the relationship between creatures and Creator, excluding, as Lossky says, "every external combination of the ideas of nature and grace. They interpenetrate each other, exist in one another" (Lossky, *Orthodox*, p. 130). To then argue for a "natural law" in Irenaeus, as Benedict Guevin does, is to miss the point. Benedict Guevin, "The Natural Law in Irenaeus of Lyons' *Adversus Haereses:* A Metaphysical or Soteriological Reality?" in *Studia Patristica* 36 (Leuven, 2001): 222-25.

134. *SC* 153:466.

the Word made flesh as he moves through this human existence towards his cross, death, resurrection and ascension."[135]

Irenaeus can be maddeningly imprecise in the word pictures that he paints, especially for those of us after Nicaea. He seems to grasp for words to describe such a radical reciprocity with God to which humans are being "accustomed" to enjoy; nevertheless, the direction of his pressure of interpretation remains steadfast. Creation's being enabled to "bear God" is only because God has first borne creation:

> invisibly it is itself borne [*portatur*] by the Father. And so the Church's preaching alone is true, namely, that it was creation itself, which derives its existence from the power and the art and the wisdom of God, which bore [*portavit*] him; while invisibly it is itself borne [*portatur*] by the Father, in the visible world, reversing the roles, it bears [*portat*] his word which is true. But the Father bears [*portat*] creation and his Word together, and the Word borne [*portatum*] by the Father gives the Spirit to all. (*AH* V.18.1-2)[136]

There is an interpenetration of created and Uncreated here that stems not from principle or potential but from God's own willingness to bear his creation and continually sustain it.[137] Irenaeus recognizes that it is not a "natural" thing for humanity to be able to bear the things of God; rather, it is always profoundly unnatural. And yet, this unnatural state of affairs — full participation in God — is precisely what God intends, for nothing, not even the "weakness of the flesh[,] can prevail against the will of God" (*AH* V.5.2), who formed creation for increase.

The divine drama by which humanity is accustomed to the Spirit is suspenseful precisely because the drama's resolution involves an impossibility. Irenaeus savored this irony, as does Orbe: "Closeness of substance compromises the liberality of the divine *dispensatio*, whose implicit postulate is: the further, in the natural order, man is from the Deity, the more will the divine shine out in the human Economy, and the more this will be

135. MacKenzie, *Demonstration*, p. 73.
136. *SC* 153:238 (trans. von Balthasar, *Glory II*, p. 57).
137. Without question, Irenaeus does not base this, as Osborn seems to think, on the fact "that all men have a point of contact with God" (Osborn, *Irenaeus*, p. 213). Instead, he injects the *Deus facit; homo fit* distinction: "God is not subject to created things, but created things to God" (*AH* V.5.2).

worthy of God."[138] Despite Irenaeus's sometimes violent language, this does not transgress the Creator-creature boundary, but fulfills it. It is that for which all creation has been straining — "even in the fulfillment the original opposition persists, but stilled."[139]

Seizing the Spirit: Adoptive Filiation

Accordingly, Irenaeus pinpoints the Spirit as humanity's *scala ascensionis ad Deum* — ladder of ascent to God (*AH* III.24.1). This is a weighty theological move, whereby Irenaeus places the adoptive work of Christ in its ongoing context of our filiation. Or, in more technical terms, the "completeness" of christology is pneumatologically (and thus eschatologically) conceived. Now it becomes clear why Irenaeus does not stop with Christ's descent to seize humanity (adoption) but presses forward to the time when humanity is also, in turn, enabled to *seize him* (adoptive sonship).

> The Son of God being made the Son of man, that through Him we may receive the adoption — humanity sustaining [*portante*], and receiving [*capiente*, "seizing"], and embracing [*complectente*] the Son of God. (*AH* III.16.3)[140]

Here we find Irenaeus pressing into the pneumatological effects of the exchange that Christ made with us, which is not of status or gifts, but of an ascending way of being with God. Precisely by receiving the Spirit, we have a mounting capacity to "seize" the things of God. It is a strictly pneumatological capacity, but one in which we actually become players on the stage. "But we do now receive a certain portion of His Spirit, tending towards perfection, and preparing us for incorruption, being little by little accustomed to receive and bear [*capere et portare*, seize and carry] God; which also the apostle terms 'an earnest'" (*AH* V.8.1). To "seize" God is thus to relate to him from a transformed, "pneumatized" state in which our actions flow forth from a new pneumatological-ontological reality. "Receiving" (*ANF* translation) the things of God and "seizing" (*SC* trans-

138. Orbe, "Irenaeus," p. 414.
139. Von Balthasar, *Glory II*, p. 63.
140. *SC* 211:298.

lation) the things of God become equivalent when under the "new manner" of the Spirit (*Epideixis* 6).[141]

In what way shall we seize God in the Spirit? We have stepped onto the stage now as *sons*. This is reflected in Irenaeus's distinction between our adoption *en Christo* and the ascending process of "filiation" or adoptive sonship whereby the Spirit works us into this identity in ever-increasing ways. Irenaeus's division between adoption and filiation is quite possibly drawn from distinctions made by Paul. While Romans 8:15 ("you received the Spirit of sonship. And by him we cry, '*Abba*, Father'") refers to our adoption in present time, Romans 8:23 refers to our adoption in the future (". . . groan inwardly as we wait eagerly for our adoption as sons . . ."). Therefore the present and future aspects of adoption in Romans 8 reflect, as Scott argues, "successive stages of participation in the Son by the Spirit."[142] Adoption is not a finished reality, Lassiat argues, but is consistently "in view of filiation."[143] We receive the Spirit, says Irenaeus, in order that we might seize Christ and ascend to the Father — elsewhere termed as "seizing" the Father (*AH* III.20.2).

> If therefore, at the present time, having the earnest, we do cry, "Abba, Father," what shall it be when, on rising again, we behold Him face to face; when all members shall burst out into a continuous hymn of triumph . . . ? For if the earnest, gathering man into itself, does even now cause him to cry, "Abba, Father," what shall the complete grace of the Spirit effect, which shall be given to men by God? It will render us like unto Him, and accomplish the will of the Father; for it shall make man after the image and likeness of God. (*AH* V.8.1)

While the Son has revealed the Father to humanity (*AH* IV.6.4-7), it is the Spirit who enables us now to cry "Father" by making us sons. (Again, we note how Irenaeus consistently moves humanity from the state of having something done to it or revealed to it, to the place where it is participating in this new reality — here encapsulated in the cry of "Abba.") And this is in anticipation of an even more glorious day, for presently we only see the Father "through a glass," but we "increase . . . and make progress . . ." until

---

141. See also Irenaeus's delightful discussion of our "inheriting" the Spirit, which he then corrects as our "being inherited" by the Spirit (*AH* IV.9.3).

142. Scott, "Adoption," p. 17.

143. Lassiat, *Promotion*, p. 208, my translation.

we at last enjoy him "face to face" (*AH* IV.9.2).[144] It is not only the Son who gives us the vision of the Father (as the theologians of Antioch would later express it), but the Spirit gives us eyes to see this vision by transforming us into sons.[145] This vision "face to face" is a masterpiece of the entire Trinity and is the final stage of the Irenaean economies called adoptive sonship or "filiation," in which we stand before the Father as sons, partaking of the "paternal vision" for which the Spirit — the earnest — has been preparing us.

Because he has made the Spirit the ladder of our ascent, Irenaeus gives himself elbow room to maneuver between the "completion" of the work of Christ and our eschatological anthropology. What sonship implies is a correspondence between anthropology, christology, and pneumatology, where the Spirit's work is not to do things to or reveal them to humanity but rather to make them progressively true of a new humanity. Here Irenaeus avoids a passive relationship between christology and pneumatology, in which the Spirit applies a completed christological reality back onto humanity. Rather, the Spirit prepares *caro* to receive and seize these things, so that Irenaeus can say simultaneously that we "inherit" the Spirit, and then correct himself and say that "we are inherited by him" (*AH* V.9.4). Both are equally true in Irenaean pneumatology, which ushers in a radical noncompetitive participation of the creature in the Creator. To this end, Irenaeus can even speak of the eschatological end of our sonship — not as the revelation of, but our being "invested with[,] the paternal light" (*AH* IV.20.2). For not only do we see the paternal light, but our ability to see light at all comes from our condition of being *within* the light:

> For as those who see the light are within the light, and partake [*metechousin*] of its brilliancy; even so, those who see God are in God, and receive [*metechontes*] of His splendor. But [His] splendor vivifies them; those, therefore, who see God, do receive life. And for this rea-

144. One could easily write this chapter in terms of the economy of "vision" that Irenaeus details, from the prophets who "prayed that they might attain to that period in which they should see their Lord face to face" (*AH* IV.11.1), to Christ, who himself is the revelation of the Father and grants this vision to us (*AH* IV.6.6-7), and then to our future filiation, in which we participate in the "paternal vision" (*AH* IV.20.5).

145. See Lossky, "Face," pp. 245-50. The Trinitarian controls on this "vision" reveal Irenaeus's conception of the "vision of God" to be an anti-Stoic polemic as well. For an overview of the Stoic concept, see M. Spanneut, *Le Stoicisme des Pères de l'Église de Clément de Rome à Clément d'Alexandrie* (Paris: Le Seuil, 1957).

son, He . . . rendered Himself visible. . . . It is not possible to live apart from life, and the means of life is found in fellowship [*participatione/metochēs*] with God; but fellowship [*participatio/metochē*] with God is to know God and to enjoy His goodness. (*AH* IV.20.5)[146]

It is perhaps unfortunate that the Ante-Nicene Fathers edition of *Against Heresies* (1885) consistently translates *participatio* (*metochē*) as "fellowship," a word whose semantic range includes both "membership of a society" and "participation, sharing" (*Oxford English Dictionary*). It is obvious that Irenaeus's use of the term tends away from the Latin *societas,* in which individuals gather together, and toward ontological incorporation, or *koinōnia.* We do not "fellowship" with light as two distinct and equal substances; we are either enveloped in light and thus see, or we are in darkness and cannot. Yet to be enveloped in light is not to lose ourselves. Light illuminates; it highlights what is in the light. It does not eclipse it.

"Bearing the Spirit" is the entry point and condition for this filial ascent: "For those who bear [*portant*] the Spirit of God are led to the Word, that is to the Son, while the Son presents them to the Father, and the Father furnishes incorruptibility" (*Epideixis* 7).[147] Although the Father is the final stage in the economies, Irenaeus gives no sense of "arrival," but of beginning, for God's *koinōnia* is infinite.[148] Nor is it to be read into Irenaeus that one "advances" past the Spirit and Son to the Father, for one is rather gathered into them in order to "progress" to the Father. It is an entirely Trinitarian ascent, with the "Spirit truly preparing man in the Son of God, and the Son leading him to the Father" (*AH* IV.20.5). "Father" is not a title for God but is the evidence of an ascending relationship that we have entered, for crying the name is evidence of our being in the very *imago* of the Son. Ysabel de Andia confirms the participatory inference of "Father," functioning as a term of union and communion of humanity with God, fashioned by the Son and the Spirit.[149] The Gnostics, too, spoke of prog-

146. *SC* 100(2): 638-42.

147. *SC* 406:92.

148. Irenaean progress to the Father is not Gnostic progress to a more "pure" experience of unmediated divinity. On the contrary, it is into greater *koinōnia* that will never come to an end, because God Himself — the source of our *koinōnia* — is infinite. (It is noteworthy that Irenaeus grounds God's infinity in the triune *koinōnia* [*Epideixis* 10], not in some unchangeable attribute appropriate to the divine. See also *AH* IV.20.7; II.28.3.)

149. De Andia, *Homo vivens,* p. 167.

ress, but it was of a different kind. "But if this be to make progress, namely, to find out another Father . . . he who thinks that he is always making progress of such a kind, will never rest in God" (*AH* IV.9.3).

This Trinitarian advance to the Father is the goal of our salvation. In his classic study on glory, Thierry Scherrer has shown us that this is the very glory that Christ desired to share with his disciples and for which creation came into being. Scherrer homes in on the striking audacity of Irenaeus, whose definition of glory is that of the "trinitarian *koinōnia*: relation of fatherhood-sonship in the Spirit."[150] We were created and intended for this glory, "but it was still a future thing that man . . . [might be received] into that glory which shall afterwards be revealed in those who love God" (*AH* IV.20.8). In typical Irenaean style, the revelation of glory is not merely shown to the church, but the church actually *becomes* the revelation of God's glory. The Spirit is maintained as the ladder of ascent: "Having embraced the Spirit of God, [the church] might pass into the glory of the Father" (*AH* IV.20.4).

The Food of Ascent

Irenaeus has scored a symphony of salvation, with humanity ascending through three interwoven melodies: that of its created vocation to grow, through the recapitulation of Christ, and through the accustoming of the Spirit to the divine things. None can be singled out, especially when we detect how Irenaeus blends them beautifully together in his doctrine of the Eucharist.[151] In the Eucharist we have a concrete realization of creation's destiny to "bear God" in the present time. Von Balthasar observes:

> [God's art] happens in reality too, when the living second Adam finally also enters into bread and wine, into products of the earth, in order to recapitulate in himself not just man but also nature and the cosmos, the most deeply realistic earth. The Eucharist is therefore the culmination of the case against Gnosticism.[152]

150. Scherrer, *Gloire*, p. 291.

151. Joseph Caillot makes much the same discovery of Irenaeus's "completely original" eucharistic theology in which Irenaeus "ties the knot of creation, incarnation, and resurrection" (Caillot, "Grâce," p. 407). The *imago Dei* is another source in Irenaeus's thought where he brings the three strands together seamlessly.

152. Von Balthasar, *Glory II*, p. 55.

Yet this is not only his final "proof" against the Gnostics; we discover that it has been guiding his theology all along. "But our opinion is in accordance with the Eucharist and the Eucharist establishes our opinion. For we offer to Him His own, announcing consistently the fellowship [*koinōnian*] and union of the flesh and Spirit" (*AH* IV.18.5). All three "ascending economies" have been pressing toward this point, in defiance of the Gnostic denial of creation as suitable home for the Spirit. In the Eucharist, creation not only exhibits the harmony between flesh and Spirit, but has become the very means by which God nourishes us ("yet not," Irenaeus interjects, "according to substance but the power of God," *AH* V.6.2). In the Eucharist, the Word presents himself to us as a man in the dimension of the Spirit, whose en-Spirited flesh is given to us as food for the journey. "He has acknowledged the cup (which is a part of the creation) as His own blood, from which He bedews our blood; and the bread (which is a part of the creation) He has established as His own body, from which He gives increase to our bodies" (*AH* V.2.2). In the Eucharist, the Spirit comes upon creaturely structures (*epiklesis*, *AH* IV.18.5) to alter them and bring them (and us!) into the Trinitarian *koinōnia*.

It is crucial to recognize that, for Irenaeus, the Eucharist is not the symbol of the new creation; rather, it *is* the new creation, bound up in the way the present order has been invaded by the two hands. "Just as a corn of wheat falling into the earth and becoming decomposed, rises with manifold increase by the Spirit of God . . ." (*AH* V.2.3), so Irenaeus relates the Eucharist to the Spirit's power to alter creaturely reality.[153] Irenaeus does not mention that this act is a bringing forward of some past grace but, rather, being taken *upward* (if I may be so crude) into the triune presence, where past, present, and future form a new reality centered on the risen Jesus. This is supremely the result of when, in the words of William Cavanaugh, "the historical imagination is superseded by the eschatological imagination."[154] It enters the heart of Farrow's insight that in Irenaeus we are not dealing with one homogeneous world history but with two: one still on its course of "decrease," while the other is taken into the Spirit's "increase."[155] The Eucharist is throwing our lot in with — and declaring ourselves taken into —

153. Douglas Farrow, "Eucharist, Eschatology, and Ethics," in *The Future as God's Gift*, ed. David Fergusson and Marcel Sarot (Edinburgh: T. & T. Clark, 2000), pp. 119-215; Farrow, *Ascension and Ecclesia*, pp. 69-71.

154. William Cavanaugh, "Eucharistic Sacrifice and the Social Imagination in Early Modern Europe," *Journal of Medieval and Early Modern Studies* 31 (2001): 599.

155. Farrow, *Ascension and Ecclesia*, pp. 66-81; Farrow, "Eucharist, Eschatology," pp. 206-10.

the latter history of increase and ascent, entering it again and again by means of the only way we can: Jesus Christ. Irenaeus thinks it marvelous that we are "nourished by means of creation" (*AH* V.2.2), but here he refers not to the old but to the new: creation having reached its goal as fully in the dimension of the Spirit. (This is made clear by the following phrase, where he refers to the bread "as His own body, from which He gives increase to our bodies.") In consonance with the creation, the eucharistic new creation is not, as Williams would suggest, a *tertium quid* or "fusion of earthly and heavenly realities,"[156] but is a new relationship *(koinōnia)* between the "two realities, earthly and heavenly" (*AH* IV.18.5).[157] Through it we participate in Jesus, who is the reconciled being of creation and the paradigm for a fully en-Spirited materiality.[158]

The Eucharist also brings to a climax that other aspect of participation uncovered in the pneumatological ascent. We began this synopsis with the *Deus facit, homo fit* distinction, where the purpose of creation is to receive from God all his benefits that are interpreted as God himself. When seen through this initial lens of creation, there is only *receiving* — no human capacity. Or, as von Balthasar notes for Irenaeus, there is "no natural salvation, no 'divine core' in man, no overlap between God and the world."[159] When it comes to the lens of the Spirit, Irenaeus reinterprets our initial vocation of "receiving" as also being brought into God's life such that we are true participants. We are seized and yet we seize; we are offered the Eucharist and yet we also offer. What is it that we offer? "For we offer to Him His own" (*AH* IV.18.5). As high priest before the Father, Christ bids us participate in his high-priestly vocation, providing even the things we are to offer. "For it behooves us to make an oblation to God, and in all things to be found grateful to God our Maker . . . offering the first-fruits of His own created things" (*AH* IV.18.4). This is no Christian harvest festival, as Williams reminds us, offering God the first portion of the land. This is offering the very first fruits of the "new creation perfectly

156. Rowan Williams, *Eucharistic Sacrifice — The Roots of a Metaphor,* Grove Liturgical Studies 31 (Bramcote, UK: Grove, 1982), p. 10.

157. It is not an ascent out of createdness, but its fulfillment: "that each and every thing should bring its divinely ordained work to completion . . ." (*Epideixis* 10 [trans. von Balthasar, *Glory II,* p. 76]).

158. This is why the Eucharist is so strongly linked to incorruptibility, which is the en-Spirited future for our bodies. Incorruptibility is always seen as a participation in the Spirit, that "Bread of immortality which is the Spirit of the Father" (*AH* IV.38.1).

159. Von Balthasar, *Glory II,* p. 62.

present in his person" — Christ's reconciled body — as the "first portion" of a new life lived in the Spirit.[160]

The Eucharist stands at the heart of the Christian life and discipleship, where we are beckoned to participate in Christ's own self-offering to the Father. Through it, we proclaim that the goal of creation is precisely this "stilled opposition" between flesh and Spirit and are renewed in hope as we ourselves are worked into the Spirit's ascending economy. It is also, in true Irenaean style, profoundly practical. Three critical things for Christian praxis are to be noted (all from *AH* IV.18.6).

First, the rendering of the offering is for *our sake*. "For even as God does not need our possessions, so do we need to offer something to God." Christian offering is placed on a footing of participation, where sacrifice does nothing to bribe, propitiate, or activate God's grace. It is we who need tangible ways to enter into God's economy — "lest we be unfruitful." (Whether or not it is Irenaeus's intent, it is tantalizing to note that our actions are "unfruitful" precisely when they cease participating in Christ. Irenaeus is not just urging people to "do something," but to do it in the right way.)

Second, "rendering thanks for His gift," we are now in a position to see the Eucharist as a gift that elicits our gratitude. Williams notes that, for Irenaeus, the Eucharist is a participation in the Son's praise. Therefore, for us it is "a gift which therefore shares the character of the Son's eternal praise of the Father in being an act of gratuitous love, and thus may be called an offering of the Son to the Father."[161] Even this "sacrifice of praise" rests on a more foundational relationship, keeping our praise from obligatory categories.

Third, our praise is not superfluous to the Son's praise but is given the dignity of becoming "divine work" by inhabiting creation, "rendering thanks for His gift, and thus sanctifying what has been created."[162] Here Irenaeus picks up strands from the Garden narrative and interweaves them into the Eucharist, for we — in the steps trodden by the Second Adam — are once again offering the praise intrinsic to our status as *homo fit*. As Farrow summarizes it, "Together with the ascended one, in the doxological ferment of the Spirit, able to offer a genuine oblation of thanksgiving on behalf of creation."[163] Thanksgiving sanctifies creation

160. Williams, *Eucharistic Sacrifice*, p. 10.
161. Williams, *Eucharistic Sacrifice*, p. 12.
162. The Irenaean overtones in Jeremy Begbie's book *Voicing Creation's Praise* (Edinburgh: T. & T. Clark, 1991) are detectable here.
163. Farrow, *Ascension and Ecclesia*, p. 70.

because it opposes Adam's initial ingratitude and reverses creation's descent, so that creation is once again released into its original identity as recipient partner of a Trinitarian God who never ceases to give.

Yet the Eucharist is not our only means to sanctify creation. Just as we offer the eucharistic gift at his altar ("that is in heaven"), so we offer our humble and loving deeds to the ascended Christ, who stands in the shoes, as it were, of the person we serve to receive our offering. Irenaeus here inserts: "Come, ye blessed of My Father, receive the kingdom prepared for you. For I was hungered, and ye gave Me to eat. . . ." We witness to our participation in the new creation by offering the Eucharist and our deeds, neither of which God needs, but which are part of our ascending journey. Both are tangible ways that we are drawn into the divine life as members of creation — and for creation.

*   *   *

In the first section, I observed that Gnostic cosmology was structured to protect divine transcendence from material corruptibility. Irenaeus, on the other hand, uses precisely the material creation against the Gnostics as proof of salvation and of God's transcendence. Going far beyond the Gnostic dualism of flesh and spirit, Irenaeus draws a much starker "dualism" between God and his creation. Yet Irenaeus is no dualist theologian — far from it; rather, he is supremely the theologian of relationship, of harmony, of unity. His theological sensitivity and perceptivity for his time lies in the *way* he forges this relationship between heaven and earth, the Uncreated and the created. Everything rides on Irenaeus's willingness to take the Holy Spirit seriously, as the one in whom the things of heaven and earth are united and brought to perfection.

Central to Irenaeus's counternarrative of *koinōnia* is his conviction that creation's true being is found in God's life. The very "imperfection" of newly created Adam is God's design to ensure humanity's ongoing future with the Trinity. Yet if Adam's original anthropology was a provisional harmony between flesh and Spirit, such that he was to grow into "genuine" human (en-Spirited) existence, Jesus' mission is an obvious recapitulation of this anthropology. Growth is returned to humanity through an exchange with Christ, whose strenuous life of obedience and suffering reworked the Spirit into the darkest places of human existence. Christ redirects humanity by restoring this mislaid "faculty of increase" and stabilizing the Spirit in his person (*AH* III.17.1).

In the third section, we observed how, incorporated into Christ, humanity continues this ascending relationship of *Deus facit, homo fit,* whereby the gifts of the Father continue to be given, and humanity continues to receive. Taken into the Spirit's new creation, we find ourselves in a dynamic reality where God's life is not just passively received but brings with it an active, wholly pneumatological "capacity." In quite remarkable language, Irenaeus speaks of this as a mutual containing, taking place, of course, in the person of the Word. Participation in God thus functions as a threat neither to our creatureliness nor to the Creator's divinity, but it is the very means by which the creation *becomes* itself. The sacraments parallel human nature, whereby the stuff of earth is taken into Christ, by the Spirit to "bear God," becoming food for our ascent toward ever greater *koinōnia* with God.

Chapter Six

Reforming Ascent:
Calvin, Irenaeus, and Christian Spirituality

We are on an entirely different level when we speak of Irenaeus. He was the only one of the ecclesiastical writers of the second century to grasp the depth of Paul's idea about the Son of Man. His entire Christology is dominated by the contrast between Adam and Christ, and he makes the only attempt in the whole history of doctrine to build a Christology on the concept "Man."[1]

As remarkable as it may sound when I say this about Calvin, he thinks initially not from God but from the human person and his situation. Yet the situation of *humanity* cannot be considered with any seriousness at all without thinking immediately of *God*. For what purpose is the human created?[2]

Backward and Forward with Descent and Ascent

Our study has brought us into contact with two lively theologies of participation, articulated in radically differing contexts. While Calvin

1. Oscar Cullmann, *The Christology of the New Testament* (London: SCM, 1963), p. 189.
2. Karl Barth, *The Theology of the Reformed Confessions, 1923*, trans. Darrell and Judith Guder (Louisville: Westminster John Knox, 2002), p. 94.

found himself up against a humanism that overexalted the creature, Irenaeus contended against the Gnostic contempt for the creature.[3] Nevertheless, both theologians fought their opponents using the same resources: a correct Creator-creature relationship that would ensure humanity's intended participation *(koinōnia)* in the divine life. Both Irenaeus and Calvin responded to the heresies of their day by burrowing deeper into creation and its fundamentally incomplete, derived status. By radically delineating between Creator and creature, they cleared the ground for a proper anthropology based on *difference*. Only then could humanity's true ascent begin and a correct doctrine of participation in the divine life flourish.[4] They found that "ascent" was not the ascent of the individual soul but humanity's participation in the triune communion, a participation that had been decisively opened in the historical Ascension of Jesus.

For Irenaeus, the story of ascent is told via the narrative of humanity; for Calvin, it is the story of Christ. Yet for both theologians the goal of humanity is the same: participation in the triune communion, as made available in the Son by the Spirit.

From Irenaeus's *Adversus haereses*, V.36.2:

This is the gradation and arrangement of those who are saved, and that they advance through steps of this nature: also that they ascend through the Spirit to the Son, and through the Son to the Father.

---

3. The legacy of theologians such as Gabriel Biel caused those in the Protestant Reformation to emphasize the creature's "negative capacity" (Kathryn Tanner, *God and Creation in Christian Theology: Tyranny or Empowerment?* [Oxford: Blackwell, 1988], pp. 132-41, 152).

4. This can be seen in the way that both responded to their various enemies with theologies of participation. Gnostic salvation was a matter of consubstantiality with the divine; Irenaeus argued, instead, for the *koinōnia* of nonidentical things: flesh and spirit. In Calvin's time, one could argue that a theology of participation was threatened on at least three fronts. Against scholastic speculations on "created grace" and grace-infused virtue, Calvin asserted a participation in God himself (*Comm. Col.* 1:19; *Comm. John* 6:26). Against Osiander's overly open anthropology, Calvin insisted that we are not infused by Christ; rather, we are indwelt by the Spirit of Christ and participate in the Son through the Spirit alone. Against Zwingli's symbolic doctrine of the Eucharist, Calvin insisted on a real presence of Christ in which we participate by the Spirit.

From Calvin's *Responsum ad fratres Polonos:*

Christ, for this reason, is said to send the Spirit from his Father (John 16:7) to raise us, by degrees, up to the Father.[5]

Both theologians insist with persistence and precision that humanity was created for communion and that all of human life and history projects toward (or is pulled toward) this *koinōnia*. Despite their differences, both Irenaeus and Calvin saw christology serving this theological anthropology of participation: the human vocation of union with the triune God.[6] The Holy Spirit serves as the only way into this ascending vocation, and both theologians were equally sensitive to any transgressions on this front. Says Calvin, "These men devise a Christianity that does not require the Spirit of Christ" (III.2.39), while Irenaeus protests, "These men do, in fact, set the Spirit aside altogether" (*AH* III.17.4).

Where a comparison proves especially tantalizing is the extent to which it exposes how they applied this ascent to their radically differing contexts.[7] For Calvin, ascent functioned to remind the church of its vocation: union with the ascended Christ rather than a misplaced focus on the things of this earth. "For thus they leave nothing to the secret working of the Spirit, which unites Christ himself to us. To them Christ does not seem present unless he descends to us. As though, if he should lift us to himself, we should not just as much enjoy his presence!" (IV.17.31). Accordingly, the language of "descent" comes to represent the means by which sinful humans wish to manipulate God, rather than trusting God's chosen means of ascent — the Holy Spirit.

5. Joseph Tylenda, "Christ the Mediator: Calvin Versus Stancaro," *Calvin Theological Journal* 8 (1973): 16.

6. This is why, as I have previously argued (chap. 4), Calvin's insistence on *unio cum Christo* must not be turned into a mechanism for salvation and thus a natural theology. It functionalizes christology for an anthropocentric end rather than placing it in its proper theocentric context: the triune God's desire for us.

7. Given Calvin's early modern context, he emphasizes the Spirit's appropriation of the gospel for the *individual*. This is not Cartesian hyper-individualism but, as Heiko Oberman makes clear, answers to the challenge of late medieval individualism (Oberman, "Reformation, Preaching, and *Ex Opere Operato*," in *Christianity Divided*, ed. Daniel Callahan [New York: Sheed & Ward, 1961], p. 228). For how the sin-anguished conscience was already a "mass phenomenon in the Latin world" in the fourteenth century, see James McCue, "*Simul justus et peccator* in Augustine, Aquinas, and Luther: Towards Putting the Debate in Context," *Journal of the American Academy of Religion* 48 (1980): 90.

Yet Irenaeus goes where Calvin does not dare, given the polemics of his situation, and it is here that their comparison proves especially fruitful. Specifically, in Irenaeus's time, creation was under attack. Under these antagonistic circumstances, when the "spiritual" was preferred to the material, Irenaeus undertakes a colorful exploration of the relationship of the Holy Spirit to the created realm.[8] Ascent functions as the entire creation's vocation *in* the Spirit and is proof that the fleshly is not opposed to the spiritual but is intended for communion with God. This progressive relationship of the creation with the Creator does not involve a change (or abandonment) of physicality, but is its fulfillment. "This, however, does not take place by a casting away of the flesh, but by the impartation [*communionem*] of the Spirit" (*AH* V.8.1).

Both of these perspectives complement and sharpen one another, offering different emphases and correctives to a doctrine of participation. Calvin gives structure and definition to participation in ways that Irenaeus could not, especially given Calvin's historical position after Nicaea. Although Irenaeus lodges participation *en Christō* in startling ways, it is Calvin who magisterially works out the breadth and depth of this relationship in a way unparalleled by any theologian, except perhaps Karl Barth. It is also Calvin whom we have to thank for working out a soteriology that draws heavily on both imputation and participation rather than allowing those categories to stand in two streams opposing one another. So whereas Rusch can say that Eastern theologians — while building on Irenaeus — were the "developers of a theology of salvation outside the framework of justification categories," Calvin brings emphases that are dear to both the West and East into his soteriology.[9] In making imputation a distinctively *participationist* category, Calvin was able to reckon both with the non-necessary character of justification and its grounding in *unio cum Christo*. Irenaeus had a general view of humanity's participation in Christ's victory over sin, but it was left to Calvin and the Reformers to work out how Christ's human righteousness became our own, thereby justifying us.

However, we will look to Irenaeus for help when Calvin hesitates to sufficiently honor the integrity of the created realm — for obvious polem-

8. Even Calvin notes this, and he explains (away) Irenaeus's commitment to free will on this basis (*CO* 6.281-82).

9. William Rusch, "How the Eastern Fathers Understood What the Western Church Meant by Justification," in *Justification by Faith*, ed. H. George Anderson, T. Austin Murphy, and Joseph A. Burgess (Minneapolis: Augsburg, 1985), p. 133.

ical reasons. While both see the Spirit as threshold to participation in God, this proved to Calvin that the divine and human do not fuse; for Irenaeus, this proved the intimate compatibility of the divine and human. For those of us in an era concerned with the particularity, freedom, and integrity of the material sphere, Irenaeus serves to articulate new (old!) ways of applying participation to the creaturely realm. With the broadened lens that Irenaeus gives us, we can give renewed attention to Calvin's pneumatology, even correcting him, where needed, to do greater justice to anthropology and creation.

Recapitulating Ascent in Calvin

Although Irenaeus is more renowned for his doctrine of human ascent, Calvin's anthropology also brings this to the fore.[10] Drawing from conventional medieval (and Irenaean) imagery, his earlier works portray the soul's "increase" to the "vision of God,"[11] while his later works incorporate Pauline imagery of the "childhood" of the church and its slow "maturation" by the Word and Spirit.[12] We will briefly look at the common moves that Irenaeus and Calvin make in their conceptions of (1) creation and (2) christology for their similar grounding of participatory ascent; then we will be able to assess the differences in how they conceive of (3) the Spirit's relationship to the created realm.

The Triune Mediation of Creation

Neither Irenaeus nor Calvin began with participation as a metaphysical principle. Instead, they both looked to a doctrine of creation to provide clues for the divine-human relationship and found themselves face to face with a material world ensconced in divine *koinōnia*. Equally convinced of the creature's total dependence on the Creator, they argued that this

10. On Christ's "perfecting" work as a necessity regardless of the Fall, see Peter Wyatt, *Jesus Christ and Creation* (Allison Park, PA: Pickwick, 1996), chapter 2.

11. Souls "always increase till they see God, and pass from that increase to the vision of God" (Calvin, "Psychopannychia," *T&T* III.441).

12. See T. H. L. Parker, *Calvin's Old Testament Commentaries* (Edinburgh: T. & T. Clark, 1986), pp. 63, 83, 100, 115.

stemmed not from a flaw in the human condition but from its glory — its being the recipient of divine love. Thus the "metaphysical given" for both Calvin and Irenaeus is a radical doctrine of the triune relationships. In the words of Irenaeus, "In the beginning, therefore, did God form Adam, not as if He stood in need of man, but that He might have some one upon whom to confer His benefits" (*AH* IV.14.1). Calvin's doctrine of the Spirit in creation complements this participatory anthropology; from it we find that God does not give us things other than himself: "God sendeth forth that [S]pirit which remains with him whither he pleases; and as soon as he has sent it forth, all things are created. In this way, what was his own he makes to be ours."[13] This strong pneumatological rendering of creation has profound ramifications for how we think of the self: to be a creature is to participate in God and the things of God.

Adam becomes a test case of sorts for this participation, the emblematic figure who has no grounding or basis outside of the "two hands" (Irenaeus) or the "mediator" (Calvin). Both ascribe to Adam a certain instability and fragility: Calvin calls it "lowliness" (II.12.1), and Irenaeus more generously calls it "infancy" (*AH* IV.38.1). Either way, this signals the need for God's ongoing involvement in human life even before the Fall. By design, the normative human condition is participation in God and all his gifts. Calvin looks specifically to Irenaeus for substantiation here:

> For when we say that the spirit of man is immortal, we do not affirm that it can stand against the hand of God, or subsist without his agency. Far from us be such blasphemy! But we say that it is sustained by his hand and blessing. Thus Irenaeus, who with us asserts the immortality of the spirit, (Irenaeus adv. Haeres. V) wishes us, however, to learn that by nature we are mortal, and God alone immortal. And in the same place he says, "Let us not be inflated and raise ourselves up against God, as if we had life of ourselves; and let us learn by experience that we have endurance for eternity through his goodness, and not from our nature."[14]

Immortality does not differ from all the other gifts that Adam enjoyed in the Garden by participation. In Calvin, this participation is disciplined strictly to the Word (*Comm. Gen.* 2:9), who mediates all creation, while in

---

13. *Comm. Ps.* 104:29 (*CO* 32.96). An external relationship between the Spirit and creation must not be read into the text here.

14. Calvin, "Psychopannychia," *T&T* III.478; Calvin is quoting *AH* V.2.3.

Irenaeus this participation is linked to Christ *and* "receiving the Spirit" and his gifts in progressively firmer ways (*AH* IV.38.2). Yet Irenaeus does not lack the christological thrust that Calvin's doctrine of creation affords; his notion of the two hands consistently orders creation to Christ, in whom creation will find its true stability and being.[15]

Christ's Mediation of the New Creation

What is similarly remarkable about Calvin and Irenaeus is how this general God-world relationship is grounded in the person of Christ. The mediation of the Word in the Garden is "prefiguring the future" (Irenaeus, *Epideixis* 12), when the Word would dwell with humanity, and humanity would be "perfected" in him. Calvin says that

> ... the state of man was not perfected in the person of Adam; but it is a peculiar benefit conferred by Christ, that we may be renewed to a life which is *celestial*, whereas before the fall of Adam, man's life was only earthly, seeing it had no firm and settled constancy.[16]

Christ's recapitulatory work not only did away with sin and guilt but was the formation of a new humanity in his person.

> The proper condition of creatures is to keep close to God. Such a *gathering together* [recapitulation — ἀνακεφαλαίωσις] as might bring us back to regular order, the apostle tells us, has been made in Christ. Formed into one body, we are united to God, and closely connected with each other. Without Christ, on the other hand, the whole world is a shapeless chaos and frightful confusion.[17]

15. But as an improvement on Calvin, Irenaeus's pneumatology directs creation more than does predestination — that "other hand" of God in Calvin. See the analysis by Colin Gunton, *Christ and Creation* (Grand Rapids: Eerdmans, 1992), pp. 95-98. While both Irenaeus and Calvin place Jesus Christ at the center of creation, Irenaeus's pneumatology consistently relates everything to Christ without reducing creation to an instrument of the divine will. Calvin's good desire to emphasize God's sovereignty against a self-sufficient humanism can at times render creation — and even the human Jesus — as instruments in God's divine plan.

16. *Comm. Gen.* 2:7; see also the discussion in chap. 2 above.

17. *Comm. Eph.* 1:10.

Therefore, for Calvin, it is self-evident that recapitulation happens *in* the person of Christ. Humanity's *telos* is to "ascend," united to the one who is the center of the new creation. "Now, we know, that out of Christ there is nothing but confusion in the world; and though Christ had already begun to erect the kingdom of God, yet his death was the commencement of a well-regulated condition and the full restoration of the world."[18] Hence, as Calvin says in his commentary on Acts, "We must seek Christ nowhere else save only in heaven, whilst we hope for the last restoring of all things."[19] All "growth," all "progress" will only happen through union with him who is the center of the restored world and a restored humanity.[20]

Both Irenaeus and Calvin emphasize that ascent takes place only as humanity once again is joined to its head — re-headed (re-*capit*-ulated) — by the Spirit, which is also the reestablishment of human anthropology: "The proper condition of creatures is to keep close to God."[21] But the head of humanity is also the Son of God, a convergence that caused them to take adoption seriously: it is his sonship that forms us and defines human ascent.

From *Adversus haereses*, III.19.1:

For it was for this end that the Word of God was made man, and He who was the Son of God became the Son of man, that man, having been taken into the Word, and receiving the adoption, might become the son of God.

From the *Institutes*, IV.17.2:

This is the wonderful exchange which, out of his measureless benevolence, he has made with us; that, becoming Son of man with us, he has made us sons of God with him; that, by his descent to earth, he has prepared an ascent to heaven for us. . . .

Irenaeus and Calvin both use the patristic formula that has become associated with deification, what McLelland calls "an instance of bad Latin for

18. *Comm. John* 12:31.
19. *Comm. Acts* 3:21.
20. See David E. Holwerda, "Eschatology and History: A Look at Calvin's Eschatological Vision," in *Exploring the Heritage of John Calvin*, ed. David E. Holwerda (Grand Rapids: Baker, 1976), pp. 110-39.
21. *Comm. Eph.* 1:10.

good Greek."[22] Regardless of the term, the theological concept has always functioned to communicate that for which humanity has been created: a relationship of *koinōnia* with the triune God. It is common (as, e.g., in the writings of Wilhelm Niesel) to classify Osiander's pantheism as "deification" and to juxtapose it to Calvin's "orthodoxy." I should note that Osiander's theology is far from the patristic, orthodox doctrine of deification; rather, it is a caricature of it, more akin to pagan pantheism. Calvin's response is much more in line with classical patristic deification than is Osiander's. Calvin can even go so far as to say:

> For we must consider from whence it is that God raises us up to such a height of honor. We know how abject is the condition of our nature; that God, then, should make himself ours, so that all his things should in a manner become our things, the greatness of his grace cannot be sufficiently conceived by our minds. Therefore this consideration alone ought to be abundantly sufficient to make us to renounce the world and to carry us aloft to heaven. Let us then mark, that the end of the gospel is, to render us eventually conformable to God, and, if we may so speak, to deify us. (*Comm. II Pet.* 1:4, *CO* 55.446)

But in disciplining ascent specifically to the Son, both Irenaeus and Calvin preserve the Creator-creature distinction vital to their conceptions of participation. Ascent is into *sonship*, but never as *the Son*.[23]

In Irenaeus, adoption functions as proof of deification — God's decision to bring humanity into his own life. For Calvin, adoption is what safeguards us from being deified, or fused into the divine, in that it is grounded in Trinitarian differentiation. Yet it is clear that for neither theologian is this adoptive ascent something that has to do with some abstract divinization of nature; rather, it is ascent into deeper *koinōnia* with God and his benefits. Everything depends on their theology of the Spirit,

---

22. "By this term the Fathers meant to signify what happens when man is graciously dealt with by the living God: Father, Son, and Spirit" (Joseph C. McLelland, "Sailing to Byzantium," in *The New Man: An Orthodox and Reformed Dialogue*, ed. John Meyendorff and J. C. McLelland [New Brunswick, NJ: Agora, 1973], p. 20).

23. Both use the nature/grace distinction for adoption: Calvin (II.14.5), Irenaeus (*AH* III.6.1). Yet we have seen that each considers adoption as true participation in the divine life: Calvin argues that this is "not a matter of figures" (II.14.5), and he relates it to the Son's relationship with the Father (III.2.22); Irenaeus specifically associates adoption with the Jewish deification, Psalm 86 (*AH* III.6.1).

as both the one who preserves the contingency of creation and the one who ensures that this is the personal activity of God on and within humanity. But it is how they then conceive of the Spirit's work with respect to the new creation and the church where their emphases diverge so widely. While this can in part be explained polemically and methodologically, it goes beyond mere "emphasis" to theological consequence.

Locus of Ascent: The Church

While Calvin's ascent follows a strictly Trinitarian structure, it is by no means theoretical. Calvin speaks of the church as our "mother," on whose bosom we "grow" until we reach "perfect manhood" (IV.1.4-5). Preaching is one such "spiritual food" whereby Christ presents himself to us, choosing "human means" and an "ordinary manner" of giving us divine life.

> Surely, this is because believers have no greater help than public worship, for by it God raises his own folk upward step by step. . . . As if it were not in God's power somehow to come down to us, in order to be near us, yet without changing place or confining us to earthly means; but rather by these to bear us up as if in chariots to his heavenly glory, a glory that fills all things with its immeasurableness and even surpasses the heavens in height! (IV.1.5)

Ascent is neither for the individual person nor for the disembodied soul, but is for the people of God. Bound together by the Spirit into one body, "all — from the highest to the lowest — aspire toward the Head!" If through worship God raises us "step by step," then sacraments are the physical "steps of the ladder."[24] In language redolent of Irenaean imagery, Calvin says: "For although the faithful come into this Communion [koinōnia] on the very first day of their calling; nevertheless, inasmuch as the life of Christ increases in them, He daily offers Himself to be enjoyed by them. This is the Communion [koinōnia] which they receive in the Sacred Supper."[25] The "increase" that the church enjoys on its ascending journey is the very life of Christ, offered to the church by the Spirit.[26]

---

24. *Serm. 2 Sam.* 6:1-7.
25. *Letter to Peter Martyr,* 8 August 1555 (*CO* 15.723).
26. The sacrament of baptism is understood in this way as well. Calvin says, "By

The radical — even watershed — role that Calvin gave to the Spirit in the Lord's Supper cannot be overstated. As had not been done since perhaps the patristic fathers, Calvin attempted to take seriously the pneumatological dimensions of presence: the Spirit is not the Pentecostal replacement *for* Christ but the way *to* him. It is not we who need to alter God's reality, but it is God who alters ours by taking us into the triune *koinōnia* via the Spirit. Thus, in the Lord's Supper, the Spirit comes upon creation and makes it a means to union with Christ — lifting us "up" to him. There is thus no need for the bread to change and become something else, for that would be "no slight insult" to the Spirit (IV.17.33). For support, Calvin cites Irenaeus:

> This ought not to seem incredible or contradictory to reason (Irenaeus, Lib. iv. cap. 34); because, as the whole kingdom of Christ is spiritual, so whatever he does in his Church is not to be tested by the wisdom of this world. . . . Such, I say, is the corporeal presence which the nature of the sacrament requires, and which we say is here displayed in such power and efficacy, that it not only gives our minds undoubted assurance of eternal life, but also secures the immortality of our flesh, since it is now quickened by his immortal flesh, and in a manner shines in his immortality. (IV.17.32, Beveridge trans.)[27]

The passage to which Calvin makes a parenthetical reference is from *Adversus haereses*, IV.18.5, where Irenaeus speaks of the Eucharist as "consisting of two realities, earthly and heavenly." For both theologians, it was critical that the eucharistic bread not change; and both considered the Eucharist as the perfect expression of the divine-human relationship. For Calvin, any change in the bread would signify an end of God's sovereignty (God enclosed in the elements) and an end to Christ's mediation. "While they feign an immense fantasy instead of the flesh, we defend the reality of the human nature on which our faith is founded."[28]

For Irenaeus, any change in the good, physical substance of bread would signify a fundamental deficiency in creation, as not worthy of "bear-

---

baptism they are admitted into the fold of Christ, and the symbol of adoption is sufficient for them, until they grow up and become fit to bear solid food" (IV.16.31).

27. See also Calvin's use of Irenaeus in "True Partaking . . . ," *T&T* II.537-38; "Last Admonition . . . ," *T&T* II.435-36; and "Adultero-German Interim . . . ," *T&T* III.226.

28. Calvin, "Last Admonition . . . ," *T&T* II.436.

ing" the Spirit and being irreconcilable with God: "For how can they be consistent with themselves when they say that the bread over which thanks have been given is the body of their Lord, and the cup His blood, if they do not call Himself the Son of the Creator of the world, that is, His Word, through whom the wood fructifies, and the fountains gush forth . . ." (*AH* IV.18.4). Irenaeus and Calvin both turn to the Holy Spirit as the one who accomplishes the "reality" of the eucharistic presence, without changing the integrity of creation.

We are in familiar territory, and it is just here that the divergence between Calvin and Irenaeus may be of some genuine use. What is interesting to note is how Calvin tweaks Irenaeus for his own purposes here (IV.17.32, quoted above), for they are not really saying the same thing.[29] In this passage Irenaeus insists that the Eucharist proclaims one thing: "the fellowship [*koinōnian*] and union of the flesh and Spirit."

> For as the bread, which is produced from the earth, when it receives the invocation of God, is no longer common bread, but the Eucharist, consisting of two realities, earthly and heavenly; so also our bodies, when they receive the Eucharist, are no longer corruptible, having the hope of the resurrection to eternity. (*AH* IV.18.5)

Irenaeus's point is that creation *as creation* participates in God. When the Spirit comes upon creation, there is forged an enduring relationship between the two such that the bread is no longer "common bread." Creation, under the impact of the Spirit, does not give way to a higher reality that is other than itself; rather, it becomes more itself as it participates in the new creation. For Irenaeus, the Eucharist is the ultimate proof that the creaturely participates in the divine life in the here and now as the new creation, and is moved closer to its *telos* of "the *koinōnian* of the flesh and Spirit." It is not a new substance, but it is in a new relationship *(koinōnia)* that alters — and yet does not alter — creation. As the bread receives the blessing of the Spirit, and is put in this new relationship, so the church, as it partakes of the Eucharist, is also participating via the Spirit in the new creation — the life of incorruptibility.[30]

---

29. This is a relic from the medieval *auctoritates* method of reading the fathers. See the chapter on Calvin in Irena Backus, *Historical Method and Confessional Identity in the Era of the Reformation (1378-1615)* (Leiden: Brill, 2003), pp. 63-129.

30. For sources on how Irenaeus's phrase *ex duabus rebus constans* has been used

Calvin, on the other hand, called on this passage to emphasize the separateness — the particularity — of the earthly and heavenly. Whereas for Irenaeus the two realities of earthly and heavenly are shown as eschatologically related (in terms of participating in the new creation), for Calvin the two realities exist more or less side by side: the earthly — the bread (IV.17.14), and the heavenly — the "assurance of eternal life."[31] Although this assurance "in a sense partakes of his immortality" (IV.17.32), nevertheless the point is that the Eucharist, by the Holy Spirit, consists of two distinct things.

Calvin's interpretation here reflects not only his polemical situation but also his anthropology, which tended to move along more dualist lines of soul/body, nobler/lower, spiritual/physical.[32] The sacraments parallel the nature of humanity, whose "nobler part" (I.15.2) is the soul: "[B]ecause we have souls engrafted in bodies, he imparts spiritual things under visible ones" (IV.14.3). Thus the "believer does not halt at the physical sight of them, but rises up to lofty mysteries" (IV.14.5). The ministry of the sacraments thus "increase[s] faith" (IV.14.9), as "God accomplishes *within* what the minister represents and attests by *outward* action . . ." (IV.14.17 [emphasis added]).

Irenaeus's anthropology, of course, informs (or is informed by) his notion of the sacraments as well. While Calvin concedes that "the body is not excluded from participation in glory, in so far as it is connected to the soul" (*Comm. 1 Pet.* 1:9), Irenaeus insists that "both are necessary, since both contribute towards the life of God" (*AH* III.18.2). The soul does not have priority over the body, but serves the body in receiving the "Spirit of the Father" (*AH* III.18.2). For Calvin, the Lord's Supper has become the supreme example of how the "visible" participates by the Spirit in the "invisible." Irenaeus, on the other hand, bound the two

---

throughout church history, see Mary Ann Donovan, *One Right Reading? A Guide to Irenaeus* (Collegeville, MN: Liturgical Press, 1997), p. 113 n. 18.

31. Calvin probably has the Lutheran *Fleischbrot* (fleshbread) in mind here, which formed a singular new substance. For how Calvin used Irenaeus against Lutheran ubiquitousness, see Irena Backus, "Irenaeus, Calvin and Calvinist Orthodoxy: The Patristic Manual of Abraham Scultetus (1598)," *Reformation and Renaissance Review* 1 (June 1999): 43-44. Irena Backus finds "Calvin's doctrine of the soul [to be] an amalgam of Plato, Aristotle and the Stoics" (Backus, *Historical Method*, p. 90).

32. Perhaps it is this dualist anthropology that is the root of Calvin's oscillation between the "two views" of the Spirit that are in tension with one another throughout his works.

earthly and heavenly realities together not through sign/signified, but through the pneumatological notion of the first fruits of the new creation (*AH* IV.18.1.4).

"First fruits" invites reflection on the ways in which the present physical creation participates in the ascended Lord. Calvin rightly emphasizes communion with the risen Lord, but this was not always matched by an equal pneumatological insistence on its material dimension. For whereas Calvin's insistence on "Christ the true sacrament"[33] led him to de-emphasize the materiality of the sacrament, it is precisely Christ the true sacrament that allowed Irenaeus to affirm the material. His emphasis on the physicality of the sacraments was never directly identified with Christ. Without taking away from Christ's preeminence, the sacraments participate *in him* and thus are wholly valid, present actions of God *among us*.

Furthermore, for Irenaeus, we are not only recipients of this gift but we are invited to participate in Christ's priestly action to the Father. As opposed to the potential for altruism in Calvin's rendering of the "sacrifice of gratitude," Irenaeus recognizes the noncompetitive nature of human and divine action. From this he is able to recognize the sacrament as our invitation to participate in Christ's self-offering to the Father.[34] In offering back to God what is his own, our human, earthly actions are sanctified by Christ's, and they bring all of creation into this sanctification. Calvin failed to see how our participation in the ascended Christ, the center of the new creation, brings our present materiality into this new eschatological reality. The Ascension does not merely locate Christ in heaven; rather, the risen, *human* Jesus also sends his Spirit to accomplish in creation what was accomplished first in him. By doing so, he transforms the physical from serving as a barrier to participation into becoming the very means by which we enjoy Christ in the Spirit.

33. "Christ is the matter or (if you prefer) the substance of all the sacraments; for in him they have all their firmness, and they do not promise anything apart from him" (IV.14.16). See also George Hunsinger's critique of Barth along these lines: Hunsinger, "Baptism and the Soteriology of Forgiveness," *International Journal of Systematic Theology* 2 (2000): 254-56.

34. See chapter 5 above.

Participation and Its Challenges

A backward glance to Irenaeus has served two purposes. First, it has confirmed participation to be a key concept emerging out of the Christian resources, rather than operating as a mere relic from Platonism. As Colin Gunton notes:

> Despite what some may expect, Christians in the Reformed tradition are often able to engage with Orthodox theology in ways not so readily available to the Catholic tradition. The reason is that John Calvin, despite his heavy dependence upon Augustine, was also a careful reader of the Eastern, including the Cappadocian, Fathers, especially in matters Trinitarian.[35]

Participation takes us to the heart of Calvin's vision of the Christian life, since it has an integrative power to bind together disparate doctrines such as creation, anthropology, soteriology, ecclesiology (sacraments), and eschatology. We have seen just how pivotal a consideration of this very conceptuality is in Calvin. Without an understanding of the nature of participation and of its cohesive power, Calvin's theology is left open to penal versions of the atonement, dialectical renditions of the divine-human relation, anthropologies of exclusive depravity, moralistic interpretations of the Christian life, and sacramental superficiality — to mention just a few deviants. Calvin studies can be enriched by embracing and pursuing this significant theme in their forefather, not least in the service of ecumenical dialogue and theologically rigorous spiritual formation.

Second, the ways in which each theologian articulated a doctrine of participation, in the midst of opposing contexts, serves to show how they found this to be the central core of the Christian faith. Both Calvin's creaturely "pessimism" and Irenaeus's creaturely "optimism" have their place in an understanding of Christian participation. Indeed, their differences highlight the defining force of the doctrine across varying centuries and polemical challenges to the church.

Finally, the centrality of the Trinity for their articulation of participation gives Calvin and Irenaeus an important voice in the contemporary debate. Yet Irenaeus also highlights an unfinished agenda in Reformed

---

35. Gunton, *Father, Son, and Holy Spirit* (Edinburgh: T. & T. Clark, 2002), pp. 41, 51.

theology, which can contribute a great deal to an ecumenically minded and self-critical Reformed perspective. Barth also saw the potential of this legacy:

> What I have already intimated here and there to good friends, would be the possibility of a theology of the third article, in other words, a theology predominantly and decisively of the Holy Spirit. Everything which needs to be said, considered, and believed about God the Father and God the Son in an understanding of the first and second articles might be shown and illuminated in its foundations through God the Holy Spirit, the *vinculum pacis inter Patrem et Filium.* The entire work of God for his creatures, for, in, and with human beings, might be made visible in terms of its one teleology in which all contingency is excluded. . . . Might not even the christology which dominates everything be illuminated on this basis *(conceptus de Spiritu Sancto!)?*[36]

We have in Calvin the seeds of a robust pneumatology that Irenaeus complements. Neither theology is explicable without participatory — and hence pneumatological — categories; yet, whereas one may argue that Calvin only tentatively explores the relationship of the Spirit to the created realm, Irenaeus made this the bulwark of his theological defense. This corrective has enormous implications for Reformed spirituality, different sectors of which continue to reflect an ambiguous understanding of their relationship to the material sphere.[37] This can be observed in a variety of ways: a historical reticence toward the arts and images;[38] confusion as to the appropriateness of social justice (as perceived to be poised over against evangelism);[39] a preference for private (immaterial) rather than

---

36. Karl Barth, "Concluding Unscientific Postscript on Schleiermacher," in *The Theology of Schleiermacher* (Grand Rapids: Eerdmans, 1982), p. 278.

37. "Calvinism" is a massively diverse sphere of practices and beliefs. Across that spectrum, there are shared "family characteristics" that take their cue from both Calvin's strengths and weaknesses.

38. Failure to integrate creation and redemption at this very practical level reveals the need for an appreciation of the way Calvin related them through his category of participation/*koinōnia*.

39. This is related to the Calvinist equivalent of the Lutheran doctrine of the "two kingdoms." Relating to the world through the category of the "sphere of sovereignty" rather than participation has proved disastrous, as the Dutch Calvinist defense of apartheid in South Africa recently exhibited.

corporate (material) means of relating to God; wariness toward the sacraments; and relative neglect of the body's role in spiritual formation, to name a few.

Dare one suggest that, in an age beset by a plethora of "spiritualities," careful theological reflection can have a significant voice? The contemporary hunger for all forms of "spirituality" only underscores the church's need for a revitalized doctrine of the Holy Spirit and a coming to terms with the significance of pneumatology for both the spiritual and material realms. Calvin's own pneumatology, I believe, has its own means of dealing with these ambiguities — and not only for his namesake tradition, but for the broader concerns of the world as well. I wish to close this study with some concluding hints as to what a more decisive "theology of the third article" might mean not only for Reformed theology but for the wider church.

Ascent, Calvin, and Contemporary Spirituality

Can Calvin's "ladder to heaven" be of any use to contemporary spirituality today? The structure of Calvin's ladder is really the fundamental link in all of his thought: *participatio Christi*. But what can this mean for those of us in the twenty-first century who experience "increasing difficulty . . . in translating Paul's imagery of incorporation into another person" into language meaningful within our individualistic notions of the self?[40] Calvin, too, realized that the concept of *koinōnia* (participation) could be easily misinterpreted in his own era, even as he toyed with the extremities of relationship — extreme communion with God and extreme differentiation from him — to evoke the profound mystery of the human being. For "Christian" spirituality to have an authentic voice, it needs to find within its resources the means to resist the generalizing (pantheistic) and privatizing (alienating) tendencies amidst the contemporary din.

---

40. James Dunn, *The Theology of Paul the Apostle* (Grand Rapids: Eerdmans, 1998), p. 393. E. P. Sanders also notes that "the participationist way of thinking is less easily appropriated today than the language of acquittal and the like . . . [thus] it has not infrequently been dismissed or played down" (Sanders, *Paul and Palestinian Judaism* [Philadelphia: Fortress, 1977], p. 520).

Combating Pantheism: The Ascent by the Spirit into the Son

Calvin's insistence that it is only "by means of [the Spirit] that we come to participate in God" (I.13.14) is crucial. The Spirit is he who brings us into the very life of God, and is himself the "first step" of humanity's ascent to the Son, and with the Son to the Father. Yet Calvin's unique emphasis was to show that this ascending relationship is marked not by assimilation and fusion, but by difference and particularity. "For if flesh were divinity itself, it would cease to be the temple of divinity" (II.14.8). It is to our advantage that many of Calvin's enemies tended to err on the side of fusion, forcing Calvin to articulate a radical doctrine of participation based on Trinitarian difference, with the Spirit acting as agent of this differentiation (I.15.5). Against Servetus, Osiander, and various "Papists," Calvin argued that a relationship of *koinōnia* is far more intimate than infusion of righteousness, fleshly eating, or absorption. In his theology, the Spirit functions supremely as this "agent of particularity," relating things even as he keeps them separate.

This is instructive today, when multiple spiritualities (even those within the church) are based not on differentiation and uniqueness, but rather on sameness — either the sameness of moral prescription or the sameness of self-emptying. Spiritual formation within the church needs to be attentive to its namesake, the Spirit, who enables creation to participate in God while also remaining (and becoming) truly itself. If the Spirit is not only the agent of differentiation but also the *Creator Spiritus*, then spiritual formation is based precisely on difference and entrusting our particularity to the Spirit, who upholds it as he upholds all of creation in its uniqueness.

More often than not in Christian spirituality, the ascetic discipline of "self-emptying" is seen as the necessary abandonment of particularity and uniqueness. It is the act by which "I must become less, that he might become greater." Based on a competitive understanding of the God-creation relationship, physicality and uniqueness is seen as a barrier to God's will in our lives. What is needed, it is thought, is a total self-emptying that God might overwhelm us, possess us thoroughly, and override our natural inclinations and thoughts. The Spirit acts in this role as the one who does not ground and transform our createdness, but overrides it. Because this is not a particularizing process (more often than not, oppressive images of God, rather than God himself, fill the vacuum), we are left to our own devices to grasp after our own uniqueness — often in ways defined by secular humanism. "Be yourself" and "staying true to yourself" are the modern mantras that weave their way in and out of the church.

Calvin's anthropology hints at a much more profound relationship: he defines the fulfillment of "human potential" — to use a secular slogan — precisely as staying in intimacy with the God who created it, is still creating it, and is the ground of its uniqueness. The Spirit does not fill vacated beings, but enables creatures to live into the fullness of the new creation, which is not a charade but a new en-Spirited human existence based on the ascended humanity of the Son. Participation in God is not the dissolving of the self in God but the finding of the self in God, because it is only truly "human" as it exists in this deep communion of receiving and giving. Because it is governed by the Trinity, *koinōnia*-participation does not annihilate particularity but is the way to step into our uniqueness. It is an entire reorientation from the autonomous self (that is, the ungrounded self) to the self-in-relationship.[41] A deep appreciation of Calvin's pneumatological doctrine of creation can combat ascetic tendencies within the church (and yes, within Calvin) that are based on "abandonment to God" — to the loss of createdness and particularity.

What is more, it is not just a doctrine of createdness that upholds human particularity, but one emerging from the reality of *participatio Christi*. We are particularized neither by grasping after our identity, nor merely by being "creatures," but only through intimacy: by being firmly ensconced in the *koinōnia* of Christ.[42] Calvin's doctrine of participation finds as its focal point the church's participation in Christ. The bounds of the Christian self are no longer realized by looking within but by looking to the one in whom we have a joint identity. "They shall constitute one person."[43] The Spirit maintains this identity for us, as persons-in-Christ, by not only serving as the one in whom we are brought into Christ, but as the "Spirit of adoption," who works this identity deeper and deeper into the church's consciousness. This new reality of adoption is not merely a synonym for

41. The fertile crossover with John Zizioulas here should be evident, and it holds much promise for ecumenical dialogue (Zizioulas, *Being as Communion* [Crestwood, NY: St Vladimir's Seminary Press, 1985]), as does the recent work by Reformed theologian F. LeRon Shults, *Reforming Theological Anthropology* (Grand Rapids: Eerdmans, 2003).

42. A "relational anthropology" can be as much a product of the age as have past "rational anthropologies" or "dualistic anthropologies."

43. ". . . not because, like ourselves, he has a human nature, but because, by the power of his Spirit, he makes us a part of his body, so that from him we derive our life" (*Comm. Eph.* 5:31).

salvation but for this new reality of participation and the anthropology that it implies. "Surely this is so: We ought not to separate Christ from ourselves or ourselves from him. Rather we ought to hold fast bravely with both hands to that fellowship by which he has bound himself to us" (III.2.24). Truly human freedom is held out to us not as individuals but as ones who discover our identities the more we live in another: *en Christo* and, correspondingly, in others.

Yet much of this is in competition with Calvin's own reticence about the integrity of the material realm, a suspicion that we know was provoked by the self-asserting humanism of his time. Calvin struggled to uphold the Spirit's relationship to creation as being not only "spiritual" but also (and simultaneously) "material." He moved in this direction by assigning "ascent" not to the individual soul but to the concrete realm of the church, where its structures and sacraments are not extraneous to ascent, but the very "good" material things that make our ascent possible.

Perhaps where the difference between Calvin and Irenaeus becomes most pronounced is in the seemingly neutral arena of methodology. Calvin expends three books on the Trinitarian structure of participation, and only then does he begin to speak of its practical outworking — the church. Irenaeus, on the other hand, begins with the reality of participation in the church: "But our opinion is in accordance with the Eucharist, and the Eucharist in turn establishes our opinion" (*AH* V.18.5). This methodological starting point in Calvin could explain why the church can seem so extraneous to what is "really real," and why in the Reformed tradition the sacraments are at times observed merely out of obedience. In many ways, the structure of the *Institutes* reflects Calvin's Platonic language of "interior/exterior," by beginning with the spiritual core and only then working outward to its external manifestation. Book IV, not inconsequentially, is called "The *External* Means or Aims by Which God Invites Us Into the Society of Christ and Holds Us Therein" (emphasis added).

The upshot of this was that Calvin also tended to use the Holy Spirit to deflect attention away from creation and (upward) to its divine source; thus he risked emphasizing a salvation *out* of the world. He acknowledges creation as wholly dependent on God's presence and even participating in God's gifts. Yet, as Tanner notes, "[i]n Reformation theology, however, this principle takes on a negative cast: worry that creatures will not thank God for all that they are deflates reveling in the gifts themselves. So, for example, Calvin [III.15.3]: 'because all his things are ours and we have all things in him, in us there is nothing.'"[44] This has left the Reformed church with a legacy of an ambiguous relationship to the physical world, where various tendencies to anthropological reductionism are paralleled by eucharistic ones. Does Christ work through me and my particularity, or despite me? Does Christ manifest himself through the sacramental elements, or despite them?

These questions reflect a basic ambivalence toward creation and the Spirit's role within it: it is unclear whether the physical is the divinely appointed realm for our participation in God or whether the physical must be bypassed for such a relationship. Calvin's relentless emphasis on the source *behind* the sacramental present did not always validate the present. It is no wonder that "self-emptying" is then seen as a way to overcome a physicality that can only be construed as a barrier to God — whether they be our desires, our gifts, or our human agency. The sacraments and church often do not fare much better than does anthropology as things that are inessential for the "real work" that God does behind the scenes. One such way this uniqueness manifests itself is in human agency, a topic that proved especially troublesome for Calvin due to his profound regard for the completion of the work of Christ.[45] Yet this is precisely where participation enables one to steer clear of both the dangers of activism and of passivity, as Irenaeus displayed so beautifully in his treatment of the Eucharist, where our grateful use of the material is allowed to reclaim creation for God. Calvin balked at giving a role to humanity just here, although his own theology (especially his commentary on Hebrews) would have us brought, by the Spirit, precisely into the ascended one who stands before the Father — not only receiving but also *offering* our humanity back to God.

It is here that Irenaeus's lack of suspicion about the material, his joyful

---

44. Kathryn Tanner, *Jesus, Humanity and the Trinity* (Edinburgh: T. & T. Clark, 2001), p. 3. So, while for Irenaeus the Spirit's presence in the world required its hallowing ("For the glory of God is a human fully alive," *AH* IV.20.7), Calvin — for fear of jeopardizing God's sovereignty — could not go that far. Humanity is not the glory of God, but is a *mirror* of the glory of God. The world is also called "the mirror of divinity" and "the theatre of divine glory" (*Comm. Heb.* 11:3). This in itself is not a problematic perspective, but one that needs supporting theology to work out a positive relationship of creation to God.

45. "Besides, we must remember this principle, that from the time when Christ once appeared, there is nothing left for the faithful, but with suspended minds ever to look forward to his second coming" (*Comm. 1 Pet.* 4:7).

realization that God's will is done precisely in (not despite) the material, can be of help in contemporary spiritual formation. If indeed the "glory of God is a human fully alive" (*AH* IV.20.7), then God's glory and human redeemed particularity are bound together in an enduring relationship. All rests on the ascended, human Christ, who raises our hearts upward to him that we may experience the power of his Spirit in our present circumstances, whether they be bread and wine or human particularity and agency. It is this Spirit who moves us from a spirituality of emptying ourselves to the reality of the self-in-Christ, and past even that to a deepened understanding of how the self-in-Christ is the only safeguard of our particular uniqueness in the here and now. As Irenaeus says, "[N]either is the substance nor the essence of the creation annihilated, for faithful and true is He who has established it" (*AH* V.36.1).

Combating Alienation: The Ascent in the Son to the Father

Calvin's fears were rooted in the pantheistic notions of nature/grace that his era manifested, and his doctrine of participation was crafted in that polemical light. Yet we must go further than this reactionary interpretation: his emphasis on Trinitarian differentiation not only combated fusion but also functioned as a necessary ingredient of intimacy.[46] The struggle of our own era, as that of Irenaeus, is not only with pantheism but with alienation — alienation from the created world, from one another, and from the self.[47] Whereas it is vital that we understand the ways in which participation resists pantheism, a truly mature and fruitful response to our culture will also plumb the depths of *koinōnia* as a response to modern alienation.

Modernity's problem of alienation has been recognized by the Existentialists (Sartre, Camus, etc.), combated by the Personalists (Buber, Mounier, Levinas, etc.), and embraced to dizzying heights by the post-

46. It is perhaps in this way that Calvin's model of participation (with its associated anthropology, christology, and doctrine of creation) best complements and challenges the model advanced by Radical Orthodoxy. One must not begin with Platonism, but with the perichoresis *(koinōnia)* of the Trinity as a metaphysical given. In so doing, participation avoids any impersonal vestiges of Greek participation and is given a dynamic trajectory toward relational fullness.

47. Paul Lebeau, "Koinōnia: la signification du salut selon saint Irénée," in *Epektasis* (Paris: Beauchesne, 1972), pp. 121-27.

modernists (Foucault, Derrida, etc.). The *koinōnia* of God, offered to a humanity that is on a self-destructive course of autonomy and alienation, constitutes a radical alternative. However, participation in this *koinōnia* is not a new Gnostic answer for the enlightened; instead, it is a qualitatively different form of existence. Going beyond all modern and postmodern attempts to find "personal fulfillment" (most often through the actualization of potential), participation in the divine life of the Trinity offers to take us out of ourselves in order to find ourselves in truth in Another. It is a way of living and being, such that our suicidal and autonomous tendencies are taken into divine love and healed. In becoming part of something much greater than ourselves — specifically the One who is the ground of our being — we find ourselves and are found. This is the secret of the "double-knowledge" with which Calvin opened his magisterial *Institutes:* "Nearly all the wisdom we possess, that is to say, true and sound wisdom, consists of two parts: the knowledge of God and of ourselves" (I.1.1).

Calvin's refusal to make salvation the narcissistic goal of human existence expresses the extent to which he attempted to reframe human existence in the broadest possible terms. In so doing, he challenges the utilitarianism of our culture with the notion of worship, and he challenges the functionalism of our culture with the notion of intimacy (to be dealt with, respectively, below).

It is the Father who is the goal of our ascent and who provides the framework for human life. We are to live *in another* — not egocentrically but exocentrically. For this reason, the "glory of God" has pride of place in Reformed theology, because worship is the recognition of the uniqueness of the Other. "His ways are not our ways."[48] It is the appreciation of God's uniqueness that draws us into a relationship of love with him. By emphasizing God's sovereignty, Calvin attempts to ground human *koinōnia* with him in a way that would impede manipulation and instead allow true intimacy to flourish, through the appreciation of his distinctiveness and particularity. The Spirit is the one who maintains both God's uniqueness and our own, for the purpose of drawing us into this much larger reality of triune *koinōnia*.

Just as salvation is not the goal of human existence (utilitarianism),

---

48. Calvin's *Comm. Isa.* 55:8 gives wonderful depth to God's perspective: "My thoughts are very different from yours. If you are implacable, and can with difficulty be brought back to a state of friendship with those from whom you have received an injury, I am not like you, that I should treat you so cruelly."

neither is morality or Christian ministry the goal of the Christian life (functionalism). The triune ascent laid out by Calvin combats both these modern trends by challenging us to interpret our present ascent with God in terms of deepened communion. "But what? It is only an entrance! We must march further in it. . . . So, then, it is not all to have entered, but we must follow further, until we are fully united to Jesus Christ."[49] Ascent is thus characterized not so much by privatized obedience; rather, it is our participation in Jesus' "return" to the Father.[50] Calvin's greatest contribution here is his insistence that the Christian life (ascent) is not merely a response to Christ's descent. Grace *includes* our response. In this light, sanctification can never be one's own personal quest for holiness; rather, it is the transformation wrought through deepened *koinōnia* with God and others, and it is characterized by the move from loneliness to an "others-consciousness." The Spirit governs this ascent by bringing the church to live in and through the Son in his relationship to the Father. As in the Eucharist, it is not the transformation of our substance that is required, but the Spirit's work to help two unlikes come together in intimacy and communion. For as Calvin affirms, "there must be some difference between the head and the members. . . ."[51] Even after death, when our communion with the triune God will be most intimate, there will be no "sinking into God," but instead a reaffirmation of our particularity through *koinōnia* with God.

49. *Serm. Acts* 1:1-4.

50. When obedience is seen as response rather than participation, we end up with exhaustion. Furthermore, when obedience is not seen as a participation in Christ's own sonship, it is rendered contentless, only to be filled by a reaction to whatever is perceived to be vices in the culture of that time.

51. *Comm. 1 John* 3:2. The quotation closes as follows: ". . . the distance between us and him will be even then very great."

Bibliography

No, we cannot read the writings of the ancients on these subjects without great admiration. We marvel at them because we are compelled to recognize how preeminent they are. But shall we count anything praiseworthy or noble without recognizing at the same time that it comes from God? Let us be ashamed of such ingratitude. . . .

Calvin, *Institutes* II.2.15

Original, Edited, and Translated Works by John Calvin

The Bondage and Liberation of the Will. Translated by G. I. Davies. Edited by A. N. S. Lane. Grand Rapids: Baker Book House, 1996.

Calvin's Commentaries. Edited by the Calvin Translation Society. 22 vols. Edinburgh, 1843-55. Reprint, Grand Rapids: Baker, 1979.

Calvin's New Testament Commentaries. Edited by David W. Torrance and T. F. Torrance. 12 vols. Edinburgh: Oliver & Boyd, 1959-72.

"Calvinus Vermilio" [Letter 2266, 8 August 1555]. In *Gleanings of a Few Scattered Ears, during the period of the Reformation in England and of the times immediately succeeding, A.D. 1533 to A.D. 1588.* Translated by George Gorham. London: Bell & Daldy, 1857.

The Deity of Christ and Other Sermons. Translated by Leroy Nixon. The Comprehensive John Calvin Collection 2.0: Old Paths Publications, 1997. Reprint, Ages Digital Library, 2002.

Institutes of the Christian Religion (1536). Translated by F. L. Battles. Grand Rapids: Eerdmans, 1986.

Institutes of the Christian Religion (1559). Translated by F. L. Battles. Edited by J. T. McNeill. Library of Christian Classics 20-21. Philadelphia: Westminster, 1960.

Institutes of the Christian Religion (1559). Translated by Henry Beveridge. Edinburgh, 1845. Reprint, Grand Rapids: Eerdmans, 1989.

Institutes of the Christian Religion of John Calvin 1559, Text and Concordance. Edited by Richard F. Wevers. 4 vols. Grand Rapids: Meeter Center for Calvin Studies, 1998. Reprint, CD-Rom, 2002.

Instruction in Faith (1537). Translated by Paul T. Fuhrmann. Louisville: Westminster John Knox, 1992.

Ioannis Calvini opera quae supersunt omnia [*CO* 1-59]. In *Corpus Reformatorum* [*CR* 29-87]. Edited by G. Baum, E. Cunitz, and E. Ruess. Brunswick, 1863-1900.

Letters of John Calvin. Translated by David Constable and Marcus Robert Gilchrist. Edited by Jules Bonnet. 4 vols. New York: B. Franklin, 1973.

A Reformation Debate: Sadoleto's Letter to the Genevans and Calvin's Reply. Edited by John C. Olin. New York: Harper & Row, 1966.

Sermons on 2 Samuel: 1-13. Translated by Douglas Kelly. Edinburgh: Banner of Truth, 1992.

Tracts and Treatises in Defence of the Reformed Faith. Edited by Henry Beveridge. 3 vols. Grand Rapids: Eerdmans, 1958.

Original, Edited, and Translated Works by Irenaeus

The Apostolic Fathers with Justin Martyr and Irenaeus. Edited by Alexander Roberts and James Donaldson. Ante-Nicene Fathers [ANF] I. Grand Rapids: Eerdmans, 1996.

Contre les hérésies (Adversus haereses). Edited by Adelin Rousseau and Louis Doutreleau. Sources chrétiennes [SC] 100, 152-53, 210-11, 263-64, 293-94. Paris: Cerf, 1952-82.

Démonstration de la prédication apostolique (Epideixis). Edited by Adelin Rousseau. Sources chrétiennes [SC] 406. Paris: Cerf, 1995.

On the Apostolic Preaching. Translated by John Behr. Crestwood, NY: St. Vladimir's Seminary Press, 1997.

Proof of the Apostolic Preaching. Translated by Joseph Smith. Ancient Christian Writers 16. New York: Paulist, 1952.

Other Original, Edited, and Translated Sources

Aquinas, Thomas. *Summa Theologiæ*. Edited by Thomas Gilby and Thomas C. O'Brien. 61 vols. London: Blackfriars [with Eyre & Spottiswoode], 1964-81.

———. *Summa Theologiæ: A Concise Translation*. Edited by Timothy McDermott. London: Methuen, 1989.

Bibliography

Augustine. *Confessions.* Translated by Henry Chadwick. Oxford: Oxford University Press, 1998.

———. *Soliloquies and Immortality of the Soul.* Translated by Gerard Watson. Oxford: Aris & Phillips, 1990.

Clement of Alexandria. *Extraits de Théodote.* Edited by F. Sagnard. Sources chrétiennes [SC] 23. Paris: Cerf, 1948.

Migne, J. P. *Patrologia Latina.* Paris: Garnier, 1844-1965.

Origen. *The Song of Songs: Commentary and Homilies.* Edited by R. P. Lawson. London: Longmans, Green, 1957.

———. *Homélies sur le cantiques des cantiques.* Edited by O. Rousseau. Sources chrétiennes [SC] 37. 2nd ed. Paris: Cerf, 1966.

———. *Traité des principes (De principiis).* Edited by Henri Crouzel and Manlio Simonetti. Sources chrétiennes [SC] 252, 253, 268, 269, 312. Paris: Cerf, 1978-84.

Plato. *Plato: Theaetetus, Sophist.* Translated by H. N. Fowler. Loeb Classical Library 123. London: Heinemann, 1921.

———. *Plato: Lysis, Symposium, Gorgias.* Translated by W. R. M. Lamb. Loeb Classical Library 166. London: Harvard University Press, 1984.

Plotinus. *Plotinus: Enneads.* Translated by A. H. Armstrong. Loeb Classical Library 440-445, 468. London: Heinemann, 1984.

Proclus. *Elements of Theology.* Translated by E. R. Dodds. Oxford: Clarendon, 1933.

Seneca. *Ad Lucilium Epistulae Morales.* Translated by Richard M. Gummere. Loeb Classical Library 77. London: Heinemann, 1918.

Secondary Sources

Alès, Adhémar d'. "La doctrine de la récapitulation en S. Irénée." *Recherches de Science Religieuse* 6 (1916): 185-211.

———. "La doctrine de l'Esprit en S. Irénée." *Recherches de Science Religieuse* 14 (1924): 497-538.

———. "La doctrine eucharistique en S. Irénée." *Recherches de Science Religieuse* 13 (1923): 24-46.

Anatolios, Khaled. "The Immediately Triune God: A Patristic Response to Schleiermacher." *Pro Ecclesia* 10 (2001): 159-178.

Andia, Ysabel de. "La résurrection de la chair selon les Valentiniens et Irénée de Lyon." *Les Quatre Fleuves* 15-16 (1982): 59-70.

———. *Homo vivens.* Paris: Études augustiniennes, 1986.

———. "La gnose au nom menteur: séduction et divisions." *Communio* 24, no. 2 (1999): 13-34.

Asiedu, F. "The Song of Songs and the Ascent of the Soul: Ambrose, Augustine, and the Language of Mysticism." *Vigiliae Christianae* 55 (2001): 299-317.

Aubineau, M. "Incorruptibilité et divinisation selon S. Irénée." *Recherches de Science Religieuse* 44 (1956): 25-52.

Backus, Irena. "Irenaeus, Calvin and Calvinist Orthodoxy: The Patristic Manual of

Abraham Scultetus (1598)." *Reformation and Renaissance Review* no. 1 (June 1999): 41-53.

———. "Calvin and the Greek Fathers." In *Continuity and Change,* edited by Robert James Bast and Andrew Colin Gow, pp. 253-76. Leiden: Brill, 2000.

———. *Historical Method and Confessional Identity in the Era of the Reformation (1378-1615).* Leiden: Brill, 2003.

Badcock, Gary. "The Anointing of Christ and the *Filioque* Doctrine." *Irish Theological Quarterly* 60 (1994): 241-58.

———. *Light of Truth and Fire of Love.* Grand Rapids: Eerdmans, 1997.

Balás, David L. "Christian Transformation of Greek Philosophy Illustrated by Gregory of Nyssa's Use of the Notion of Participation." In *Proceedings of the American Catholic Philosophical Association, 1966,* edited by George McLean, pp. 40, 152-57. Washington, DC: Catholic University of America Press, 1966.

———. *Metousia Theou: Man's Participation in God's Perfections According to Saint Gregory of Nyssa.* Studia Anselmiana 55. Rome: IB Libreria Herder, 1966.

———. "Encounter Between Christianity and Contemporary Philosophy in the Second Century." *Anglican Theological Review* 50 (1968): 131-43.

———. "Participation." In *Encyclopedia of Early Christianity,* edited by Everett Ferguson, pp. 692-95. London: St James, 1990.

Barfield, Owen. *Saving the Appearances: A Study in Idolatry.* New York: Harcourt Brace Jovanovich, 1965.

Barth, Karl. *Church Dogmatics.* 13 vols. Edinburgh: T. & T. Clark, 1956-75.

———. "Concluding Unscientific Postscript on Schleiermacher." In *The Theology of Schleiermacher,* pp. 261-79. Grand Rapids: Eerdmans, 1982.

———. *Protestant Theology in the Nineteenth Century.* London: SCM, 2001.

———. *The Theology of John Calvin.* Grand Rapids: Eerdmans, 1995.

———. *The Theology of the Reformed Confessions, 1923.* Translated by Darrell and Judith Guder. Louisville: Westminster John Knox, 2002.

Barth, Karl, and E. Thurneysen. *Revolutionary Theology in the Making: The Barth-Thurneysen Correspondence, 1914-1925.* London: Epworth, 1964.

Bates, Gordon. "The Typology of Adam and Christ in John Calvin." *Hartford Quarterly* 5 (1964): 42-57.

Battles, Ford Lewis. *Analysis of the Institutes of the Christian Religion of John Calvin.* Grand Rapids: Baker, 1980.

Beardslee, John W., III. "Sanctification in Reformed Theology." In *The New Man: An Orthodox and Reformed Dialogue,* edited by John Meyendorff and J. C. McLelland, pp. 132-48. New Brunswick, NJ: Agora, 1973.

Begbie, Jeremy. "Repetition and Eucharist." In *Theology, Music, and Time,* pp. 155-75. Cambridge: Cambridge University Press, 2000.

———. *Voicing Creation's Praise.* Edinburgh: T. & T. Clark, 1991.

Behr, John. "The Word of God in the Second Century." *Pro Ecclesia* 9 (2000): 85-107.

Benko, Stephen. *The Meaning of Sanctorum Communio.* Studies in Historical Theology 3. London: SCM, 1964.

Bibliography

Berger, Klaus. *Identity and Experience in the New Testament.* Minneapolis: Augsburg Fortress, 2003.

Bertaud, Émile, and André Rayez. "Échelle Spirituelle." *Dictionnaire de Spiritualité* 4 (1961): 62-86.

Berthouzoz, Roger. *Liberté et grâce suivant la théologie d'Irénée de Lyon.* Paris: Cerf, 1980.

Billings, Todd. *Calvin, Participation, and the Gift: The Activity of Believers in Union with Christ.* New York: Oxford University Press, 2008.

Bird, Michael. "Incorporated Righteousness: A Response to Recent Evangelical Discussion Concerning the Imputation of Christ's Righteousness in Justification." *Journal of the Evangelical Theological Society* 47 (2004): 253-76.

Bonhoeffer, Dietrich. *Christology.* London: Collins, 1966.

Bos, Abraham. "'Aristotelian' and 'Platonic' Dualism in Hellenistic and Early Christian Philosophy and in Gnosticism." *Vigiliae Christianae* 56 (2002): 273-91.

Bousset, Wilhelm. *Kyrios Christos.* Nashville: Abingdon, 1970.

Bouwsma, William J. *John Calvin: A Sixteenth-Century Portrait.* New York: Oxford University Press, 1988.

Bouyer, Louis. *A History of Christian Spirituality* III. London: Burns & Oates, 1969.

Braaten, Carl, and Robert Jenson, eds. *Union with Christ: The New Finnish Interpretation of Luther.* Grand Rapids: Eerdmans, 1998.

Bray, Gerald. *The Doctrine of God.* Downers Grove, IL: InterVarsity Press, 1993.

Breck, John. "Trinitarian Liturgical Formulas in the New Testament." In *The Power of the Word.* Crestwood, NY: St Vladimir's Seminary Press, 1986.

———. "'The Two Hands of God': Christ and the Spirit in Orthodox Theology." *St Vladimir's Theological Quarterly* 40 (1996): 231-46.

Brown, Robert. "On the Necessary Imperfection of Creation: Irenaeus' *Adversus Haereses* IV,38." *Scottish Journal of Theology* 28 (1975): 17-25.

Brunner, Emil. *The Mediator.* Philadelphia: Westminster, 1947.

Butin, Philip W. "Constructive Iconoclasm: Trinitarian Concern in Reformed Worship." *Studia Liturgica* 19 (1989): 133-42.

———. "Two Early Reformed Catechisms, the Threefold Office, and the Shape of Karl Barth's Christology." *Scottish Journal of Theology* 44 (1991): 195-214.

———. *Revelation, Redemption, and Response: Calvin's Trinitarian Understanding of the Divine-Human Relationship.* New York: Oxford University Press, 1995.

Caillot, Joseph. "La grâce de l'union selon saint Irénée." In *Penser la foi,* edited by Joseph Doré and Christoph Theobald, pp. 391-412. Paris: Cerf, 1993.

Cairns, David. *The Image of God in Man.* Revised ed. London: Collins, 1973.

Campbell, J. Y. "Koinonia and its Cognates in the New Testament." *Journal of Biblical Literature* 51 (1932): 352-82.

Canlis, Julie. "Being Made Human: The Significance of Creation for Irenaeus' Doctrine of Participation." *Scottish Journal of Theology* 58 (2005): 434-67.

Carpenter, Craig. "A Question of Union with Christ? Calvin and Trent on Justification." *Westminster Theological Journal* 64 (2002): 363-86.

Carr, Wesley. "A Theology of the Holy Spirit." *Scottish Journal of Theology* 28 (1975): 501-16.

Cavadini, John. "The Structure and Intention of Augustine's *De trinitate.*" *Augustinian Studies* 23 (1992): 103-23.

Cavanaugh, William. "A Joint Declaration? Justification as Theosis in Aquinas and Luther." *Heythrop Journal* 41 (2000): 265-80.

―――. "Eucharistic Sacrifice and the Social Imagination in Early Modern Europe." *Journal of Medieval and Early Modern Studies* 31 (2001): 585-605.

Chung, Paul. *Spirituality and Social Ethics in John Calvin: A Pneumatological Perspective.* Lanham, MD: University Press of America, 2000.

Coffey, David. "A Proper Mission of the Holy Spirit." *Theological Studies* 47 (1986): 227-50.

Collins, John. "A Throne in the Heavens." In *Death, Ecstasy, and Other Worldly Journeys,* edited by John Collins and Michael Fishbane. New York: State University of New York Press, 1995.

Conradt, Nancy. *John Calvin, Theodore Beza, and the Reformation in Poland.* Ann Arbor, MI: Univ. Micro., 1975.

Coppens, J. "La *koinonia* dans l'église primitive." *Ephemerides Theologicae Lovanienses* 46 (1970): 116-21.

Courcelle, Pierre. *Recherches sur les Confessions de saint Augustin.* Paris: Boccard, 1968.

Cullmann, Oscar. *Immortality of the Soul, or Resurrection from the Dead? The Witness of the New Testament.* London: Epworth, 1952.

―――. *The Christology of the New Testament.* London: SCM, 1963.

Daniélou, Jean. "Histoire des origines Chrétiennes." *Recherches de Science Religieuse* 58 (1970): 113-54.

―――. "Adam et le Christ chez St Irénée." In *Sacramentum Futuri.* Paris: Beauchesne, 1950.

Davis, Thomas J. *The Clearest Promises of God: The Development of Calvin's Eucharistic Teaching.* AMS Studies in Religious Tradition 1. New York: AMS, 1995.

Delling, G. "μεταλαμβάνω, μετάληψις." In *Theological Dictionary of the New Testament,* edited by G. Kittel, 4:10-11. Grand Rapids: Eerdmans, 1967.

DeVries, Dawn. "The Incarnation and the Sacramental Word." In *Towards the Future of Reformed Theology,* edited by David Willis and Michael Welker, pp. 386-405. Grand Rapids: Eerdmans, 1999.

Donovan, Mary Ann. "Irenaeus in Recent Scholarship." *Second Century* 4 (1984): 219-41.

―――. *One Right Reading? A Guide to Irenaeus.* Collegeville, MN: Liturgical Press, 1997.

Douglass, Jane Dempsey. *Women, Freedom, and Calvin.* Philadelphia: Westminster, 1985.

Dunn, James. *The Theology of Paul the Apostle.* Grand Rapids: Eerdmans, 1998.

Eichler, J. "Fellowship, Have, Share, Participate." In *New International Dictionary of New Testament Theology,* edited by Colin Brown, 1:635-39. Grand Rapids: Zondervan, 1975-85.

Eire, Carlos M. N. "John Calvin's Attack on Idolatry." In *War Against the Idols,* pp. 195-233. Cambridge: Cambridge University Press, 1986.

Bibliography

Engel, Mary Potter. *John Calvin's Perspectival Anthropology*. Atlanta: Scholars Press, 1988.

Evans, William Borden. "Imputation and Impartation: The Problem of Union with Christ in Nineteenth-Century American Reformed Theology." Ph.D. dissertation, Vanderbilt University, 1996.

Évieux, Pierre. "Théologie de l'accoutumance chez saint Irénée." *Recherches de Science Religieuse* 55 (1967): 5-54.

Faber, Jelle. *Essays in Reformed Doctrine*. Neerlandia, Alberta: Inheritance, 1990.

Fabro, Cornelio. *La nozione metafisica di partecipazione secondo S. Tommaso d'Aquino*. Torino: Societa Editrice Internazionale, 1950.

Farrow, Douglas. "St. Irenaeus of Lyons: The Church and the World." *Pro Ecclesia* 4 (1995): 333-55.

————. "The Doctrine of the Ascension in Irenaeus and Origen." *ARC* 26 (1998): 31-50.

————. *Ascension and Ecclesia*. Grand Rapids: Eerdmans, 1999.

————. "Eucharist, Eschatology, and Ethics." In *The Future as God's Gift*, edited by David Fergusson and Marcel Sarot, pp. 199-215. Edinburgh: T. & T. Clark, 2000.

————. "Between the Rock and a Hard Place: In Support of (something like) a Reformed View of the Eucharist." *International Journal of Systematic Theology* 3 (2001): 167-86.

Ferguson, Sinclair B. "The Reformed Doctrine of Sonship." In *Pulpit and People*, edited by William Still, Nigel Cameron, and Sinclair Ferguson, pp. 81-88. Edinburgh: Rutherford House, 1986.

Feuillet, A. "La participation actuelle à la vie divine d'après le quatrième évangile." In *Johannine Studies*. New York: Alba House, 1964.

Finance, Joseph de. *Être et Agir dans la philosophie de S. Thomas*. Paris: Beauchesne, 1954.

Fuller, Reginald. "Justification in Recent Pauline Studies." *Anglican Theological Review* 84 (2002): 411-16.

Gaffin, Richard. "Biblical Theology and the Westminster Standards." *Westminster Theological Journal* 65 (2003): 165-79.

Ganoczy, Alexandre. *Calvin, Théologien de l'Église et du Ministère*. Paris: Cerf, 1964.

————. *The Young Calvin*. Edinburgh: T. & T. Clark, 1987.

————. "Observations on Calvin's Trinitarian Doctrine of Grace." In *Probing the Reformed Tradition*, edited by Elsie Anne McKee and Brian G. Armstrong, pp. 96-107. Louisville: Westminster John Knox, 1989.

Garcia, Mark. *Life in Christ: Union with Christ and Twofold Grace in Calvin's Theology*. Studies in Christian History and Thought. Carlisle, UK: Paternoster, 2008.

Geiger, L. B. *La participation dans la philosophie de S. Thomas d'Aquin*. Paris: Vrin, 1953.

Gerrish, B. A. "The Mirror of God's Goodness: Man in the Theology of Calvin." *Concordia Theological Quarterly* 45 (1981): 211-22.

————. "Sign and Reality: The Lord's Supper in the Reformed Confessions." In *The Old Protestantism and the New: Essays on the Reformation Heritage*, pp. 118-49. Chicago: University of Chicago Press, 1982.

————. *Grace and Gratitude: The Eucharistic Theology of John Calvin*. Minneapolis: Fortress, 1993.

Gorringe, Timothy. *God's Just Vengeance*. Cambridge: Cambridge University Press, 1996.

Griffith, Howard. "'The First Title of the Spirit': Adoption in Calvin's Soteriology." *Evangelical Quarterly* 73, no. 2 (2001): 135-53.

Guevin, Benedict. "The Natural Law in Irenaeus of Lyons' *Adversus Haereses:* A Metaphysical or Soteriological Reality?" In *Studia Patristica* 36 (Leuven, 2001): 222-25.

Gunton, Colin. *Christ and Creation*. Grand Rapids: Eerdmans, 1992.

————. *The One, the Three, and the Many*. Cambridge: Cambridge University Press, 1993.

————. "God, Grace and Freedom." In *God and Freedom*, edited by Colin Gunton, pp. 119-33. Edinburgh: T. & T. Clark, 1995.

————. "Aspects of Salvation: Some Unscholastic Themes from Calvin's Institutes." *International Journal of Systematic Theology* 1 (1999): 253-65.

————. "Creation and Mediation in the Theology of Robert W. Jenson: An Encounter and a Convergence." In *Trinity, Time, and Church*, edited by Colin Gunton, pp. 80-93. Grand Rapids: Eerdmans, 2000.

————. *Father, Son, and Holy Spirit*. Edinburgh: T. & T. Clark, 2002.

————. "'One Mediator . . . the Man Jesus Christ': Reconciliation, Mediation, and Life in Community." *Pro Ecclesia* 11 (2002): 146-58.

Hadot, Pierre. *Philosophy as a Way of Life*. Translated by Michael Chase. Oxford: Blackwell, 1995.

Hainz, J. *Koinonia: 'Kirche' als Gemeinschaft bei Paulus*. Regensburg: Pustet, 1982.

Hampson, Daphne. *Christian Contradictions*. London: Cambridge University Press, 2001.

Hanse, H. "μετέχω." In *Theological Dictionary of the New Testament*. Edited by G. Kittel. Translated by Geoffrey W. Bromiley, 2:830-32. Grand Rapids: Eerdmans, 1964-76.

Harnack, Adolph. *History of Dogma*. Vol. II. London: Williams & Norgate, 1894.

Hart, Trevor. "Humankind in Christ and Christ in Humankind: Salvation as Participation in Our Substitute in the Theology of John Calvin." *Scottish Journal of Theology* 42 (1989): 67-84.

————. "Irenaeus, Recapitulation, and Physical Redemption." In *Christ in Our Place*, edited by Trevor Hart and Daniel Thimell, pp. 152-81. Exeter, UK: Paternoster, 1989.

————. "Redemption and Fall." In *The Cambridge Companion to Christian Doctrine*, edited by Colin E. Gunton, pp. 189-206. Cambridge: Cambridge University Press, 1997.

Hauck, F. "κοινωνός." In *Theological Dictionary of the New Testament*. Edited by G. Kittel. Translated by Geoffrey W. Bromiley, 3:789-809. Grand Rapids: Eerdmans, 1964-76.

Hays, Richard. "*PISTIS* and Pauline Theology: What Is at Stake?" In *The Society of*

Bibliography

Biblical Literature Seminar Papers 1991, edited by Eugene Lovering, pp. 714-29. Atlanta: Scholars Press, 1991.

Hendry, George. *The Gospel of the Incarnation*. London: SCM, 1959.

Henle, R. J. *Saint Thomas and Platonism*. The Hague: Nijhoff, 1956.

Heron, Alasdair. *Table and Tradition*. Edinburgh: Handsel Press, 1983.

Hesselink, John. "Governed and Guided by the Spirit." In *Reformiertes Erbe*, edited by Heiko Oberman. Zurich: Theologischer Verlag, 1993.

Hick, John. *Evil and the God of Love*. London: Macmillan, 1985.

Holmes, Stephen R. "On the Communion of Saints." In *Listening to the Past*, pp. 18-36. Carlisle, UK: Paternoster, 2002.

Holwerda, David E. "Eschatology and History: A Look at Calvin's Eschatological Vision." In *Exploring the Heritage of John Calvin*, edited by David E. Holwerda, pp. 110-39. Grand Rapids: Baker, 1976.

Hooker, Morna. "Interchange in Christ." *Journal of Theological Studies* 22 (1971): 349-61.

Hopkins, Gerard Manley. *The Poems of Gerard Manley Hopkins*. Edited by W. H. Gardner and N. H. MacKenzie. 4th ed. London: Oxford University Press, 1967.

Houssiau, Albert. *La christologie de saint Irénée*. Louvain: Publications Universitaires de Louvain, 1955.

Hunsinger, George. "Baptism and the Soteriology of Forgiveness." *International Journal of Systematic Theology* 2 (2000): 247-69.

————. "Calvin's Doctrine of Justification: Is it Really Forensic?" Unpublished manuscript, 2005.

————. *Disruptive Grace*. Grand Rapids: Eerdmans, 2000.

————. "The Dimension of Depth: Thomas F. Torrance on the Sacraments of Baptism and the Lord's Supper." *Scottish Journal of Theology* 54 (2001): 155-76.

————. "A Tale of Two Simultaneities: Justification and Sanctification in Calvin and Barth." *Zeitschrift für dialektische Theologie* 18 (2002): 316-38.

————. "The Bread that We Break: Toward a Chalcedonian Resolution of the Eucharistic Controversies." *Princeton Seminary Bulletin* 24 (2003): 241-58.

Janssens, L. "Notre filiation divine d'après Cyrille d'Alexandrie." *Ephemerides Theologicae Lovanienses* 15 (1938): 233-78.

Jenson, Robert W. "The Initial Christianizing of Hellenism." In *Christian Dogmatics I*, edited by Carl E. Braaten and Robert W. Jenson, pp. 118-24. Philadelphia: Fortress, 1984.

————. "Pneumatological Soteriology." In *Christian Dogmatics II*, edited by Carl E. Braaten and Robert W. Jenson, pp. 125-42. Philadelphia: Fortress, 1984.

————. "Autobiographical Reflections on the Relation of Theology, Science, and Philosophy; or, You Wonder Where the Body Went." In *Essays in Theology of Culture*, pp. 216-24. Grand Rapids: Eerdmans, 1995.

————. *Systematic Theology I: The Triune God*. Oxford: Oxford University Press, 1997.

————. *Systematic Theology II: The Works of God*. Oxford: Oxford University Press, 1999.

————. "Response to Mark Seifrid, Paul Metzger, and Carl Trueman on Finnish Luther Research." *Westminster Theological Journal* 65 (2003): 245-50.

Jenson, Robert W., and Eric W. Gritsch. *Lutheranism: The Theological Movement and Its Confessional Writings.* Philadelphia: Fortress, 1976.

Jüngel, Eberhard. *Justification: The Heart of the Christian Faith.* Translated by Jeffrey F. Cayzer. Edinburgh: T. & T. Clark, 2001.

Kaiser, Christopher. "Climbing Jacob's Ladder: John Calvin and the Early Church on Our Eucharistic Ascent to Heaven." *Scottish Journal of Theology* 56 (2003): 247-67.

Kang, P-S. "The Concept of the Vicarious Humanity of Christ in the Theology of Thomas Forsyth Torrance." Ph.D. dissertation, University of Aberdeen, 1983.

Kasper, Walter. *Jesus the Christ.* London: Burns & Oates, 1976.

———. *The God of Jesus Christ.* New York: Crossroad, 1984.

Keller, Carl-Albert. *Calvin mystique: au coeur de la pensée du réformateur.* Geneva: Labor et Fides, 2001.

Kim, Jae Sung. "*Unio Cum Christo:* The Work of the Holy Spirit in Calvin's Theology." Ph.D. dissertation, Westminster Theological Seminary, 1998.

Kolb, Robert. "'Not Without the Satisfaction of God's Righteousness': The Atonement and the Generation Gap between Luther and His Students." In *Archiv für Reformationsgeschichte, Sonderband,* edited by Hans R. Guggisberg and Gottfried G. Krodel, pp. 136-56. Gütersloh, Germany: Gütersloher, 1993.

Kolfhaus, Wilhelm. *Christusgemeinschaft bei Johannes Calvin.* Beiträge zur Geschichte und Lehre der Reformierten Kirche 3. Neukirchen, Germany: Buchhandlung des Erziehungsvereins K. Moers, 1939.

Lane, A. N. S. *John Calvin: Student of the Church Fathers.* Edinburgh: T. & T. Clark, 1999.

Lanne, D. E. "Le vision de Dieu dans l'oeuvre de saint Irénée." *Irenikon* 33 (1963): 311-20.

Laporte, Jean-Marc, S.J. "Christ in the *Summa.*" *The Thomist* 67 (2003): 221-48.

Lassiat, Henri. *Promotion de l'homme en Jésus-Christ d'après Irénée de Lyon.* Paris: Mame, 1974.

———. "L'anthropologie d'Irénée." *Nouvelle Revue Théologique* 100 (1978): 399-417.

Lawrenz, Carl J. "On Justification, Osiander's Doctrine of the Indwelling Christ." In *No Other Gospel,* edited by Arnold J. Koelpin, pp. 149-73, 350-52. Milwaukee: Northwestern Publishing House, 1980.

Lawson, John. *The Biblical Theology of Saint Irenaeus.* London: Epworth, 1948.

Layton, Bentley, ed. *The Rediscovery of Gnosticism: The School of Valentinus.* Leiden: Brill, 1980.

Lebeau, Paul. "Koinonia: la signification du salut selon saint Irénée." In *Epektasis,* pp. 121-27. Paris: Beauchesne, 1972.

Leclercq, Jean. *The Love of Learning and the Desire for God: A Study of Monastic Culture.* New York: Fordham University Press, 1961.

Lidgett, J. Scott. *The Fatherhood of God.* Edinburgh: T. & T. Clark, 1902.

Loewe, William P. "Myth and Counter Myth: Irenaeus' Story of Salvation." In *Interpreting Tradition,* edited by J. Kopas, pp. 39-54. Chico: Scholars, 1984.

Löhr, Winrich Alfried. "Gnostic Determinism Reconsidered." *Vigiliae Christianae* 46 (1992): 381-90.

Lossky, Vladimir. *The Vision of God*. London: Faith Press, 1963.

———. "The Problem of the Vision Face to Face and Byzantine Patristic Tradition." *Greek Orthodox Theological Review* 17 (1972): 231-54.

———. *Orthodox Theology: An Introduction*. Translated by Ian and Ihita Kesarcodi-Watson. Crestwood, NY: St Vladimir's Seminary Press, 1989.

Louth, Andrew. *The Origins of the Christian Mystical Tradition*. Oxford: Clarendon, 1981.

MacKenzie, Iain. *Irenaeus's Demonstration of the Apostolic Preaching*. Translated by J. Armitage Robinson. Aldershot, Hants: Ashgate, 2002.

Mangum, R. Todd. "Is There a Reformed Way to get the Benefits of the Atonement to 'Those Who Have Never Heard'?" *Journal of the Evangelical Theological Society* 47 (2004): 121-36.

Markschies, C. "Valentinian Gnosticism: Toward the Anatomy of a School." In *The Nag Hammadi Library After Fifty Years*, edited by J. D. Turner and A. McGuire, pp. 401-38. Leiden: Brill, 1997.

Marshall, Bruce. "Action and Person: Do Palamas and Aquinas Agree About the Spirit?" *St Vladimir's Theological Quarterly* 39 (1995): 379-408.

———. "Justification as Declaration and Deification." *International Journal of Systematic Theology* 4 (2002): 3-28.

May, Gerhard. *Creatio ex Nihilo*. Edinburgh: T. & T. Clark, 1994.

McCormack, Bruce. *For Us and Our Salvation: Incarnation and Atonement in the Reformed Tradition*. Princeton: Princeton Theological Seminary, 1993.

———. "The End of Reformed Theology?" In *Reformed Theology*, edited by Wallace Alston and Michael Welker, pp. 46-64. Grand Rapids: Eerdmans, 2003.

———. "What's at Stake in Current Debates over Justification? The Crisis of Protestantism in the West." In *Justification*, edited by Mark Husbands and Daniel Treier, pp. 81-117. Downers Grove, IL: InterVarsity Press, 2004.

McCue, James. "*Simul justus et peccator* in Augustine, Aquinas, and Luther: Towards Putting the Debate in Context." *Journal of the American Academy of Religion* 48 (1980): 81-96.

McDermott, John Michael. "The Biblical Doctrine of Koinonia." *Biblische Zeitschrift* 19 (1975): 64-77, 219-33.

McDonnell, Kilian. *John Calvin, the Church, and the Eucharist*. Princeton, NJ: Princeton University Press, 1967.

———. "Jesus' Baptism in the Jordan." *Theological Studies* 56 (1995): 209-36.

———. "Quaesto Disputata: Irenaeus on the Baptism of Jesus." *Theological Studies* 59 (1998): 317-19.

McGinn, Bernard. *The Foundations of Mysticism*. New York: Crossroad, 1991.

———. "God as Eros: Metaphysical Foundations of Christian Mysticism." In *New Perspectives on Historical Theology*, edited by Bradley Nassif, pp. 189-209. Grand Rapids: Eerdmans, 1996.

———. *The Flowering of Mysticism*. New York: Crossroad, 1998.

McGowan, Andrew. "Justification and the *Ordo Salutis*." In *Justification in Perspective*, edited by Bruce McCormack. Grand Rapids: Baker, 2006.

McGrath, Alister E. *Iustitia Dei: A History of the Christian Doctrine of Justification.* Cambridge: Cambridge University Press, 1998.

McLelland, Joseph C. *The Visible Words of God.* Edinburgh: Oliver and Boyd, 1957.

———. "Lutheran-Reformed Debate on the Eucharist and Christology." In *Marburg Revisited,* edited by Paul C. Empie and James I. McCord, pp. 39-54. Minneapolis: Augsburg, 1966.

———. "Sailing to Byzantium." In *The New Man: An Orthodox and Reformed Dialogue,* edited by John Meyendorff and J. C. McLelland, pp. 10-25. New Brunswick, NJ: Agora, 1973.

Meconi, David Vincent. "The Incarnation and the Role of Participation in St. Augustine's *Confessions.*" *Augustinian Studies* 29, no. 2 (1998): 61-75.

Meyendorff, John. "Greek Philosophy and Christian Theology in the Early Church." In *Catholicity and the Church,* pp. 31-47. Crestwood, NY: St Vladimir's Seminary Press, 1983.

———. "The Significance of the Reformation in the History of Christendom." In *Catholicity and the Church,* pp. 65-82. Crestwood, NY: St Vladimir's Seminary Press, 1983.

———. "Humanity: 'Old' and 'New' — Anthropological Considerations." In *Salvation in Christ: A Lutheran-Orthodox Dialogue,* edited by John Meyendorff and Robert Tobias, pp. 59-65. Minneapolis: Augsburg, 1992.

Milbank, John. *Being Reconciled: Ontology and Pardon.* London: Routledge, 2003.

Milbank, John, Catherine Pickstock, and Graham Ward, eds. *Radical Orthodoxy.* London: Routledge, 1999.

Mongrain, Kevin. *The Systematic Thought of Hans Urs von Balthasar: An Irenaean Retrieval.* New York: Crossroad, 2002.

Mooi, Remko Jan. *Het kerk, en dogmahistorisch element in de werken van Johannes Calvijn [The church and the dogma-historical aspect of the works of John Calvin].* Wageningen, Netherlands: H. Veenman, 1965.

Mosser, Carl. "The Greatest Possible Blessing: Calvin and Deification." *Scottish Journal of Theology* 55, no. 1 (2002): 36-57.

———. "Mormonism and the Christian Doctrine of Deification." Th.M. thesis, Fuller Theological Seminary, 2002.

———. "The Earliest Patristic Interpretations of Psalm 82, Jewish Antecedents and the Origin of Christian Deification." *Journal of Theological Studies* 56 (2005): 30-74.

Muller, Richard A. "Christ in the Eschaton: Calvin and Moltmann on the Duration of the *Munus Regium.*" *Harvard Theological Review* 74 (1981): 31-59.

———. *Christ and the Decree.* Durham, NC: Labyrinth, 1986.

———. *The Unaccommodated Calvin.* Oxford: Oxford University Press, 2000.

———. "The Starting Point of Calvin's Theology: An Essay-Review." *Calvin Theological Journal* 36 (2001): 314-41.

Niesel, Wilhelm. "Union with Christ." In *Reformed Symbolics,* pp. 181-200. Edinburgh: Oliver & Boyd, 1962.

———. *The Theology of Calvin.* Grand Rapids: Baker, 1980.

————, ed. *Bekenntnisschriften und Kirchenordnungen.* Zurich: Evangelischer Verlag, 1938.

Norris, Richard A. "Irenaeus and Plotinus Answer the Gnostics: A Note on the Relation Between Christian Thought and Platonism." *Union Seminary Quarterly Review* 36 (Fall 1980): 13-24.

Nussbaum, Martha. "Augustine and Dante on the Ascent of Love." In *The Augustinian Tradition,* edited by Gareth Matthews, pp. 61-90. Berkeley: University of California Press, 1999.

Nygren, Anders. *Agape and Eros.* Vol. II/II. London: SPCK, 1939.

Oberman, Heiko. "Reformation, Preaching, and *Ex Opere Operato.*" In *Christianity Divided,* edited by Daniel Callahan, pp. 223-39. New York: Sheed & Ward, 1961.

————. "The *'Extra'* Dimension in the Theology of Calvin." *Journal of Ecclesiastical History* 21 (1970): 43-64.

————. *The Harvest of Medieval Theology.* Durham, NC: Labyrinth Press, 1983.

————. "The Pursuit of Happiness: Calvin Between Humanism and Reformation." In *Humanity and Divinity in Renaissance and Reformation,* edited by John O'Malley, pp. 251-83. New York: Brill, 1993.

————. "*Initia Calvini:* The Matrix of Calvin's Reformation." In *Calvinus Sacrae Scripturae Professor,* edited by Wilhelm Neuser, pp. 113-54. Grand Rapids: Eerdmans, 1994.

————. "The Meaning of Mysticism from Meister Eckhart to Martin Luther." In *The Reformation: Roots and Ramifications,* pp. 77-90. Grand Rapids: Eerdmans, 1994.

O'Connell, R. J. "The Plotinian Fall of the Soul in St. Augustine." *Traditio* 19 (1963): 1-35.

————. "The Riddle of Augustine's 'Confessions': A Plotinian Key." *International Philosophical Quarterly* 4, nos. 327-372 (1964).

————. *St. Augustine's Early Theory of Man.* Cambridge: Harvard University Press, 1968.

O'Keefe, Bernard J. "Casel and Calvin on the Eucharist." *Canadian Journal of Theology* 11 (1965): 8-24.

Old, Hughes Oliphant. *The Patristic Roots of Reformed Worship.* Zürcher Beiträge zur Reformationsgeschichte 5. Zürich: Theologischer Verlag, 1975.

O'Meara, J. J. *The Young Augustine.* London: Longmans, Green, 1954.

Oort, Johannes van. "John Calvin and the Church Fathers." In *The Reception of the Church Fathers in the West II,* edited by Irena Dorota Backus, pp. 661-700. Leiden: Brill, 1997.

Orbe, Antonio. *La Uncion del Verbo.* Estudios Valentinianos III. Rome: Gregorian University, 1961.

————. "La definición del hombre en la teología del s.II." *Gregorianum* 48 (1967): 522-76.

————. *Antropologia de San Ireneo.* Madrid: Biblioteca de Autores Cristianos, 1969.

————. "Irenaeus." In *Encyclopedia of the Early Church,* edited by Angelo di Berardino, pp. 413-16. Cambridge: James Clark, 1992.

———. "El Espiritu en el bautismo de Jesus (en torno a san Ireneo)." *Gregorianum* 76 (1995): 663-99.

Osborn, Eric. "The Logic of Recapitulation." In *Pléroma: Salus carnis, Homenaje a Antonio Orbe,* edited by Eugenio Romero-Rose, pp. 321-35. Santiago de Compostella, Spain: Aldecoa, 1990.

———. "Irenaeus: God as Intellect and Love." In *Prayer and Spirituality in the Early Church, I,* edited by Pauline Allen et al., pp. 175-86. Brisbane: Australian Catholic University, 1998.

———. *Irenaeus of Lyons.* Cambridge: Cambridge University Press, 2002.

Ozment, Steven. *Homo spiritualis: A Comparative Study of the Anthropology of Johannes Tauler, Jean Gerson and Martin Luther.* Leiden: Brill, 1969.

Pagels, Elaine. "Conflicting Versions of Valentinian Eschatology." *Harvard Theological Review* 67 (1974): 35-53.

Panikulam, George. *Koinonia in the New Testament: A Dynamic Expression of Christian Life.* Analecta Biblica 85. Rome: Pontificio Instituto Biblico, 1979.

Parker, T. H. L. *Calvin's Doctrine of the Knowledge of God.* Edinburgh: Oliver & Boyd, 1969.

———. *Calvin's Old Testament Commentaries.* Edinburgh: T. & T. Clark, 1986.

Partee, Charles. "Soul and Body in Anthropology." In *Calvin and Classical Philosophy,* pp. 51-90. Leiden: Brill, 1977.

———. "Calvin's Central Dogma Again." *Sixteenth Century Journal* 18 (1987): 191-99.

Perkins, Pheme. "Irenaeus and the Gnostics: Rhetoric and Composition in *Adversus haereses* Book One." *Vigiliae Christianae* 30 (1976): 193-200.

Peterson, Robert A. *Calvin's Doctrine of the Atonement.* Phillipsburg, NJ: Presbyterian and Reformed, 1983.

Philippou, A. J. "The Mystery of Pentecost." In *The Orthodox Ethos,* edited by A. J. Philippou, pp. 70-97. Oxford: Holywell Press, 1964.

Pollard, Paul. "The 'Faith of Christ' in Current Discussion." *Concordia Journal* 23 (1997): 213-28.

Porter, Jean. "Desire for God: Ground of the Moral Life in Aquinas." *Theological Studies* 47 (1986): 48-68.

Powers, Daniel G. *Salvation Through Participation: An Examination of the Notion of the Believers' Corporate Unity with Christ in Early Christian Soteriology.* Leuven: Peeters, 2001.

Pruett, Gordon. "A Protestant Doctrine of the Eucharistic Presence." *Calvin Theological Journal* 10 (1975): 142-74.

Puntel, Lourencino Bruno. "Participation." In *Sacramentum Mundi: An Encyclopedia of Theology,* edited by Karl Rahner, pp. 347-50. London: Burns & Oates, 1969.

Purves, James G. M. "The Spirit and the *Imago Dei:* Reviewing the Anthropology of Irenaeus of Lyons." *Evangelical Quarterly* 68 (1996): 99-120.

Quasten, J. *Patrology.* Utrecht: Spectrum, 1962.

Raitt, Jill. "The Person of the Mediator: Calvin's Christology and Beza's Fidelity." In *Occasional Papers of the American Society for Reformation Research,* edited by R. C.

Walton, vol. 1, pp. 53-80. St. Louis: American Society for Reformation Research, 1977.

———. "Calvin's Use of Persona." In *Calvinus Ecclesiae Genevensis Custos,* edited by Wilhelm Neuser, pp. 273-87. New York: Lang, 1984.

Rankin, William Duncan. "Carnal Union with Christ in the Theology of T. F. Torrance." Ph.D. dissertation, University of Edinburgh, 1997.

Refoulé, F. "Immortalité de l'âme et résurrection de la chair." *Revue de l'Histoire des Religions* 163 (1963): 11-52.

Reumann, John. "Koinonia in Scripture: Survey of Biblical Text." In *On the Way to Fuller Koinonia,* edited by Thomas Best and Günther Gassmann. Geneva: World Council of Churches, 1994.

Reynders, D. Bruno. *Lexique comparé du texte grec et des versions latine, arménienne, et syriaque de l'Adversus Haereses de saint Irénée.* Corpus Scriptorum Christianorum Orientalium 141. Louvain: Imprimerie orientaliste, 1954.

Richard, Lucien. *The Spirituality of John Calvin.* Atlanta: John Knox, 1974.

Robinson, James, ed. *The Beginnings of Dialectic Theology I.* Richmond, VA: John Knox, 1968.

Rogers, Eugene. "The Mystery of the Spirit in Three Traditions: Calvin, Rahner, Florensky or, You *Keep* Wondering Where the Spirit Went." *Modern Theology* 19 (2003): 243-58.

Rorem, Paul. "Pseudo-Dionysius." In *Christian Spirituality I,* edited by Bernard McGinn and John Meyendorff, pp. 132-151. London: Routledge, 1986.

———. "'Procession and Return' in Thomas Aquinas and His Predecessors." *Princeton Seminary Bulletin* 13 (1992): 147-63.

———. "The *Consensus Tigurinus* (1549): Did Calvin Compromise?" In *Calvinus Sacrae Scripturae Professor,* edited by Wilhelm Neuser, pp. 72-90. Grand Rapids: Eerdmans, 1994.

Rousseau, Adelin. "L'éternité des peines de l'enfer et l'immortalité naturelle de l'âme selon saint Irénée." *Nouvelle Revue Théologique* 99 (1977): 834-64.

Rudolph, Kurt. *Gnosis.* San Francisco: Harper & Row, 1977.

Rusch, William. *The Trinitarian Controversy.* Philadelphia: Fortress, 1980.

———. "How the Eastern Fathers Understood What the Western Church Meant by Justification." In *Justification by Faith,* edited by H. George Anderson, T. Austin Murphy, and Joseph A. Burgess, pp. 131-42. Minneapolis: Augsburg, 1985.

Russell, Norman. "The Concept of Deification in the Early Greek Fathers." D.Phil. dissertation, University of Oxford, 1988.

———. "'Partakers of the Divine Nature' (2 Peter 1:4) in the Byzantine Tradition." In ΚΑΘΗΓΗΤΡΙΑ, edited by J. M. Hussey, pp. 51-67. Camberley, UK: Porphyrogenitus, 1988.

Sanders, E. P. *Paul and Palestinian Judaism.* Philadelphia: Fortress, 1977.

Schattenmann, J. "κοινωνία." In *New International Dictionary of New Testament Theology,* edited by Colin Brown, 1:639-44. Grand Rapids: Zondervan, 1975-85.

Scherrer, Thierry. *La Gloire de Dieu dans l'oeuvre de Saint Irénée.* Rome: Gregorian University Press, 1997.

Schoedel, William R. "Topological Theology and Some Monistic Trends in Gnosticism." In *Essays on the Nag Hammadi Texts*, edited by M. Krause, pp. 88-108. Leiden: Brill, 1972.

————. "Enclosing, Not Enclosed: The Early Christian Doctrine of God." In *Early Christian Literature and the Classical Intellectual Tradition*. Paris: Beauchesne, 1979.

————. "Gnostic Monism and the Gospel of Truth." In *Rediscovery of Gnosticism*, pp. 379-90. Leiden: Brill, 1980.

Scholl, Hans. *Calvinus Catholicus*. Freiburg: Herder, 1974.

————. "Karl Barth as Interpreter of Calvin's *Psychopannychia*." In *Calvinus Sincerioris Religionis Vindex*, edited by Wilhelm H. Neuser and Brian G. Armstrong, pp. 291-308. Kirksville, MO: Sixteenth Century Journal, 1997.

Schreiner, Susan. "Exegesis and Double Justice in Calvin's Sermons on Job." *Church History* 58 (1989): 322-38.

Schurr, George M. "On the Logic of Ante-Nicene Affirmations of the 'Deification' of the Christian." *Anglican Theological Review* 51 (1969): 97-105.

Schwöbel, Christoph. "The Creature of the Word: Recovering the Ecclesiology of the Reformers." In *On Being the Church*, edited by Colin Gunton and Daniel Hardy, pp. 110-55. Edinburgh: T. & T. Clark, 1989.

————. "The Triune God of Grace: The Doctrine of the Trinity in the Theology of the Reformers." In *The Christian Understanding of God Today*, edited by James Bryne, pp. 49-64. Dublin: Columba, 1993.

————. "Christology and Trinitarian Thought." In *Trinitarian Theology Today*, edited by Christoph Schwöbel, pp. 113-46. Edinburgh: T. & T. Clark, 1995.

————. "Reconciliation: From Biblical Observations to Dogmatic Reconstruction." In *The Theology of Reconciliation*, edited by Colin Gunton, pp. 13-38. Edinburgh: T. & T. Clark, 2003.

Scott, J. M. "Adoption, Sonship." In *A Dictionary of Paul and his Letters*, edited by Gerald F. Hawthorne and Ralph P. Martin, pp. 15-18. Downers Grove, IL: InterVarsity Press, 1993.

Seeberg, Reinhold. *Textbook of the History of Doctrines*. Translated by Charles E. Hay. Philadelphia: Lutheran Publication Society, 1905.

Segal, Alan. "Paul and the Beginning of Jewish Mysticism." In *Death, Ecstasy, and Other Worldly Journeys*, edited by John Collins and Michael Fishbane, pp. 95-122. New York: State University Press, 1995.

Seifrid, Mark A. *Justification by Faith: The Origin and Development of a Central Pauline Theme*. Leiden: Brill, 1992.

————. "Luther, Melanchthon, and Paul on the Question of Imputation." In *Justification*, edited by Mark Husbands and Daniel Treier, pp. 137-152. Downers Grove, IL: InterVarsity Press, 2004.

Shults, F. LeRon. *Reforming Theological Anthropology*. Grand Rapids: Eerdmans, 2003.

Skinner, Quentin. "Meaning and Understanding in the History of Ideas." In *Visions of Politics I*, pp. 57-89. Cambridge: Cambridge University Press, 2002.

Smalbrugge, Matthias. "La notion de la participation chez Augustin. Quelques observations sur le rapport Christianisme-Platonisme." *Augustiniana* 40/41 (1990): 333-47.

Smith, Christopher R. "The Life-of-Christ Structure of Athanasius' *De Incarnatione Verbi*." *The Patristic and Byzantine Review* 10 (1991): 7-24.

Smith, Daniel A. "Irenaeus and the Baptism of Jesus." *Theological Studies* 58 (1997): 618-42.

Sommers, Paula. *Celestial Ladders: Readings in Marguerite de Navarre's Poetry of Spiritual Ascent*. Geneva: Droz, 1989.

Steenberg, M. C. "The Role of Mary as Co-Recapitulator in St Irenaeus of Lyons." *Vigiliae Christianae* 58 (2004): 117-37.

Steenkamp, J. J. "A Review of the Concept of Progress in Calvin's Institutes." In *Calvin: Erbe und Auftrag*, edited by W. van 't Spijker, pp. 69-76. Kampen: Kok Pharos, 1991.

Steinmetz, David. "Andreas Osiander." In *Reformers in the Wings*, pp. 91-99. Grand Rapids: Baker, 1971.

―――. "Calvin and the Absolute Power of God." *Journal of Medieval and Renaissance Studies* 18 (1988): 65-79.

―――. "Calvin among the Thomists." In *Calvin in Context*, pp. 141-46. Oxford: Oxford University Press, 1995.

―――. "Calvin and His Lutheran Critics." In *Calvin in Context*, pp. 172-86. Oxford: Oxford University Press, 1995.

Strehle, Stephen. "Imputatio iustitiae: Its Origin in Melanchthon, Its Opposition in Osiander." *Theologische Zeitschrift* 50 (1994): 201-19.

Stroumsa, Guy. "Mystical Descents." In *Death, Ecstasy, and Other Worldly Journeys*, edited by John Collins and Michael Fishbane. New York: State University of New York Press, 1995.

Stubbs, David. "Sanctification as Participation in Christ." Ph.D. dissertation, Duke University, 2001.

Tamburello, Dennis. *Union with Christ: John Calvin and the Mysticism of St. Bernard*. Louisville: Westminster John Knox, 1994.

Tan, Seng-Kong. "Calvin's Doctrine of our Union with Christ." *Quodlibet* (http://www.quodlibet.net/tan-union.shtml) 5, no. 4 (2003): 1-14.

Tanner, Kathryn. *God and Creation in Christian Theology: Tyranny or Empowerment?* Oxford: Blackwell, 1988.

―――. *Jesus, Humanity and the Trinity*. Edinburgh: T. & T. Clark, 2001.

Tavard, George. *Les Jardins de saint Augustin. Lecture des Confessions*. Paris: Cerf, 1988.

―――. *The Starting Point of Calvin's Theology*. Grand Rapids: Eerdmans, 2000.

Taylor, Charles. *Sources of the Self: The Making of Modernity Identity*. Cambridge: Harvard University Press, 1989.

Thysell, Carol. *The Pleasure of Discernment: Marguerite de Navarre as Theologian*. Oxford: Oxford University Press, 2000.

Torrance, T. F. *Calvin's Doctrine of Man*. Grand Rapids: Eerdmans, 1957.

―――. *The School of Faith*. London: Camelot, 1959.

————. "Justification: Its Radical Nature and Place in Reformed Doctrine and Life." *Scottish Journal of Theology* 13 (1960): 225-46.

————. *Theology in Reconstruction.* London: SCM, 1965.

————. *Space, Time and Incarnation.* London: Oxford University Press, 1969.

————. "The Paschal Mystery of Christ and the Eucharist." In *Theology in Reconciliation*, pp. 106-38. Grand Rapids: Eerdmans, 1975.

————. "Calvin's Doctrine of the Trinity." *Calvin Theological Journal* 25 (1990): 165-93.

————. "The Doctrine of the Holy Trinity in Gregory Nazianzen and John Calvin." In *Trinitarian Perspectives*, pp. 21-40. Edinburgh: T. & T. Clark, 1994.

————. "Legal and Evangelical Priests." In *Calvin's Books*, edited by W. H. Neuser, pp. 63-74. Heerenveen, Netherlands: Groen, 1997.

Torrance, T. F., ed. *Theological Dialogue Between Orthodox and Reformed Churches.* Edinburgh: Scottish Academic, 1985.

Tour, Pierre Imbart de la. *Origines de la Reforme.* Vol. IV. Paris, 1935.

Trumper, Tim. "The Theological History of Adoption I: An Account." *Scottish Bulletin of Evangelical Theology* 20 (2002): 4-28.

————. "The Theological History of Adoption II: A Rationale." *Scottish Bulletin of Evangelical Theology* 20 (2002): 177-202.

Tylenda, Joseph. "Christ the Mediator: Calvin Versus Stancaro." *Calvin Theological Journal* 8 (1973): 5-16.

————. "The Controversy on Christ the Mediator: Calvin's Second Reply to Stancaro." *Calvin Theological Journal* 8 (1973): 131-57.

————. "Calvin and Christ's Presence in the Supper — True or Real." *Scottish Journal of Theology* 27 (1974): 65-75.

————. "Calvin's Understanding of Communication of Properties." *Westminster Theological Journal* 38 (1975): 54-65.

————. "Calvin and Westphal: Two Eucharistic Theologies in Conflict." In *Calvin's Books*, edited by Wilhelm Neuser, pp. 9-22. Heerenveen, Netherlands: Groen, 1997.

Van Fleteren, Frederick. "The Ascent of the Soul in the Augustinian Tradition." In *Paradigms in Medieval Thought, Applications in Medieval Disciplines*, edited by N. VanDeusen, pp. 93-110. Lewiston, NY: Edwin Mellen Press, 1990.

Von Balthasar, Hans Urs. *The Glory of the Lord II: A Theological Aesthetics.* Edinburgh: T. & T. Clark, 1982.

————. *The Grain of Wheat.* San Francisco: Ignatius, 1995.

————. "The Fathers, the Scholastics, and Ourselves." *Communio* 24 (1997): 347-96.

————. *Origen: Spirit and Fire.* Edinburgh: T. & T. Clark, 2001.

Wainwright, Geoffrey. "The Doctrine of the Trinity: Where the Church Stands or Falls." *Interpretation* 45 (1991): 117-32.

Wallace, Ronald S. *Calvin's Doctrine of the Christian Life.* Grand Rapids: Eerdmans, 1961.

————. *Calvin's Doctrine of the Word and Sacrament.* Edinburgh: Scottish Academic Press, 1995.

Wawrykow, Joseph. "John Calvin and Condign Merit." *Archiv für Reformationsge-schichte* 83 (1992): 73-90.

Webster, John. *Holiness.* Grand Rapids: Eerdmans, 2003.

Weis, James. "Calvin versus Osiander on Justification." *Springfielder* 30 (1965): 31-47.

Wendel, François. *Calvin: The Origins and Development of his Religious Thought.* London: Collins, 1963.

Westhead, Nigel. "Adoption in the Thought of John Calvin." *Scottish Bulletin of Evangelical Theology* 13 (1995): 102-15.

Wilken, Robert L. *The Spirit of Early Christian Thought.* London: Yale University Press, 2003.

Williams, Anna. "Mystical Theology Redux: The Pattern of Aquinas' *Summa Theologiæ.*" *Modern Theology* 13 (1997): 53-74.

————. *The Ground of Union.* Oxford: Oxford University Press, 1999.

Williams, Rowan. "Barth on the Triune God." In *Karl Barth: Studies of his Theological Method,* edited by S. W. Sykes, pp. 147-93. Oxford: Clarendon, 1979.

————. *Eucharistic Sacrifice — The Roots of a Metaphor.* Grove Liturgical Studies 31. Bramcote, UK: Grove, 1982.

————. "Analogy and Participation." In *Arius,* pp. 215-29. London: Darton, Longman, & Todd, 1987.

————. "The Nicene Heritage." In *The Christian Understanding of God Today,* edited by James Bryne, pp. 45-48. Dublin: Columba, 1993.

————. "The Paradoxes of Self-Knowledge in De trinitate." In *Augustine,* edited by J. Lienhard et al., pp. 121-34. New York: Peter Lang, 1993.

————. "Word and Spirit." In *On Christian Theology,* pp. 105-127. Oxford: Blackwell, 2000.

Willis, E. David. *Calvin's Catholic Christology.* Leiden: Brill, 1967.

Willis-Watkins, D. "The Unio Mystica and the Assurance of Faith According to Calvin." In *Calvin: Erbe und Auftrag,* edited by W. van 't Spijker, pp. 77-84. Kampen: Kok Pharos, 1991.

————. *Notes on the Holiness of God.* Grand Rapids: Eerdmans, 2002.

Wilson-Kastner, Patricia. "Grace as Participation in the Divine Life in Augustine of Hippo." *Augustinian Studies* 7 (1976): 135-52.

————. "Andreas Osiander's Theology of Grace in the Perspective of the Influence of Augustine of Hippo." *Sixteenth Century Journal* 10 (1979): 72-91.

————. "On Partaking of the Divine Nature: Luther's Dependence on Augustine." *Andrews University Seminary Studies* 22 (1984): 113-24.

Wilterdink, G. A. *Tyrant or Father? A Study of Calvin's Doctrine of God.* Lima, OH: Wyndham Hall Press, 1985.

Wingren, Gustaf. *Man and the Incarnation.* Edinburgh: Oliver & Boyd, 1959.

Winling, R. "Une façon de dire le salut: la formule 'être avec Dieu, être avec Jesus Christ' dans les écrits de saint Irénée." *Revue des Sciences Religieuses* 58 (1984): 105-35.

Witvliet, John. "Sursum Corda: Images and Themes in John Calvin's Theology of Liturgy." In *Worship Seeking Understanding,* pp. 127-48. Grand Rapids: Baker, 2003.

Wyatt, Peter. *Jesus Christ and Creation*. Allison Park, PA: Pickwick, 1996.

Yates, John. "Role of the Holy Spirit in the Lord's Supper." *Churchman* 105 (1991): 350-59.

Zachman, Randall. *The Assurance of Faith*. Minneapolis: Fortress, 1993.

Zizioulas, John. *Being as Communion*. Crestwood, NY: St Vladimir's Seminary Press, 1985.

Index of Names

Index of Subjects

Adoption and ascent into the Trinity (Calvin), 130-59, 237-38, 247-48; and baptism narrative, 134-35; Calvin in contrast to Aquinas, 137; Calvin in contrast to Luther's nuptial union, 136-37; and Calvin-Osiander debate regarding participation, 69-70, 81, 139-46, 164, 237; and christological participation in God, 136-47; and doctrine of mediation, 134; and God's fatherhood, 131-33; human "sonship" and union with God, 137-38; implications for Calvin's theological anthropology, 145-47; and role of the Holy Spirit, 148-59, 237-38

Adoption and Irenaeus's christology: adoptive ethics, 208-9; the adoptive exchange and ascent in Christ, 205-9; adoptive filiation and humanity's capacity to "seize" God, 219-23; and "growth," 205; the Son and the Spirit, 205-7

Agency, human, 103-4, 249

Alienation, contemporary, 250-52

Altruism, 169-70, 242

Aquinas's golden circle ascent pattern, 37-42, 43-45; and Calvin's ascent, 43-45; critiques of, 40-41; and Neo-

Platonism, 39; and Plotinian procession-return scheme, 37-38, 39-41, 62

Ascent, Calvin's paradigm of, 2-5, 233-42; and adoption, 130-59, 237-38, 247-48; appropriation and transformation of earlier patterns, 42-51; and Aquinas's golden circle, 43-45; church as locus of ascent, 238-42, 248; and communion, 44-45; comparing to Irenaeus, 21-24, 229-33, 248; and contemporary spirituality, 245-52; and evangelical approach/sapiential approach, 42-43, 80-81; the lack of scholarly attention by Reformed theologians, 45-46; participation in Christ's ascent, 3-5, 43-44, 47-51; and Platonic ascent, 46-47, 49; and *Psychopannychia*, 46-50; threefold path of ascent, 49-50. *See also* Creation and ascent (Calvin); Humanity's ascent (Calvin)

Ascent traditions (history of), 2-3, 25-51; Aquinas's golden circle, 37-42, 43-45; "ascent of the soul," 3-5; Calvin's appropriation/transformation of earlier patterns, 42-51; challenges posed by Greek typologies, 29-31, 36; early Christian appropriation of Greek patterns, 29-42; Greek patterns, 26-

227-28, 230; and "deification," 188-91, 236-38; *Deus facit* (God makes), 180-84; and God's glory, 182-83; and God's transcendence, 181; and "growth," 188-91; *Homo fit* (humanity is made), 184-88; and human "thankfulness," 185-86; and immortality, 186; receiving God's gift, 190-91

Daimones, 17, 174-75
Deification, Irenaeus's doctrine of, 188-91, 236-38

Eucharistic ascent (Calvin), 159-70, 238-42; and Chalcedon, 160-61; sacraments, Holy Spirit, and participation, 160-67, 241-42; sign and symbols, 164-67; and the Spirit, 166-67, 171, 238-42; the three eucharistic temptations of ascent, 167-70
Eucharist (Irenaeus), 223-27, 239-42; and first fruits, 225, 242; and new creation, 224-26
Existentialists, 250-51

Fall of Adam, 83-87, 88

Garden of Eden: Adam and Calvin's anthropology of mediation, 59, 64, 65, 74-88, 235-38; Adam's fall and the loss of communion/immortality, 83-87, 88; *imago Dei* and Adam's life in, 3, 8, 65, 76-83; and immortality/communion, 76-83, 234-35; and Irenaeus's Creator-creature distinction, 186-87, 215; and participation, 74-83; the tree of life, 75, 83, 85-86
Gnostics, 174-76, 227, 230; and dualism, 179-80, 183-84; and intellectualized ascent, 179-80, 193-94; and Irenaeus's ascending economy of the Holy Spirit, 211-13, 223-24; and Irenaeus's ascending vision of creation/humanity, 179-80, 183-85, 188-92; and Irenaeus's christology, 193-95, 203; and Jesus' humanity, 195-96; myths of

descents/ascents, 193-95, 203; and participation, 173, 183-84; and salvation/redemption, 179
Greek patterns of ascent, 26-31; challenges for Christianity, 29-31, 36; Christian appropriation of, 29-42; Plato's ladder, 26-27, 29, 32-36, 39, 46-47, 49; Plotinus's golden circle (procession-return scheme), 27-31, 34, 37, 39-41
Greeks and *koinonia*-consciousness, 6-7, 19-20

Heaven and ascent, 118-21
Holy Spirit: adoption into the Trinity, 148-59, 237-38; and adoptive filiation (Irenaeus), 219-23; and the benefits of Christ *(beneficia Christi)*, 153-57; and Calvin-Osiander debate regarding participation, 141-45; and Calvin's christology, 96-98, 101-3, 115-18; and Calvin's doctrine of creation and mediation, 59-61; Calvin's doctrine of the Spirit in creation, 234; competing interpretations of (as "bridge" vs. agent of participation), 150-59, 167; and the Eucharist, 166-67, 171, 238-42; and humanity's ascent, 148-59, 166-67, 171, 237-42; *imago Dei* and immortality/communion, 77; Irenaeus and the ascending economy of, 210-27, 228, 244; and Irenaeus's christology, 195-96, 198-202, 203-7, 234-35, 244; and Irenaeus's doctrine of the Eucharist, 223-27, 239-42; role in the ascent/descent of Christ, 96-98, 195-96, 198-202, 203-5
Humanity's ascent (Calvin), 123-71; adoption/ascent into the Trinity, 130-59, 237-38; ascent by the Trinity, 124-30; and ascent in Reformed tradition, 129-30, 159; bidirectionality, 124-25; binding Christ's descent to, 126-28; and Calvin's alternative to moral philosophers, 128-29; and Calvin's antidote to eucharistic idolatry, 159-

Index of Calvin's Works

Index of Calvin's Works

Ref	Pages
II.14.5	131, 132-33, 137, 237
II.14.8	246
II.15	106
II.15.6	169
II.16.1	118
II.16.2	107, 108
II.16.3	109
II.16.4	107, 117
II.16.5	98, 104, 106, 108
II.16.6	106
II.16.8	106
II.16.12	105
II.16.14	114, 116
II.17	111
II.17.1	111
II.17.4	106
III.1.1	98
III.1.2	63, 148, 159
III.1.3	148
III.2.1	124
III.2.12	105
III.2.22	237
III.2.24	248
III.2.25	68
III.2.30	132
III.2.32	132, 135
III.2.39	149, 231
III.3.2	84, 108
III.3.9	109
III.3.20	108
III.6.3	124, 128-29, 130, 133
III.7.1	147
III.9.5	116
III.9.6	120
III.11.5	70, 98, 140, 141, 142
III.11.6	133, 143, 161
III.11.7	143
III.11.8	97, 116, 133
III.11.8-9	103
III.11.9	142, 143
III.11.10	98, 141, 142, 143, 164
III.13.4	149
III.14.11	43
III.14.21	58
III.15.3	80, 248
III.15.5	129, 142, 146
III.16.1	161
III.17.8	109
III.18.1	150
III.19.2-5	150
III.19.5	150
III.20.14	150
III.20.37	132, 149
III.20.38	135
III.25.1	118
III.25.2	118
III.25.4	133
III.25.7	116
III.25.10	4
IV.1.4-5	238
IV.1.5	238
IV.6.10	117
IV.14.2	176
IV.14.3	241
IV.14.5	241
IV.14.9	241
IV.14.12	77, 86
IV.14.16	242
IV.14.17	241
IV.15.1	135
IV.15.5	93, 99
IV.15.6	58, 107, 133
IV.16.31	239
IV.16.44	170
IV.17.2	5, 108, 162, 236
IV.17.5	165
IV.17.8	77
IV.17.9	93, 101, 102, 164
IV.17.10	98, 162, 164
IV.17.12	102
IV.17.14	114, 116, 241
IV.17.26	118
IV.17.27	116
IV.17.29	116, 120
IV.17.31	116, 231
IV.17.32	116, 164, 166, 169, 239, 240, 241
IV.17.33	162, 164, 239
IV.18.5	239
IV.18.7	169
IV.18.13	169
IV.18.16	169
IV.19.15	165
IV.24	91, 93
IV.27	161

Ioannis Calvini opera quae supersunt omnia [CO]

Ref	Pages
2.102	60
2.317	76
3.352	167
5.165-232	46
6.9	84
6.25	98
6.281-82	232
7.545-674	135
7.735-44	162
9.192	14
9.333-42	55
9.338	57
9.339	59, 71, 90
9.345-58	55
9.349	56
9.351	136
10a.7	170
10a.25	170
15.723	13, 101, 113, 115, 238
22.36	83
23.391	91
24.966	103
29.353	138
31.237B	130
31.87	130
32.96	60, 234
46.966	162
47.472	120
47.479	65, 85
47.479-80	61
48.590	72
48.596	119, 129
48.618	112, 115